FIRESIDE

By Henry Pleasants

VIENNA'S GOLDEN YEARS OF MUSIC—*translated, selected and edited from the collected works of Eduard Hanslick* (1950)

THE AGONY OF MODERN MUSIC (1955)

THE MUSICAL JOURNEYS OF LOUIS SPOHR—*translated, selected and edited from Louis Spohr's* Selbstbiographie (1961)

DEATH OF A MUSIC?—*The Decline of the European Tradition and the Rise of Jazz* (1961)

THE MUSICAL WORLD OF ROBERT SCHUMANN—*translated, selected and edited from the critical writings of Robert Schumann* (1965)

HENRY PLEASANTS

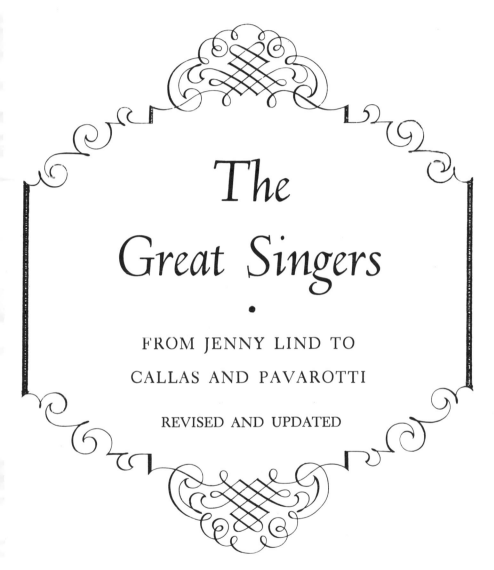

The Great Singers

·

FROM JENNY LIND TO

CALLAS AND PAVAROTTI

REVISED AND UPDATED

A FIRESIDE BOOK
published by
SIMON AND SCHUSTER
New York

A Fireside Book
Published by Simon and Schuster
A Division of Gulf & Western Corporation
Simon & Schuster Building
Rockefeller Center
1230 Avenue of the Americas
New York, New York 10020
FIRESIDE and colophon are trademarks of Simon & Schuster
Manufactured in the United States of America
1   2   3   4   5   6   7   8   9   10
Library of Congress Cataloging in Publication Data

Pleasants, Henry.
   The great singers.
   "A Fireside book."
   Bibliography: p.
   Includes index.
   1. Singers.   I. Title.
ML400.P65   1981   782.1'092'2   [B]   81–5260
ISBN 0–671–42160–3   AACR2

Contents

ACKNOWLEDGMENTS

To William Anderson, George Jellinek, H. C. Robbins Landon, George and Nora London, Dr. William B. Ober, Max de Schauensee, Daniel Schorr, Maria W. Smith and my wife, Virginia, who read the typescript, or parts of it, in various stages of its preparation, and who offered valuable corrections, suggestions and encouragement.

To Miss Edith Adams of the Cooper Union Library; Sidney Beck, head of the Rare Book and Manuscript Collection, Music Division, New York Public Library; Harry R. Beard, proprietor of the Harry R. Beard Theater Collection, Little Eversden, Cambridge, England; Dr. Otto Bettmann, proprietor of Bettmann Archive, New York; Mlle. H. Bosch, of the Musée de l'Opéra, Paris; Seymour Freidin, of London; James Goodfriend; Dr. Richard Logsden, Director of Libraries, Columbia University, and his department heads; Messrs. Raymond Mander and Joe Mitchenson of London; George W. Nash, Curator of the Endhoven Theater Collection, Victoria and Albert Museum, London; Mrs. John Dewitt Peltz, archivist of the Metropolitan Opera; Mr. Janos Scholz; Miss Donna Sustendal, of *Opera News*; Giampiero Tintori, of the Museo Teatrale alla Scala, Milan; Ides Van der Gracht, of Pully; Mrs. Alice Weaver, of the New York Academy of Medicine; Miss Helen Willard, of the Harvard College Library Theater Collection; Miss Caroline P. Wistar, of the Boston Museum of Fine Arts, and the staffs of the Music Research Division of the New York Public Library, the Frick Art Reference Library, New York, and the British Museum Print Room, for their assistance in finding and making available pictures and other illustrative material.

To Edward Waters and the staff of the Music Division of the Library of Congress and to the staff of the Music Research Division of the New York Public Library for general library and research assistance.

To Max de Schauensee, again, for his generosity in playing for me whatever I wanted to hear from his unique collection of recordings by the singers of the last "golden age," for calling to my attention certain pertinent records and for supplying much first-hand information about singers of that period.

To Mrs. Ann Maulsby, Mrs. Sophie Sorkin and Mrs. Edith Fowler, of Simon and Schuster, for their editorial assistance.

To the late Henry W. Simon, with whom the idea for this book originated and whose guidance, encouragement and advice were indispensable.

To the late Janet Schott for her devoted enthusiasm and encouragement.

To John Davis for his care in preparing the musical examples.

To Harold Rosenthal and William H. Seltsam, whose *Two Hundred Years of Covent Garden* and *Annals of the Metropolitan* have provided invaluable sources of statistical and factual material.

H.P.

List of Illustrations

Preface

MOST OF US, when we think of the great singers, will not look backward beyond Giuditta Pasta, whose prime was between 1825 and 1835, and who is now remembered primarily as the first Norma. Only the names of Farinelli and, less commonly, Caffarelli have survived to remind us that the art of *bel canto*, as cultivated by the castrati and their female colleagues, was already two centuries old when Pasta came along.

We are accustomed, similarly, to think of the "golden age" as that period of vocal prosperity extending roughly from 1880 to the First World War. Some of the great singers of that era continued their careers well into the twentieth century. There are still some among us who heard many of them, and there are many among us who heard some of them. The voices of most of them have been preserved, however inadequately, on phonograph records.

We are not often aware that the singers surrounding Pasta represented an earlier "golden age"—Maria Malibran, Giulia Grisi, Henriette Sontag, Fanny Persiani, Laure Cinti-Damoreau, Henriette Méric-Lalande, Joséphine Fodor-Mainvielle, Caroline Unger, Benedetta Pisaroni, Giovanni-Battista Rubini, Manuel García, Luigi Lablache, Antonio Tamburini, Adolphe Nourrit and Gilbert-Louis Duprez among many others.

There had been, in fact, at least two even earlier "golden ages." One was the period between 1720 and 1740, when not only Farinelli and Caffarelli but also Senesino, Bernacchi and Carestini flourished, along with the prima donnas, Faustina and Cuzzoni. And fifty years later, between 1770 and 1790, there was another flowering, dominated by the castrati Guadagni, Pacchierotti, Marchesi and Crescentini, and by the prima donnas Mara, Todi, Banti and Catalani.

It is easy to understand why these earlier "golden ages," insofar as we are aware of them at all, have been relegated to a category of prehistory. What the singers sang, in opera and concert, is forgotten, barring the occasional and inevitably unsatisfactory revival of some of Handel's operas, and information about who and what they were is fragmentary, out of print and hard to come by.

We can relate a Maria Callas and a Joan Sutherland to Pasta and Malibran because the music that Callas and Sutherland sing—from *Norma* and *I Puritani*, for example, or from *Lucia* and *Anna Bolena*— was written for Pasta and Malibran or for their contemporaries. But there is little in the repertoire, even of a Sutherland or a Callas, to remind us of the art of the great castrati and the prima donnas of the seventeenth and eighteenth centuries.

And yet there has been a continuity in the vocal art from the very beginning. A Pasta, for example, was schooled in the eighteenth-century style. As a singing actress she heralded the great dramatic sopranos of more recent times; but purely as a singer she was a lineal descendant of Farinelli, Guadagni, Pacchierotti and Crescentini. This was true, also, of her contemporaries.

An awareness of a continuity of objectives, technique and criteria extending back more than three centuries is pertinent today as it would not have been even twenty-five years ago. A new appreciation of the beauties of florid song is evident in the achievements and the success of such contemporary singers as Callas, Sutherland, Giulietta Simionato, Teresa Berganza, Marilyn Horne and Montserrat Caballé.

The vocal art seems, indeed, to be coming full circle. The art of *fioritura*, anathematized by Robert Schumann, Hans von Bülow and Wagner, and incompatible with the requirements of the lyric theater as envisioned by Wagner and Strauss, and by the later Verdi and his *verismo* Italian successors, is experiencing an incipient revival. We are learning that there must have been art as well as artifice in the virtuoso accomplishments of the age of *bel canto*.

The plan of this book has been, accordingly, to trace the line of the great singers from farther back than has been the custom heretofore, and to place them in historical perspective. The same plan has governed the selection of some seventy singers from the several hundred who, over a span of three centuries, might have been thought of properly as great singers.

Those have been selected who seem to have contributed most importantly to the decisive phases in the evolution of the vocal art, or to have represented those phases most vividly. That certain singers have been omitted, or included only incidentally to present a selected singer in the company of his peers, is no reflection upon those thus apparently slighted. If the emphasis is almost exclusively upon opera singers this is because the song recital is an institution of comparatively recent origin and because the great singers have been, with very few exceptions, opera singers. If contemporary singers, with the exception of those few already mentioned, appear to have been neglected, it is because, with so many of them still in mid-career, the perspective essential to evaluation is lacking.

It is a curious phenomenon of contemporary music appreciation that the study of history is concentrated upon composers to the virtual exclusion of performers—unless, of course, the performers were also composers. This is only partially rationalized by the fact that the accomplishments of the composers are documented in legible notation while what the performers did before the maturity of the phonograph could be impressed upon nothing more durable or reliable than the memories of their listeners.

It is also a reflection of the separation of composition and performance that has been growing ever more conspicuous since the turn of the nineteenth century, with the composer gaining an almost autonomous status as a source of creative initiative—which is unjust to the great performers. What Haydn, Mozart, Chopin, Liszt, Anton Rubinstein and even Wagner owed to the singers of their time is documented in their compositions and their letters.

Composers today could hardly derive comparable inspiration from contemporary performers, and not solely because so few of the most prosperous are performing contemporary music. The end result of the separation of composer and performer has been an inhibition of the performer's creative impulses and an impoverishment of his creative imagination. He has for too long been admonished to stick to what is written, right down to the last dot. It has inhibited the composer, too, depriving him not only of that immediate contact with the public which he enjoyed when he was also a performer, but even the indirect contact which he could establish through the performer as collaborator and intermediary.

And so this book is about performers—singers—many of them of conspicuously creative disposition. And it is also about theater professionals out there on the stage, experiencing success and failure, as creative artists must, in the verdict of the public.

PART ONE

The Age
of
Bel Canto

The eighteenth century required such a development of singing; it deemed it absolutely indispensable; and in that day of artistic strength and riches, the genius spent in an extemporized vocal ornament which was never transmitted to paper, in the delivery of a few notes which lasted but a second; the genius squandered in the most evanescent performance, the memory of which died with those who had heard it—all this seemed no waste, and indeed it could well be afforded; but when we read of it—we, who can only read of it—we feel an indefinable sense of dissatisfaction, a wistful dreary sense of envy for what did not fall to our lot, and of pain at the thought that all that feeling, all that imagination, all that careful culture, has left no trace behind it. In turning over the leaves of memoirs and music-books we try, we strain as it were, to obtain an echo of that superbly wasted vocal genius; nay, sometimes the vague figures of those we have never heard, and never can hear, will almost haunt us.

—Vernon Lee (pseudonym of Violet Paget)
in *Studies of the Eighteenth Century in Italy*

· I ·

Singer and Setting

FEW DEVICES of musical terminology, with the exception of tempo rubato (which means stolen or borrowed time, not changed time), are employed less precisely than *bel canto*; there is none whose origin is so obscure.

It means simply, and in curiously idiomatic Italian, beautiful song. And it is associated with a kind of singing that flourished in Italian throats in the seventeenth and eighteenth centuries when song was expected to be beautiful—and not much else. But at that time, when the whole purpose of *canto* was that it be *bel*, the term did not exist. It would have been redundant.

Just when it came into general usage has never been determined. The Oxford English Dictionary gives the date of its first appearance in English as 1908, which is demonstrably too late. The Grand Larousse attributes it to nineteenth-century dilettantes, which is probably accurate, but hardly precise. The Oxford English Dictionary, however, offers an important clue to the origin of the term, citing an article in the New York *Daily Chronicle* about the complaints of music critics that "audiences do not want Wagner" and that "the public flocks to the Italian *bel canto*."

There were, in the latter half of the nineteenth century, many connoisseurs who felt that the kind of singing required by Wagner—or accorded him by many Wagnerian singers—was not beautiful, just as there were many Wagnerians who felt that merely beautiful singing was not enough. It is probably a reasonable supposition, therefore, that the term *bel canto* evolved from the sulphur of pro- and anti-Wagnerian invective, employed by the Wagnerians pejoratively, by others as a symbol of the assumed virtues of the older Italian vocal tradition.

The term is exposed, therefore, in its nonpejorative usage, to appropriation by any teacher satisfied that he possesses the secret of beautiful singing or by any singer who thinks that he sings beautifully. When teachers and singers use it they have in mind, as a rule, a mellifluous kind of singing aimed at an agreeable, well-rounded tone, an even scale from bottom to top, an unbroken legato, a nicety of intonation, an eloquence of phrase and cadence, a purity of vowels and a disciplined avoidance of shouting, nasality, harsh or open sounds, disjointed registers, undue vehemence and any other evidence of vulgarity or bad or negligent schooling. Within this frame of reference *bel canto* can be applied even to the best singers of Wagner.

But most of those who use the term pride themselves on representing, in their singing or their pedagogy, a survival and perpetuation of the principles of vocalism developed in Italian opera in the seventeenth and eighteenth centuries. In some considerable degree they do. The basic criteria of good singing evolved in Italy have never been abandoned, however much they may have been relaxed to admit the dramatic urgency of Verdi's operas, the parlando style of Verdi's Italian successors, and the recitative and declamatory requirements of Wagner and Strauss. But while the old criteria have survived, they have been applied to operatic objectives conspicuously different from those of the early Italian singers.

Prior to the dawn of grand opera in the mature works of Rossini, Cherubini, Halévy, Spontini, Auber, Donizetti, Bellini, Meyerbeer and Weber in the first decades of the nineteenth century—with all their delight in spectacular melodrama—good singing, or *bel canto*, was its own objective, and it bred its own lyrical and dramatic excitement. One looked not so much to the composer or the librettist as the source of suspense and tension as to the singer; and he, a soloist, had to make do without the harmonic vocabulary and the articulate orchestra of nineteenth-century opera. He was on his own.

He had to develop his own devices and techniques, and he employed them to a large extent improvisationally, whether in the theater, at court, in the church or in the salon. The mere aria or cantata, the printed or, as was more usual, handwritten notes, provided a melodic skeleton or frame completed by the singer from his own repertoire of ornaments, embellishments, graces, roulades, trills, portamenti, arpeggios, octave skips, melodic deviations and alterations, variations, cadences, and so on.

The principal setting for such exhibitions of vocal virtuosity was the theater, either the appurtenance of a court or an urban establishment open to the public but guaranteed by aristocratic subscribers who were also the box holders. A kind of opera dedicated to mythological and classical subjects, known as *opera seria*, provided the dramatic and scenic setting. This, in its barest essentials, was the European lyric theater in the seventeenth and eighteenth centuries; and it is the vocal art that flourished there to which the musical historian refers when he speaks of "the age of *bel canto*."

Most of its musical devices, if not the tradition of improvisation, have survived in a somewhat sublimated form in Handel's oratorios, in Bach's cantatas and Passions and in Mozart's operas. But even in music of such enduring substance, we accept them today as old-fashioned conventions somehow ennobled by the genius of great composers. They survive, too, and in a more instructive form, in what we still hear of Rossini, Bellini and Donizetti. These composers stood at the crossroads of *opera seria* and grand opera; and, with the art of improvisation in decline or disrepute, they put into notation much that had formerly been left to the discretion—or indiscretion—of the singers.

We do not and cannot hear the devices of *bel canto* with eighteenth-century ears, nor are they now commonly employed with the purposes and objectives of the greatest of the seventeenth- and eighteenth-century singers. We tend today to think of florid song as a purely mechanical, decorative, emotionally empty, vain display of vocal prowess. It was denounced on these grounds in the nineteenth century, particularly in Germany. But in fact most, if not all, the devices of *bel canto* originated in an expressive purpose.

Brilliant roulades, or "divisions," lent themselves to the expression of fury, rage, vengeance and resolve, or, given the requisite harmony and figuration, jubilance and satisfaction. Trills and turns served to give emphasis to closes and cadences. Appoggiaturas brought dignity and gravity and sustenance to a long melodic line. Slurs, portamenti, and rapid scale passages, diatonic and chromatic, ascending and descending, could give weight and pathos to a climactic note. And embellishments could be fashioned according to situation and personality, thus becoming a constituent element of characterization.

The expressive purposes of florid song, and the basic devices employed in their service, were well established and generally understood by singers and listeners alike well before the end of the seventeenth century. Indeed, they would seem to have emerged almost simultaneously with the new fashion of monodic song in Italy just before and after the turn of the seventeenth century. It was this fashion that marked the end of the contrapuntal era. From it is dated the "modern" era of European music, and from it evolved the melodic conventions of baroque opera and of vocal music in the church and the salon.

Giulio Caccini (*circa* 1560–*circa* 1615), also known as Giulio Romano, from his birthplace, was the most decisively influential figure in this evolution. Rebelling against the artificiality of the multiple-voiced music of his time, and particularly against the want of any expressive relationship between text and melodic contour, he devised a style of solo singing over an instrumental accompaniment (*Stile rappresentativo*) in which the florid conventions of multiple-voiced song were harnessed to prosody and made subservient to the elucidation of text and to the expression of the appropriate emotions.

Caccini's principles were laid down in a discourse, *Le nuove musiche*, written in 1602. The character and effect of the kind of singing at which Caccini aimed is reflected more persuasively, however, in the *Discorso sopra la musica* of Vincenzo Giustiniani, Marchese da Bassano, a noble dilettante who lived in Rome during the early decades of the seventeenth century. His discourse is dated about 1628. Describing the singing of certain ladies of Mantua and Ferrara, he says that they "vied with each other not only in regard to the timbre and training of their voices, but also in the design of exquisite passages delivered at opportune points but not in excess.

"Furthermore," he goes on, "they moderated or increased their voices, loud or soft, heavy or light, according to the demands of the piece they were singing; now slow, breaking off with sometimes a gentle sigh, now singing long passages legato or detached, now groups, now leaps, now with long trills, now with short, and again with sweet running passages sung softly, to which sometimes one heard an echo answer unexpectedly. They accompanied the music and the sentiment with appropriate facial expressions, glances and gestures, with no awkward movements of the mouth or hand or body which might not express the feeling of the song. They made the words clear in such a way that one could hear even the last syllable of every word, which was never interrupted or suppressed by passages and embellishments."

It was Pier Francesco Tosi (*circa* 1650–1730), however, nearly a century later, and after Caccini's innovations had been exposed to elaboration by several generations of vocal virtuosos, who left us the most useful documentation of the devices and the basic criteria of florid song in the baroque era. Tosi's *Observations on the Florid Song* (*Opinioni de' cantori antichi e moderni, o sieno osservazioni sopra il canto figurato*) was published in the original Italian in Bologna in 1723 and translated into English by John Ernest Galliard (*circa* 1687–1749) twenty years later.

Tosi was himself a man of notable accomplishments, not only as a castrato soprano but also as a composer and teacher. He traveled widely, arriving finally in London about 1693, where he resided for most of the remainder of his eighty-odd years. His basic philosophy of the vocal art is summarized in the consoling words he offers to those who come to it without an extraordinary endowment.

"Let him," he says, "who studies under the disadvantage of an ungrateful genius remember for his comfort that singing in tune, expression, *messa di voce*, the appoggiaturas, trills, divisions and accompanying himself are the principal qualifications; and no such insuperable difficulties but what may be overcome. I know they are not sufficient to enable one to sing in perfection, and that it would be weakness to content one's self with only singing tolerably well; but embellishments must be called to their aid, which seldom refuse the call, and sometimes come unsought. Study will do the business."

Each of these principal devices is dealt with by Tosi in a separate chapter. The appoggiatura he defines as a note inserted between two other notes to give grace and elegance to the movement from one to the other. Of the trill, or shake, as it is called in Galliard's translation, in conformity with past and even present British terminology, he says:

"Whoever has a fine trill, tho' wanting in every other grace, always enjoys the advantage of conducting himself without giving distaste to the end or cadences, where, for the most part, it is very essential; and who wants it, or has it imperfectly, will never be a great singer, let his knowledge be ever so great."

Those long, rapid vocal excursions known as roulades or divisions, the inescapable device of every *aria di bravura*, the glory of the truly great singers and the despair of all others, are divided by Tosi into two types, the "marked" and the "gliding," or, as one would say nowadays, non-legato and legato. They were expected to be absolutely even, the non-legato not too obviously marked, in time and in tune, uninterrupted by breath-snatching, accomplished without grimaces or convulsive movements of the body.

Of the *messa di voce*, in which the singer attacked a given tone pianissimo, swelled it out to the fullest sound of which he was capable, and then diminished it gradually to the initial pianissimo, sometimes rounding it off with a cascade of pyrotechnics, he says: "A beautiful *messa di voce*, from a singer that uses it sparingly, and only on the open vowels, can never fail of having an exquisite effect." It was a favorite device of the castrati, whose extraordinary lung capacity made it possible for them to sustain such a crescendo and decrescendo far beyond normal limits.

Such were the basic devices with which the singers of the age of *bel canto* sought to animate, vary and embellish a simple melodic line. Their employment was governed by fairly rigid conventions, the latter dictated, in turn, by the plan of the *da capo* aria (in two contrasted parts, closing with a repetition of the first part), the dominant song form of *opera seria*. It was only the improvisatory art of the singers that saved this essentially static and easily tedious form from intolerable monotony. But, at the same time, the *da capo* aria provided a congenial setting for the extemporaneous invention that placed the singers above most of the composers as the creative source of *opera seria*. Here is how Tosi wished his singers to approach a *da capo* aria:

"Among things worthy of consideration, the first to be taken notice of is the manner in which all airs divided into three parts are to be sung. In the first part they require nothing but the simplest ornaments, of a good taste and few, that the composition may remain simple, plain and pure; in the second part they expect that to their purity some artful graces be added, by which the judicious may hear that the ability of the singer is greater; and in repeating the air, he that does not vary it for the better is no great master.

"Let a student, therefore, accustom himself to repeat them always differently, for, if I mistake not, one that abounds in invention, though a moderate singer, deserves much more esteem than a better who is barren of it; for this last pleases the connoisseurs but for once, whereas the other, if he does not surprise by the rareness of his productions, will at least gratify your attention with variety."

Bel canto was, in other words, a performer's art, with the composer serving the singer as the song writer or arranger serves the popular singer or instrumental jazz soloist today, and with the singer granted a liberty to depart from the written notes conceivable today only in popular music or in the art of the older generation of Jewish cantors. In the composition of an opera, and in rehearsal, all was shaped to the singer's art and convenience. In performance he was on his own and, to some extent at least, his own composer. He was expected, even required, to depart from the letter of the score, and he was judged by the imagination, taste, daring and refinement of his invention. This view of the singer's inventive privilege and responsibility persisted well into the nineteenth century, and was still embodied in the younger Manuel García's *Traité complet de l'art du chant*, first published in 1847.

We do not know, and we never shall know, just how all this worked out in performance. The *opere serie*, in which the art of the great singers of the seventeenth and eighteenth centuries flourished, are virtually extinct, even the *opere serie* of such masters as Handel, Gluck and Mozart (*Idomeneo* and *La Clemenza di Tito*). And the occasional revival or excavation can give us only the frame and the form, but not the substance. The genius of the singers who animated them is gone. The castrated male sopranos, mezzo-sopranos and contraltos, who were their principal ornament, have been extinct for a century and a half. There are few female and no male singers who now meet the virtuoso requirements, and none of either sex, probably, sufficiently identified with the idiom to improvise with either the invention or the stylistic security of those earlier singers.

Hundreds, even thousands, of scores are available in the libraries. We know what was written. But we also know that there was more to them than meets the eye, that what we can see and examine today are mere skeletons. And we know that what is missing was supplied by the singers. We even know, in a general way, what it was that the singers added, sometimes even specifically, thanks to the written recollections of contemporary composers and lay listeners.

But the actual sound, the music of the phrase, with all those expressive resources of dynamics and inflection that elude documentation, and the effect that the sound had upon the listener, we can only surmise from contemporary accounts, and these are difficult to evaluate. We who have been brought up on Verdi, Wagner, Strauss and Puccini can hardly apprehend the perceptions and reactions of writers long dead when Verdi and Wagner were born.

Our problem is that we have become accustomed—thanks to the achievements of composers, primarily German, from Bach to Strauss—to think in terms of written composition. We think of the performer as the more or less self-effacing servant of the composer, as an interpreter rather than as a creator in his own right. We tend to forget that in the time of the fullest flower of European music many of the greatest composers—Bach, Mozart, Beethoven, Spohr, Mendelssohn, Liszt and Chopin, for example—were also the greatest performers, and that composition often proceeded from their requirements as professional virtuosos.

Composers and librettists of the age of *bel canto* have been taxed with their failure to provide cohesive, cumulative, credibly motivated dramatic structure. And from the point of view of the modern critic the censure is just. Operas were little more than concerts in costume, pursuing a rigid course of predictable situations developed in such a way that each member of the cast received the arias due his station in the vocal hierarchy (*primo uomo*, prima donna, tenor, *secondo uomo*, *seconda donna* and bass) and of such variety (*aria parlante, aria cantabile, aria di mezzo carattere* and *aria di bravura*, or *aria d'agilità*) as to exhibit all facets of his art and virtuosity. Even the positions the singers could occupy on the stage—center, right, left—were determined by rank and according to protocol. And they seldom left them.

Pietro Antonio Metastasio (1698–1782), the foremost librettist of the eighteenth century, in a letter dated February 10, 1748, offers these suggestions as to how the singers should be placed in the first act of his opera *Demofoönte*:

RIGHT	*Scene I* CENTER	LEFT
Matusio		Dircea
	Scene II	
Dircea		Timante
	Scene III	
Adrasto	Demofoönte	Timante
	Scene IV Timante	
	Scene V	
Creusa		Cherinto
	Scene VI	
Creusa	Timante	Cherinto

Finale
Demofoönte

Dircea   Cherinto
Matusio   Adrasto

Metastasio offers some flexibility by pointing out that the more illustrious character may be at the left, since the right hand is not considered the most eminent position by every nation. "Even if it were," he concludes, "the character could make the left the most distinguished merely by walking across the stage."

This sort of rigidity, associated with the dignity and, curiously, the identity of the individual singer as distinguished from the character the singer was supposed to be impersonating, was characteristic of *opera seria* almost from the first. As early as 1720 it was the target of a satirical treatise, "Il teatro alla moda," by the composer Benedetto Marcello (1686–1739):

"The singers, male and female, are to keep their dignity above all things, never listening to any other actor; saluting the people in the boxes, joking with the orchestra, etc., that people may clearly understand that he or she is not the Prince Zoroaster but Signor Forconi; not the Empress Filastroca but Signora Giandussa Pelatutti. . . . If the singer plays the part of a prisoner, or slave, he must take care always to appear well powdered, with many jewels on his dress, a very high plume, nice shining sword and chains, which latter he is to clatter frequently in order to awaken compassion in the audience; the prima donna must always raise one arm, then the other, constantly changing her fan from one hand to the other; and if she perform the part of a man she must always be buttoning one of her gloves, must have plenty of patches on her face, must very frequently, on entering the stage, forget her sword, helmet, wig. . . ."

The chorus, if any, had little to do, and the orchestra, small and primitive by modern standards—strings, oboes, bassoons, horns, trumpets and percussion, with only a *maestro al cembalo* (harpsichord) as supervisor—was expected to be an unobtrusive and permissive accompanist. Many of the arias were supported only by the harpsichord and a double bass or cello, others by continuo and solo instrumental obbligato, as in so many of Bach's arias.

The theatrical substance of the operas themselves was as stereotyped and stilted as were the musical forms and the style of the musical performance. The plots, dealing with the fortunes and misfortunes of mythological gods and goddesses, Greek, Trojan, Roman and Persian heroes and heroines, medieval kings and queens, and so on, were both complex and incredible. But certain conventions were inviolable, and the outcome always predictable. Good triumphed over evil, the institution of monarchy was treated with respect, and, as in literature, only exalted personages were acceptable as subjects of epic treatment.

Much use was made of mistaken identity and disguise, such tedious devices being rendered either more credible or more incredible by the appearance of both castrati and prima donnas as both males and females. Characters assumed to be dead turned up suddenly among the living, either as spirits or as more or less unmortified flesh and blood. Entrances and exits occurred at the librettist's—or the singers'—whim, without regard to probability or motivation.

It should be remembered, however, that the librettist's purpose was to supply situations rather than continuity. He was serving the singers, not drama as we understand it, and the situations, in themselves, could be dramatic enough, often the revelation to a principal character of some unexpected change of fortune, for better or worse, prompting a few moments of reflection, expressed in a recitative, and then an exposition of the appropriate emotional reaction—rage, resolve, tenderness, nostalgia, remorse, despair, jubilation, as the case might be—usually concluding with an extensive cadenza and a vehement exit. With the best singers, not only were the individual situations felt as dramatic but also the singing itself; individual scenes could be sung with persuasive dramatic conviction and art.

With a structure at once so arbitrary and so loose, however, and with everything geared to the singers' virtuosity and convenience, extensive tampering with book and music was both possible and inevitable. Arias from other operas and by other composers were introduced at the discretion of the singers. Even the rightful composer took no umbrage at being asked to delete an aria and replace it with another if the original was inconvenient to the singer of the moment.

This was true even of Mozart. He deleted "Il mio tesoro intanto" from the Vienna production of Don Giovanni, for example, and replaced it with "Dalla sua pace" when the original aria proved to be too much for the Vienna tenor, as it has for many tenors since then. Elvira's "Mi tradì" was added to the Vienna production for the convenience of Katharina Cavalieri, an excellent soprano, who had been his first Konstanze.

The Royal Opera House at Dresden, one of the most consistently brilliant centers of Italian *opera seria* in the first half of the 18th century, is shown during a performance of Antonio Lotti's *Teofane* in 1719. The arrangement of the stage, orchestra pit, boxes and parquet is typical of opera houses of that time. Boxes on the stage provided a temptation to social intercourse, not always resisted, between singers and listeners. Performance is directed from the harpsichord, on this occasion probably by Lotti himself.

The first theater at Covent Garden was opened in 1732 and was destroyed by fire in 1808. It was modeled on the King's Theater in the Haymarket, where most of Handel's operas were given. The expenses of the performance of Thomas Arne's *Artaxerxes*, shown here, prompted the management to suspend a policy of half price for admission. The ensuing riot caused damages estimated at £2,000.

It should not be surprising, therefore, that the *pasticcio*—a potpourri of scenes and arias from a variety of operas and a variety of composers—was common and popular.

One may well suppose, and correctly, that such a succession of scenes and arias could hardly provide either the continuity or the variety required to sustain an audience's interest through performances that began early and often lasted until well after midnight. It was not expected to. There were other diversions, not all of them artistic.

In its formative years in the seventeenth century, *opera seria* was more spectacle than music, and the early Venetian stage mechanics and scene painters contrived wondrous representations of battles, earthquakes, floods, thunder and lightning, conflagrations and fat clouds bursting to reveal heavenly choirs. Live animals were brought upon the stage, and birds were released.

The most elaborate of such productions were reserved for special occasions—a coronation, a royal wedding or birth, a state visit—when all the human, material and financial resources of a court establishment could be drafted for the enterprise. But poorer theaters followed the princely example as best they could. The importance of spectacle in relation to the music declined as the art of the vocal virtuoso matured, and as the singer became the attraction, but visual delights continued to be provided in the form of magnificent sets and drops and resplendent costuming, with much emphasis on flowing robes, elaborate coiffures and gloriously plumed helmets, and with no emphasis at all on period authenticity.

Further variety was provided by ballet divertissements and scenes of *opera buffa* given between the acts, the function of the latter being documented by their original designation as intermezzi. Pergolesi's *La Serva Padrona*, for example, the oldest surviving specimen of these diversions, was first performed between the acts of Pergolesi's own *opera seria*, *Il Prigionier Superbo*, in Naples in 1733. *Opera buffa* became self-sufficient toward the end of the eighteenth century, and its vitality, as demonstrated in the *opere buffe* of Haydn, Cimarosa, Mozart, Paisiello and Rossini, contributed decisively to the decline and fall of the parent *opera seria*.

Not even this wealth of scenic, terpsichorean and musical diversion would have sufficed to enliven so many hours had audiences assembled in darkened theaters, as they do today, to devote their entire attention to a musical performance in respectful and dutiful silence. In the seventeenth and eighteenth centuries such reverence was neither demonstrated nor expected. The theater was the meeting place of society; and the box, or loge, often owned by a family and passed on from generation to generation, was a living room, or salon, away from home.

The houses were usually well lighted—as they continued to be until comparatively recently—and all the rites of social intercourse were celebrated in the boxes, the more elaborate of them equipped with an anteroom where refreshments could be served, business and politics discussed, introductions made and so on. While the performance was in progress, especially during the recitatives, there were conversation, gossip, drinking, dining, gambling, lovemaking, eavesdropping and spying.

"The box," notes Simon Towneley Worsthorne in his valuable *Venetian Opera in the Seventeenth Century*, "had an influence that permeated through the whole organization. . . . It became simply another room in a rambling mansion, the obvious means of cramming as many people as possible into a confined space, yet preserving the amenities of a civilized social life. For, if St. Mark's Square can be considered today the drawing room of Europe, the box was then the boudoir from which the world of politics and fashion could be discussed and plans for future policies laid." It filled, in other words, some of the functions of today's cocktail party—and many more.

Charles Burney, the English musical historian, attended the opera in Milan in 1770, and thus described the arrangements of the theater (not today's La Scala) in his *The Present State of Music in France and Italy*:

"The theater here is very large and splendid; it has five rows of boxes on each side, one hundred in each row; and parallel to these runs a broad gallery round the house, as an avenue to every row of boxes: each box will contain six persons, who sit at the sides, facing each other. Across the gallery of communication is a complete room to every box with a fireplace in it, and all conveniences for refreshments and cards. In the fourth row is a faro table on each side of the house, which is used during the performance of the opera."

Obviously, in such circumstances, listening to music was an intermittent preoccupation. There might be silence and rapt attention while the castrato star or prima donna of the day sang the principal arias and duets, but the remainder of the cast would sing to a background of social chatter and box-hopping. "The noise," Burney recalled of his evening in Milan, "was abominable, except while two or three airs and a duet were singing, with which everyone was in raptures."

Such behavior is conceivable only if we acknowledge that in the age of *bel canto* people did not "go to the opera" as we do today. They went to a social gathering for which operatic and other entertainment was provided. Nor was the gathering so exclusive as we may tend to picture it. Opera was performed in public as well as in private theaters, and, excepting the court theaters, which were usually open to the public under a variety of arrangements, it was a commercial enterprise. Aristocracy and the mercantile rich were the guarantors and box holders, but there were other, less expensive accommodations, often in the parterre, with or without seats. In Italy, opera was the diversion and passion of all classes, which need not imply that it was always listened to reverently.

It was everywhere a social occasion. The participation of a celebrated virtuoso lent the occasion a special glamour. The celebrity would command attention and harvest applause and money. But his presence imposed no obligation upon the public to forswear less elevated diversion when others were performing, or to defer to the celebrity himself if he failed to please. Hissing, whistling and catcalls were the reward of those considered inadequate. Against this background it is easier to condone the sometimes casual and indifferent behavior of the singers, who, while on stage, might converse among themselves when a colleague was singing, or exchange greetings with friends in the boxes. Since some boxes were actually on stage, there were obvious temptations to such intercourse.

The singers led an itinerant life. The "season" in Italy, and throughout most of Europe, was from December 26 to the beginning of Lent, in other words, the carnival season of Catholic countries, and singers were engaged for the season at a specific theater. Supplementary seasons might be held in some theaters between Easter and June 15 and between September 1 and November 30. And a festival indigenous to a certain locality might be the occasion for a special season of opera. Composers were similarly engaged to provide a new opera, to establish residence for the time being, to work out the details of the opera with the singers, to supervise rehearsals and to direct the first three performances from the harpsichord.

In Germany, Spain, Portugal, Austria, Scandinavia and Russia, and in some Italian kingdoms, principalities and duchies, both singers and composers could become fixed members of a court establishment—Farinelli in Madrid, Mara in Berlin, Faustina in Dresden, for example; and, among the composers, Hasse in Dresden, Haydn at Esterháza, Jommelli

Olivero's picture of the Royal Theater at Turin, about 1740, shows a typical depth-perspective stage set and an atypically large double orchestra. Refreshments are served while the performance is in progress. Conversation is general and apparently animated.

This picture of the opera house in Verona in 1770 shows a plan typical for the time but gives an exaggerated impression of its size.

in Stuttgart, Graun at Berlin, Traetta at Parma and Sarti at St. Petersburg. But their contracts normally included a "leave" clause permitting their absence for stipulated periods, during which they could nourish their international reputations while, at the same time, bringing a reflected glory to their employers.

Nor was the singers' activity restricted to opera. Those employed at courts were expected to sing at private musicales for the delectation of their employers and their guests, and to participate in religious and secular musical festivities; hence the terms *virtuoso di camera* or *Kammersänger* (chamber singer) usually applied to them. From the earliest days of *bel canto*, special airs, originally known as cantatas, were provided for vocal chamber music. Surviving examples are the so-called concert arias of Haydn, Mozart and Beethoven.

It should not be supposed that the deportment of the listeners on such occasions was necessarily superior to that of the public in an opera house. It depended upon the musicality of the ruler. It may be assumed that Frederick the Great played his flute to respectful silence, and that he demanded as much for the excellent artists of his establishment. But elsewhere there might be the inevitable card-playing, gambling and gossip, the noise augmented by the clatter of knives and forks on royal porcelain and by the traffic of servants. Nor, of course, were the artists received among the guests. They were hired help, and were expected to know their station. Impudence and insubordination were dealt with firmly, even brutally.

There were public concerts, too, variously designated as *concerts spirituels, accademie* and *Akademien,* modeled on the *concerts spirituels* founded in Paris in 1725. Outstanding among such concerts were those of the Tonkünstler-Societät in Vienna, the Professional Concerts in London, the Felix Meritis Concerts in Amsterdam and the Gewandhaus Concerts in Leipzig. In cities where there was opera, public concerts were usually restricted to those days when the opera house, for reasons of religion or custom, was closed, and, initially at least, the performance of operatic music was forbidden.

The performance of oratorio offered a way around this restriction, and oratorio continued to be popular under such auspices. But the ruling was soon relaxed, and the format of overtures, symphonies, instrumental and vocal solos, duets, including opera arias, quickly emerged, which would be typical of public concerts until comparatively recently. The song recital as we know it now did not exist. When we read of a singer's "giving a concert," we may assume an orchestra and one or more assisting artists even if no other participants are mentioned. Not until Liszt's heyday did a virtuoso presume to carry an entire program on his own shoulders. Liszt himself thought it a daring and even presumptuous enterprise, and others, including the most celebrated singers, were hesitant to follow his example.

But the *bel canto* virtuoso's most congenial arena was always the opera. One speaks of an arena advisedly. Denied the concentrated attention now accorded even mediocre performers as a matter of course and courtesy, and required to compete with such compelling distractions of social intercourse as conversation, dining, drinking and gambling, the singing star may be pardoned for having sought to surprise and astound. And the accomplishments which could always be counted upon to secure these objectives were inevitably athletic as well as musical.

The chaste delivery of a lovely air, sparingly embellished and free of extraneous melodic deviations, may have assured him the approbation of the connoisseurs, but a *messa di voce* of lung-bursting length, roulades of stunning rapidity, incisive and prolonged trills, and ascents to improbable vocal heights provided a more predictable guarantee of the public's attention and applause, just as the resplendent high note does today.

The musical world was divided as early as Tosi's time about the aesthetic admissibility of such displays, and it has remained so divided ever since. Sheer virtuosity in the athletic sense has always been attractive so long as one performer could surpass all others. In the nineteenth century the vocal matadors were joined by instrumentalists—Liszt, Paganini, Rubinstein, Wieniawski, for example—whose triumphs were often scorned by those who understood and treasured a more musical and less obvious kind of virtuosity. If this latter view would seem today to have prevailed, it may well be only because the athletic limits have been reached, and because hundreds of pianists and violinists can play what, a century ago, was the prerogative of Liszt and Paganini alone.

Tosi's *Observations* have a significant subtitle: "Sentiments on the Ancient and Modern Singers." He treasures the "ancients" for their restraint, taste and musicianship, and he denounces the "moderns" for their musical carelessness and vulgar athleticism. "The study of the singers of the present times," he says, "consists in terminating the cadence of the first part [of a *da capo* aria] with an overflowing of passages and divisions at pleasure, and the orchestra waits; in that of the second

the dose is increased, and the orchestra grows tired; but on the last cadence the throat is set going like a weather-cock in a whirlwind, and the
orchestra yawns."

Things were not quite so bad as Tosi claimed. Vocal trumpery continued to be attractive to a large public. But in the 1730s for a Caffarelli
there was a Carestini; in the 1780s for a Marchesi there was a Pacchierotti, and at the turn of the century for a Velluti there was a Crescentini,
and so it has always been. Vocal trumpery flourishes to this day, if
principally in the form of trumpetry. What else can one say of the gra-
tuitously interpolated high C's of "Di quella pira" and the A-flat and
the G in the *Pagliacci* Prologue?

The capacity of the single high note to inspire wonder and rapture
seems to be inexhaustible, however little it may have to do with music,
and however much at odds it may be with musical phrase and textual
sense. This may well be because a singer's security is both less predictable
and less enduring than the instrumentalist's mastery of technical difficulties, and because his failure is more conspicuous and more disgraceful.
Suspense breeds its own excitement.

Feats of derring-do stimulate emulation in every field. Even those for
whom such aspiration is distasteful are encouraged to follow suit, if only
to prove that they can. This is particularly true of male singers, with
whom vocal prowess is associated inevitably with virility. But the musical
world, including the vocal world, has never been without performers who
could combine their athletic accomplishments with a respect for the
bounds of taste and propriety. Nor has it ever been without those once
great artists who have sensed and pronounced in their own decline the
end of all virtuous tradition.

We who approach opera and singing with requirements, expectations
and criteria governed by nineteenth-century German concern for psychological and philosophical profundity tend to think of the art of *bel
canto* as superficial and vain. But our appreciation of what the Germans
sought and found in a musical idiom identified primarily with the resources of chromatic harmony and the symphony orchestra should not
blind us to that idiom's inherent melodic austerity.

As we review the lives of the castrati and the prima donnas, particularly of those who flourished between 1720 and 1790, when the art of
florid song was at its height, and as we learn how their contemporaries
were touched and delighted by their singing, it must become evident
that many of them offered more than mere blandishment, and that the
greatest of them served an ideal of beauty in music as noble as any.

· II ·

The Castrati

"LET YOUR WOMEN keep silence in the churches," St. Paul wrote to the Corinthians (I Corinthians 14:34). And he echoed the injunction in his epistle to St. Timothy: "Let the woman," he said (I Timothy 2:11-12), "learn in silence with all subjection. But I suffer not a woman to teach, nor to usurp authority over men, but to be in silence."

St. Paul, in the view of contemporary theology, meant simply that women should not participate in theological disputation, or presume to teach men. He is not thought to have been otherwise unappreciative of women's contribution to the early Christian communities. But in the interpretation of the Church of Rome the injunction was absolute, and women were forbidden, accordingly, not only to speak in church, but also to sing. Delighted, possibly, with the ensuing serenity, the Church extended the prohibition to the theater, too; and this latter restriction endured, in Rome, at least, well into the eighteenth century.

The absence of female voices in the music of the church was accommodated easily enough in the relatively simple strains of the Middle Ages. One could make do with men and boys. But in the latter half of the sixteenth century, the prosperity and complexity of multiple-voiced song, an inheritance from the Netherlands contrapuntalists, created a problem susceptible only of a surgical solution. The boys' voices were not strong enough to hold up the treble parts; and the musicianship required for the secure execution of this exacting music was such that the boys, by the time they had acquired it, were either boys no longer or had, at best, no more than a year or so to go.

Attempts were made to master the difficulty with male falsettists. The art of falsetto singing was, for a time, a Spanish monopoly, and in the

Sistine Chapel the monopoly of falsettists imported from Spain was absolute. The Spaniards seemed to have discovered a secret for making the falsetto male soprano, or alto, sound sweeter than it normally does, and for giving it greater range and flexibility. It has been suggested that the secret was, in fact, surgical, that the Spanish falsettists were really castrati. Some of them probably were. But in 1599, two Italian castrati, Pietro Paolo Folignato and Girolamo Rossini, were admitted to the Sistine Chapel—over the vehement protests of the Spanish falsettists—and the age of the castrati was born with the new century.

Folignato and Rossini were not the first castrati to sing in church, nor even in the Sistine Chapel—a Spanish soprano, Francisco Soto, admitted into the chapel choir in 1562, is known to have been a castrato. Orlando Lassus had had six castrati in his choir at Munich in the 1560s and 1570s. There were others elsewhere, including some Spanish castrati in Lisbon. But the acceptance of Folignato and Rossini into the choir of the Sistine Chapel seems to have given the employment of castrati a special sanction, particularly since it had required the explicit intervention of Pope Clement VIII to overrule the objections of the Spanish falsettists. Other Roman Catholic churches throughout Europe followed suit, among them the court chapels, where splendid music was a desirable regal distinction.

Castration itself—excepting a disputed pronouncement by Clement VIII—was never sanctioned. Indeed, the operation was punishable by death, and any association with such surgery, e.g., as an accomplice, called for excommunication. But the Church's attitude seems to have been that the victim, once the irrevocable deed was done, might as well be encouraged to serve both the Church and himself in the most congenial and profitable field thereafter open to him.

Since a castrato's earnings could be enormous—in the Church, initially, and as an appurtenance of a church dignitary's private musical entertainment, later in opera—there grew up, inevitably, a flourishing black market. Impoverished parents sought out surgeons, or, as we shall learn, did the job themselves, in the hope of securing a comfortable old age supported by a famous castrato's fortune. At a time during the eighteenth century, when the reign of the castrati was supreme, it is estimated that as many as four thousand boys were castrated in Italy each year. Very few of them became either famous or rich.

The practice of castration is nearly as old as mankind. In earlier times it had been inflicted as punishment or imposed upon slaves to make them suitable as companions, tutors and servants to highly placed females and as guardians of harems (Mozart once toyed with the idea of casting Osmin, in *Die Entführung aus dem Serail*, as a eunuch, the role to be sung by a castrato.) It was sometimes a ritual sacrifice, and it has figured in the beliefs of certain religious sects. But it had never before been used systematically to preserve a boy's treble voice into manhood.

There are two principal types of emasculation. The more severe, involving the removal of all the genital parts, and usually inflicted as punishment, was often fatal. The other involves the removal of the testes only. It was this latter operation that was performed on boys destined to be singers—before puberty, and usually between the ages of seven and twelve. Some boys were castrated in infancy during the earliest years of the practice, obviously on the assumption that castration alone would make them good singers. Later on, they had to display both voice and musical talent before a decision for castration was made.

Few specifics have come down to us about just where and how the surgery was accomplished, which is hardly surprising in view of its illegality and the delicacy—or indelicacy—of the subject. Burney looked into the matter during his travels in Italy in 1770 without success: "I was told at Milan that it was at Venice; at Venice that it was at Bologna; but at Bologna the fact was denied, and I was referred to Florence; from Florence to Rome, and from Rome I was sent to Naples. The operation most certainly is against law in all these places, as well as against nature; and all the Italians are so much ashamed of it that in every province they transfer it to some other."

Burney may not have known that the subject had been looked into more thoroughly sixty years earlier by a French lawyer, Charles d'Ancillon (1659–1715) and by d'Ancillon's anonymous English translator. D'Ancillon's study had been prompted by an unidentified castrato who wished to marry. His task was to give an opinion, on the basis of such physiological and legal facts as could be determined, as to whether marriage to a castrato was physically, morally and legally admissible. His report, published in 1707 as *"Traité des eunuques,"* concluded that such a marriage, since it could not have procreation as its mission, was contrary to both Church and civil law.

The English version of d'Ancillon's book, published in 1718, the title oddly given as *Eunuchism Displayed*, is a curious document. Although essentially a translation, it makes no reference to the original, and it includes interpolations written in the first person by someone who is demonstrably not d'Ancillon. It would seem to be, in other words, a piracy, possibly justified in the translator's view by the fact that d'Ancillon himself had preserved a coy anonymity. The authorship of the original is ascribed to a "M. ***," and a dedicatory epistle is signed anagrammatically, "C. Ollincan." The English edition, or version, is credited simply to "a person of honor," an attribution the more curious in view of the absence of any reference to a French original. It purports to have been "occasion'd," moreover, "by a young lady's falling in love with Nicolini, who sung in the opera at the Haymarket, and to whom she had like to have been married."

The English translator, by his own account, was in Rome in 1705–06, and to him we are indebted for the following description of castration as it was practiced in Italy at that time:

A boy's testicles were removed, he writes, "by putting the patient into a bath of warm water, to soften and supple the parts, and make them more tractable. Some small time after, they pressed the jugular veins, which made the party so stupid and insensible that he fell into a kind of apoplexy, and then the action could be performed with scarce any pain to the patient; and this was generally done by the mother or nurse in the most tender infancy."

There is no way of determining how frequently this comparatively simple operation was performed by parents rather than by surgeons. Most other accounts speak of surgeons. But d'Ancillon's translator was told by a castrato in Rome how he had been castrated by his own uncle, himself a castrato. The uncle, acting without the child's knowledge, had drugged him with opium. According to the translator's account, opium was sometimes used as an anesthetic, but the practice was discouraged because the dose was so often fatal.

The illegality of the deed, and the shame of the parents' complicity, inspired many a tortured excuse. In some cases the infirmity was alleged to have stemmed from injury in a childhood fracas. In others the boy was the victim of dog bite or a fall from a horse, or some pathological circumstance that made the operation necessary. One castrato was supposed to have been bitten by a wild pig, and another to have been attacked thus grievously by a goose, an attribution more treasurable, certainly, for its imagery than its candor.

The vocal consequences of castration went well beyond the mere perpetuation of a boyish treble. The child continued to grow, and so did his voice; or at least his physical powers to exploit the voice he already had.

This scene, probably from Handel's *Flavio* (1723), in a caricature attributed to John Vanderbank, shows two castrati and a prima donna. Senesino, as *primo uomo*, has the position on the *right*. The prima donna is Francesca Cuzzoni. The *secondo uomo* is Gaetano Berenstadt, a German born in Italy, and one of the very few non-Italian castrati.

A young castrato usually made his debut in a female role and took advantage of a slender figure while it lasted, which was, in most cases, not for long. Here Farinelli, greatest of all the castrati, is caricatured by Pier Leone Ghezzi as he appeared in Rome in 1724, when he would have been 18 or 19.

Under the rigid discipline to which he would now be exposed, his lung capacity and diaphragmatic support would be augmented to an extraordinary degree, enabling him to sustain the emission of breath in the projection of tone up to a minute or more, which is beyond the ability of most normal adult male and female singers. The mature castrato was a boy soprano or alto with all the physical resources of a grown man, although there was, of course—as a castrato acquaintance expressed it, wistfully, to the anonymous translator—"something missing."

The translator singles out three of the castrati whom he heard in Rome in 1705–06—Pauluccio, Pasqualino and Jeronimo. While we shall encounter many professional appreciations of more famous castrati in subsequent chapters, his report is better than theirs—who took the sound for granted—in conveying some idea of just what it was about that sound which inspired such ecstasy and made castrati the undisputed rulers of the operatic roost for nearly two centuries.

Of Pauluccio, for instance, he writes that "this eunuch, who was then about nineteen years of age, was indeed the wonder of the world. For besides that his voice was higher than anyone else's, it had all the warblings of a nightingale, but with only this difference, that it was much finer; and did not a man know the contrary, he would believe it impossible such a tone could proceed from the throat of anything that was human." Jeronimo's voice he described as "so soft and ravishingly mellow that nothing can better represent it than the flute stops of some organ." Elsewhere he compares Jeronimo's sound with "the gentle fallings of water I have somewhere in Italy often heard, lulling the mind with a perfect calm and peace."

From the foregoing it may be inferred that Pauluccio was a soprano, Jeronimo a mezzo-soprano or contralto. Some theorists have held that those castrated closest to the age of puberty were more likely to become altos than sopranos; others that whether the castrated boy became an alto or soprano was determined by the length of his vocal cords, just as this determines whether normal males become tenors or basses, and that the boy's age at the time of castration had nothing to do with it. The fact that many of those castrated at an early age became altos or mezzo-sopranos would seem to support the latter view. A number of castrati, it should be added, who began as sopranos became contraltos or mezzo-sopranos in the course of their careers. A beautiful lower range was often late in developing, and, as with unmutilated men, the top notes were commonly the first to go.

The stilted attitude affected by the castrati, the music held daintily in a relaxed hand, one arm resting on a hip, curved like a caudle cup, is reflected in this painting by Casali of Angelo Maria Monticelli.

Beyond the preservation of a boy's treble voice, the effects of castration upon his further physical development were considerable. He would be beardless, of course, but the hair on his head would be thicker and more luxuriant. He would probably grow to above an average height, and in middle age would be more prone than normal men to obesity. His movements might—but not necessarily—be somewhat ungainly. An anonymous *Reflections upon Theatrical Expression in Tragedy*, published in London in 1755, for instance, includes the following reminiscence of Farinelli as an actor:

"What a pipe! What modulation! What ecstasy to the ear! But heavens! What clumsiness! What stupidity! What offence to the eye! . . . If thou art within the environs of St. James's thou must have observed in the park with what ease and agility a cow, heavy with calf, has arose up at the command of the milkwoman's foot: Thus from the mossy bank sprang up the divine Farinelli. Then with long strides advancing a few paces, his left hand settled upon his hip, in a beautiful bend like that of the handle of an old-fashioned caudle-cup, his right remained immovable across his manly breast, till numbness called its partner to supply the place; when it relieved itself in the portion of the other handle of the caudle-cup."

In a number of the castrati an extraordinary chest development, encouraged by systematic breathing exercises and an attendant enlargement of the rib cage, was accompanied by the appearance of an almost womanly breast (gynecomastia). Casanova, writing from Rome in 1762, thus describes a castrato whom he saw and heard at the Aliberti Theater:

"In a well-made corset, he had the waist of a nymph and, what was almost incredible, his breast was in no way inferior, either in form or in beauty, to any woman's; and it was above all by this means that the monster made such ravages. Though one knew the negative nature of this unfortunate, curiosity made one glance at his chest, and an inexpressible charm acted upon one, so that you were madly in love before you realized it.

"To resist the temptation, or not to feel it, one would have had to be cold and earthbound as a German. When he walked about the stage during the ritornello of the aria he was to sing, his step was majestic and at the same time voluptuous; and when he favored the boxes with his glances, the tender and modest rolling of his black eyes brought a ravishment to the heart."

From other observations made by Casanova about this singer, not otherwise identified, it is clear that he was also a homosexual. As such he was not an isolated case. Another, cited by Angus Heriot in his informative *The Castrati in Opera*, was that of the castrato Cecchino de' Castris, who, in the latter half of the seventeenth century, obtained such a hold over Ferdinand de' Medici, brother of Giovan Gastone, the last native Grand Duke of Tuscany, that Ferdinand's wife was heard to remark: "I would marvel greatly if matters were properly conducted at court while they are regulated by a *castrone*."

Generally speaking, however, homosexuality does not seem to have been more common among castrati than among unmutilated men. The effects of castration upon their sexual appetites seem to have been various. The sexual drive was not, as a rule, extinguished. The operation deprived castrati of the power of procreation, but of neither the possibility nor the pleasure of engaging in unfruitful intercourse. Since they could not achieve real or full sexual satisfaction, modern endocrinology takes a skeptical view of the many legends of their sexual activity and prowess. It seems not unlikely, however, that some of them, reacting to a consciousness of inferiority, salved their egos by simulating a greater degree of sexuality than was biologically possible.

Women sought them out, impelled, no doubt, by various combinations of curiosity, prurience, compassion and, presumably, security from conception. Since the castrato could bring only an immature member to such an intimacy, there were doubtless many deviations from normal sexual intercourse. The love affairs of the castrati were, nevertheless, numerous, often with women of high birth and position, and accounts of many such affairs have come down to us among the more amusing and bizarre scandals of the seventeenth and eighteenth centuries.

Indeed, the castrato was virtually condemned to scandalous relationships, for the Catholic Church could not, and never did, countenance a castrato's marriage, and the Protestant denominations were hardly less adamant. Some castrati and the women they loved sought papal indulgences, but in vain. An exception was Filippo Finazzi (1710–1776), who became a Protestant and married a Protestant woman in Hamburg. Giusto Tenducci (*circa* 1736–?) and an Irish Protestant eloped and were married by a Catholic priest at Cork. The scandal was resolved by Tenducci's recantation and a "legal" Protestant ceremony. The marriage was annulled.

For the rest, the castrati were normal enough. In character and disposition they manifested the familiar attributes of good and evil in the usual proportions. There were the mean and vicious among them, but others of noble character and extensive cultivation. Farinelli, during his long stay at the Spanish court, proved himself to be both an excellent politician and statesman and a man of exceptional humility, integrity and devotion.

Much has been made of the castrati's alleged arrogance, vanity and pompous posturing; but this would seem to be one of those cases where the notorious excesses of a few came to be associated with the generality. Nor should it be surprising that among those deprived of the appurtenances and faculties about which men tend to be, either privately or publicly, most vain, some should have been inordinately concerned with such accomplishments as were still within their reach. Among the latter, certainly, was Luigi Marchesi (1754–1829), a star of the last generation of the castrati, who is supposed to have insisted upon making his first entrance descending a hill on horseback—or at least descending a hill—and wearing a helmet with plumes a yard high.

Not surprisingly, they could be jealous, too. Michael Kelly (1762–1826), the Irish tenor who sang the roles of Basilio and Don Curzio in the first performance of *The Marriage of Figaro*, and the English soprano, Nancy Storace (1766–1817), Mozart's first Susanna, were in Florence, about 1780, where Storace was second woman to Marchesi in an opera by Francesco Bianchi (1752–1810). As Kelly tells us in his *Reminiscences:*

"Bianchi had composed the celebrated cavatina, 'Sembianza amabile del mio bel sole,' which Marchesi sang with the most ravishing taste; in one passage he ran up a flight of semitone octaves, the last note of which he gave with such exquisite power and strength that it was ever after called *la bomba di Marchesi!* Immediately after this song, Storace had to sing one, and was determined to show the audience that she could bring a *bomba* into the field also.

"She attempted it, and executed it, to the admiration and astonishment of the audience, but to the dismay of poor Marchesi. The manager requested her to discontinue it, but she peremptorily refused, saying that she had as good a right to show the power of her *bomba* as anyone else. The contention was brought to a close by Marchesi's declaring that if she did not leave the theater, he would; and, unjust as it was, the manager was obliged to dismiss her and engage another lady who was not so ambitious of exhibiting a *bomba*."

But vainglory, arrogance, impertinence and pompous airs have never been confined in this world to singers, nor, among singers, to castrati. Vain

Giusto Tenducci's marriage to a Protestant became a famous scandal. Tenducci was, for a time, imprisoned. The marriage was first "legalized" and then annulled.

singers are with us today, male and female. How long has it been since Giuseppe di Stefano threatened to cancel an appearance in Philadelphia because an advertisement in the program book at the Academy of Music billed Franco Corelli as the world's greatest tenor? (He finally agreed to sing on condition that distribution of the offending program book be stopped.)

The life of a castrato followed a fairly predictable course, beginning with tough and exacting schooling. The centers of musical education in Italy were the musical conservatories, originally charitable institutions, the most celebrated being those of Venice and Naples. The Venetian schools were largely for females, the Neapolitan for boys. Burney visited the Conservatorio of Sant' Onofrio in Naples in 1770, and his account leaves one astonished that such institutions could have produced not only a long list of illustrious singers, but also a succession of fine composers.

"This morning I went . . . to the Conservatorio of Sant' Onofrio," he wrote, "and visited all the rooms where the boys practice, sleep and eat. On the first flight of stairs was a trumpeter, screaming upon his instrument till he was ready to burst; on the second was a French horn, bellowing in the same manner. In the common practicing room there was a Dutch concert, consisting of seven or eight harpsichords, more than as many violins, and several voices, all performing different things in different keys: other boys were writing in the same room; but it being holiday time, many were absent who usually study and practice in this room.

"The jumbling them all together in this manner may be convenient for the house, and may teach the boys to attend to their own parts with firmness, whatever else may be going forward at the same time: it may likewise give them force by obliging them to play loud in order to hear themselves; but in the midst of such jargon and continued dissonance, it is wholly impossible to give any kind of polish or finishing to their performance; hence the slovenly coarseness so remarkable in their public exhibitions, and the total want of taste, neatness and expression in all these young musicians till they have acquired them elsewhere.

"The beds, which are in the same room, serve for seats to the harpsichords and other instruments. Out of thirty or forty boys who were practicing I could discover but two that were playing the same piece. The violoncellos practice in another room; and the flutes, hautbois and other wind instruments in a third, except the trumpets and horns, which are obliged to fag together on the stairs or on the top of the house. There are in this college sixteen young castrati, and these lie upstairs by themselves, in warmer apartments than the other boys, for fear of colds, which might not only render their delicate voices unfit for exercise at present, but hazard the entire loss of them forever.

"The only vacation in these schools in the whole year is in autumn, and that for a few days only: during winter the boys rise two hours before it is light, from which time they continue their exercise, an hour and a half at dinner excepted, till eight o'clock at night; and this constant perseverance, for a number of years, with genius and good teaching, must produce great musicians."

Kelly, who visited Sant' Onofrio ten years later, gave a similar account. "I left the place in disgust," he wrote, "and swore to myself never to become an inmate of it." Louis Spohr inspected the amalgamated Royal College of Music in 1817 and found the instruction execrable. In healthier times it must have been good. Certainly it was thorough.

Heriot, for instance, cites the following regimen for the young Caffarelli as a pupil of Porpora: In the morning an hour of singing difficult passages, an hour of letters (diction and enunciation) and an hour of singing exercises before a mirror; in the afternoon a half hour of theory, a half hour of counterpoint on a *canto fermo* (improvisation), an hour of counterpoint with the *cartella* (blackboard), and another hour of letters. The rest of the day was spent in exercise at the harpsichord and in the composition of psalms, motets, etc.

If this was typical, and there is no reason to doubt that it was, it is hardly surprising that so many of the castrati were also composers of sorts, and considered themselves qualified to make their own decisions in regard to ornamentations, appoggiaturas, cadences, melodic variants, and so on. Nor should it be surprising that composers felt no compunction about consulting with the better singers in shaping their recitatives and arias. Some of the castrati studied privately, with Pistocchi in Bologna, for example, and some teachers at the conservatories took private pupils, as did Porpora in Naples, but it may be assumed that the regimen was no less severe, however less squalid the circumstances.

When the master felt that his pupil was sufficiently advanced, by which time the boy would normally be fifteen or sixteen, he would arrange for an operatic debut, usually in a female role, in which his pupil's youth, fresh appearance and unblemished voice might best be exploited. At that time, if he had not already done so, the boy would take a pseudonym, derived, as a rule, from the name of his patron, or benefactor, his teacher or his birthplace. The pseudonym was not, however, obligatory, and some castrati sang under their own names.

The young castrato's initial success or failure would determine whether he was destined for a career in the theater, for a life of drudgery and indignity in churches and chapel choirs—or worse. "Nothing in Italy is so contemptible," d'Ancillon's translator noted, "as a eunuch that cannot sing." Assuming a decent success, he would then do a good deal of traveling, gaining experience and establishing his credentials and building a reputation.

If all went well, he would accept a position in some court, where he would be distinguished from other singers in the court records by the designation *musico*, a euphemistic avoidance of the all too explicit castrato or *evirato*. The term *musico*, after the disappearance of the castrati from opera, was passed on, curiously, to female mezzo-sopranos and contraltos specializing in male roles.

The careers of the castrati were longer, as a rule, than those of unmutilated men. They started earlier, and vocal decay set in rather later, although not invariably; Angelo Maria Monticelli (1715–1758) was only thirty-seven when a Neapolitan impresario wrote of him that "he neither wishes to, nor should, be heard." But all voices eventually deteriorate, and the chronicles are full of references to castrati who clung to their careers longer than was prudent. In due course, they would retire, usually to settle down in a pleasant villa in their native Italy, often in the place of their birth, possibly to teach, certainly to welcome visitors and relive with them the hours of their glory, deploring the estate into which the vocal art had fallen—as singers have done ever since, and probably not without reason.

The castrati seem to have been somewhat longer-lived than normal males of the time. Many of them lived well into their seventies, and not a few into their eighties. One of them, Antonio Bannieri (1643–1740)— who was brought to the court of Louis XIV as a boy soprano and enjoyed such favor there that (allegedly but not demonstrably) he had himself castrated on his own initiative in order to perpetuate his privileges—lived to be ninety-seven. (Castrati were never fashionable in France, to which fact is attributed the allegedly ghastly sound of French singing in the seventeenth and eighteenth centuries; but they were not unknown, either in church or at court, and visitors were heard from time to time, without, however, exciting much pleasure.)

The last of the Spanish soprano falsettists in Rome died in 1625.

Spanish contralto falsettists survived at the Sistine Chapel until near the end of the century. Castrati, on the other hand, continued there for another two centuries, and long beyond their disappearance from the opera scene. The last of the operatic castrati was Giovanni-Battista Velluti, for whom Meyerbeer wrote his early *Il Crociato in Egitto*, produced in Venice in 1824. The last of the great church castrati was Domenico Mustafà (1829–1912), who was director of the papal music until his retirement in 1902.

It was from Mustafà, apparently, that Emma Calvé learned the secret of what she used to call her "fourth voice." She described this voice, as employed by Mustafà, as consisting of "certain curious notes . . . strange, sexless, superhuman, uncanny." It would appear to have been a greatly refined falsetto. Calvé's, if not Mustafà's, "fourth voice" can be heard on some of Calvé's records.

The last of the line at the Sistine Chapel was Alessandro Moreschi (1858–1922), who retired in 1913. His voice may be heard on a number of records made by the Sistine Chapel Choir under his direction shortly after the turn of the century. Although once the possessor of a voice of great beauty, Moreschi was not a brilliant performer, and he was past his prime when these records were made.

They are treasurable as the only clue we have to how the castrati really sounded. It is important, however, when listening to them, to remember that it is a man in his mid-forties that we are hearing, not a Farinelli or a Caffarelli in his early twenties, and that in the age of *bel canto* Moreschi, even in his prime, would probably not have been numbered among the great singers.

Some Early Virtuosos

FERRI · SIFACE · NICOLINO

OPERA IS DATED conventionally from the *Eurydice* of Jacopo Peri (1561–1633), first produced in Florence on February 9, 1600. This was a recitative work designed to rediscover the lyric-dramatic art of Hellenic tragedy. Aside from its being sung throughout, it bore little resemblance to the kind of opera dominated by the singer and the *da capo* aria which subsequently provided the frame within which flourished the great singers of the seventeenth and eighteenth centuries. But it did include a foretaste of what was to come in the form of some airs with florid passages composed by Caccini for his daughter Francesca, one of the principals in the Peri première.

Opera remained a rare and exclusively courtly phenomenon until 1637, when the opening of the Teatro San Cassiano in Venice with the *Andromeda* of Francesco Manelli (1595–1667) touched off a flame of popular enthusiasm that spread almost immediately to other Italian cities. From that time until the end of the century some three hundred or more operas were produced in seventeen theaters in Venice, and as many more by Venetian composers in other cities. While the Venetian operas, with their delight in earthquakes, naval battles, celestial revelations and other examples of scenic extravagance, were initially more notable for mechanical than for vocal wonders, it was probably inevitable that an art so nourished by popular enthusiasm should soon eschew the lofty recitative structure of what the Florentines had thought was Hellenic melodrama in favor of something at once more tuneful and more virtuosic.

The musical evolution of the Venetian opera in the works of Monteverdi (1567–1643), (Pietro) Francesco Cavalli (1602–1676) and Marcantonio Cesti (1620–1669) was clearly toward the later conventions of *opera seria*, with its dependence upon the dramatically static *aria da capo* and its prescribed distribution of opportunities for individual accomplishment throughout the cast and according to rank. It is pertinent to note that both Cavalli and Cesti were, for a time, singers in the choir of St. Mark's in Venice, and that with them began the reign of the composer over the dramatist—the objective of the early Florentine experiments had been precisely the reverse—and of the singer over both, which was to characterize Italian opera for the next two centuries.

Castrati were prominent in Venetian opera from the very beginning. The singers for Manelli's *Andromeda* had been drawn from the choir of St. Mark's, and all the female roles were sung by castrati. Although women were not everywhere in Italy forbidden to appear on the stage in public, as they were in Rome, there was a considerable prejudice against them—on moral rather than religious grounds—and in some other cities they were barred from the stage until well into the eighteenth century. The consequent shortage of qualified female singers made it inevitable that the castrati, already established in the Church, should be called upon to fill the gap.

Less inevitable, it would seem, was their assumption of male roles, which can be documented from as early as 1641, in Cavalli's *Didone*. There was, after all, no prejudice against the appearance of normal males in the theater, on either religious or moral grounds. Indeed, in the legitimate theater, such as it was in seventeenth-century Italy, female roles were often played by unmutilated men. The Italian preference for the castrato in male roles is usually attributed to a predilection for the high voice.

Until the end of the eighteenth century, the bass had little standing in *opera seria*, and even the tenor was cast in secondary roles and rated accordingly in the distribution of arias. The Italians seem to have felt that the soprano, having the highest voice, should be cast in the principal part, even if this were a hero rather than a heroine. Thus, not only castrati but also female sopranos were frequently cast as heroic males. The practice persisted into the nineteenth century, as reflected in Rossini's *Tancredi*, written for a female contralto and remembered as one of Pasta's great roles.

Italians, to this day, prefer tenors to basses as heroes, despite Verdi's elevation of the lower male voices in *Nabucco, Macbeth, Rigoletto* and *Simon Boccanegra*, none of whose heroes, incidentally, is a lover. The incongruity of an Alexander the Great or Hercules singing soprano seems not to have disturbed the Italians, and some of their indifference has come down to us in our own easy acceptance of Octavian, Niklaus, Oscar and Cherubino, not to mention the Orpheus of Gluck's opera, originally sung by a castrato and now entrusted by custom to a female mezzo-soprano.

1. BALDASSARE FERRI

Curiously, the first of the castrati to attain international eminence, and to receive both the popular acclaim and the marks of royal favor that the great castrati of later generations came to expect as no more than their due, was not a product of the Venetian opera, and did not make his career in Italy. He was Baldassare Ferri, who was born in Perugia in 1610 and died there in 1680.

Ferri had been a child prodigy. As a boy soprano he entered the service of Cardinal Crescienzi at Orvieto at the age of eleven. He left it, and Italy, four years later to serve Prince (later King) Ladislas IV of Poland at the court of Sigismund III at Warsaw. He remained in the service of Ladislas and his successor, John Casimir, for thirty years. His only subsequent appearances in Italy are believed to have been in 1643, for the marriage of Ladislas to Maria Lusia of Mantua at Venice. Of his reception at public appearances there we read for the first time of a singer's carriage being strewn with flowers and, later, at Florence, of his being met by the townspeople three miles from the city and given honors customarily reserved for high personages. (This sort of thing became common later on, and will not again be specially noted.)

When Poland was invaded by the Swedes in 1655, and the court compelled to withdraw to Silesia, Ferri moved on to Vienna, where he was employed and greatly favored by Ferdinand III and Leopold I. He retired to Italy in 1675. The most persuasive account of his singing is that of Giovanni Bontempi (1624–1705) in his *Istoria Musica*, published in Perugia in 1695. Bontempi was not only roughly a contemporary of Ferri, but also, apparently, himself a castrato, who sang in the choir at St. Mark's in Venice from 1643 until 1647, or even later. The

accuracy of some of his biographical details on Ferri has been questioned, including his reference to an appearance in England in 1669 or
1673, but there is no reason to doubt so knowledgeable a contemporary
on his singing. According to Bontempi:

"What this noble singer expressed with his voice is beyond description. There was, to begin with, the purity of his voice and his success
with every kind of passage, the impact of the trills and the ease and grace
with which he achieved every note. But beyond all that, after a very
long, sustained and lovely passage beyond the lung capacity of any other
singer, he would, without taking a breath, go into a very long and lovely
trill and then into still another passage, more brilliant and beautiful
than the first, and all this while remaining still as a statue, without any
movement of the brow, the mouth or the body.

"To sing a descending chromatic scale, trilling on each note, from the
high G and A to the same notes in the lower octave, a feat, if not impossible, certainly very difficult for any other singer, was child's play for
Ferri; for again, without taking a breath, he would continue on to other
trills, passages and artistic wonders. He often added a soft crescendo to
these chromatic scales, building out the trills at the same time, a feat
never previously accomplished or heard of."

According to Esteban Arteaga (1747–1799), whose life work was a
study of the Italian musical theater (Le Rivoluzioni del teatro musicale
italiano, dalla sua origine fino al presente), it was Ferri's singing that led
to the adoption of the da capo aria in Italian opera seria. If so, in terms
of the development of the lyric theater as a dramatic art, he had quite a
lot to answer for.

Whether or not Ferri was the greatest as well as the first of the great
singers of the seventeenth century, Bontempi's exuberant appreciation
suggests that his style and his accomplishments may have contributed
decisively to the establishment of the basic criteria against which subsequent singers were judged.

In trying to imagine for ourselves just how fine and brilliant a singer
Ferri may have been, it is well to remember that Bontempi could not
have heard the great singers of later generations, who brought the art of
bel canto to its maturity toward the middle of the eighteenth century,
and that even before the prime of Farinelli and Caffarelli in the 1730s,
the devices and accomplishments of Ferri and his immediate successors
were regarded as old-fashioned and crude.

2. SIFACE (GIOVANNI FRANCESCO GROSSI)

To Siface belongs the distinction of having been the first of his kind to establish himself in England, although he never sang in opera there. Born in a little town near Pistoia in 1653, he derived his stage name from the role of Siface (Syphax) in Cavalli's opera *Scipione Africano*, with which he enjoyed a sensational success in Venice in 1678. He was impetuous and impudent, but the beauty of his voice and, according to Galliard, a manner of singing "remarkably plain, consisting particularly in *messa di voce* and the expression," seem always to have redeemed the offenses of his temper and tongue.

As an appurtenance of the court of the Duke of Modena, he was sent in 1688 to Queen Mary of England, the duke's sister. The London climate bothered him, and he sang only rarely, but when he did sing he delighted everyone. The queen, in an enthusiastic thank-you letter, assured her brother that she believed Siface to be "the finest *musico* in the world." And a charming souvenir of his visit has come down to us in the form of a short keyboard composition by Henry Purcell bearing the affectionate title "Farewell to Siphauci [*sic*]."

Siface ended badly by becoming the lover of a countess, Elena Forni, née Marsilii, the widow of a Modenese nobleman. The lady's horrified family put her away in a convent, but Siface found ways of gaining admittance and continuing their trysts. The family learned of it, apparently as a result of the castrato's own indiscreet boasting, and had him done away with by the local Sparafucile, a common and convenient means of disposal in those libertine days.

3. NICOLINO (NICOLÒ GRIMALDI)

It is to Nicolino, however, whose English lady love had "occasion'd" d'Ancillon's English translator's piracy of *"Traité des eunuques,"* that is credited not only the enthusiasm of the British public for *bel canto*, which was to bring fame and fortune to most of the great castrati of the eighteenth century, but also the very acceptance of Italian *opera seria* in England, soon to flourish there under the inspired leadership of Handel, that greatest of all early composers of Italian opera. Nicolino, who was born in 1673, came to London in 1708, Handel in 1710, and the singer's performance in the title role of *Rinaldo*, with which Handel introduced himself to the London public on February 24, 1711, at the old Haymarket Theater, had much to do with the success of that venture.

More has come down to us about the acting of Nicolino (or Nicolini, as his name was often spelled) than about his singing. He was the first, and one of the few, of the castrati about whom this could be said. When he made his debut in Alessandro Scarlatti's *Pyrrhus and Demetrius* in December, 1708, Steele, who found the proceedings otherwise ridiculous, and who did not, on another occasion, shy at referring to the "squeak" of the "eunuchs," said of Nicolino in No. 115 of *The Tatler:*

"I was fully satisfied with the sight of an actor who, by the grace and propriety of his action and gestures, does honor to the human figure. Everyone will imagine I mean Signor Nicolini, who sets off the character he bears in an opera by his action as much as he does the words by his voice. Every limb and every finger contributes to the part he acts, insomuch that a deaf man may go along with him in the sense of it. There is scarce a beautiful posture in an old statue which he does not plant himself in, as the different circumstances of the story give occasion for it.

"He performs the most ordinary action in a manner suitable to the greatness of his character, and shews the prince even in the giving of a letter, or dispatching of a messenger. . . . Our best actors are somewhat at a loss to support themselves with proper gesture as they move from any considerable distance to the front of the stage; but I have seen the person of whom I am now speaking, enter alone at the remotest part of it, and advance from it with such greatness of air and mien as seemed to fill the stage, and at the same time commanded the attention of the audience with the majesty of his appearance."

This suggests posturing and attitudinizing rather than acting as we think of it today, but again we should remember that this was the very early eighteenth century, and that the textual frame within which Nicolino worked probably inspired or permitted little else. Within that frame his accomplishments must have been formidable if he could survive the celebrated scene with the lion in Francesco Mancini's *Hydaspes*, thus described by George Hogarth (1783–1870) in his *Memoirs of the Musical Drama:*

"Hydaspes addressed the lion in a long bravura song, full of divisions and flourishes; first calling on the 'cruel monster' in a tone of defiance to come on, and then telling him, with a sentimental air, and in a largo movement in the minor key, that he may tear his bosom but shall not touch his heart, which he has kept faithful to his beloved. The exhibition of Nicolino, alternately vaporing and gesticulating to a poor biped in a lion's skin, then breathing a love-tale in the pseudo-monster's ear, and at last fairly throttling him on the stage, must have been ludicrous in the extreme, and sufficient to throw ridicule on the Italian opera."

Even Addison, while he could not approve the episode, or condone Nicolino's participation in such a travesty, was awed by his accomplishments. "It gives me a great indignation," he wrote in *The Spectator*, "to see a person whose action gives new majesty to kings, resolution to heroes and softness to lovers thus sinking from the greatness of his behavior, and degraded into the character of the London *prentice*. I have often wished that our tragedians would copy after this great master in action.

"Could they make the same use of their arms and legs, and inform their faces with as significant looks and passions, how glorious would an English tragedy appear with that action which is capable of giving a dignity to the forced thoughts, cold conceits and unnatural expressions of an Italian opera!"

Could Addison not have known that it was Nicolino himself who had

This is a "division," or roulade, sung by the castrato Nicolino, in Giovanni-Battista Buononcini's *Etearco* in 1711. Compared with the bravura passages sung by virtuosos of succeeding generations, it is primitive in both its rhythmic and harmonic invention, but it would have required the long breath that was one of the fundamentals of a castrato's technique.

brought *Hydaspes,* or *Idaspe Fedele,* to London? In any case, when Nicolino left England for the first time in 1712, Addison regretted the departure of "the greatest performer in dramatic music that is now living, or that perhaps ever appeared upon a stage."

Nicolino was back in London in 1715, but left again two years later to divide the remainder of a long career between Venice and Naples. His last appearance was in Venice in 1730, when he was fifty-seven, and when it can only have been his accomplishments as an actor that made tolerable his performing on the same stage with Farinelli, then approaching his prime.

How good a singer he was, even under the best of circumstances, is hard to tell. Burney, writing toward the end of the century, remarks that "in Nicolini's best songs the longest division is but the same series of notes repeated above or below their first station in the movement," and he associates them with a kind of invention "to our ears at present very dull and tiresome."

But Galliard, in whose opera *Calypso and Telemachus* Nicolino had sung, said of him that he combined the qualities of singer and actor "more than any that have come here since. He acted to perfection and did not sing much inferior." And Galliard's experience covered the prime of Senesino, Bernacchi, Carestini, Farinelli and Caffarelli.

· IV ·

Virtuosos of the First "Golden Age"

PISTOCCHI · BERNACCHI · SENESINO

CARESTINI · PORPORA · FARINELLI

CAFFARELLI · GUADAGNI

Tosi's *Observations* provided the theoretical and aesthetic basis of subsequent vocal instruction, as well as enduring criteria for the evaluation of vocal accomplishment. But the men who put these fundamentals into pedagogical practice most effectively were Antonio Pistocchi (1659–1726), of Bologna, and Niccolò Porpora (1686–1767), a Neapolitan.

1. ANTONIO PISTOCCHI

Pistocchi, as a singer, belongs among the early virtuosos, but it was as a teacher of the virtuosos of the first "golden age" that he made his greatest contribution. Tosi describes him as "the most famous singer of our own or any other time, who rendered his name immortal as the inventor of a mature and inimitable taste," and as the one who "taught how to achieve all the beauties of vocal art without singing out of time." Pistocchi probably went farther than Tosi in the encouragement of virtuoso passages of an instrumental character.

Franz Haböck, the Viennese pedagogue whose death in 1921 left incomplete his vast study, *Die Kastraten und ihre Gesangskunst*, the principal source for anyone investigating the life, art and times of the castrati, attributed Pistocchi's predilection for instrumental effects to his experience as leader of the excellent orchestra of the Margrave of Brandenburg at Ansbach. Whatever its inspiration, the new virtuosity brought fame to Pistocchi's pupils and came to be recognized as a Bolognese way of singing. Pistocchi himself knew how to employ it with taste and discretion. But not all his pupils were of a similarly chaste disposition, and their abuses exposed Pistocchi to charges of having contributed to the corruption of the vocal art by introducing empty gymnastics.

2. ANTONIO BERNACCHI

The most celebrated, and probably the guiltiest, of these pupils was Antonio Bernacchi, a mezzo-soprano, who concluded a brilliant career by passing on the Bolognese tradition as the teacher of Senesino, Carestini and the German tenor, Anton Raaff.

Bernacchi's birth date is given variously as 1685, 1690 and 1700. Such details of his career as can be established, and the ages of those reputed to have been his pupils, indicate 1690, or thereabouts, as the most plausible. (The birth dates of some other castrati are similarly uncertain, due, we may assume, to the obscure origins of so many of these singers and to the familiar tendency of singers to add a few years to their competitors' ages while subtracting a few from their own.)

Tosi declines to identify the sinners among his exasperating "moderns," but the tenor of resignation and frustration in his utterances suggests that he had prominent and successful singers in mind, and one is tempted to assume that Bernacchi was one of them. The fact that Tosi does single out Pistocchi as an example of "ancient" virtues may have been intended as a reproach to Bernacchi. In any case, Pistocchi, when he heard Bernacchi at the peak of his career, hailed in Italy as the "king of singers," is said to have exclaimed: "Ah, poor me! I taught you to sing, and you want to be an instrumentalist (*tu vuoi suonare*)."

Bernacchi must still have been under Pistocchi's chastening influence when he first came to London in 1716, for Burney says: "This performer's voice seems by nature to have been feeble and defective, but he supplied the defects of nature by so much art that his performances were always much more admired by professors than by the public in general." His prime was already past when Handel brought him back to London in 1729. The vehicle for his reappearance was *Lotario*, a new opera by Handel, and a curious light is thrown upon his endowment in Burney's account: "Bernacchi's first song, 'Rammentati, cor mio,' is an air of great dignity, and susceptible of much taste and expression, particularly as Handel judiciously left this singer to himself, undisturbed by instruments, through which his voice had not sufficient force to penetrate."

It may have been this frailty that prompted Bernacchi to sing his divisions with a full chest voice instead of the lighter head voice or mixed voice previously considered more suitable for such rapid and florid passages. And it was this device, presumably, that had enabled him to compete successfully a few years earlier with the younger and more generously endowed Farinelli. The practice was followed by his pupils, and constituted one of his important and enduring innovations.

The most vivid, and also the most reliable, evidence of Bernacchi's capacities is the well-documented account of a meeting with Farinelli in Bologna in 1727. Farinelli was then twenty-two, and had already triumphed in Naples, Rome, Venice and Vienna. An appearance in Bologna with the celebrated Bernacchi must have been an exciting challenge to the young prodigy, and such challenges were accepted in those days in a manner for which the only modern parallel would be the "cutting sessions" of old-time jazz musicians. Battle was joined in the course of an opera, each singer attempting to outdo the other in art, in the invention and skill of his ornamentation, and in feats of vocal athleticism.

Farinelli had the first aria—perhaps the first inning would be the more appropriate term—and employed all the devices and flourishes that Porpora, imitation and experience had taught him. Bernacchi, following, did everything that Farinelli had done, improving on his challenger in taste and finish, and then went on to additional *fioriture* of his own. The two singers became good friends, and Bernacchi even passed on some of his secrets, including the singing of divisions from the chest. Farinelli subsequently employed them with such zeal that he was, for a time, charged with excessive acrobatic display.

3. SENESINO (FRANCESCO BERNARDI)

Bernacchi retired in 1736 and died in 1756. His two most famous pupils, Senesino and Carestini, were very nearly his contemporaries; and being also contraltos, or mezzo-sopranos, they were likewise his competitors. In London, where the Royal Academy under Handel at the Haymarket had become to Italian singers of that time what the Metropolitan in New York is today, they were preferred to their teacher. Senesino, born probably about 1700, was chosen over Bernacchi as successor to Nicolino in 1720. Ten years later, with Senesino away, Bernacchi again failed to please, and Senesino was recalled. And in 1733, when Senesino and most of Handel's singers deserted to the opposition at Lincoln's Inn Fields under Porpora, it was Carestini rather than Bernacchi whom Handel chose to enter the lists against Farinelli and the truants.

Johann Joachim Quantz (1697–1773), later to achieve fame as Frederick the Great's flute master, heard Senesino in Dresden in 1718–19 and again in London in 1727. "He had a powerful, clear, equal and sweet contralto voice," Quantz told Burney during the latter's visit to Berlin in 1772, "with a perfect intonation and an excellent trill. His manner of singing was masterly and his elocution unrivalled. He never loaded adagios with too many ornaments, but he delivered the original and essential notes with the utmost refinement. He sang allegros with great fire, and marked rapid divisions from the chest in an articulate and pleasing manner. His countenance was well adapted to the stage, and his action was natural and noble. To these qualities he joined a majestic figure; but his aspect and deportment were more suited to the part of a hero than a lover."

Senesino (the name was derived from Siena, his birthplace) was vain, contentious and arrogant. Handel had his troubles with him, but the fact that their partnership endured beyond a decade suggests that each was aware of the advantages of the association. John Mainwaring, in his *Memoirs of the Life of the Late George Frederick Handel* (1760), wrote: "I am as far from asserting as I am from believing that any other person could have shown such a singer to equal advantage." And Burney, speaking of an aria in Handel's *Admeto* (1727), notes: "The air is slow, simple, and often without any other accompaniment than a bass, in order to furnish an opportunity for unfolding his whole volume of voice in all its purity and force."

4. GIOVANNI CARESTINI

The last, and probably the finest, of the great Bolognese singers of the first "golden age" was Giovanni Carestini, who was born at Filottrano, near Ancona, *circa* 1705 and died there *circa* 1759. He was exceptional among the castrati in that, while he had a pseudonym, Cusanino—derived from the Cusani family, who had helped him as a boy—he was usually known by his real name. Even more exceptional was a long and distinguished career—in Italy, Germany, England and, at the last, Russia—almost totally devoid of dramatic or scandalous incident. Like the other pupils of Pistocchi and Bernacchi, he began as a soprano, with a range extending to the soprano high C, but emerged as a contralto in his prime. Was there something about the Bolognese schooling that tended to rob the voice of its highest notes? Could it have been the practice of singing lengthy and rapid divisions from the chest?

Burney describes his voice as "the fullest, finest and deepest countertenor [the term was not usually applied to mutilated males] that has, perhaps, ever been heard," and he goes on to say: "Carestini's person was tall, beautiful and majestic. He was a very animated and intelligent actor, and having a considerable portion of enthusiasm in his composition, with a lively and inventive imagination, he rendered everything he sang interesting by good taste, energy and judicious embellishments. He manifested great agility in the execution of difficult divisions from the chest in a most articulate and admirable manner. It was the opinion of Hasse, as well as of many other eminent professors, that whoever had not heard Carestini was unacquainted with the most perfect style of singing."

Burney adds that the aria "Salda quercia," from Handel's *Arianna in Creta*, which Carestini sang a tone lower than the subsequently printed version, "contained longer and more difficult divisions than had been heard on our stage before the arrival of Farinelli." It also "put into action his low notes and fine trill," another of the countless examples of Handel's solicitous behavior toward his singers.

How times change! Mozart was still considerate enough and resourceful enough to make the melodic alterations necessary to accommodate his singers' virtues and frailties, and if one aria did not suit a singer at all, he would give him another. But Beethoven was unmoved by the pleas of Henriette Sontag and Caroline Unger to moderate the *tessitura* of certain passages of the Ninth Symphony and the *Missa Solemnis*. Sontag was eighteen at the time, and Unger all of twenty. "Learn it," Beethoven told Unger about a note she felt was beyond her reach, "and it will come." At the performance it came; probably unfortunately, for Beethoven seemed to be vindicated, and composers ever since have tended to behave as though the accommodation of singers were beneath the dignity of a composer's calling. Neither vocal art nor vocal health has profited from this presumption.

Senesino (above left) was Handel's *primo uomo* at the King's Theater in London in the 1720s. Handel wrote for him some of his finest arias in the mezzo-soprano range.

Giovanni Carestini (above right) was considered by connoisseurs the finest singer of the Bolognese school. The German composer Hasse said that "whoever had not heard him was unacquainted with the most perfect style of singing."

After Farinelli the most famous of the castrati of the first "golden age" was Caffarelli (right) for whom Handel wrote "Ombra mai fù," the famous Largo from *Xerxes*.

5. NICCOLÒ PORPORA

Even while Carestini was at the height of his career, the center of vocal virtuosity was passing from Bologna to Naples, thanks to Porpora's extraordinarily productive pedagogy. Porpora was the first—he would not be the last—to become a great teacher without himself having been a great singer. Insofar as he was a singer at all he was a tenor, and this in a time when tenors did not count for much. And he confined his singing to the chamber and the church. But among his pupils were Porporino, Farinelli, Caffarelli, Appiani and Salimbeni, five of the greatest castrati of the eighteenth century; the female sopranos Regina Mingotti and Catterina Gabrielli; and Antonio Montagnana, one of the first of the great bassos.

He was a versatile, restless, difficult, probably even exasperating man. Himself a pupil of Alessandro Scarlatti (1658–1725), he composed a great number of operas, but for all his skill and learning, he seems to have lacked a truly creative flair, and he was doomed, as a composer, to be overshadowed by Hasse in Dresden and Handel in London. Once he had prepared and launched Farinelli and Caffarelli, he was constantly on the move, promoting himself as composer and teacher, and volunteering more or less welcome postgraduate guidance to his star pupils.

He taught at the conservatories in Venice as well as those of his native Naples. He early sought employment in Vienna, but his penchant for floridity was uncongenial to the musical taste of Charles VI. In Dresden, then one of the most brilliant centers of Italian opera in Europe, he fared better, remaining off and on from 1728 to 1733 and from 1748 to 1752. There was friction, however, between him and Hasse, who had come to Naples in 1724 to study with him but had deserted him in favor of Scarlatti. And during Porpora's later sojourn in Dresden there was trouble between his pupil, Regina Mingotti, and Faustina, who was Hasse's wife. In London, from 1733 to 1736, he led that opposition to Handel's company, assisted by Farinelli, which brought financial ruin upon all concerned.

To his pupils Porpora was father, friend, impresario and tyrant. While none ever denied his genius as a teacher, as alumni they found his possessiveness tedious. His pedagogical objectives did not differ notably from those of Pistocchi and Tosi, with which he was, of course, familiar. He was obviously influenced by the example of Bernacchi in emphasizing—probably overemphasizing—*fioriture*. But he thought, as Tosi did, that the heart must come before the throat, and he was strict about recitative and a proper regard for the words.

His greatest gift, however, seems to have been his ability to sense or detect a pupil's peculiar aptitudes, and to fashion his instruction accordingly. All sources agree on his almost exclusive concern for fundamentals, and the account given by François Joseph Fétis (1784–1871), in his *Curiosités historiques de la musique*, is illuminating, if probably not precisely accurate:

"Porpora became fond of one of his pupils, a young castrato. He asked him if he had the courage to follow the path prescribed for him, as tedious as it might seem. Upon the boy's affirmative reply, Porpora wrote out on a piece of paper the diatonic and chromatic scales, ascending and descending, skips of the third, fourth, fifth, etc., for the mastery of intervals and the sustaining of the tone; then trills, turns, appoggiaturas and vocalises. This piece of paper occupied teacher and pupil for the ensuing year; also the next. In the third year nothing was said about a change. The pupil began to grumble, but the teacher reminded him of his promise. The fourth year passes, and then the fifth, and always the same piece of paper. In the sixth year they continue, but add exercises in articulation, enunciation and, finally, declamation. At the end of this year the pupil, still thinking himself a beginner, is surprised to hear his teacher say: 'Go, my son, you have no more to learn. You are the first singer of Italy and of the world.' He spoke the truth, for this singer was Caffarelli."

This story has been passed down in various versions by many other sources. Porpora's "famous piece of paper" was supposed to have been preserved in the library of the Royal College of Music in Naples, and an English singing teacher, Marcia Harris, in 1858, published an edition allegedly drawn from the original. Haböck copied out this latter edition in the British Museum in 1913, omitting interpolated piano accompaniments, and took it to Naples, hoping to be able to compare it with the original. But the library catalogue contained no reference to any such thing, and the librarian could shed no light on it.

Haböck was inclined, nevertheless, to accept the authenticity of the Harris edition, and reprinted it in *Die Kastraten und ihre Gesangskunst*. Heriot doubts the whole story, suggesting that the "piece of paper," or *foglia*, may have been, in fact, a *cartella*, a sort of glazed tile with music staves, on which exercises could be written or erased—the equivalent, in other words, of a school slate. Both Heriot and Haböck point to the many solfeggi, or vocalises, by Porpora, of various degrees of difficulty, which have survived, and which, indeed, have served as models for singing teachers from Porpora's time to the present. They are far more sophisticated and comprehensive than the elementary scale exercises offered in the Harris edition. Also preserved are many solo cantatas obviously conceived as studies in vocal virtuosity, contrived, presumably, to illustrate the virtues of individual pupils, or to assist others in overcoming their special deficiencies.

Our last and, indeed, our only intimate glimpse of Porpora is through the eyes of no less illustrious a commentator than Joseph Haydn, who was his pupil, and assisted him as accompanist and even as servant during Porpora's stay in Vienna from 1753 to 1757. Porpora had come to Vienna in the retinue of the Venetian ambassador, as singing teacher to the latter's mistress. Haydn was boarding in the same house as Metastasio at that time, and the poet brought them together.

Porpora, as recounted in Georg August Griesinger's *Biographical Notes Concerning Joseph Haydn*, based on conversations with Haydn when the latter was an old man, was "too grand and too fond of his ease to accompany at the keyboard himself, and entrusted this business to the young Haydn," who discharged it in exchange for instruction in singing and composition. In Haydn's own words, as quoted by Griesinger, "there was no lack of *asino, coglione, birbante* (ass, boob, rascal) and pokes in the ribs, but I put up with it all, for I profited greatly with Porpora in singing, in composition and in the Italian language." Porpora is remembered, however, as the teacher not of Haydn but of Farinelli and Caffarelli. Of these Farinelli was probably the greater singer—he is commonly spoken of as the greatest singer who ever lived—and he certainly was the finer character.

6. FARINELLI (CARLO BROSCHI)

There were, to be sure, certain circumstances in Farinelli's career beside his public triumphs that set him apart from all his excellent contemporaries, particularly his celebrated success in assuaging the crippling melancholy of Philip V of Spain by singing the same four songs to him every night for nearly ten years. His engagement at the Spanish court in 1737 meant his withdrawal from the international circuit and, indeed, from the theater, at the age of thirty-two, and spared him those indifferent or deplorable twilight performances which blighted the remembrance of other illustrious castrati.

Under Philip V's successor, Ferdinand VI, Farinelli—both as director of an opera ensemble that must have been matched at the time only in Dresden, and as a gray eminence deeply and usefully concerned in such nonmusical matters as public works and foreign affairs—achieved much that was beyond the range or even the comprehension of most singers of his own or any other time. As one foreign observer reported, "Farinelli drills tenors and sopranos one day and ambassadors and ministers the next."

His withdrawal from the Spanish scene in 1759 was prompted not by decaying vocal or administrative prowess but by differences with Charles III, Ferdinand's successor, on foreign policy. Even his dismissal was dignified—overlooking Charles's snide observation that "capons are for eating." Farinelli was retired at full pension, the only condition being that he settle at Bologna rather than his native Naples, then under Spanish dominion.

The circumstances of Farinelli's origin may help to explain this extraordinary career, particularly with respect to the tact, diplomacy and political acumen that so distinguished his services to Ferdinand VI. Unlike the majority of the castrati, he came of a "reputable" family—possibly also slightly disreputable. The pseudonym Farinello was applied to the Broschi family, not just the singer, and it means, in Italian, rascal or rogue.

The elder Broschi, Salvatore, was governor of the towns of Maratea and Cisternino from 1706 to 1709, which means that his governorship survived the Austrian conquest of the Kingdom of Naples in 1707. Heriot suggests that this must have involved some adroit political footwork on the part of Salvatore Broschi, and that Broschi's subsequent disappearance from public life may have proceeded from disgrace. It may also explain why young Carlo, born in Andria, near Bari, in 1705, was surrendered to the knife, at the age of seven, an unusual fate for a boy of good family.

In any case, Farinelli was brought to Naples so early in his childhood that he always claimed it as his birthplace. His musical education began in his infancy, first from his father and his brother Riccardo, who was later to write several of his most compelling showpieces, and subsequently from Porpora. He made his debut in Naples in 1720 in a serenata

No other castrato was the subject of so many flattering portraits as Farinelli, seen here as painted by Jacopo Amiconi (or Amigoni) wearing the white mantle of the Order of Calatrava, conferred upon him by Ferdinand VI of Spain. In background are Ferdinand VI and Queen Maria Barbara.

by Porpora to a text by Metastasio. This was also Metastasio's debut as a librettist, and it was this circumstance of a double debut that prompted Farinelli and Metastasio to address each other as "Dear twin" in the exchange of correspondence kept up throughout their lives. They died within a few months of each other in 1782.

Farinelli was only fifteen at the time of this Neapolitan debut, and it was not until two years later, when Porpora took him to Rome to appear in one of his own operas, that he established himself as a singer of extraordinary gifts. Here occurred that competition between Farinelli and a trumpet player which has survived as a legend of the age of *bel canto*. This, more than any other legend of the time, gives us an idea of the singular combination of musical virtuosity and athleticism that distinguished the accomplishments of the great castrati from those of any other singers. Although the record is not clear, it seems that Porpora, with precocious showmanship, set the stage for his pupil by providing him a solo with trumpet obbligato. Burney leaves this, but little else, to the imagination:

"During the run of an opera there was a struggle every night between Farinelli and a famous player on the trumpet in a song accompanied by that instrument; this, at first, seemed amicable and merely sportive, till the audience began to interest themselves in the contest, and to take different sides. After severally swelling a note in which each manifested the power of his lungs and tried to rival the other in brilliancy and force, they had both a swell and shake together, by thirds, which was continued so long, while the audience eagerly waited the event, that both seemed exhausted; and, in fact, the trumpeter, wholly spent, gave it up, thinking, however, his antagonist as much tired as himself, and that it would be a drawn battle; when Farinelli, with a smile on his countenance, showing he had only been sporting with him all that time, broke out all at once in the same breath, with fresh vigor, and not only swelled and shook the note, but ran the most rapid and difficult divisions and was at last silenced only by the acclamations of the audience. From this period may be dated that superiority which he ever maintained over all his contemporaries."

His career henceforth was that of the itinerant vocal matador. His profitable encounter with Bernacchi has been mentioned. It is probably too much to assume that he was ever Bernacchi's pupil in any formal sense; Porpora would hardly have permitted it. But they often sang together, including what must have been a memorable appearance in

In al-to mar si con-fon - de e spa-ven - ta-ta va sol-can-do in al-to mar, in al-to mar, in al-to mar

Unprecedented agility and flexibility contributed to Farinelli's unique status. This is an excerpt from the aria "Son qual nave," written for him by his brother, Riccardo Broschi, and sung in the *pasticcio* in which Farinelli made his London debut in 1734. It includes many of the devices that subsequently became clichés of virtuoso singing: scales, trills, repeated notes, octave leaps and syncopations. All these were child's play to Farinelli. On the opposite page are measures 19 to 23 of the above as elaborated by Farinelli in performance.

Parma in 1728, when Leonardo Vinci (1690–1730) wrote a trio for them and an unidentified colleague with parts of equal difficulty for each.

What these difficulties may have been is illustrated in music written for Farinelli by his brother, particularly an aria, "Qual guerriero in campo armato," referred to at the time as a "concerto for larynx," which included skips of a tenth, repeated notes, syncopation (all devices frowned upon by Tosi), arpeggios and a high E. There are many appreciations of Farinelli's art and style at this time, the most reliable, probably, being that of the knowledgeable Quantz, who heard him in Naples in 1726:

"Farinello [the name was originally spelled in this fashion, the "i" probably including the whole family] had a penetrating, well-rounded, luscious, clear and even soprano whose range at that time was from the low A to the D above high C. In later years it was extended several tones below without the loss of the high notes. The result was that in many operas there would usually be an adagio for him in the contralto range, and another in the soprano. His intonation was pure, his trill beautiful, his lung capacity extraordinary and his throat very flexible, so that he could sing the most distant intervals in fast tempi and with the greatest ease and accuracy. Interrupted and all other passages were no problem. In arbitrary embellishment of an adagio he was very inventive. The fire of youth, his great talent, universal applause and an accomplished throat led him from time to time to excessive display. His appearance was advantageous, his action perfunctory."

Burney visited Farinelli at his villa in Bologna in 1770 and was told by his host that an imperial admonition given him by Charles VI in Vienna in 1731 had been of more service to him than all the precepts of his master or examples of his competitors for fame. "Those gigantic strides," the emperor had told him, "those never-ending notes and passages, only surprise; and it is now time for you to please; you are too lavish of the gifts with which nature has endowed you; if you wish to reach the heart you must take a more plain and simple road." These few words, Burney reported, brought about an entire change in Farinelli's manner of singing, and from this time on he mixed the pathetic with the spirited, the simple with the sublime, and by these means delighted as well as astonished every listener.

How well he succeeded in both is illustrated by occurrences at his debut in London in 1734 in a *pasticcio* put together from music by Hasse, Riccardo Broschi and others. At the first rehearsal the members of the orchestra were so astonished that they forgot to play—or were unable to keep pace—and at the first performance Senesino, playing the part of a tyrant to Farinelli's captive in chains, was so moved by Farinelli's first aria that he stepped out of character and embraced him on the stage.

One of the arias of this production was Riccardo Broschi's "Son qual nave," in which, according to Burney, "the first note was taken with such delicacy, swelled by minute degrees to such an amazing volume, and afterwards diminished in the same manner, that it was applauded for full five minutes. He afterwards set off with such brilliancy and rapidity of execution that it was difficult for the violins of those days to keep pace with him." The bravura passages of this aria were designed to give the impression of a voyage at sea.

The most persuasive contemporary appreciation of Farinelli's art at the time of his London triumphs is contained in a letter by the often caustic Paolo Antonio Rolli, an Italian poet resident in London, who was, moreover, Senesino's friend and ally: "I must have you know—for it deserves to be known—that Farinello was a revelation to me, for I realized that till then I had heard only a small part of what human song can achieve, whereas I now conceive I have heard all there is to hear. He has, besides, the most agreeable and clever manners, hence I take the greatest pleasure in his company and acquaintance. He has also made me a present. . . ." All of which indicates that Farinelli's diplomatic propensities were well advanced before his arrival at the untidy court of Philip V.

His engagement there—the idea of the queen, Elizabeth Farnese, who had heard him at Parma (she was the daughter of the Duke of Parma)— begins prettily enough. There is the shrewdly planned recital in a chamber adjacent to the king's at the palace at La Granja, near Segovia. To quote from Sir William Coxe, the British ambassador at that time: "Philip was struck by the first air sung by Farinelli, and at the conclusion of the second sent for him, loaded him with praises and promised to grant whatever he should demand. The musician, who had been tutored by the queen, entreated him to rise from his bed, suffer himself to be shaven and dressed and attend council. Philip complied, and from that moment his disorder took a more favorable turn."

In fact, the circumstances of Farinelli's service were anything but pretty. He could help, but he could not cure, and the king remained a singular specimen. Among his persistent aversions were bathing, shaving, changing his clothes or permitting his bed linen to be changed. He is reported to have worn the same clothes for a year and a half, and it seems not unlikely that he also wore them in bed. He dined at 3 A.M., retired at 5 A.M., arose to hear Mass, retired again at 10 A.M., and arose at 5 P.M. Farinelli was with him every night from midnight until 5 A.M., treasured not only for his song but also for his conversation.

Musicologists and historians have been tempted to doubt that Farinelli really sang the same four songs every night throughout this tedious and probably disgusting decade. It has been surmised that he may have sung just one of the four every night, adding others at his discretion. But given the king's peculiarities and Farinelli's characteristic humility and self-effacing dedication—which survived even the king's habit of attempting to emulate Farinelli's singing—it seems not impossible.

Two of these songs were "Pallido il sole" and "Per questo dolce amplesso," both from Hasse's *Artaserse*, the opera which had provided the nucleus for the *pasticcio* in which he made his London debut. A third was a minuet by Attilio Ariosti (*circa* 1666–*circa* 1740), "Fortunate passate mie pene," inserted in the *pasticcio* by Farinelli. The fourth was

Quell' u - si - gnuo - lo che in - na - mo - ra - - - - to se can - - - - - - - - - ta _ so - lo tra fron - da e fron - da spie - ga del fa - to la cru - del - tà spie - ga del fa - to la cru - del - tà la cru - del - tà

The imitation of birds, specifically the nightingale, was an inevitable tour de force of the castrati. Farinelli's nightingale was this elaboration of an aria from Geminiano Giacomelli's opera *Merope*. It was one of the four songs that he is said to have sung every night for a decade for the melancholy Philip V of Spain.

"Quell' usignuolo," by Geminiano Giacomelli (1686–1743), an imitation of the nightingale with *fioriture* added by Farinelli.

Under Ferdinand VI, who had a taste for spectacle, Farinelli, no longer confined by contract to the king's chamber, devoted himself to the production of opera and the organization of aquatic extravaganzas. He brought many of the finest singers of the time to Spain, including Caffarelli, Gizziello, Mingotti, Montagnana and Raaff; he commissioned libretti from Metastasio to be set by the court composers; he summoned painters as scenic designers, including Jacopo Amiconi, who did several of Farinelli's best—and doubtless flattering—portraits, and certain stage mechanics whose accomplishments must have recalled the scenic wonders of the Venetian theaters of the preceding century.

In recognition of these splendid productions, and especially for those celebrating the wedding of the Infanta Maria Antonia in 1750, he was admitted to the Order of Calatrava, one of the highest orders of knighthood in Spain. This required the furnishing of proof of noble birth, and Farinelli's ability to comply is cited as evidence of his family's aristocracy. But since the future Charles III was then ruling in Naples as King of the Two Sicilies, such documentation need not have been very persuasive or of very ancient origin.

Ferdinand VI died on August 10, 1759, and although Elizabeth Farnese, who had brought Farinelli to Spain, was Charles III's mother, Farinelli's day was done. Charles III had, indeed, built the first San Carlo Theater in Naples, destroyed by fire in 1816, but his attitude toward music is betrayed by the fact that he had his own box placed where he would be least exposed to disturbance by the sound of any other voice than his own.

Farinelli had retired from the public stage in 1737, and now he retired altogether. His villa at Bologna, where he spent the remainder of

Farinelli was uniquely fortunate in having a composer for a brother. An *aria di bravura*, usually on a militant subject, was essential to every castrato's stable of war-horses. One of Farinelli's most faithful steeds was his brother's "Qual guerriero in campo armato." The fragment above shows why it came to be known as a "concerto for larynx."

his life, still stands, but without the lovely harpsichords that he had brought with him from Spain, a reminder of his recent magnificence. His declining days must have been comforted by Burney's remarkable tribute: "His talents had effects upon his hearers beyond those of any musical performer in modern times, and it may be doubted whether the most celebrated musicians of antiquity, Orpheus, Linus or Amphion, however miraculous their powers over the heart of man, ever excited such splendid and solid munificence in their hearers."

7. CAFFARELLI (GAETANO MAJORANO)

If Farinelli was distinguished by every characteristic commonly thought of as virtuous, Caffarelli, born in 1710, for whom Handel wrote the famous "Largo" from *Xerxes*, was equally distinguished by most of those we think of as vicious. He was vain, arrogant, impertinent, insubordinate and given to brawling. In Rome, early in his career, he was surprised by a duped husband and spent the rest of the night hiding out in a cistern. Even his singing, as magnificent as it certainly must have been at its best, was inconsistent, and when not in good voice he resorted to forcing.

One exasperatingly inexplicit reference to "a ridiculous tone of lamentation which can turn the most cheerful allegro sour" in a letter from Metastasio to Farinelli, describing the impression made by Caffarelli in Vienna in 1749, leaves the reader wondering if he may not have been the first to affect that sobbing inflection so characteristic of later Italian tenors, particularly Neapolitans.

He took his pseudonym from a certain Domenico Caffarelli, who presumably arranged for his castration at Norcia—which seems to have been a center for this operation—when he was twelve, and for his subsequent studies with Porpora, previously described. It seems not impossible that his mutilation was voluntary. The usual stories about a fall from a horse, or an attack by a dog or a pig, etc., were not told about, or by, Caffarelli.

An early high point in Caffarelli's career was his appearance with Farinelli in Venice in 1734. The opera was Giacomelli's *Merope*, and it may have been Caffarelli's presence that prompted Farinelli to make that elaboration of "Quell' usignuolo" which later so delighted the public in London and eased the sordid doldrums of Philip V. In London, in 1738, Caffarelli experienced his only decisive failure. The memory of

Farinelli was too fresh, and the Londoners were apparently unaffected by Caffarelli's more vehement song and action. He returned to Italy and settled in Naples, so greatly admired that his sins were overlooked or pardoned.

At one performance there, according to the official report of the theater director, he disgraced himself by "disturbing the other performers, acting in a manner bordering on lasciviousness with one of the female singers, conversing with the spectators in the boxes from the stage, ironically echoing whichever member of the company was singing an aria, and finally refusing to sing in the ensembles with the others." On another occasion, again according to an official account, "when he came to the duet at the end of the second act, the *musico* Caffarelli began to sing the first two verses in a manner quite different from that written by the Saxon maestro [Hasse]; but the prima donna, [Giovanna] Astrua . . . though thus obliged to improvise, managed as well as she could. . . .

"At the repeat, however, Caffarelli produced a new version different from his first one, and full of rhythmic variations and syncopations, with anticipation of a beat. When Astrua, in responding, tried to get back into the proper tempo, Caffarelli had the audacity not only to remonstrate with his hands, how she should keep time, but even suggested vocally how she should sing. . . . There was a universal murmur of outrage from the boxes and the pit. . . ."

For the first of these offensive performances he was imprisoned for three days. It should be remembered that Naples was then ruled by the future Charles III of Spain, whose exasperation with Caffarelli may have encouraged his determination to get rid of Farinelli upon his assumption of the Spanish throne in 1759.

And there were other episodes—a near duel with Gianambrosio Migliavacca, poet laureate at the court in Dresden, during a rehearsal in Vienna, averted only by the intervention of the prima donna, Vittoria Tesi, when she literally presented her person between the two swords; an actual duel in Paris with the poet Ballot de Sauvet, arising from an argument about the relative merits of Italian and French music; an insult to Louis XV about the size of a snuff box, a royal gift, which resulted in an exit visa valid for only three days, and an uncooperative performance at Turin for the wedding of the Prince of Savoy and the Spanish Infanta, turned into a triumph by the diplomacy of the King of Sardinia, who reminded him that the Infanta had expressed doubts that any other singer could equal Farinelli.

Niccolò Porpora (left) was one of the earliest and one of the greatest of singing teachers. Among his pupils were Farinelli and Caffarelli.

The first of Pistocchi's great pupils was Antonio Bernacchi (below left), noted for his delivery of divisions from the chest. He is shown here with the prima donna Vittoria Tesi, famous for the masculine strength of her low notes.

Antonio Pistocchi (below center, to the right of the picture) was an early virtuoso and the first of the great singing teachers. He founded the so-called Bolognese school. Shown with him are Farinelli, in a youthful likeness, and Maria Bulgari, or Bulgarelli, an early prima donna.

Gaetano Guadagni (below right), an alto castrato, was the original Orpheus of Gluck's opera. With him, to the left, is Giovanni Manzuoli, who gave singing lessons to the child Mozart in London in 1764-65.

Toward the end of his career, Caffarelli, who had eagerly submitted to Porpora's exacting regimen, became lazy and sloppy, no longer bothering with the expression in recitatives, and demanding easy pieces in moderate tempi. He had grown rich, and had purchased the domain of San Dorato in Calabria and the dukedom that went with it. Here he built an appropriately immodest *palazzo*, with the inscription over the portal: AMPHION THEBAS, EGO DOMUM (Amphion built Thebes, I this house), prompting, among the irrepressible Neapolitans, the ribald extension: *"Ille cum, tu sine"* (He with, you without).

He became more amiable, too. Burney met him at a private party in Naples in 1770 and reported: "The whole company had given Caffarelli over when, behold! he arrived in great good humor; and contrary to all expectations, was, with little entreaty, prevailed upon to sing. Many notes in his voice are now thin, but there are still traits in his performance sufficient to convince those who hear him of his having been an amazingly fine singer; he accompanied himself, and sang without any other instrument than the harpsichord; expression and grace, with great neatness in all he attempts, are his characteristics." Caffarelli was then probably sixty.

He died in 1783. But his memory is perpetuated, curiously, in *The Barber of Seville*. Not one opera lover in a thousand, probably, catches the reference when, following Rosina's offering in the lesson scene, Bartolo exclaims: "But that song, what a bore! Music in my time was something else again. Ah, when, for example, Caffariello [Caffarelli] used to sing that heavenly air! . . ."

8. GAETANO GUADAGNI

Although from our distance in time from the eighteenth century we are inclined to think of the great castrati collectively, and to accept the term "golden age" as including them all, there appear, on closer acquaintance, to have been two distinct peaks. The first of these culminated in the careers of Farinelli and Caffarelli. The second came much later. But there was a continuity of fine singers, and the school of Porpora and his contemporaries among the Neapolitan vocal pedagogues was, at mid-century, still far from the sterility discovered by Spohr and bemoaned by Crescentini in 1817.

Among the castrati of the interim, the one whom we have the most compelling reason to remember is Gaetano Guadagni, if only because he was the original Orpheus of Gluck's opera. The music written for him by Gluck provides the contemporary music lover's only truly surviving link with the castrati of the age of *bel canto*. It is a tenuous link, to be sure, for Guadagni distinguished himself in this role from all other castrati by adding nothing to what Gluck had written.

But the lovely "Chiamo il mio ben così" and the famous "Che farò" cannot help but give some idea of the sustained lyricism and lofty sentiment of which the castrato voice was capable. Indeed, it speaks for this unique capacity that no substitution has ever been judged entirely satisfactory, either Gluck's own of a tenor, for the Paris production of 1774, or that of a mezzo-soprano (Pauline Viardot) for the Paris production of 1859. Experiments with baritones have been even less successful. The castrato contralto, or mezzo-soprano, seems to have had a certain disembodied sound particularly suited to the legend of Orpheus and Eurydice.

Guadagni was not, to be sure, a Neapolitan by birth. He was born in Lodi, near Milan, *circa* 1725. But he was a pupil of Gizziello (Gioacchino Conti) who had been a pupil of Domenico Gizzi, a Neapolitan contemporary of Porpora, and he belongs, accordingly, to the Neapolitan line. Initially, he seems to have had no schooling at all. He began his career, curiously, as the juvenile lead in a *buffa* company, with which he arrived in England in 1748. He was described then as of fine voice and appearance, but wanting in technique of any kind. He remained in England until 1755, profiting greatly as an actor from an appearance with David Garrick in John Christopher Smith's *The Fairies*, a musical setting of *A Mid-Summer Night's Dream*, in 1755.

His studies with Gizziello seem to have taken place in Rome between 1755 and 1762, in which latter year he turned up in Vienna, a finished singer, and ready for his historic accomplishment as Orpheus. This is not a bravura part, and Guadagni, for all his great art as singer and actor, was never a vocal matador. "Though his manner of singing was perfectly delicate, polished and refined," wrote Burney when Guadagni reappeared in London in 1769, "his voice seemed at first to disappoint every hearer." But "his figure was uncommonly elegant and noble; his countenance replete with beauty, intelligence and dignity; and his attitudes and gestures were so full of grace and propriety that they would have made excellent studies for a statuary. . . .

"The music he sang was the most simple imaginable; a few notes with frequent pauses, and opportunities of being liberated from the composer

and the band [orchestra] were all he wanted. And in these seemingly extemporaneous effusions he proved the inherent power of melody totally
divorced from harmony and unassisted even by a unisonous accompaniment. Surprised at such great effects from causes apparently so small, I
frequently tried to analyze the pleasure he communicated to the audience, and found it chiefly arose from the artful manner of diminishing
the tones of his voice, like the dying notes of the aeolian harp. Most
other singers captivate by a swell or *messa di voce*; but Guadagni, after
beginning a note or passage with all the force he could safely exert,
fined it off to a thread, and gave it all the effect of extreme distance."

Although as a person Guadagni had none of the less edifying vices of
some other castrati, he could be difficult. He was proud of his art and of
himself as an artist, and he demanded respect for both at a time when
such expectations on the part of an artist were regarded by society as
impudent. He spoke often of the dignity of a singer, and he even refused to take curtain calls when he felt that they were inappropriate to
the course of the drama. The story that he once kept a monarch cooling
his heels in an anteroom while he finished whatever he had under way
with a lady friend is probably apocryphal, if only because a castrato's
anteroom is an unlikely place for a monarch to have been; but there is
no reason to doubt Burney when he says, "He had strong resentments
and high notions of his own importance, which revolted many of his
warmest friends and augmented the malice of his enemies."

Guadagni left England in 1771, attaching himself to the retinue of
the dowager Maria Antonia of Saxony in Munich. He retired to Padua
in 1777, singing at the Cathedral of San Antonio, and amusing himself
and his visitors with a puppet theater, himself manipulating the puppets.
The *pièce de résistance* was Gluck's *Orfeo*, with Guadagni behind the
scenes, singing the music that he had launched on its course down
through the ages. He died in 1792.

V

The Last Full Flower

PACCHIEROTTI · MARCHESI
CRESCENTINI · VELLUTI

NEITHER RESEARCH nor narrative, however persuasive, can disturb the security of Farinelli's reputation as the greatest of the castrati and possibly the greatest of all singers. But among the group constituting the second "golden age" in the 1770s and 1780s there was one who may well have been the greater artist. He was Gasparo Pacchierotti, who was born near Ancona in 1740 and died in Padua in 1821.

1. GASPARO PACCHIEROTTI

Of no other singer, not even of Farinelli, are there comparable accounts of the effect his singing had on those who heard him, nor is there a comparable unanimity in the hyperbole expended upon any other singer by informed listeners of varying nationality, experience and disposition. Pacchierotti, like Farinelli, seems to have had everything that a singer can offer; and, unlike Farinelli, he was also an affecting actor.

Burney, who heard him often, tells of his experience in attending Pacchierotti's first rehearsal in London in 1778, when, "though he sang *sotto voce* under a bad cold in extreme severe weather, my pleasure was such as I had never experienced before. The natural tone of his voice was so interesting, sweet and pathetic, that when he had a long note, or *messa di voce*, I never wished him to change it or do anything but swell, diminish or prolong it in whatever way he pleased to the utmost limit of his lungs. A great compass of voice downward, with an ascent up to B flat and sometimes to C, with an unbounded fancy, and a power not only of executing the most refined and difficult passages of other singers, but of inventing new embellishments, which as far as my musical reading and experience extended, had never then been put on paper, made him during his long residence here a new singer to me every time I heard him."

Lord Mount-Edgcumbe, in his *Musical Reminiscences*, offers detailed corroboration: "Pacchierotti's voice was an extensive soprano, full and sweet in the highest degree. His powers of execution were great, but he had far too good taste and good sense to make a display of them where it would have been misapplied, confining it to one *aria d'agilità* in each opera, confident that the chief delight of singing and his own supreme excellence lay in touching expression and exquisite pathos. Yet he was so thorough a musician that nothing came amiss to him.

"Every style was to him equally easy, and he could sing at sight all songs of the most opposite characters, not merely with the facility and correctness which a complete knowledge of music must give, but entering at once into the views of the composer and giving them all the spirit and expression he had designed. Such was his genius in his embellishments and cadences that their variety was inexhaustible. He could not sing a song twice exactly the same way, yet never did he introduce an ornament that was not judicious and appropriate to the composition."

It is curious that the writer refers to Pacchierotti here as a soprano. He was commonly thought to be a contralto. But the normal range of the castrato contraltos was the two-octave G to G of today's baritones, although an octave higher, of course, and, as we learn from Burney, Pacchierotti sang up to a B flat or even a C. Burney also notes the fullness and flexibility of his low voice, and remembers hearing him sing tenor arias in their original pitch, descending to the B flat. This would indicate a range of at least three octaves. In other words, his voice must have provided a foretaste of those female mezzo-sopranos of the nineteenth century who inspired such wide-ranging roles as Cenerentola, Rosina, Malcolm Graeme (in *La Donna del Lago*) and Fidès (in *Le Prophète*), the delight of their originators and the despair of most of those who followed.

Lord Mount-Edgcumbe not only heard Pacchierotti frequently but also knew him intimately, and he speaks highly of his character and cultivation, as, indeed, did all who knew him. Like Farinelli, again, he seems to have neither borne malice nor earned any. Nor was he guilty of vanity, arrogance or envy. The consciousness of supremacy does not always bring a sense of security and humility, but in some great artists these rare characteristics seem to add a dimension to their communicative resources.

One is tempted to assume something of the kind in Pacchierotti's case, for of no other singer are there so many accounts of listeners—even the most hardened—being moved to tears. The story is told of a performance in Rome where in one scene he had to sing the words: *Eppur, son innocente*, to be followed by an instrumental interlude leading to the aria. But the orchestra was silent. Pacchierotti turned inquiringly to the *maestro di capella*. "We are all in tears," said the conductor through his own. This was obviously at the close of a recitative, and may be attributable to Pacchierotti's habit, by artful melodic improvisation, of giving certain recitatives an aria-like character.

As might be expected of a man of his excellent disposition, Pacchierotti precipitated no scandals; but some were thrust upon him. Despite an unprepossessing physique—he was tall, thin and awkward—he was attractive to women. An impressionable countess in Naples, according to Kelly, who heard the story there, fell in love with him, and Pacchierotti was lucky to escape assassination by her lover. Kelly also tells of a well-born English lady who was "fervently attached to him" and assuaged his inadequacies with large sums of money. This was presumably the Lady Mary Duncan, described by the English writer, William Beckford, as being "more preciously fond of Pacchierotti than a she-bear of its suckling."

Also in Naples, when Pacchierotti was singing there with Catterina Gabrielli (1730–1796), a prima donna as celebrated for her alleged promiscuity as for her evident beauty, one of her innumerable fans—or one of her apparently innumerable lovers—insulted him in the street. Pacchierotti, an excellent swordsman in addition to all his other accomplishments, challenged him to a duel and extracted an apology. According to some accounts they actually crossed swords. It seems likely, for the singer was imprisoned briefly. He was jailed again late in life, while living in retirement in Padua, when a letter he had written to the soprano Angelica Catalani was intercepted by the police and found to contain some real or fancied political indiscretion.

He sang at the opening of La Scala in Milan in 1778, and his last public appearance was at the opening of the Fenice in Venice in 1792. Both theaters still stand; but how many of the thousands who visit them each year, and the millions who pass them, remember or have ever known that their walls first resounded to the voice of the mutilated creature who may have been the greatest singer of them all?

One who knew and would have remembered was Violet Paget, who wrote (under the pseudonym of Vernon Lee) in *Studies of the Eighteenth Century in Italy:* "Of all those dim figures of long-forgotten singers which arise, tremulous and hazy, from out of the faded pages of biographies and scores, evoked by some intense word of admiration or some pathetic snatch of melody, there is one more poetical than the rest—for all such ghosts of forgotten genius are poetical—that of Gasparo Pacchierotti."

And it was Miss Paget, of all people, who, while rambling one day through a quiet corner of Padua, stumbled into a "beautiful tangle of trees and grass and flowers" and was informed by a gardener's boy that this garden had once belonged to a famous singer, by name Gasparo Pacchierotti.

"The gardener," she recalled, "let us into the house, a battered house, covered with creepers and amorphae, and sentimental inscriptions from the works of the poets and philosophers in vogue a hundred years ago. He showed us into a long narrow room in which was a large, slender harpsichord—the harpsichord, he informed us, which had belonged to Pacchierotti, the singer. It was open, and looked as if it might just have been touched, but no sound could be drawn from it.

"The gardener then led us into a darkened lumber-room where hung the portrait of the singer, thickly covered with dust: a mass of dark blurs, from out of which appeared scarcely more than the pale, thin face—a face with deep dreamy eyes and tremulously tender lips, full of vague, wistful, contemplative poetry, as if of aspirations after something sweeter, fairer—aspirations never fulfilled but never disappointed, and forming in themselves a sort of perfection."

2. LUIGI MARCHESI

The second "golden age" bore many resemblances to the first, even to an approximate duplication of the cast of characters. For Farinelli we have Pacchierotti; for Carestini we have Crescentini, and for Caffarelli we have Marchesi. But the requirements, if not the standards, were probably higher, as suggested by a curious statement of Burney that "such execution as many of Farinelli's songs contain, and which excited such astonishment in 1734, would be hardly thought sufficiently brilliant in 1788 for a third-rate singer at the opera. The dose of difficulties to produce the same effects as fifty years ago must be more than double."

Significantly, 1788 was the year that brought Luigi Marchesi to London. We have encountered him before, disputing the right, or the propriety, of Nancy Storace's duplication of his *bomba* in Florence, and insisting upon entrances and helmets of appropriate magnificence. These and other examples of a vanity extraordinary even among singers have made him a symbol of the sort of behavior that gave the castrati a bad name. But when we read what discerning contemporaries had to say about his singing, it is plain that the notoriety of his failings distorts the picture of his place in vocal history.

"His voice," according to Ernst Ludwig Gerber, the German historian and Marchesi's contemporary, "is perfectly pure and silvery, and extends from the low C to the D above high C. With the loveliest declamation and deportment, he combines much musical insight. In the execution of passages and the so-called hammer-stroke (*il martello*) he is commonly reckoned superior to Farinelli." This specialty was obviously the device of repeated notes which occurs in the music written for Farinelli by his brother and in much music composed for subsequent virtuosos, both male and female.

Lord Mount-Edgcumbe adds: "Marchesi was at this time [1788] a very well-looking man, of good figure and graceful deportment. His acting was spirited and expressive. His vocal powers were very great, his voice of extensive compass, but a little inclined to be thick. His execution was very considerable, and he was rather too fond of displaying it; nor was his cantabile singing equal to his bravura. In recitative and scenes of energy and passion he was incomparable, and had he been less lavish of ornaments, which were not always appropriate, and possessed a more pure and simple taste, his performance would have been faultless; it was always striking, animated and effective." Later on, the writer observed that Marchesi's flowery style was an absolute simplicity compared to what one grew accustomed to hear in later days—a reference, no doubt, to the extravagance of Catalani and the castrato Velluti, which blemished and probably hastened the end of the age of *bel canto*.

Marchesi had begun his career as a boy soprano in the cathedral at Milan, and some critics have speculated that the exercise of singing in so large an auditorium may have contributed to the size and brilliance

Luigi Marchesi (above left) was one of the handsomest of the castrati—and one of the most vain. He insisted on making his first entrance descending a hill and wearing a helmet crowned with plumes at least a yard high, his arrival heralded by a fanfare of trumpets.

The most tasteful singer of the last generation of operatic castrati was Girolamo Crescentini (above right). Alfred de Vigny heard him in Paris and wrote of "a seraph's voice that came from an emaciated and wrinkled face."

Last of the great castrati was Giovanni-Battista Velluti, whose license in embellishment prompted Rossini to put into notation his own embellishments and insist, not always successfully, that his singers adhere to them. Velluti, seen (below right) in street attire and (below left) as Trajan in Giuseppe Niccolini's *Traiano in Dacia*, was probably more handsome than Marchesi.

of his voice. He may have belonged to that small number of *evirati*—Pacchierotti is also supposed to have been among them—whose castration was voluntary. He had extraordinarily fine features, predestining him to early success in female roles, and he retained them into his maturity—with predictable amorous consequences. A Mrs. Conway, wife of a reputable miniaturist, deserted husband and children when Marchesi left England, and followed him about Europe.

3. GIROLAMO CRESCENTINI

The Carestini of this quartet, as previously noted, was Girolamo Crescentini (1762–1846). Napoleon was so taken with his voice and his singing when he heard him in Vienna in 1805 that he packed him off to Paris, where he was knighted and sang at court (but not in the theater) until 1812, the only castrato to have prevailed in the French capital since Bannieri a century and a half before. He is described there by Alfred de Vigny as singing "with a seraph's voice that came from an emaciated and wrinkled face." He also earned the following entry in the diary of the youthful Schopenhauer, who heard him in Vienna: "His supernaturally beautiful voice cannot be compared with that of any woman: there can be no fuller and more beautiful tone, and in its silver purity he yet achieves indescribable power."

A more professional commentary was provided by the *Allgemeine Musikalische Zeitung* when Crescentini appeared in Vienna in 1804: "His voice, employed with discreet restraint, is indescribably agreeable, round, pure and flexible; his embellishments rich in noble art and aesthetic propriety, without being overly elaborated. Especially beautiful is the pure, even, ever stronger pulsation of his heavenly voice, with which, in one passage, he makes a crescendo to the high A and then holds the tone at full voice for several measures."

Nor, probably, is heavenly too strong a word, as demonstrated in this passage from a story in E. T. A. Hoffmann's *Kreisleriana*, based on Crescentini's singing in the third act of Zingarelli's *Giulietta e Romeo*: "The song flows like a silvery stream amid blossoming flowers. But is it not precisely this master's mysterious magic that enables him to endow the simplest melody, the most artless structure, with this indescribable power, irresistible in its effect upon every susceptible nature?"

We last encounter Crescentini in Naples, where he settled as a teacher at the Royal College of Music in 1816. Spohr met him there in the following year. "I was," Spohr recorded in his diary, "pleased to have my judgment of the present state of music in Italy confirmed by him. . . . He complained that in recent times the good vocal school, which formerly had alone distinguished the Italians, had become rarer and rarer. On his last return to Italy he had found Italian taste so frivolous that not a trace was left of the simple, grand method of former times."

Nor, it seems, of a proper sense of a great castrato's dignity. On one occasion Crescentini even had to insist on exchanging costumes with the tenor, because the latter's was trimmed in patrician red, his own in plebeian black. A mere tenor!

4. GIOVANNI-BATTISTA VELLUTI

Giovanni-Battista Velluti (1781–1861) could hardly have afforded this patronizing attitude toward tenors; for it was both his distinction and his misfortune to be the last of his kind to grace the opera stage. He was surrounded by excellent tenors throughout his career, and he lived to see tenors assume that supreme station among males in the operatic hierarchy that they have enjoyed and abused to this day.

It is not only as the last of his kind, however, that Velluti's place in history is assured. This circumstance, however distinctive, is a mere statistic. Far more important in its consequences was his encounter with Rossini, from which is dated the inhibition of the singer's privilege of improvisation. This encounter took place in 1813, when Velluti appeared in the première of Rossini's *Aureliano in Palmira* in Milan. This is how Stendhal tells the story in his *Life of Rossini:*

"Velluti was then in the full bloom of his youth and vigor, at the very height of his genius, and, incidentally, one of the handsomest men of his century; and he made shameless abuse of his prodigious gifts. Rossini had never actually heard this outstanding singer on the stage; none the less, he sat down straight away and composed the main cavatina which was to belong to the role.

"At the first rehearsal with the orchestra, Velluti sang the aria straight through, and Rossini was dazzled with admiration; at the second rehearsal, Velluti began to embroider the melody, and Rossini, finding the result both exquisite in performance and well in keeping with his own intentions as composer, approved; but at the third rehearsal, the

The Teatro alla Scala in Milan, more familiarly known simply as La Scala, opened in 1778, became one of the principal centers of opera in Italy, as it has been ever since.

Some critics considered Gasparo Pacchierotti to be the greatest of all the castrati. He is shown here at a Sunday concert in London in 1782, performing under the watchful eye of Lady Mary Duncan, who was much attached to him. Dr. Burney (lower right) seems to have found more substantial diversion. At the harpsichord is the composer Ferdinando Bertoni.

original pattern of the melody had almost entirely disappeared beneath a marvelous filigree-work of embroidery and arabesque.

"At last there dawned the great day of the première: the cavatina itself, and in fact Velluti's whole performance, created a furore; but Rossini found himself confronted with insuperable difficulties in trying to identify what Velluti was supposed to be singing; his own music, in fact, had grown completely unrecognizable. For all that, however, Velluti's performance was a thing of unparalleled beauty, and enjoyed popularity with the audience, which, after all, can never be blamed for applauding something which it so wholeheartedly enjoys.

"The young composer's vanity was deeply wounded: his opera was a failure, and all the applause had gone to Velluti, his soprano. Rossini was always quick to size up a situation, and instantly drew the inevitable conclusions from an experience which had proved so unspeakably humiliating."

At this point in his narrative Stendhal does a bit of improvising on his own—an imaginary soliloquy in which Rossini ponders the lessons to be drawn from this experience. Velluti, he concedes, knows what he is about, and has good taste and admirable invention. But similar liberties granted to singers of lesser accomplishment could mean not only the mutilation of a composer's work, but also a public disaster. It behooves the composer, therefore, to anticipate such contingencies by writing down his own ornamentation and insisting that the singers use it and nothing else.

Stendhal concedes that Rossini never uttered these sentiments in his presence; but it is inconceivable, he modestly insists, that he should never have uttered them at all, adding that his scores prove it. Nor did Stendhal applaud. Bad or reckless singers could cause much mischief, but so could a composer, even Rossini. For ornamentation suitable to one singer might not be equally congenial to another, nor the same ornamentation be equally appropriate to every singer every night. (Velluti, Stendhal tells us, had three sets of ornaments for every passage that called for embellishment.) And he points to the arias and ornamentation written subsequently for Isabella-Angela Colbran (1785–1845), the future Signora Rossini, designed specifically to expose her virtues and disguise her very considerable deficiencies.

Why should future singers of the same roles, Stendhal asks, be governed by the vocal idiosyncracies of Colbran? He seems to have foreseen that the requirement of conformity, the acknowledgment of the notes once written as immutable, would inhibit the singer's art, demanding that all sing the same music in more or less the same way, stifling spontaneous invention and denying that special inspiration which is drawn from the excitement of an occasion or the blessed assurance of exceptional vocal condition.

But the argument was academic almost before it began. Stendhal concedes that not even Velluti could boast the noble style attributed to the best of the castrati from Ferri to Crescentini, nor was such a style any longer attractive. Popular taste in the theater was already demanding more than the concert in costume that had been a prerequisite for an institution in which the singers could call the turns. Velluti's taste in opera, for example, was evidence of his obsolescence. He traveled from city to city and—for a time—from triumph to triumph with operas by Giuseppe Niccolini (1763–1842) and Francesco Morlacchi (1784–1841), which might have been sufficient as vehicles for a celebrated castrato fifty years before, but could hardly be expected to survive against the headier dramatic stuff already being offered by Cherubini, Auber, Spontini, Rossini and Donizetti. Opera was now dealing with sentiments beyond the capacity of *fioritura*, however expressive, to convey.

Neither by his statements nor by his practice of writing in his own ornamentation did Rossini put an immediate end to the singer's prerogative of improvisatory embellishment. It continued to be exercised in the operas of the older Italian repertoire throughout the century, although the tendency was more and more to restrict it to *ad libitum* cadenzas. Rossini never ceased to hate it, and he expressed his displeasure to both Malibran and Patti, when they had embroidered his arias to their own tastes, by asking them who had been the composer of the pieces they had just sung—much to their bewilderment and embarrassment.

It is proof enough of Velluti's artistic and vocal prowess that—already something of a freak—he could have stood his ground alone and shared the stage honorably with such prodigies of a new era as Pasta, Malibran and Sontag. But for all the applause he harvested, there was also much distaste. The castrato, as an institution, and the sterile *opera seria* in which he had flourished, were unacceptable to the more or less enlightened middle-class society emerging from the cataclysms of the French Revolution and the Napoleonic wars.

Velluti left the stage about 1830 to become a gentleman farmer on the Brenta, between Padua and Venice, where, in their declining years,

Guadagni had tended his puppets and Pacchierotti had sung in the cathedral. Let us not take leave of Velluti, however, and the great company of which he was the last, without being reminded that there was music in their art and art in their music. Describing Velluti's singing of an aria from Morlacchi's *Tebaldo ed Isolina,* Stendahl wrote:

"The first three bars which Velluti sings are prayers addressed by a lover to his mistress in her displeasure; and the passage concludes with a sudden fortissimo, when the lover, tormented by the object of his love, implores her forgiveness in the name of memory—the memory of the first fair morning of their new-discovered joy. The two opening bars, in Velluti's interpretation, are filled to the brim with *fioriture,* expressing, to begin with, extreme timidity, and later, profound despair; he strews every note with descending scales in semitones, with *scale trillate;* and then, at the third bar, resolves them all into a clear, unembellished, strong and sustained fortissimo, which, on the occasions when he is at the height of his powers, is a miracle of freedom and confidence. No woman who truly loved could resist such a *cri de coeur!*"

Nor can the historian! For it was a cry that would soon pass into history. There was another cry, similarly and happily doomed. This was the *"Viva il coltello!—*Long live the knife!" which Italians, in their rapture, used to shout when a castrato had sung surpassingly well.

VI

Some Early Prima Donnas

CUZZONI · FAUSTINA

TESI · MARA

WHILE REVIEWING the lives and times of the castrati, we have had occasional glimpses of some of the more notable females who—from the earliest beginnings of Italian opera—shared the stage with them and competed for the highest honors and the highest fees.

We have admired the intrepid Vittoria Tesi, preventing the duel between Caffarelli and the poet Migliavacca in Vienna. We have seen the same Caffarelli disgracing a performance in Naples by giving audible and visible instruction to Giovanna Astrua. And we have been told by Michael Kelly how Nancy Storace was dismissed from a theater for stealing Marchesi's *bomba*.

It must seem odd that in a time when women were available and many of them, in the eighteenth century if not in the seventeenth, certainly very good, there should have been any place for castrati in the theater. But it should be remembered that in the seventeenth century, with women barred from the church choir and sometimes from the theater (as they had been in the Greek and even the early English theater), they were neither so available, initially, nor so good as they later became. Nor were they considered especially necessary. The theatrical conventions of the time accepted men in female roles just as, with the emergence of the prima donna, they accepted females in male roles. And the castrati were, as a rule, better singers. But there were exceptions.

Most of the females of the age of *bel canto* were pupils of castrati or learned from the castrati in performance and by observation and imitation. They sang the same type of music—and often even the same music. They practiced the same embellishments. They gloried or despaired in the same *fioritura* throughout the same vocal range. And they were judged by the same criteria. These criteria, moreover, favored those advantages of strength and stamina that men normally enjoy over women.

If the early prima donnas excelled the castrati in any single respect, it was in contentiousness. Certainly there was much rivalry among the great castrati, some of it chivalrous, some of it petty, but even at its worst, it rarely equaled the antagonism and the rivalry of Cuzzoni and Faustina in London and Venice, of Mingotti and Faustina in Dresden, of Mara and the composer Giuseppe Sarti (1729–1802) in St. Petersburg and of Mara and La Todi in Paris. Nor did their hostility provoke such vicious partisanship among their followers.

1. FRANCESCA CUZZONI AND FAUSTINA BORDONI

How much more agreeable would life have been for so many prima donnas had the greatest of them been decently spaced in time, had each been granted a decade or so of untroubled supremacy! But for Callas there have been a Tebaldi and a Nilsson; for Melba there were an Eames and a Sembrich, for Grisi a Lind and a Viardot, and for Pasta a Malibran. And so it was for Francesca Cuzzoni and Faustina Bordoni, the first prima donnas to achieve international fame and to hold their own with the greatest castrati of their generation. They had each other.

They are always spoken of together, for neither was properly queen or challenger as long as both were in their prime and in the same city, as they were in Venice, then in London and again in Venice. Each had her absolute moments in the other's absence. Faustina, as she was always called, made her debut in Venice in 1716 and was unchallenged until the arrival of Cuzzoni two or three years later. Cuzzoni preceded Faustina to London, arriving in 1723, three years ahead of Faustina, but the latter threw a long shadow. Following Cuzzoni's benefit on March 26, 1723 (the "benefit" was a performance customarily guaranteed in every singer's contract, all the proceeds going to the singer), the London *Journal* reported that "as soon as Cuzzoni's time is out we are to have another over; for we are assured Faustina, the fine songstress at Venice, is invited, whose voice, they say, exceeds that we have already here."

Faustina did not reach London until 1726, taking time out to conquer Vienna; but, once she had been heard, all London was divided, and there began that rivalry which, in Burney's words, led to "the destruction of theatrical tranquillity and, indeed, of good neighborhood among the adherents of the attending parties." It reached an untidy climax at a performance of Buononcini's *Astianatte* on June 6, 1727, in which both ladies sang and, according to the more lurid accounts, ended by pulling each other's hair. It was described in the British *Journal* of June 10:

"On Tuesday night last, a great disturbance happened at the opera, occasioned by the partisans of the two celebrated rival ladies, Cuzzoni and Faustina. The contention at first was only carried on by hissing on one side and clapping on the other; but proceeded at length to catcalls and other great indecencies: And notwithstanding the Princess Caroline was present, no regards were of force to restrain the rudeness of the opponents."

A wealth of knowledgeable and authoritative contemporary commentary provides us with more precise information about the respective merits and distinctive characteristics of Cuzzoni and Faustina than is commonly available for singers of that period. Tosi describes them as "of a merit superior to all praise; who with equal force, in a different style, help to keep up the tottering profession from immediately falling into ruin. The one [Faustina] is inimitable for a privileged gift of singing and for enchanting the world with a prodigious felicity in executing and with a singular brilliancy (I know not whether from nature or art) which pleases to excess. The delightful, soothing cantabile of the other, joined with the sweetness of a fine voice, a perfect intonation, strictness of time, and the rarest productions of a genius, are qualifications as particular and uncommon as they are difficult to be imitated. The *pathetic* of the one and the *allegro* of the other are the qualities the most to be admired respectively in each of them. What a beautiful mixture would it be if the excellence of these two angelic creatures could be united in one person!"

More precise is Quantz, who heard them both in London, as quoted by Burney:

Cuzzoni, he remembered, had a "very agreeable and clear soprano voice, a pure intonation and a fine trill. Her compass extended two octaves, from C to C. Her style of singing was innocent and affecting. Her graces did not seem artificial, from the easy and neat manner in which she executed them. However, they took possession of the soul of every auditor by her tender and touching expression. She had not great rapidity of execution in allegros; but there was a roundness and smoothness which were neat and pleasing. Yet, with all these advantages, it must be owned that she was rather cold in her action, and that her figure was not advantageous for the stage.

"Faustina," Quantz continues, "had a mezzo-soprano voice that was less clear than penetrating. Her compass was now only from B flat to G [below high C], but after this time [i.e., 1727] she extended its limits downward. Her execution was articulate and brilliant. She had a fluent tongue for pronouncing words rapidly and distinctly, and a flexible throat for divisions, with so beautiful a trill that she could put it in motion upon short notice just when she would. The passages might be smooth or by leaps, or consist of iterations of the same tone. She sang adagios with great passion and expression, but was not equally successful if such deep sorrow were to be impressed on the hearer as might require dragging, sliding, or notes of syncopation and tempo rubato. In her action she was very happy; and as she perfectly possessed that flexibility of muscles and features which constitutes face-playing, she succeeded equally well in furious, amorous and tender parts; in short, she was born for singing and for acting."

More or less equally gifted and accomplished as singers they may have been, but in every other respect Faustina was the more abundantly favored. Indeed, upon few women in musical history has fortune smiled so consistently throughout a long life. Unlike most prima donnas of her own or any other time, she was well born, coming of a distinguished Venetian family, and enjoying, in addition to her musical and vocal endowment, great personal beauty and a charming and gracious presence. Composers were ever at her service. As a student in Venice she was a protégée of Benedetto Marcello. Handel and Buononcini wrote for her in London, and after the Haymarket company broke up in 1728, she returned to Venice and married Johann Adolph Hasse (1699–1783), a German composer already on his way to becoming the most popular composer of Italian operas in the middle third of the eighteenth century.

They were soon established in Dresden, he as director of the Opera, she as prima donna, and there, at the most sumptuous and brilliant musical court in Europe, she reigned for twenty years, her absolute supremacy challenged only by the arrival of Mingotti in 1747. She retired from the stage in 1751. At that time Saxon losses during the Seven Years' War brought an end to the Dresden musical establishment. Hasse was pensioned, and he and Faustina withdrew, first to Vienna and then to Venice, where they lived comfortably into their eighties and in 1783, died.

How different is the story of Cuzzoni, whose origins were so humble that it is not recorded exactly when she was born (it was about 1700, at Parma). Her person and manners were such that Horace Walpole, who saw her in Handel's *Rodelinda*, would remember her as "short and squat, with a doughy cross face!" She was not a good actress, he added; she dressed ill, and was "silly and fantastical." If there was a loser in the London fracas it was she, particularly if the story is true that the directors of the Royal Academy of Music, in 1728, offered Faustina one guinea a year more than her rival, who had taken an oath not to accept a penny less than was offered to Faustina.

With Faustina's marriage and removal to Dresden, this shadow vanished from Cuzzoni's life, but it was too late. Her time was past. In London in the 1720s, she and Faustina could more than hold their own against Senesino, but when Cuzzoni returned for the seasons of 1734 to 1736 she was overshadowed by Farinelli and Carestini, beside whom she probably appeared old-fashioned. Thereafter her path is hard to follow, and distressing when discovered. She turned up at the court of Charles Eugene, Duke of Württemberg, toward the end of 1745, where her behavior and fortune are described by Alan Yorke-Long in his instructive book, *Music at Court:*

"She was expected to sing in the private chamber concerts of the duke and in the services of the Ducal Chapel; but when her contract was renewed for three years in March, 1747, the significant proviso was inserted that if she lost her voice the contract was void. She anticipated this by absconding in the autumn of 1748, leaving behind her a sizable pile of debts; from Bologna she sent an impudent offer to return if her salary were doubled, but this was curtly refused by the duke."

From then on it was more of the same—and worse. She was back in London in the spring of 1750, and a benefit concert was arranged for her. The receipts must have been insufficient, for in a letter dated August 2, 1750, Horace Walpole says: "Another celebrated Polly has been arrested for thirty pounds, even the old Cuzzoni. The Prince of Wales bailed her—who will do as much for him?" A second benefit in the following year was presumably similarly inadequate.

She was now past fifty and voiceless, and her appearances were artistically and financially disastrous. She went to Holland, but fell into debt again and landed in debtors' prison, from which she was released from time to time, just long enough to give concerts for whoever was still gullible enough or kind enough to pay to hear her. From these concerts she did earn at least enough to buy her release. She continued on to her native Italy, settling in Bologna, where her ultimate occupation was making buttons in the workhouse. She died in 1770.

2. VITTORIA TESI

Of the contemporaries of Cuzzoni and Faustina, only Vittoria Tesi achieved comparable eminence. She was born in Florence in 1700. Like

Francesca Cuzzoni (above right) and Faustina Bordoni were the first prima donnas to achieve great international reputations. Their rivalry in London in the 1720s "led to the destruction of theatrical tranquility." Faustina's celebrated beauty is confirmed in the portrait (above left) by Giovanna Fratellini in the Uffizi Gallery at Florence.

Elisabeth Mara was not the first, but she was the most celebrated, of the early German prima donnas. Her costume as Mandane (below left) in a setting of Metastasio's *Artaserse*, probably Hasse's, gives a vivid impression of the flowing robes and plumed headdress affected by prima donnas of that time.

Mara is shown (below right) even more fancifully as the partner of the alto castrato Rubinelli on the occasion of his London debut on May 14, 1786.

Cuzzoni, she studied in Bologna with Francesco Campeggi; and both Cuzzoni and Tesi, presumably reflected, if they did not actually enjoy, the schooling of Pistocchi. Tesi did the rounds of the Italian and German theaters, appearing on an equal footing with all the great singers, female and castrati, of her time.

Described by Quantz, who heard her in Dresden in 1719, as a "contralto of masculine strength," she had an extensive compass and sang with fire, force and dramatic expression, although without the virtuosity in *fioritura* that so distinguished Cuzzoni and Faustina. She excelled in male roles, and the masculinity of her contralto voice may have been a reflection of other masculine characteristics. This would help to explain the readiness of Caffarelli and Migliavacca to accept her bold intervention in their abortive duel in Vienna. Among her distinctions was a predilection for singing (an octave higher, of course) arias originally written for basses.

In 1743, fairly late in life, Tesi married a barber named Tramontini, apparently only to escape marriage to a nobleman who was not content to have her merely as his mistress. He was, presumably, the same "man of great rank" with whom, according to Burney, she had been living for many years, "probably in a very chaste and innocent manner," when Burney met her in Vienna in 1772. She had settled there about the middle of the century and had established a singing school. She died in Vienna in 1775.

3. MARA

Although she was not quite the first great German singer, Gertrud Elisabeth Schmeling, eventually to become famous under her husband's name of Mara, was the first German to achieve and sustain a career of international eminence without having grown up in the atmosphere of a court theater or serving an apprenticeship in Italy, or, for that matter, ever singing in Italy at all, except briefly in Venice and Turin when her career was well advanced.

Schmeling, or Mara, was the daughter of an obscure violin maker in Kassel. Born in 1749, she spent her childhood touring the Continental and British provinces as a probably not very wondrous *Wunderkind* on the violin, trying—not always successfully—to keep her father out of debtors' prison. After many vicissitudes and some vocal training, first in London with Pietro Paradisi (1707–1791), a pupil of Porpora, and later in Leipzig with Johann Adam Hiller (1728–1804), founder of the German *Singspiel*, she braved the court of Frederick the Great, armed with a letter to Frederick from Maria Antonia Walpurgis, Electress of Saxony. The letter assured Frederick of Schmeling's facility and admirable voice, concluding: "As she now finds herself at the fountainhead of good taste, Your Majesty will soon have the most brilliant singer of the century."

The proprietor of the fountainhead of good taste, who had been known to observe that he would rather hear his horse neigh than a German woman sing, was skeptical. "He believed," the singer recalled in her autobiography, "that a German woman must sing with the German method and a German manner of interpretation, and this was not to his taste—nor was it to mine! If a German were to sing with the Italian method, which is the only true one, she must please him despite his prejudices."

She did please him, and was to remain in Berlin for a turbulent decade. Frederick was always delighted with her singing, which improved under the guidance of Porporino, Frederick's castrato-in-residence. Burney, when he was in Berlin in the summer of 1772, heard her sing several songs "of uncommon rapidity and compass. Her powers in these particulars," he noted, "are truly astonishing; but she is frequently compelled to abuse them by the airs that are given her to execute, in which she has passages that degrade the voice into an instrument, indeed, often such as a player of taste would be ashamed to execute upon any instrument. . . . If Mme. Schmeling were to go to Italy she would not, perhaps, meet with greater powers than her own in any one performer; but by adopting the peculiar excellencies of many performers, of different schools and talents, her style . . . would be an aggregate of all that is exquisite and beautiful."

Elisabeth had always wanted to visit Italy, but Frederick, who liked to keep his nightingales within hearing distance, had no intention of letting her go; and she played into his possessive hands by marrying, in defiance of his wishes, Giovanni-Battista Mara (1744–1808), a cellist in the orchestra of Frederick's brother, Prince Henry of Prussia. Thenceforward, whenever Frederick had any difficulty with either of them, which was often, he would put Mara in jail or send him off to play the drum in a regimental band. In this manner he frustrated her acceptance of all invitations for foreign engagements except for brief visits to Leipzig and Kassel in 1777 and to Strasbourg in 1778, where she met and heard her future rival, Todi.

The most spectacular of many tests of will occurred in 1776 upon the visit to Berlin of Grand Duke Paul of Russia. Frederick chose to crown the occasion with an opera by his new *Kapellmeister*, Johann Friedrich Reichardt (1752–1814). Mara, as she was now called, returned an aria written especially for her by Reichardt with a curt note saying that she would not sing such stuff. Her husband encouraged her in this impudence. When Frederick heard of it he had Mara arrested again, and sent off an official communication to the intendant, adding in his own hand that "she is paid to sing and not to write."

There are many versions of what happened thereafter. According to one of them Elisabeth developed, or feigned, a severe indisposition and took to her bed, only to be hauled off to the performance, mattress and all, by eight dragoons acting on order of the king. According to others, she sang the opera, including the aria, listlessly, having arrived on her own two feet, and then disgraced herself and her master by singing all but inaudibly at a court concert a few days later. Frederick had wished to show his guest that he had a singer as good as, or better than, Gabrielli, then gracing the court of the grand duke's mother, Catherine the Great. The grand duke complimented her, Elisabeth recalled, "presumably only out of politeness or ignorance—for he certainly did not hear me." In her own view she had demonstrated to the king that *lèse majesté* can apply to prima donnas, too.

The end came in 1780, when Mara's physician prescribed a cure at Teplitz in Bohemia. Frederick's view was that the waters of nearby Freienwalde would suffice to relieve his prima donna's pleurisy. This was the last straw for the strong-willed Mara. Using the coach placed at her disposal to take her and her husband to Freienwalde, they managed to escape through Saxony to Bohemia. The journey is described vividly in Elisabeth Mara's autobiography, but she was probably guilty of some overdramatization. Frederick, soon afterward, released her from her contract. He was losing his breath and his teeth, and, thus inhibited as a flute virtuoso, is said to have lost his former intense interest in music. He may well have been content to see the last of a presumptuous prima donna and her offensive husband.

For the next two years the Maras divided their time between Vienna and Munich, Elisabeth's singing much admired, their deportment often deplored. In 1782 they were in Paris, where Elisabeth's rivalry with Todi (1753–1833), a Portuguese mezzo-soprano born Luiza Rosa d'Aguiar, aroused partisanship to a pitch that recalled the excesses of the Gluckists and the Piccinnists a generation earlier. It was inconclusive, but profitable for all, as such contentions have usually been.

Mara and her husband arrived in London in 1784, where she would remain, except for occasional excursions to France and Italy, for the next eighteen years, dominant in opera, unsurpassed in the oratorios of Handel and Haydn, much admired for her singing in concerts (including many appearances with Haydn), and encumbered by a husband whose alcoholic, spendthrift and ruffianly ways prompted her to divorce him. He drank himself to death in sailors' dives in Holland. But his widow had a soft spot for handsome and weak men, and the departure of the cellist merely made room for a flutist, Giovanni-Battista Florio, twenty years her junior. They may have been the first to make a family specialty of those passages of vocal coloratura with flute obbligato that have delighted the lovers of birdlike singing and mad scenes ever since.

Contemporary accounts of Mara's singing abound in hyperbole but are oddly wanting in descriptive particulars. Burney, for instance, calls her "enchanting," and refers to her as "a divinity among mortals," but neither he nor other critics of the time have much to say about how she actually sang. All agree that hers was a very beautiful, remarkably even voice of extensive range (from a B flat below middle C to the high E or F), and that it was admirably disciplined in the florid style; but not only in that. The piece by which she was most vividly remembered, both in England and in Germany, was "I know that my Redeemer liveth" from *Messiah*. She never became a good actress. Once, at the height of her career, when this deficiency was noted, she asked plaintively whether she was expected to sing with her hands and her feet, too.

She was well past her prime when she left London in 1802, at the age of fifty-three, but she sang her way to Moscow, a city which pleased her so much that she retired and settled there. Her home and her possessions were destroyed in the burning of the city in 1812, and she moved in with rich friends in Reval (Talinn), to teach and to write her memoirs. The sunset of her life was brightened by many visits of homage by artists passing through on their way to and from St. Petersburg, among them Anna Milder-Hauptmann (1785–1838), the original Leonore of Beethoven's *Fidelio*.

For her eighty-second birthday Goethe sent her two verses, one recalling the first time he had heard her in Leipzig in 1767 (he missed by four years and inscribed the date 1771), the other a tribute dated 1831. They were set to music by Goethe's neighbor in Weimar, the composer and pianist Johann Nepomuk Hummel (1778–1837). She died two years later.

VII

The End of the Era

BANTI · MRS. BILLINGTON

CATALANI

APPROACHING THE CLOSE of the age of *bel canto* and the dawn of the age of grand opera, one senses a certain decline in the dignity of the great singers. What we know of Marchesi and Velluti, for example, suggests little of the high motivation and artistic probity of Guadagni, Pacchierotti and Crescentini. Among the ladies, similarly, what we read of Brigitta Banti, Mrs. Billington and Angelica Catalani seems meretricious and trivial against contemporary appreciations of Faustina, Cuzzoni, Tesi, Astrua and Mara.

It is possible that the times had changed more than the ladies, that the later prima donnas may simply have carried over into the nineteenth century certain musical habits and personal attitudes congenial enough to pre-Revolutionary court environment, but incompatible with the expectations of a new bourgeois public whose taste in music had already been influenced by Gluck, Haydn, Mozart and Beethoven.

1. BRIGITTA BANTI

A timely retirement probably spared Brigitta Banti, oldest of the prima donnas who dominated the last decades of *opera seria*, any awareness of having become more or less ridiculous. Nor was her intelligence such as to have grasped easily so unpredictable a circumstance.

Born Brigitta Giorgi in 1756, she was allegedly the daughter of a gondolier; but since her birthplace was Monticelli d'Ongina, a considerable distance from Venice, even this tale—like almost everything else pertaining to her early life—should be accepted with reserve.

All accounts agree, however, that as a young girl she was a street singer, that she sang her way to Paris and that she began her professional career there. Her first great success came in 1778 when she was engaged to succeed Lucrezia Agujari (1743–1783), a celebrated high-note singer popularly and indelicately known as *La Bastardina* or *La Bastardella,* as principal soloist for the concerts in the London Pantheon. This was a massive entertainment establishment in Oxford Street, whose concerts were of such quality that they represented a formidable competition for the Italian opera.

There was a significant clause in Banti's contract with the Pantheon requiring the deduction of a hundred pounds a year for her musical education. This may have been prompted by a story going the rounds in Paris that she would sing *da capo* arias over and over again, not knowing how to end them. She was assigned successively to three of the finest masters in London, and one after another gave it up as a bad job. She was indolent and indifferent, rebellious and arrogant; and to her dying day she never learned to read music. The Pantheon regarded her behavior as a breach of contract and dismissed her.

She returned to the Continent and to a rapid succession of triumphs in all the major musical centers of Italy and Germany, enchanting audiences that cared little whether she could read music or not. Nor was this enchantment confined to the musically unsophisticated. Kelly, recalling an appearance in London in 1794, said: "Her acting was sublime, her singing charming; for twenty nights the opera [*Alceste*] drew crowded houses. She had a finely marked countenance and a noble soprano voice, but she was no musician. The difficulties arising from this deficiency she obviated by an extraordinary quickness and niceness of ear, perfect intonation and strong feeling."

The London *Morning Chronicle,* covering her performance as assisting artist to Haydn in a concert in 1795, reported: "It was ecstasy to listen to her sweet, powerful and impressive notes. . . . More perfect, more impassioned, more divine singing, perhaps, was never heard. The delicacy of her execution and sweetness of her taste and the enchanting discrimination of her feeling were incomparable." And Haydn thought enough of her to write for her his "Scena di Berenice."

These references to her taste, discrimination and refinement of feeling are at odds with what we read of her behavior behind the scenes, particularly the recollections of Mozart's librettist, Lorenzo da Ponte, who, as theater poet, worked with her in London in 1794.

"Banti," he recalled in his *Memoirs,* "was an ignorant, stupid, insolent woman. Accustomed from early girlhood to singing in cafés and about the streets, she brought to opera, whither only her voice had elevated her, all the habits, manners and customs of a brazen-faced Corsican. Free of speech, still freer of action, addicted to carousals, dissolute amusement and to the bottle, she showed herself in the face of everybody for what she was, knowing no measure, no restraints; and when any one of her passions was stirred by difficulties or opposition, she became an asp, a fury, a demon of Hell, capable of upsetting an empire, let alone a theater."

Elsewhere da Ponte refers to her as "that cursed woman who terrified by her perverseness as much as she pleased with her voice." This, considering da Ponte's feelings about her, speaks highly for her singing. Da Ponte was rarely guilty of either understatement or charity in his judgments of his contemporaries. What Banti thought of him is unrecorded, beyond his own allegation that she once tried to lure him away for a cozy weekend. His description is more likely a caricature. But in view of her background and her upbringing, if any, it is doubtless not without substance.

It should be added, to dress the balance, that her husband (a dancer named Zaccaria Banti) and her daughter were devoted to her; that the latter had a monument erected to her in a cemetery in Bologna, where she died in 1806; and that Banti herself left to the city of Bologna her larynx, which was of extraordinary dimensions. The city fathers are supposed to have had it preserved in alcohol; but an intensive search of the museums and the Anatomical Clinic in Bologna in the summer of 1964 failed to discover any trace of it.

2. MRS. BILLINGTON

The great prima donnas of the turn of the century represented an extraordinary variety of national origins. Mara was German, Todi Portuguese, Banti and Catalani Italians and Mrs. Billington English. There was even a French lady among them, Julie Angélique Scio (1768–1807), memorable as the creator of the title role in Cherubini's *Medée* at the Théâtre Feydeau in Paris in 1797. It is the English lady whose place in vocal history falls neatly between Banti and Catalani.

Elizabeth Billington (1768–1818) was not the first English prima

If Brigitta Banti (right) seems to be paying scant attention to the notes of this set of variations on "God Save the King," there was no reason why she should, for she never learned to read music. Her voice was one of the loveliest of history, but Mozart's librettist, Lorenzo da Ponte, called her "that cursed woman who terrified by her perverseness as much as she pleased with her voice."

Mrs. Billington, a great English prima donna, was painted by Sir Joshua Reynolds as St. Cecilia (below left) before she became a "cherub of notorious obesity." Others had a less flattering impression (below right).

donna. Mrs. Catherine Tofts (?–1756) had preceded her by a century, as had Anastasia Robinson (*circa* 1695–1755), a contralto in defense of whose honor and person the Earl of Peterborough, to whom she was secretly married, caned Senesino. Neither of these ladies, however, had extended her realm beyond the British Isles, nor was either in a class with Cuzzoni and Faustina.

Of more recent date had been Cecilia Davies (1740–1836), the first English female to achieve some fame in Italian opera in Italy. But Miss Davies devoted most of her career to an act with her sister Marianne, a celebrated virtuoso on Benjamin Franklin's glass harmonica. This was an instrument whose musical effects were achieved by the application of the fingertips to a row of graduated glass discs arranged on a spindle and revolving in a trough of water. Cecilia could so adapt her voice to the sound of the glass harmonica that listeners could not always determine which was which. Both sisters ended miserably. Marianne's nerves were affected by the vibrations of the glass discs on her fingertips, a complaint so common among the relatively few who played the glass harmonica that it was prohibited in a number of Continental cities. Cecilia lived to be ninety-six, but it was no blessing, as her later years were tormented by decrepitude, disease and poverty.

Mrs. Billington (*née* Weichsel, daughter of a German oboist at the King's Theater) held her own with the greatest non-British singers of her generation, including Mara and Banti. Kelly described her as "an angel of beauty and the Saint Cecilia of song." This extravagant impression was excited by an audition and viewing in 1787, when Mrs. Billington was nineteen. It was at about this time that Sir Joshua Reynolds painted her as St. Cecilia. She subsequently became a cherub of notorious obesity. Her vocal charms survived her angelic appearance.

Like Miss Davies, she enjoyed great success in Italy, and operas were written for her by some of the first opera composers of the time. Her debut in Naples coincided with an eruption of Mount Vesuvius and the fatal apoplexy of her husband, a double-bass virtuoso whom she had married at sixteen. The death of Mr. Billington was borne by the Neapolitans with predictable equanimity, but the eruption of Vesuvius was blamed by the superstitious natives upon the appearance of a Protestant heretic—namely, Mrs. Billington—upon the hallowed boards of the San Carlo. But Mrs. Billington persisted, and Vesuvius subsided.

Burney found her "a sweet and captivating singer. At first," he said, "in emulation of Mara and other great bravura singers, she was, perhaps, too frequently struggling with difficulties which she has, however, so totally subdued that no song seems too high [she had a three-octave range from A to A] or too rapid for her execution. But besides these powers, which the bad taste of the public tempts or obliges her to exercise, perhaps too frequently for lovers of expression and simplicity, the natural tone of her voice is so exquisitely sweet, her knowledge of music so considerable, her shake so true, her closes and embellishments so grateful that nothing but envy or apathy can hear her without delight."

She was, nevertheless, a more spectacular than moving singer, and apparently no actress at all. As one contemporary rhymester put it:

> *She oft wants the gentle assistance of ease,*
> *And seems more intent to surprise than to please.*

She retired to an estate near Venice with a second husband, and died there in 1818.

3. ANGELICA CATALANI

The singer of this generation who left the most vivid impression upon those who heard her, and who, in the early years of her career, dominated her period as had no other prima donna since Mara, was Angelica Catalani. She allowed—or required—herself to be billed as *Prima Cantatrice del Mondo*, and for the first two decades of the nineteenth century it was not an extravagant claim.

In terms of sheer voice her endowment was phenomenal. Even so critical a listener as Stendhal could describe her voice as "filling the soul with a kind of astonished wonder, as though it beheld a miracle." And Lord Mount-Edgcumbe, who had grave and specific reservations about her artistry, had none about her voice. It was, he observed, "of a most uncommon quality, and capable of exertions almost supernatural. Her throat seems endowed (as has been remarked by medical men) with a power of expansion and muscular motion by no means usual, and when she throws out all her voice to the utmost it has a volume and strength that are quite surprising; while its agility in divisions, running up and down the scale in semi-tones, and its compass in jumping two octaves at once, are equally astonishing." Queen Charlotte is reported to have said that she wanted cotton wool in her ears when Catalani sang; and there was the story of the London wit who, when asked if he was going to York to hear her, said he could hear her well enough where he was.

But for all the excitement she aroused, Catalani was a generation too late. Had hers been a short career, she might not have had to suffer

Billed, not inaccurately, as *Prima Cantatrice del Mondo*, Angelica Catalani (below), shown (left) as Semiramis in an opera of Portogallo, was the last of the great prima donnas of the age of *bel canto*.

The King's Theater in the Haymarket (after 1837 Her Majesty's) opened in 1791 (an earlier theater had been built, 1705), where Mrs. Billington, Mara, Catalani, Malibran, Sontag, Grisi, Rubini, Nourrit, Lablache and many other great singers appeared. It was overshadowed after 1847 by Covent Garden and was destroyed by fire in 1867.

A pioneer English prima donna was Anastasia Robinson (below), a contralto and a considerable beauty. She was secretly married to the Earl of Peterborough.

the consequences in the form of many unflattering critical references to her shortcomings as an actress and as a musician. But thanks to her extraordinary endowment and her basically sound vocal schooling, she remained in good form until she was close to fifty. The last decade of her active life coincided with the prime of Pasta and the initial triumphs of Sontag, Cinti-Damoreau and Malibran, and in the company of this new nineteenth-century type of singing actress Catalani was an anachronism, and her art as obsolete as that of Velluti.

Velluti, as a castrato, could hardly help himself. Catalani, as a woman, and a surpassingly handsome woman at that, might have adapted her art to the new trends. But such was not her nature, and it would probably have been beyond her intelligence. For she was not an imaginative creature. Politically her leanings were so legitimist that she refused—to his face—to sing for Napoleon; and musically she resented the new eminence given to such composers as Mozart and Rossini and the growing assertiveness of their instrumentation.

She sang Mozart, and was even reckoned a good Susanna—characteristically appropriating Cherubino's "Voi che sapete" and embellishing and altering it at will. (The theft was repeated in Vienna in 1824 by a more discriminating artist, Joséphine Fodor-Mainvielle (1789–1870). But she was never comfortable in Mozart's music, even in an *opera seria* such as *La Clemenza di Tito*. The accompaniments were obtrusive, she argued, and required her to sing in time, which she found an annoying inhibition. There is no evidence that she invented, but every reason to assume that she would have applauded, an Italian saying of those days: "German accompaniments do not constitute a guard of honor for the melody, but rather a police escort."

In the early years of her career—she was born in Sinigaglia in 1780— her companions on the stages of Italy, Portugal and Spain had included Marchesi and Crescentini. She never, apparently, studied with either of them systematically. Crescentini told Fétis, the French critic and historian, that he had offered her some advice, but that she seemed incapable of grasping it. She can hardly have escaped being influenced by their example, however, and contemporary evidence would indicate that she had been more taken with Marchesi's extravagance than with Crescentini's sobriety.

When she arrived in London in 1806 Lord Mount-Edgcumbe tempered his admiration for her voice with severe comments upon her style. "It were to be wished," he wrote, "that she was less lavish in the display of these wonderful powers, and sought to please more than surprise; but

There was no telling whose music might turn up in any opera in which Catalani sang. Here are the famous—some thought them infamous—variations she sang to Paisiello's "Nel cor più non mi sento" and which she introduced into

Il fanatico per la musica. They are a good example of the overembellishment of a simple tune that characterized the decadence of the age of *bel canto.*

her taste is vicious, her excessive love of ornament spoiling every simple air, and her greatest delight (indeed her chief merit) being in songs of bold and spirited character, where much is left to her discretion (or indiscretion), without being confined by the accompaniment, but in which she can indulge in *ad libitum* passages with a luxuriance and redundancy no other singer ever possessed or, if possessing, ever practised, and which she carries to a fantastical excess. She is fond of singing variations on some known simple air, and latterly she has pushed this taste to the height of absurdity by singing, even without accompaniment, variations composed for the fiddle."

Among the variations to which Lord Mount-Edgcumbe referred were a set by Pierre Rode (1774–1830), the foremost violinist of the pre-Spohr generation, on an air in G major of his own, and another by Giacomo Gotifredo Ferrari (1763–1842) on the lovely Paisiello tune "Nel cor più non mi sento." Catalani may, as Lord Mount-Edgcumbe said, have sung them as vocalises without accompaniment, but they have been preserved in sheet-music form with piano accompaniment, and Ferrari's variations carry a notation that they may be played as a solo on the violin or flute an octave higher. Rode's air has been given words, allegedly by Catalani.

Spohr himself heard her in Naples in 1817, and she was still singing the same pieces in the same way. His report is of special interest as that of a cultivated German musician not notably predisposed to contemporary Italian musical taste, but still sufficiently sympathetic to the Italian tradition to have composed his "Scena ed aria," more familiarly known as the "Gesangsszene," for his Italian tour.

"The arrival of Signora Catalani," he wrote in his diary, "had all the music lovers of Naples in a great state of excitement. She took advantage of it, and promptly arranged a concert in the Teatro Fiorentino with tickets at seven times the normal price. The day before the concert it was only with the greatest difficulty that I was able to get two tickets, and then only because I had ordered them in advance. Never has an audience been in such a state of intense expectation as the Neapolitan audience that evening. My wife and I, who had hoped for years to have the opportunity of hearing this admired singer, could hardly contain ourselves.

"At long last she appeared, and there was a deathly stillness throughout the auditorium. Her bearing was cold and rather pretentious, and she greeted neither the court nor the rest of the audience, which made an unpleasant impression. Possibly she had expected in her own turn to be greeted with applause, which is not customary in Naples, and was piqued when there was none. Her first song, however, was fervently applauded, and she promptly became more friendly, remaining so the rest of the evening.

"There was much sheer pleasure in the purity of her intonation, in the perfection of every kind of figuration and embellishment, and the individuality of her interpretive style. But she was not quite the prototype of the perfect singer upon which we had counted. Her voice has a respectable range from G below the staff to the B above, and in the lower and middle registers it is full and strong. The passage to the upper register, around E and F, however, is quite conspicuous, and three or four tones in this area are noticeably weaker than the very low and the very high. In order to cover this defect she sings all the figures that occur there in half-voice.

"Her trill is especially beautiful, whether in whole or semi-tones. Much admired was a run through the half-tones, actually an enharmonic scale, since each half-tone occurred twice. This is regarded as something exclusively hers. I found it more remarkable than beautiful, sounding something like the howling of the wind in a smokestack. Very beautiful was the way in which she accomplished another and not uncommon type of ornamentation, a descending scale of coupled eighths and sixteenths, pausing for breath after each sixteenth, and giving to the whole passage a most melancholy complexion. Among the variations was one in syncopation, which had a strikingly individual character, and another in triplets, which she managed with the utmost perfection.

"What I missed most in her singing was soul. Her recitatives were rendered without expression, almost carelessly, and her adagios left one cold. We were never once moved, but we did have the pleasure always associated with the spectacle of the easy mastery of mechanical difficulties. I must still mention certain unpleasant and obtrusive mannerisms which, at her age, she can hardly be expected to overcome. Among them is the habit, in passages, and particularly in full voice, of chewing out each tone in such a way that even a stone-deaf listener, if he saw her sing, could distinguish between eighths and sixteenths as she goes up and down the scale. Particularly in trills, the movement of her chin is such that each note can be counted. Secondly, in passionate episodes, she indulges in bodily movements, possibly Latin, but certainly unwomanly, from which, again, a deaf person could easily divine the figures she is singing.

"A few days later we heard her again at the rehearsal for her second concert. . . . She seemed on this occasion much less pretentious, much more engaging. She was also most gracious to the orchestra and to the people who had crowded in to hear her. Thus I was quite ready to believe what various persons told me; namely, that her pretentious bearing at her first appearance had proceeded rather from embarrassment than from pride, and was essentially a device for disguising her anxiety. A young man who had been backstage at that first concert assured me that at her first entrance she had trembled from head to foot, and had hardly been able to breathe, so intense was her nervousness."

Her lack of soul was noted by others, including Stendhal, who, having spoken of a miracle, went on to say that "the very confusion of our hearts blinds us at first to the noble and goddess-like impassivity of this unique artist." She had other blinding devices, including her wardrobe. The London *Times*, describing her appearance in *La Clemenza di Tito* in 1812, recorded:

"Her dress on her first appearance was magnificently arranged, and the glittering diadem, the head wreathed like an antique bust, her scarlet tunic and her looped and tasseled drapery gave the full impression of regal grandeur to a face and form fitted, beyond all that we have ever seen, to the expression of dignity and grace—the softness of a woman mingled with the solemn and tragic majesty of a fallen queen."

As a queen she liked to appear, and as a queen she liked to be treated. Many tales were told of the homage she expected and got—or exacted. Once, when dissatisfied with the quality of the carpet laid in her path to the piano on the stage, she ostentatiously spread her own shawl to accommodate her feet. Her gesture on this occasion was not unprecedented. In Munich, when taken to task for occupying a seat in church reserved for the royal family, she canceled her concert, swearing never to set foot in Munich again, and required that a rug be laid from the hotel door to her carriage, throwing her own shawl in her path as a final act of defiance as she flounced out.

Her policies as an impresario were similarly royalist. Probably it was her own appetite for absolutism that led her into opera management in the first place, an appetite in which she was encouraged by her husband. In Lisbon, early in her career, she had met and married a French soldier and diplomat named Valabrègue, who was ever afterward constantly at her side, assisting her in the mismanagement of her money and her own and other people's affairs.

They shared a singular vision of how an opera house should be run.

"My wife and four or five puppets—that's all you need," her husband used to say. The management of the King's Theater in London did not agree, and declined to lease them the theater in 1813. The French, with less experience of Italian opera and Catalani, thought the idea worth a try, and the Valabrègues were offered the Théâtre-Italien in Paris along with a generous subsidy.

The experiment endured, off and on, until 1818—with an interruption between Napoleon's return and the restoration—and was a disaster. Catalani and her husband saw no purpose in spending money on cast, chorus, orchestra, costumes, scenery or rehearsals. And any old opera would do, since it would, in any case, quickly be made over into a concert in costume for Catalani, complete with Rode variations and all.

Catalani may have sensed the obsolescence of herself and her ideas of production in the new operatic scheme of things; for after 1818 she devoted herself to concertizing, traveling from one end of Europe to another, singing the same old war-horses and earning for herself the designation "the trilling gypsy."

She was back in England again in 1824, when the ubiquitous Lord Mount-Edgcumbe found "her powers undiminished, her taste unimproved." In Berlin, in 1827, Sontag complained of her shouting, and by that time even Catalani must have realized that her day was done. She retired to Florence, then to Paris, where she died of cholera in 1849.

Everyone else had known for some time that her day was done. As early as 1813, when she quitted London for Paris to take over the Théâtre-Italien, a British critic wrote: "A new era began in our opera." It was a curious way of putting it, particularly since the critic was Lord Mount-Edgcumbe, who observed at the same time: "I consider Catalani to be the last great singer heard in this country whose name is likely to be recollected in musical annals."

But there is a clue. Lord Mount-Edgcumbe was of the old school. However much he may have deplored Catalani's vices, her virtues reminded him of Pacchierotti, Marchesi and Crescentini. He was, moreover, among those who felt that Mozart's accompaniments restricted a singer's fancy too severely. When he spoke of a new era, therefore, he did not imply a better one. And, in fact, London had to wait another decade for Pasta to herald an era not only new but better.

What Lord Mount-Edgcumbe meant was that when Catalani departed the old order went with her—and forever. And in that he was right enough.

· VIII ·

Epilogue for Basses and Tenors

BOSCHI · MONTAGNANA

FISCHER · FABRI · RAAFF

GARCÍA · RUBINI

THERE WERE always basses and tenors in the age of *bel canto*, some of them excellent. But the conventions of the time gave priority to treble voices, even in male roles, and favored a kind of vocalism that left the unmutilated male at a disadvantage.

If tenors fared better than basses it was because they learned, under the tutelage of the castrati, to use a light head voice and falsetto in such a way that the best of them could approximate the embellishments, cadences, portamenti, roulades, trills and turns established by the castrati as basic devices of good singing.

Basses, governed similarly by the requirements of florid song, were condemned pretty much to rumbling until the prosperity of *opera buffa* toward the end of the eighteenth century provided a more congenial and a more hospitable environment.

1. GIUSEPPE BOSCHI AND ANTONIO MONTAGNANA

Some basses rumbled better than others, or more musically. Two of the best were Giuseppe Boschi and Antonio Montagnana, about whom little is known beyond the fact that Handel brought them to London—Boschi in 1710 and again in 1720, Montagnana in 1731—and provided them with some of the finest bass arias ever written. Indeed, Handel seems to have had a predilection for the bass voice not shared by later composers of *opera seria*. "Handel's genius and fire," said Burney, "never

The "division" (above) sung by Giuseppe Boschi in Buononcini's *Etearco* in 1711, is of the same primitive and monotonous variety as those sung by the castrato Nicolino in the same opera. Far more sophisticated is Handel's writing (below) for Antonio Montagnana in *Sosarme* twenty years later, exploiting a full two-octave range and the ability to negotiate wide intervals, which was a specialty of the Bolognese school.

shine brighter than in the bass songs he composed for Boschi and Montagnana; as their voices were sufficiently powerful to penetrate through a multiplicity of instrumental parts, he set every engine to work in the orchestra to enrich the harmony and enliven the movement."

Just how fine these two singers must have been may be appreciated by any bass of our own time who attempts the arias written for them, or by any listener attending the enterprise. Of the aria "Desciolte dal piede," from Buononcini's *Astarto*, written for Boschi, for instance, Burney says: "The divisions in this air seem to imply unusual agility for a voice of such a pitch." The sentiments served by such exercises for a bass voice may be imagined. There was even a simile current in London at that time: "and Boschi-like to be always in a rage."

Burney also singles out the aria "Fra l'ombre e gl'orrorr" from Handel's *Sosarme*, sung by Montagnana, "in which the bass voice of the new singer, in its depth, power, mellowness and peculiar accuracy of intonation in hitting distant intervals were displayed, and which will ever be admired by judges of composition and heard with delight by the public whenever it is executed by a singer whose voice and abilities shall be equal to those of Montagnana. The divisions in many songs written expressly for his voice are both numerous and rapid, and sometimes extend to two octaves in compass."

2. LUDWIG FISCHER

From Montagnana to Ludwig Fischer (1745–1825) there is a gap of some forty years, during which time no basses of truly exceptional attainments are noted. What sort of singer Fischer must have been may be surmised from the role of Osmin in *Die Entführung aus dem Serail*, which Mozart wrote for him. He had an extraordinary range of two and a half octaves from the low D to the A of a tenor or high baritone, which, in his prime, he sang without resorting to falsetto. Some German commentators even credited him with three and a half octaves, which would suggest a double low D, i.e., the D an octave below the normal low D of a bass.

Such a tone, if audible, could have had no other purpose than astonishment. The possibility is supported, however, by the critics who covered his appearances in London in 1794. One of them describes his voice as descending "from his alto notes to what might almost be called the bottomless depths with a certainty and fullness of intonation that astonishes." Another critic noted that "with each descending note the audience could not but inquire: 'What, deeper yet?' " And one of them even employed the term "double low D," but without specifying precisely what he meant by it.

Although born in Mainz, and trained by the German tenor, Raaff, in Mannheim, Fischer was a singer in the Italian tradition; for Raaff had been a pupil of Bernacchi, and had passed on to Fischer the Bolognese tradition of ornamentation. This became an embarrassment to Fischer late in his career. German critics, after the turn of the century, began to find such embellishment old-fashioned and, in Mozart's music, offensive, especially Fischer's ornamentation of Sarastro's "In diesen heil'gen Hallen" from *The Magic Flute*. Mozart, however, admired him, and wrote for him, in addition to Osmin's music, the concert arias "Aspri remorsi atroci" (K. 432) and "Non so, d'onde viene" (K. 512). Figaro and Don Giovanni were his other Mozart roles, although he was not the creator of either of them.

Fischer accepted an engagement at the opera in Berlin in 1788, and made his headquarters there for the rest of his life. He sang too long— until 1817, when he was seventy-two—lost his bottom notes and developed elsewhere that quaver common to aging basses. He also composed for himself a song "Im tiefen Keller sitz' ich hier," a forerunner of such purposeful ditties as "Rocked in the Cradle of the Deep" and "The Big Bass Viol," with whose vocal depths, if hardly profundities of any other kind, later basses have sought to astonish their listeners. Fischer's song employs those wide intervals that were a specialty of the Bolognese school.

Also of the Bolognese school was the German bass Ludwig Fischer. His own song, "Im tiefen Keller sitz' ich hier," has him plunging to the cellar in leaps of octaves and tenths and ascending by even wider intervals.

3. ANNIBALE PIO FABRI

The tenor family tree has a more resplendent flowering of famous names, or at least of names famous in the eighteenth and early nineteenth centuries. Tenors had, of course, a better time of it. In addition to the vocal advantages mentioned earlier, they could be employed in parts written for, and customarily sung by, women. Since it was not usual at that time for tenors to carry their chest voices into the upper extremes of the tenor compass, moving into a head voice or falsetto above F or G, their normal voices were probably pitched lower, or trained to a lower pitch, than those of later tenors, schooled to achieve the vocal heroics of grand opera. Their natural range was normally probably closer to that of the average church choir tenor.

When Annibale Pio Fabri (1697–1760) came to London with Bernacchi in 1729, for example, he appeared in parts written both for Boschi and for Boschi's wife Francesca. Boschi himself once took a role originally written for a mezzo-soprano. This interchangeability of basses and tenors, and, more particularly, of males and females, would continue for another century and beyond. The role of Othello in Rossini's opera, written for García and created by Nozzari, both tenors, was sung by Pasta, Malibran and other prima donnas well into the 1830s. When *La Gazza Ladra*, first performed in Milan, was brought to Naples, Nozzari sang the role written for Filippo Galli, a bass. And as late as 1847 Marietta Alboni assumed the baritone role of Don Carlo in a performance of *Ernani* at Covent Garden when the part proved to be too high for Tamburini and distasteful to Ronconi.

Fabri seems to have been the first truly great tenor—great, at least, in the sense that he was generally conceded to have had no peers. He was a Bolognese and a pupil of Pistocchi. What is known of him is derived largely from his record in London, where he appeared from 1729 to 1731, and that record tells us little except that he achieved a status not previously enjoyed by a mere tenor.

4. ANTON RAAFF

Much more is known of Anton Raaff, mentioned earlier as the teacher of Fischer and a pupil of Bernacchi. Born near Bonn in 1714, he was destined for the priesthood, and was twenty before he learned to read music. His singing in an oratorio in Cologne attracted the attention of the visiting Elector of Bavaria, who became his patron and sent him to Italy. After completing his studies with Bernacchi, he sang in Italy and Germany, then went to Madrid, where he joined Farinelli's company. From 1759 to 1769 he was in Naples, and in 1770 he returned to Germany, to remain in the establishments of the Bavarian court in Mannheim and Munich for the rest of a long life.

Such had been the career of the man to whom Leopold Mozart commended young Wolfgang when the latter stopped in Mannheim on his way to Paris in 1777. Raaff soon became one of Mozart's most ardent supporters and devoted friends, and Mozart rewarded him with the title role in *Idomeneo*. References to Raaff in Mozart's letters provide an extraordinary insight into the vocal traditions and customs of the eighteenth century; and the gradual change of Mozart's tone from one of derision to one of respect and, finally, of love, offers a sympathetic view of Mozart and an instructive glimpse of an eighteenth-century composer-singer relationship.

Mozart's first reference to Raaff is in a letter to his father, dated November 14–16, 1777, when Mozart was twenty-one and Raaff sixty-three: "On one occasion Raaff sang four arias, about 450 bars in all, in such a fashion as to call forth a remark that his voice was the strongest reason why he sang so badly. Anyone who hears him begin an aria without reminding himself that it is Raaff, the once famous tenor, who is singing, is bound to burst out laughing. . . . Moreover, he has never been, so people here tell me, anything of an actor; you'd only have had to hear him without even looking at him; nor has he by any means a good presence. In the opera he had to die, and while dying sing a very very very long aria in slow time; well, he died with a grin on his face, and towards the end of the aria his voice gave out so badly that one really couldn't stand it any longer." Raaff's grin was, of course, no more than the smile prescribed by the Bolognese school as a guarantee that a singer's features would betray no evidence of effort or distress. Three months later Mozart tells his father:

"I was at Raaff's yesterday and brought him an aria which I composed for him the other day. The words are 'Se al labbro mio non credi, bella nemica mia,' etc. [(K. 295)]. . . . He liked it enormously . . . I asked him to tell me candidly if he did not like it or if it did not suit his voice, adding that I would alter it if he wished or even compose another. 'God forbid,' he said, 'the aria must remain just as it is, for nothing could be finer. But please shorten it a little, for I am no longer able to sustain my notes.' 'Most gladly,' I replied, 'as much as you like. I made it a little long on purpose, for it is always easy to cut down, but not so easy to lengthen.' After he had sung the second part, he took off his spectacles, and looking at me with wide-open eyes, said: 'Beautiful! Beautiful! That is a charming *seconda parte*.' And he sang it three times. When I took leave of him he thanked me most cordially, while I assured him that I would arrange the aria in such a way that it would give him pleasure to sing it. For I like an aria to fit a singer as perfectly as a well-made suit of clothes."

Raaff was in Paris with Mozart the following year, and in a letter to his father, dated June 12, 1778, Mozart says: "I must now say something about our Raaff. You will remember, no doubt, that I did not write too favorably about him from Mannheim, and was by no means pleased with his singing—*enfin*, that I did not like him at all. The reason, however, was that I scarcely heard him properly. . . . But when he made his debut here in the Concert Spirituel, he sang Bach's *scena* 'Non sò d'onde viene,' which, by the way, is a favorite of mine [so much so, as we have seen, that he set the words himself for Fischer]—and then for the first time I really heard him sing—and he pleased me—that is, in his particular style of singing, although the style itself—the Bernacchi school—is not to my taste. . . . I admit that when he was young and in his prime this must have been very effective and have taken people by surprise. I admit also that I like it. But he overdoes it and so to me it often seems ridiculous. What I do like is when he sings short pieces, as for example, some andantinos; and he has also certain arias, which he renders in his peculiar style. Well, each in his own way. I fancy that his forte was bravura singing—and, so far as his age permits, you can still tell this from his manner; he has a good chest and long breath; and then—these andantinos! His voice is beautiful and very pleasant. . . . In bravura singing, long passages and roulades Raaff is absolute master and he has, moreover, an excellent, clear diction, which is very beautiful."

During the rehearsals of *Idomeneo* in Munich in 1780 Mozart and Raaff had their problems. "I have just had a bad time with him over the quartet," Mozart wrote to his father in a letter dated December 27. "The more I think of this quartet, as it will be performed on the stage, the more effective I consider it; and it has pleased all those who have heard it played on the clavier. Raaff alone thinks it will produce no effect whatever. He said to me when we were by ourselves: '*Non c'e da spianar la*

Manuel García in Goya's portrait (above right), and as Othello (above left) in Rossini's opera, was the first Count Almaviva in *The Barber of Seville* and the father of Maria Malibran, Pauline Viardot and the Manuel García who became the greatest singing teacher of the 19th century.

Mozart was first repelled and then enchanted by the Bolognese-schooled singing of the German tenor Anton Raaff (left), and wrote for him the title role of *Idomeneo.*

voce—It gives me no scope.' As if in a quartet the words should not be spoken much more than sung! That kind of thing he does not understand at all. All I said was: 'My very dear friend, if I knew of one single note which ought to be altered in this quartet, I would alter it at once. But there is nothing in my opera with which I am so pleased as with this quartet; and when you have heard it sung in concert you will talk very differently. I have taken great pains to serve you well in your two arias, I shall do the same with your third one—and shall hope to succeed. But as far as trios and quartets are concerned, the composer must have a free hand.' Whereupon he said that he was satisfied."

Raaff recanted, as Mozart had thought he would, but he made further difficulties about certain words in his last aria, complaining that they gave him too many *i*'s to sing. Mozart sided with him in this matter, working behind the librettist's back to accommodate him. There is, indeed, something touching about the Mozart-Raaff relationship. Raaff was forty-two years older than Mozart, and this at a time in musical history when forty-two years represented a greater disparity in points of view than would have been the case at any previous time, once the conventions of *opera seria* had been settled in the first decades of the century. But Raaff sensed and respected the extraordinary genius of his young friend, and the latter admired in Raaff a singer who had certainly been a master, however much his former virtuosity must have faded, and however exasperating, from time to time, his adherence to old-fashioned devices and his assumption of outdated prerogatives must have been.

5. MANUEL GARCÍA

The view of the tenor as a florid singer would persist well into the nineteenth century. Among the most distinguished later practitioners of this art, or craft, were Giovanni Anzani, dates unknown, but born about the middle of the eighteenth century; the Davids, Giaccomo (1750–1830) and Giovanni (1789–1851); John Braham (1777–1856); Andrea Nozzari (1775–1832) and Manuel García (1775–1832). They all have a certain historical importance because of the roles written for most of them by Rossini in his earlier and now forgotten operas, and as transitional figures in the slow graduation of the tenor to the status of an opera star, displacing the castrato as the male counterpart of the prima donna.

A section of the aria "Ecco ridente" from *The Barber of Seville*, with two sets of embellishments and two cadenzas as given by the younger Manuel García in his *Traité complet de l'art du chant*, to show how embellishment was supposed to contribute to characterization. Of these versions García says: "It will be perceived that the style of our last example [third stave] is too languid for the character of the brilliant count." Although García does not so state, it may be assumed that the embellishments of the second stave may have been identical with, or similar to, those employed by his father, the original Almaviva.

Manuel García was the most memorable of this group. Of all the roles Rossini wrote for his tenors—discounting that of William Tell, which belongs to a later epoch—only that of Almaviva in *The Barber of Seville*, written for García, has survived to give us some idea of the singer, the voice and the style that he had in mind. But García is even more memorable as the father of Maria Malibran, Pauline Viardot and the Manuel García who became the most celebrated singing teacher of the nineteenth century, and as the man who, in 1825, introduced Italian opera to New York.

Not only one of the great tenors of his generation, but also the composer of seventy-one Spanish, nineteen Italian and seven French light operas, he was born in Seville. Both gypsy and Jewish origins have been assumed or alleged, but not documented. Gifted, restless, versatile and willful, he came to Paris in 1808, moved to Naples in 1811 (where he studied with Anzani), returned to Paris in 1816 and sang there and in London until his departure for New York.

When he returned to Paris in 1829, his vocal prime was past, but he could—and did—rejoice in the fame of Malibran, and he still had enough voice to sing an Othello to her Desdemona in London. Everyone knew that this was probably García's last appearance, and there was an emotional scene before the curtain at the end of the performance. Malibran made the most of it by kissing her father and smearing her own face with his black makeup. One of García's favorite roles, incidentally, was Don Giovanni, written for baritone or bass. Other tenors followed his example, including Donzelli, Nozzari, Braham, Nourrit and Mario, none of them with any success.

But it was as a pedagogue that his influence was most enduring. He was the teacher not only of Nourrit, but also of his children. Malibran had no pupils, but Pauline Viardot and her brother Manuel set criteria of vocalism and principles of vocal pedagogy that were to endure far into the present century. Among Manuel's pupils were such notable vocalists and teachers as Jenny Lind, Julius Stockhausen, Sir Charles Santley and Mathilde Marchesi.

One of Viardot's pupils was the late Anna Eugénie Schön-René, for many years a member of the faculty of the Juilliard School of Music in New York, and the teacher of Charles Kullman, Risë Stevens, Paul Robeson, William Horne and the late Mack Harrell. Unlike Malibran, both García and Viardot were extraordinarily long-lived. García died in 1906 at the age of 101, and Viardot in 1910, aged eighty-nine.

Greatest of the early-19th-century virtuoso tenors was Giovanni-Battista Rubini, as Arturo in *I Puritani* (above right), a part written for him by Bellini, and (above left) in an unidentified role.

John Braham (Abraham) (left), the first great English tenor, was considered the equal and even the superior of most of his Italian contemporaries. His own song, "The Death of Nelson," enjoyed great popularity as long as he was around to sing it.

6. GIOVANNI-BATTISTA RUBINI

But among all the turn-of-the-century and early nineteenth-century tenors, excellent as they must have been, Giovanni-Battista Rubini (1795–1854) was unique. He was the first normal male to achieve international renown and a popular following corresponding to that hitherto reserved for prima donnas and castrati and to command commensurate fees. Where Giovanni David, García and Nozzari had been primarily Rossinian tenors, Rubini was the tenor of Donizetti and Bellini. His female partner in some of their operas, notably *La Sonnambula* and *Anna Bolena*, was Pasta, who brought to her own parts a new dramatic dimension. From all this one would assume a new kind of tenor, introducing, or at least anticipating, the dramatic tenor or lighter-voiced *lirico spinto* of the nineteenth century. Rubini was nothing of the sort; rather an ungelded Marchesi, and not so handsome.

Not alone among the greatest singers, Rubini had initially to contend with an imperfect vocal endowment; and the voice, once mastered, yielded a prime of less than average duration. He was only thirty-six when he came to London in 1831, and Henry F. Chorley, critic of *The Athenaeum*, found his voice "hardly capable, perhaps, of being produced mezzo-forte or piano; for which reason he had adopted a style of extreme contrast betwixt soft and loud, which many ears were unable, for a long time, to relish." He had also developed a tremolo and the habit of reattacking a sustained note just before the cadence, the device by which tenors have been turning *del mio cor* into *de-hel mio cor* ever since.

Nor was he well favored in appearance. He had a pockmarked face and an awkward figure and showed neither taste nor care in dress. He was an indifferent actor, or no actor at all. In opera he walked through his parts, slighted recitatives, lent some attention to his duties in concerted numbers, blending his voice expertly with the voices of his partners, and awaited his moment—possibly just one aria in an entire opera. And then he sang!

He was simply all singer. Chorley noted happily that "there never was an artist who seemed so thoroughly and intensely to enjoy his own singing—a persuasion," he added cogently, "which cannot fail to communicate itself to audiences. . . . As a singer and nothing but a singer he is the only man of his class who deserves to be named in these pages [*Thirty Years' Musical Recollections*] as an artist of genius. No one in

my experience, so merely and exclusively a singer as he was, so entirely
enchanted our public so long as a shred of voice was left to him; no one
is more affectionately remembered."

Quoting from ecstatic notices is easy—and risky. The vocabulary of
hyperbole is not unlimited. The same adjectives are often applied to
singers of obviously different characteristics, and the evaluations tend
to be repetitive. Critics still under the spell of an exciting occasion yield
to enthusiasm and forget other occasions and other artists, claiming for
their idols powers and achievements which, within the span of a century or so, can hardly have been unique. But making due allowance for
such hazards, there is, in the commentary of those who heard Rubini,
always something that suggests a quality of communication setting him
apart from any other tenor before or since.

When *Lucia* was introduced to Paris on December 12, 1837, Rubini
was the Edgardo (Gilbert-Louis Duprez had created the role in Naples
two years before). Of that performance the French critic, Pietro (Pierre)
Scudo, wrote: "As for the scene of the malediction which forms the
dramatic nexus of the beautiful finale [of Act II], no other singer has
been able to reproduce the sob of fury which Rubini emitted from his
trembling mouth." Of the same scene another critic, Ernest Legouvé,
co-author with Scribe of *Adriana Lecouvreur*, said that Rubini "suddenly
was transformed into a tragedian by dint of being a sublime singer."

The essential question about Rubini is how a tenor noted for extravagant embellishment and improvisatory genius could have excited such
rapture right through the 1830s, while tenors of similar schooling, a
decade earlier, had been thought old-fashioned. The answer may be that
Rubini was even more old-fashioned than they; that his art was not so
much a continuation or reflection of David, García and Nozzari as a
throwback to Pacchierotti, Crescentini, Anzani and even Raaff, just as,
half a century later, the Neapolitan tenor, Fernando de Lucia (1860–
1925), would seem on the evidence of some of his recordings—notably
of the "Ecco ridente" from *The Barber of Seville*—to be a throwback to
Rubini. Some observations by Stendhal, although not dealing with Rubini, provide a clue:

"The supreme qualities of the soprani [castrati] and their pupils were
seen at their most resplendent in the execution of largo and *cantabile
spianato* passages. . . . Yet this precisely was the type of aria which
Rossini, ever since the moment when he arrived in Naples and adopted
what is known in Italy as his 'second manner,' has been at greatest pains

to eliminate from his operas. . . . The older style of singing could stir a man to the innermost recesses of his soul; but it could also prove rather boring. Rossini's style titillates the mind, and is never boring. . . . Rossini has been responsible for a musical revolution, but even his sincerest friends blame that revolution for having restricted the boundaries of the art of singing, for having limited the qualities of emotional pathos inherent in that art, and for having rendered useless, and therefore obsolete, certain technical exercises, valueless in themselves, but which could ultimately lead to those *transports of delirium and rapture* which occur so frequently in the history of Pacchierotti and other great artists of an earlier generation, and so very rarely today. The source of these miracles lay in the *mystic powers of the human voice*."

It was precisely in long cantabile passages, which he sometimes sang without embellishment, that Rubini excelled; and it was Bellini, rather than Rossini or even Donizetti, who seems to have sensed the true elements of Rubini's genius and to have provided the types of aria designed to give them the most fruitful scope. Rubini is said to have lived with Bellini while the latter was composing *Il Pirata*, and to have sung each song as it came from the young composer's hand.

From 1831 to 1843 Rubini divided his year between Paris and London. It must have been in Paris, in 1840, that Anton Rubinstein heard him and, as Rubinstein is said to have remarked to Pierre Lalo, "formed my ideas of noble and eloquent phrasing almost entirely from the example of the great tenor, Rubini." And Rubini was certainly among those who prompted Liszt to say that he had learned to phrase on the piano from listening to great singers. In 1843 Liszt and Rubini even toured together.

Later in the same year Rubini went to St. Petersburg, where he was made Director of Singing in the realm of Czar Nicholas I and a Colonel of the Imperial Music. He returned to Italy about 1845, and retired to his birthplace, Romano de Lombardia, near Bergamo, to live out his life, with one of the greatest fortunes ever amassed on the stage. There he build a splendid *palazzo*, preserved to this day as a Rubini Museum. And there on March 2, 1854, he died.

"The tradition of his method," said Chorley, "died with him."

It was rather more than that. The age of *bel canto* had been a long time dying. With Rubini's last breath it expired.

PART TWO

The Age
of
Grand Opera

A New Kind of Prima Donna

PASTA · MALIBRAN

SCHRÖDER-DEVRIENT

SOCIAL RATHER than critical stimulus spurred the transition from *opera seria* to grand opera in the first decades of the nineteenth century. If the transition was hesitant, erratic and haphazard, it was simply because neither the composers nor their singers were prepared for it, let alone prepared to guide it.

It was introduced, curiously, through the back door—or tradesmen's entrance. One is accustomed to think of this transition in terms of Gluck, Mozart, Cherubini and Beethoven. But modern musicology regards the masterpieces of *opera buffa* in the mature works of Haydn, Paisiello, Mozart, Cimarosa and Rossini as probably having been the more decisive influence.

Generalization is a hazardous means of attempting to block out phases in the evolution of European music. Boundaries are obscure, and developments in one area are not invariably paralleled or reflected in another. The spectacular growth and refinement of instrumental music in Germany and Austria at the turn of the century was little noted by the composers of *opera seria*. And the extent to which the Teutonic influence was felt at all—in a more extensive and sophisticated use of the orchestra, for example—was resented and resisted by the devotees of eighteenth-century Italian singing and, of course, by the singers, long accustomed not only to call the tunes but also to exercise some influence upon the character of the orchestral accompaniment.

In instrumental music the implications of what Haydn, Mozart, Beethoven and Schubert had accomplished were obscured in the 1820s and 1830s by a fad of instrumental virtuosity as prone to triviality and vain display as the art of the eighteenth-century singers, and without the communicative beauty of the singers' finest accomplishments. One hesitates, therefore, to ascribe the decline of *opera seria* to a sudden improvement in popular taste. Mozart's masterpieces and the reform operas of Gluck, while generally admired, did not lead to immediate emulation. Gluck's last operas, moreover, enjoyed their most resounding successes in Paris, hardly the capital to which Italian opera composers would look for instruction in composition, or singers for examples of superior vocalism.

And Mozart's best operas were, after all, either a superior kind of *Singspiel* or a sublimation of the type of *opera buffa* already well advanced by Pergolesi, Galuppi, Piccinni, Paisiello and Haydn; and the extent of Mozart's improvement over his predecessors was not instantly appreciated. *Opera buffa* was popular music, and not even such achievements as Mozart's were felt as a threat to *opera seria*. The rank and file of Italian opera composers simply moved along in the old groove, largely ignorant, probably, of the new dimensions—and especially the dramatic dimensions—discovered and exploited within the tonal, melodic and rhythmic framework of eighteenth-century music in the instrumental works of Haydn, Mozart and Beethoven. Nor were they disturbed by the originality and vitality of *opera buffa*.

But if popular taste was not improving, it was changing. The later composers of *opera seria* may not have been inferior to such older masters as Buononcini and Hasse. They may even have been better. It was not a question of quality but of fashion. Before they knew what had happened, they had become outmoded, and their singers with them. The new taste was for a livelier and more immediate kind of drama than had been implied or achieved in the predictable succession of recitatives and arias and the prescribed poses, gestures and attitudes of *opera seria*.

And it was from *opera buffa* that emerged the concerted numbers, particularly the finales: the lively participation of the orchestra, the liberation of male voices from secondary assignments, the more extensive and more flexible use of the chorus and the appearance of more or less ordinary mortals upon the stage, which would be given dramatic dignity in the serious operas of Rossini, Donizetti, Bellini, Meyerbeer and Verdi. There had been hints of assimilation in the serious operas of Domenico Cimarosa (1749–1801) and Simone Mayr (1763–1845), but the composer in whose music assimilation became decisive was Rossini.

He is remembered primarily for *The Barber of Seville*, an *opera buffa*, but his early serious operas, notably *Tancredi* and *Otello*, were more influential. By giving new prominence to the male voices, and by introducing into serious opera the exciting orchestral and ensemble devices of *opera buffa,* he hit upon a genuinely contemporary and popular style of serious opera. And it was Rossini who, in his last operas, *The Siege of Corinth* and *William Tell,* written, significantly, for Paris, pointed the way to what would become known as grand opera. The singer who did more than any other to translate the new taste for dramatic excitement into singing, and to combine the art of the singer with that of the actor, was Giuditta Pasta.

1. GIUDITTA PASTA

Operatic evolution was rapid throughout the nineteenth century, and from the time of Meyerbeer's arrival in Paris in the 1820s through all the turbulent innovations of Verdi and Wagner, composers tended to run a decade or so ahead of the singers in their vocal requirements. During the age of *bel canto,* composers had always worked with certain singers in mind, tailoring their vocal requirements accordingly. This was also true of the earlier opera composers of the nineteenth century, notably of Rossini, Donizetti, Bellini and Meyerbeer; but Verdi and Wagner wrote what they hoped to hear, without reference to the talents of specific singers, and in some cases they had to wait a generation for the ideal singer to materialize.

With Pasta it was the other way around. She had to wait until her vocal powers were already declining to discover in Bellini and Donizetti the composers who could understand her potential. Rossini, for all his contribution to the dawn of grand opera, seems to have neither understood nor liked her. For the greater part of the best years of her career her triumphs were attained despite the want of any music really adequate to her vocal gifts and interpretive predilections. She had to make do with what was at hand, to adapt her vocal resources and dramatic insights to music written for less imaginative singers. Some measure of her accomplishment may be inferred from Chorley's recollection of her "magical and fearful Medea—a part musically and dramatically composed by herself out of the faded book and correct music of Simone Mayr's opera."

Stendhal, in his *Life of Rossini,* lamented the fact that Rossini had never composed an opera for Pasta, and he did so in a paragraph that tells us more than any other critic was able to tell of this singer's unique combination of personal, vocal and dramatic gifts and accomplishments.

"If chance," he wrote, "were to present Rossini with an actress who is young and beautiful; who is both intelligent and sensitive; whose gestures

The example of Giuditta Pasta was decisive in proving how dramatic an opera could be in the art of a great singer who was primarily an actress, and capable of total identification with the part she was playing. Pasta is shown as Desdemona (above) in Rossini's *Otello*. The intensity of Pasta's acting invited such caricatures as these by A. E. Chalon, showing her as Norma (left), a part written for her by Bellini, and in the title role of Rossini's *Tancredi* (right), originally written for a contralto.

never deteriorate from the plainest and most natural modes of simplicity, and yet manage to keep faith with the purest ideals of formal beauty; if, allied to such an extraordinary wealth of dramatic talent, Rossini were to discover a voice which never fails to thrill our very souls with the passionate exaltation which we used, long ago, to capture from the masters of the golden age; a voice which can weave a spell of magic about the plainest word in the plainest recitative; a voice whose compelling inflections can subdue the most recalcitrant and obdurate of hearts, and oblige them to share in the emotions which radiate from some great aria . . . if Rossini were to discover such a world of wonder, who doubts that the miraculous would happen, that he would shed his laziness like a garment, settle down unreservedly to a study of Madame Pasta's voice, and soon start composing within the special range of her abilities?"

Stendhal, writing thus in 1823, when Pasta was twenty-five, assessed Rossini's probable reaction incorrectly. Rossini was subsequently to become well acquainted with her. She was a member of the company during his directorship of the Théâtre-Italien, and one of his first administrative acts was to engage a number of excellent singers, allegedly as "a check on the pretensions of Madame Pasta." He wrote several more operas, none of them for her.

It was left to other and younger composers to accomplish what Stendahl had desired and hoped for Rossini. Giovanni Pacini (1796–1867) wrote for Pasta the title role in his *Niobe*, an opera now remembered— and not by many—as the source of a Liszt paraphrase. Donizetti's *Anna Bolena* was more enduring. But what Stendhal had dreamed about came to pass only in Bellini's *La Sonnambula* and *Norma*. Here was vocal writing that provided the long, plastic line required for the ultimate unfolding of Pasta's interpretive genius, the sustained cantilena that she could mold and bend and embellish to her high artistic purpose. In this respect Bellini was to Pasta what he also was to Rubini, who was Pasta's partner in *La Sonnambula*.

These roles—along with the Medea noted previously—will remind the contemporary reader of Maria Callas, although Callas's Medea was Cherubini's rather than Mayr's. And, indeed, these two singers have had more in common than merely an affinity of roles. In Callas was repeated Pasta's imperfect and unruly voice, tamed, more or less, by severe discipline and training, and resourcefully managed. Both could sing badly later in their careers and, at the same time, excite enthusiasm and even ecstasy. Common to both has been the achievement of prevailing over more beautiful and more tractable voices. Pasta and Callas have had the

Here is a passage from *Norma*, the upper stave showing the Bellini original, the lower the same passage as embellished by Pasta. It is cited by Manuel García, in his *Traité complet de l'art du chant*, as an example of how slurs should be prepared. Unlike most singers of her generation, Pasta never changed her embellishments once she had hit upon what she felt to be most effective and appropriate.

glamour, or genius, as Chorley would have called it, by which great artists, as distinguished from the merely very good, cast a spell that deafens the listener to executive imperfections and inadequacies. They have been more than singers; rather tragediennes in the grand manner, big actresses and big, commanding, persuasive personalities.

Pasta (1798–1865) was born Giuditta Negri, of Jewish parents, in Saronno, near Milan. She entered the conservatory in Milan at fifteen, an average age for female singers in those days, and made her debut three years later. She was not an immediate success. She traveled the Italian provincial circuit and appeared in more distinguished company in Paris and London, making so little impression that in Paris she was even included among the nonentities with whom Catalani preferred to surround herself. Along the way she met, married and took the patronymic of a tenor named Pasta. Dissatisfied with her progress, she withdrew from the stage for further vocal study. She reappeared in Venice in 1819 and was on her way. In Paris, in 1822, she ascended the throne. And for the next decade she defended it against such formidable challengers as Pisaroni, Malibran, Schröder-Devrient, Sontag and Grisi.

How she appeared upon that eminence is a subject on which sober commentators are curiously at odds. Julian Marshall, in his article in Grove's Dictionary, says: "Below the middle height, her figure was, nevertheless, very well proportioned; she had a noble head with fine features, a high forehead, dark and expressive eyes, and a beautiful mouth." Chorley, speaking from firsthand observation, said: "Though her countenance spoke, the features were cast in that coarse mold which is common in Italy. Her arms were fine, but her figure was short and clumsy. She walked heavily, almost unequally." But the same Chorley, describing her triumph before a "gorgeous assembly" in Rossini's *Zelmira*, could write: "I remember well the central figure in the blue robe and the classical diadem adorned with cameos; who stood forth like a sovereign in the midst of her subjects, with a grace and majesty which put many a born Royalty and Ambassadress to shame."

A less sovereign but no less compelling picture was offered by the Paris correspondent of the *Allgemeine Musikalische Zeitung* in his coverage of a performance of Paisiello's *Nina* in 1824. "Not only did this enchantress hold her listeners spellbound; she was herself so seized and carried away that she collapsed before the end. She was recalled, and duly appeared; but what a sight! Too weak to walk alone, supported by helping hands, more carried than walking, tears streaming down her pale cheeks, every muscle of her expressive face in movement, and reflecting as touchingly as her singing, the depth of her emotions! The applause rose to the highest conceivable pitch—and she fainted!"

Such an ecstatic performance must inevitably exact a vocal toll, particularly from an organ blemished to begin with. And Pasta seems to have been incapable of any other kind of performance. She disliked concerts, and rarely sang in them. When she did, she was unsuccessful and was sometimes even hissed. She was a woman of the theater, through and through, requiring the trappings of the stage and the fully developed dramatic situation to ignite her interpretive fires. And even in the theater she was a slow starter. Ignaz Moscheles (1794–1840), the celebrated German pianist, composer and pedagogue, heard her in London in 1832 and wrote: "Veiled at first, the voice later breaks forth triumphantly like the sun breaking through a fogbank."

Stendhal and Chorley both recorded their detailed and professionally well-informed observations of Pasta's vocal art. Because of her unique position in vocal history, near the ill-defined boundary between *opera seria* and grand opera, and still reflecting the criteria and techniques of the old tradition while revealing new vistas for the singer as actress, it is rewarding to read what they had to say.

"Madame Pasta's voice," wrote Stendhal, when she was at the height of her vocal powers, and before any signs of decay or damage had set in, "has a considerable range. She can achieve perfect resonance on a note as low as the bottom A, and can rise as high as C sharp or even to a slightly sharpened D; and she possesses the rare ability to sing contralto as easily as she can sing soprano. I would suggest that the true designation of her voice is mezzo-soprano, and any composer who writes for her should use the mezzo-soprano range for the thematic material of his music, while exploiting, as it were, incidentally, and from time to time, notes which lie within the more peripheral areas of this remarkably rich voice. Many notes of this last category are not only extremely fine in themselves, but have the ability to produce a kind of resonant and magnetic vibration, which, through some still unexplained combination of physical phenomena, exercises an instantaneous and hypnotic effect upon the soul of the spectator.

"I think that I should despair of ever succeeding were I obliged to describe one single embellishment normally used by Madame Pasta which is not a monument of classical grace and style, or which is unfit to stand as a model of unrivalled perfection. Extremely restrained in her use of *fioriture*, she resorts to them only when they have a direct contribution to make to the dramatic expressiveness of the music; and it is worth noting that none of her *fioriture* are retained for a single instant after they have ceased to be useful. I have never known her guilty of those interminable frescoes of ornamentation which seem to remind one of some irrepressible talker in a fit of absent-mindedness, and during which one suspects that the singer's attention has wandered far out into vacancy, or else that he started out with one intention, only to change his mind upon the subject half-way through."

What Stendhal says about Pasta's ornamentation is confirmed by Chorley, who, writing many years later, also offers a clue to her economy. While still exercising the prima donna's privilege of fashioning her own ornaments, Chorley tells us, she was not among those who regarded repetition as a confession of sterility. Once she had found the ornaments best suited to her interpretive purpose, she retained them, just as many jazz musicians have retained improvisations they felt to have been especially felicitous. "Pasta never changed her readings," Chorley recalled, "nor her effects, her ornaments; what was to her true, once arrived at, remained with her true forever." And he remembered hearing her sing an aria from *Niobe* after an interval of twenty years: "Not a change, not a cadenza of the old times was left out.

"To arrive at what stood with her for truth," he continues, "she labored, made experiments, rejected, with an elaborate care, the result of which, in the meaner, or more meagre, must have been monotony. But the impression made on me was that of my being always subdued and surprised for the first time. Though I knew what was coming, when the passion broke out, or when the phrase was sung, it seemed as if they were something new, electrical, immediate."

This same care was characteristic of her recitatives. Stendhal, referring to Desdemona's entrance in Rossini's *Otello*, says: "Madame Pasta's rendering to some extent redeemed the utter idiocy of the libretto at this point; the same recitative declaimed by some northern singer might pass completely unnoticed . . . Madame Pasta contrives a subtlety of embellishment which is beyond all praise." And Chorley seconds the opinion. "Her recitative," he wrote, "from the moment she entered was riveting by its truth."

Had Pasta been similarly judicious in the expense of her physical resources, her reign might have been longer than a single decade. But she did not apply restraint and discretion to embellishments for the purpose of sparing herself, an economy foreign to her nature and incompatible with her vision of an artist's calling. And there were other considerations. If she was, as Stendhal suggests, a mezzo-soprano, she may have been the first to mistake an initially responsive upper range for a natural habitat, and to be severely penalized for the error. By 1830, moreover, formidable competitors had emerged in Malibran and Schröder-Devrient, both of them fully as much women of the theater as she, not to mention the radiant Sontag. In such company any relaxation of effort was unthinkable.

It was probably inevitable that a woman whose life was so exclusively in the theater should be reluctant to withdraw, just as it was probably inevitable that so resourceful a woman would find ways of compensating for vocal decline by dramatic revelation. She was, thus, tempted to postpone retirement too long, and, having retired, was too easily persuaded to try again, including an engagement in St. Petersburg in 1840. Chorley's account of one of her two performances in London, ten years later, when Pauline Viardot, then in her prime and hearing Pasta for the first time, was his companion in the audience, is a memorable epitaph:

"Nothing more inadvised could have been dreamed of. Madame Pasta had long ago thrown off the stage and all its belongings. Her voice, which at its best had required ceaseless watching and practice, had been long ago given up by her. Its state of utter ruin on the night in question passes description. She had been neglected by those who, at least, should have presented her person to the best advantage admitted by time. Her queenly robes (she was to sing some scenes from *Anna Bolena*) in no-wise suited or disguised her figure. Her hairdresser had done some tremendous thing or other with her head—or rather, had left everything undone. A more painful and disastrous spectacle could hardly be looked on. . . .

"The first scene was Ann Boleyn's duet with Jane Seymour. The old spirit was heard and seen in Madame Pasta's 'Sorgi!' and the gesture with which she signed to her penitent rival to rise. Later she attempted the final mad scene of the opera. . . . By that time, tired, unprepared, in ruin as she was, she had rallied a little. When, on Ann Boleyn's hearing the coronation music for her rival, the heroine searches for her own crown on her brow, Madame Pasta wildly turned in the direction of the festive sounds, the old irresistible charm broke out; nay, even in the final song, with its roulades and its scales of shakes ascending by semitones, the consummate vocalist and tragedienne, able to combine form with meaning—the moment of the situation with such personal and musical display as form an integral part of operatic art—was indicated: at least to the apprehension of a younger artist.

" 'You are right!' was Madame Viardot's quick and heartfelt response (her eyes full of tears) to a friend beside her; 'You are right! It is like the *Last Supper* of da Vinci at Milan—a wreck of a picture, but the picture is the greatest in the world!' "

2. MARIA MALIBRAN

How different was Malibran's ending: dead in Manchester at the age of twenty-eight!

Otherwise, Pasta and Malibran had much in common. They were similarly possessed by the theater. They were mezzo-sopranos, and so successful in the discipline of intractable voices that they could dominate the great soprano roles of their time. They were similarly reckless in their expenditure of physical and psychic resources. And they shared a totality of identification with their operatic heroines that brought them again and again right up to that fine line beyond which lie fustian and ham. In this perilous border area Malibran lived the more dangerously, and there were some who thought that she trespassed from time to time. Others disagreed.

Between 1828 and 1833 Malibran and Pasta were often together in

Maria Malibran (above) surpassed even Pasta in the intensity of her acting, and she was the more brilliant vocalist, but there were those who felt that she sometimes transgressed the bounds of both propriety and credibility. Malibran, as Rosina (left) in *The Barber of Seville*, was caricatured by A. E. Chalon at the time of her London debut in 1825. She "passed over the stage like a meteor," and was dead at 28. This Eugène Delacroix painting (right) is believed to be of Malibran.

Paris and London, appearing in the same repertoire. Among the roles they shared were Tancred, Semiramis, Desdemona, Othello, Norma, Amina (in *La Sonnambula*) and Romeo (in Zingarelli's opera). There was thus ample opportunity for comparison. On balance it would seem that Pasta was the nobler, the more elevated and, by the tastes of the times, the more old-fashioned of the two, and she enjoyed the preference of the more fastidious. Legouvé thought of Pasta as the daughter of Sophocles, Corneille and Racine; of Malibran as the daughter of Shakespeare, Victor Hugo, Lamartine and Alfred de Musset. Pasta, he said, was dignified, imposing and noble, while Malibran was "all spontaneity, inspiration and fermentation." This was not meant pejoratively. It was Legouvé who said of Malibran when he first heard her in Paris in 1827: "Until that time, music had been for me an amiable art, compounded of graciousness and spirit. Now, suddenly, it became the purest and most dramatic expression of poetry, of love and of pain. A new world was revealed to me."

We have, fortunately, a fund of detail about Malibran's stage business. Legouvé, comparing her Desdemona with Pasta's, recalled that "when Othello moves toward her with drawn dagger [in Rossini's opera Desdemona is stabbed, not strangled], Pasta, with the strength of her virtue and courage, advanced to meet it. Malibran tried desperately to escape, running to every window and every door, leaping through the room like a startled deer." Ludwig Börne, the German critic and *littérateur*, described the same scene: "She clings pleading to the cloak of the raging Othello, she twines her hands in its folds, she tugs on it—an iota more, and it would be ludicrous; it would look as if she wished to tear the clothes from his body. But she never crosses the line. . . ."

Eugène Delacroix thought that she did. Recalling a scene from Donizetti's *Maria Stuarda*, in which she "ripped her handkerchief and even her gloves to tatters," he observed: "That, again, is one of those effects to which a great artist will never descend; they are of the sort that delights people in the loges and wins an ephemeral reputation for those willing to indulge themselves that way. People whose minds do not rise very high, and who are not at all demanding in matters of taste—that is to say, unfortunately, the majority—always will prefer [to Pasta's] talents of a sort possessed by Malibran."

This was a cavalier dismissal of a following that included Chopin, Mendelssohn, Liszt, Schröder-Devrient, Sontag, Rossini, Donizetti, Bellini and Moscheles. Such musical artists were probably better able than Delacroix to appreciate the superlative accomplishments of both Malibran and Pasta. Liszt, for example, in a letter to his publisher Maurice

Schlesinger, dated March, 1838, when Malibran was already dead and Pasta long past her prime, recalled "those divine secrets of a Malibran or a Pasta, who gave to a single note or a single phrase a so irresistible inflection." Schumann used to say that Liszt's art was closest to that of Paganini and Malibran. And Schröder-Devrient, who was more discriminating in her choice of idols than in her selection of roles or lovers, said of Malibran: "There is an artist before whom one must bend the knee."

Malibran was brought up in the theater, as were her contemporaries, Sontag and Schröder-Devrient. Like them, she was precocious as both musician and actress, and at fifteen she began serious vocal study with her father, Manuel García. Initially, at least, her own conspicuously strong will was dominated by his. She had at that time a dark, rather rough and far from pliable contralto. But her father would acknowledge no limitations, and neither, in later life, would she. As Legouvé wrote, comparing her with Sontag: "When Sontag sang the tones emerged from her throat so translucent and pearl-like that one was reminded of a pure beam of light. Malibran's voice resembled the costliest gold, but it had to be mined, forged and stamped like metal under the hammer to make it malleable."

One of the more familiar Malibran stories—or legends—has the composer Ferdinando Paër and a friend passing the García house in Paris. The friend is alarmed at the screams of anguish issuing from a window. "It's nothing," says Paër, "just García beating trills into his daughter." At the summit of her powers and her fame she used to speak of her voice as something separate from herself, almost as an enemy. Every difficulty, every shortcoming, she regarded as an evil to be confronted and vanquished. She often sang while ill or indisposed, and seemed to relish the contest and the victory, challenging her friends to identify any passage where she had failed to disguise her infirmity.

She was possessed by a requirement to excel in all that she undertook—which included riding, painting and composition. Moderation was as distasteful to her as it was impossible. But her determination and her resourcefulness, however extraordinary, were not miraculous, and there were times when neither her voice nor her body could sustain the pace. She often had to retire for a month or so to recuperate from sheer vocal and physical exhaustion, and in 1835 her indisposition caused the postponement of the première of *Maria Stuarda* in Milan. Her "voicelessness" (Donizetti's description) when the première did take place annoyed the audience and is supposed to have contributed to the opera's failure.

Her first public performance was in Paris in 1824, when she was sixteen, at a musical club founded by her father. She made her operatic debut in London on June 7, 1825, as Rosina. Three weeks later she sang Felicia in the London première of Meyerbeer's *Il Crociato in Egitto* opposite Velluti. Her success was immediate, but due rather to the public's reaction to a new and electric personality than to already notable accomplishments.

At the end of that London season the García family went to New York to bring Italian opera to the natives. This is not the place to discuss that remarkable and amply documented venture. Suffice it to say that Maria, in a nine-month season, just passing from seventeen to eighteen, sang leading roles in *The Barber of Seville, Otello, La Donna del Lago, La Cenerentola, Semiramide, Romeo and Juliet, Il Turco in Italia* and *Don Giovanni*. It was a strenuous schooling, complicated by a disastrous and short-lived marriage to François-Eugène Malibran, a mountebank Frenchman, to whose name she brought an immortality certainly not earned by him. She stayed behind when her father and the rest of the family went on to Mexico—to be robbed of all their worldly goods by bandits on their way to Veracruz at the close of a successful season. In the fall of 1827 Maria deserted New York and her husband, and returned to Paris.

She appeared first at the Opéra on January 14, 1828, with Pisaroni in *Semiramide,* moving shortly afterward to the more congenial Théâtre-Italien, where she became immediately a fixed star. In April, 1829, she conquered London, and, in 1832, moved on to Italy, which was to be the scene of her greatest triumphs for the remainder of her brief career.

There is neither need nor space to detail her successes in Naples, Rome, Bologna, Venice, Lucca and Milan. Accounts of the honors heaped upon the greatest singers from generation to generation—and the enormous fees exacted and paid—are as alike as horse races run off in a newsreel, although in the case of Malibran they are distinguished from all others by their reflection of a certain hectic pace and fervor, a suggestion of hysteria and insatiability, both in the performer and in her admirers, as though both had an inkling that it could not endure, and must be savored to the full while it lasted.

The Malibran legend is endless. There are innumerable stories of her willfulness, her courage, her reckless daring, her versatility, her restlessness, her ambition, her spontaneous acts of generosity—and of egotism and greed. The most characteristic and illustrative, perhaps, is Legouvé's account of a private party following her marriage, on March 26, 1836, to Charles Auguste de Bériot (1802–1870), the celebrated Belgian violinist. Among the guests was the reigning piano virtuoso of the time, Sigismond Thalberg (1812–1871). She asked Thalberg to play, but he would not presume to do so until she had sung. She pleaded exhaustion and voicelessness, but he insisted, and she sang—badly. Then it was Thalberg's turn. His playing inspired her—and awakened her competitive spirit, never dormant for long. When he had finished, she sprang to the piano, exclaiming, "And now me!" Gone was fatigue; the voice was restored. Thalberg was astonished. "And now me!" he said. And so it continued by the hour, each outdoing the other in fantasy and daring. If it may seem strange that this duel took place on Malibran's wedding night, and that her husband was apparently not a participant, it should be noted that she and de Bériot had been living together for several years —awaiting her divorce from Malibran—and that she had borne him a son in 1833.

In April of 1836 she fell from a horse in London, suffering injuries from which she never fully recovered, and five months later, on September 23, she died. She had arrived in Manchester on September 11, for a choral festival, and had sung on three successive days in obvious distress. The last thing she sang in public was a duet from an opera by Giuseppe Mercadante (1795–1840) with Maria Caterina Caradori-Allan (1800–1865), and it was the opinion of Sir George Smart (1776–1867), the conductor on that occasion, that Malibran's exertions in the performance of this duet may have hastened her death. As he remembered it in his journal:

"They settled the manner at rehearsal as to how it was to be sung, but when the time came, Madame Caradori-Allan made some deviations; this prompted Malibran to do the same, in which she displayed a most wonderful execution. During the well-deserved [demands for an] encore she turned to me and said, 'If I sing it again it will kill me.' 'Then do not,' I replied, 'let me address the audience.' 'No,' said she, 'I will sing it again and annihilate her.' She was taken ill with a fainting fit after the duet and carried into her room."

The musical world was probably more shocked than surprised by the news of her death nine days later. There must have been many who sensed that no mortal could long survive such sustained and heedless extravagance. "She passed over the stage," said Chorley, "like a meteor, as an apparition of wonder rather than as one who, on her departure, left her mantle behind her for others to take up and wear."

There was no one then, and there has been no one since, who would have found that mantle becoming—or supportable.

3. WILHELMINE SCHRÖDER-DEVRIENT

The dramatic intensity brought by Pasta and Malibran to music still rooted in the traditions of *bel canto* led, in the operas of Meyerbeer and Verdi, to a kind of instrumental and vocal writing in which both the phenomenon and the propriety of such vehemence were assumed. This trend to what we now think of as melodrama—anticipated in individual operas by Cherubini and Spontini, by Beethoven in *Fidelio* and Weber in *Der Freischütz*—was despised by those for whom purity and mellifluence of vocal sound, unlabored agility, niceness of intonation and tasteful and inventive embellishment were the decisive criteria. And yet neither Verdi nor Meyerbeer, nor any other Italian or French composer of the time, broke radically with vocal tradition or denounced the blandishments of florid song. Wagner did. And the singer who inspired and encouraged him in the years when he was shaping his style was Wilhelmine Schröder-Devrient (1804–1860).

"When I review my entire life," wrote Wagner in *Mein Leben*, referring to Schröder-Devrient's appearance as Fidelio in Leipzig in 1829, "I can discover hardly another occurrence which affected me so profoundly. Whoever remembers this remarkable woman at that stage of her career will testify to the almost demoniacal warmth radiated by the human-ecstatic achievement of this incomparable artist. After the performance I dashed to the home of a friend of mine to write her a letter in which I solemnly stated that, as of that day, my life had acquired its meaning, and that if she were ever to hear my name mentioned as of consequence in the world of art, she should remember that on this evening she had made me what I herewith vowed to become. I dropped the letter at her hotel and rushed off into the night."

It had been Schröder-Devrient —or Wilhelmine Schröder, as she was at that time—who, in the revival of *Fidelio* in Vienna in 1822, when she was still a month short of eighteen, had brought an utterly new conception to the part, contributing to the success of that production and helping to launch this initially ill-starred opera on its journey through the opera houses of the world.

Recalling her performances in Berlin some years later, the critic Ludwig Rellstab (1799–1860) wrote: "Her part does not begin when she first speaks or sings, or has business to do; it never ceases so long as elements of the poem concern the character. Thus, her pantomime, in particular, establishes a chain of subtle devices which, when closely examined, are distinguished equally by organic homogeneity and imaginative

Her performance as Leonore (right) in *Fidelio* in 1822, when she was not yet 18, established the fame of Wilhelmine Schröder-Devrient (above) and contributed to the ultimate success of Beethoven's opera. Her performance in this part so inspired the young Wagner that it influenced his future approach to the lyric theater. She was the first Senta in *The Flying Dutchman* and the first Venus in *Tannhäuser*.

variety. Every reference to the fate of the prisoner, every innocent utterance of the adoring Marzelline, finds a softly awakened echo in Leonore's features."

Rellstab's observations are echoed by Chorley, who heard her in London in 1832 and 1833, and again in Dresden in 1839–40, although Chorley accords the same characteristics a more qualified approval. "There is no possibility," he wrote in *Modern German Music*, "of an opera being performed by a company, each of whom should be as resolute as she was never to rest, never for an instant to allow the spectator to forget her presence. She cared not whether she broke the flow of the composition by some cry, hardly on any note, or in any scale—by even speaking some word for which she would not trouble herself to study the right musical emphasis or inflexion—provided only she succeeded in continuing to arrest attention. Hence, in part, arose her extraordinary success in *Fidelio*. . . .

"From her first entry upon the stage, it might be seen that there was a purpose at her heart which could make the weak strong and the timid brave, quickening every sense, nerving every fibre, arming its possessor with disguise against curiosity, with persuasion more powerful than any obstacle, with expedients equal to every emergency. . . . There was a life's love in the intense and trembling eagerness with which she passed in review the prisoners when they were allowed to come forth into the air—for *he* might be among them! There was something subduing in the look of speechless affection with which she at last undid the chains of the beloved one, saved by her love—the mere remembrance of which makes the heart throb and the eyes fill."

Such dramatic achievements, suggesting the legitimate theater rather than the opera house, fall into perspective when it is remembered that she was the daughter of Sophie Bürger Schröder, an actress so famous that she is commonly referred to by theater historians as "the German Mrs. Siddons," and that Wilhelmine was herself an actress before she became a singer. (Her father, Friedrich Schröder, was a baritone, long considered the best German Don Giovanni.) Born in 1804, Wilhelmine was dancing in the theater in Hamburg at nine. Shortly afterward she was in the ballet in Prague and Vienna. All the while she was being trained in gesture and declamation by her mother. In 1819, not yet fifteen, she made her debut as an actress at the Burgtheater in Vienna as Aricia in Schiller's *Phädra*, her mother playing the title role. She appeared subsequently in Schiller's *Kabale und Liebe*, as Beatrice in Schiller's *Die Braut von Messina* and as Ophelia in *Hamlet*.

In the meantime, her mother, who had sung in opera for ten years before turning to the legitimate theater, had seen to her musical education, and on January 20, 1821, just sixteen, Wilhelmine made her opera debut as Pamina in *The Magic Flute*. In November of the same year she sang her first Agathe in *Der Freischütz*. Four months later, when she sang it again under Weber's direction, the composer is quoted as saying: "She is the best Agathe in the world, and surpassed anything that I had conceived for the role." Then came *Fidelio*.

Whatever may have been her vocal endowment, she never mastered it, as a singer must; and it did not long survive the abusive exactions of an impetuous and resolute dramatic temperament. She was always more actress than singer, and the imbalance grew as vocal deficiencies became more conspicuous. Toward the end of her career, when vocal limitations, if nothing else, forced her to become a pioneer in the public performance of songs by Beethoven, Schubert and Schumann, even German critics were to complain of *Lieder* more acted and declaimed than sung.

To say that she was predestined for German opera is not to suggest that Germans cannot sing, or that German opera may not be well sung; but the declamatory predilection of German composers, and the emphatic inflection of the German language, favor a kind of singer for whom the wide range and the plastic melodic line of the older Italian operas offer only merciless exposure. Schröder-Devrient became the first Adriano in *Rienzi*, the first Senta in *The Flying Dutchman* and the first Venus in *Tannhäuser*, but while she was still young, German opera had little to offer beyond *Fidelio*, Weber's operas, Mozart's two German operas, and Gluck's, in German translation.

An opera singer still had to sing the Italian repertoire, and Schröder-Devrient sang it—or tried to—even in Paris and London. On one occasion, in Paris in 1831, when she sang Desdemona to Malibran's Othello (Malibran had a weakness for male roles), the spectacle was physically as well as vocally incongruous. "Malibran is small," Chopin wrote to a friend, "while the German lady is huge—it looked as if *she* would strangle Othello!" In London, two years later, they reversed the roles, which was easier on the eye but not much help to the fastidious ear. Said Chorley:

"A woman, supposing she can correctly flounder through the notes of a given composition, has been allowed, too contemptuously, to take rank as a singer. Such a woman was not Sontag—neither, of later days, Mlle. Lind. The two had learned to sing; Madame Schröder-Devrient *not*. Her tones were delivered without any care, save to give them due force. Her execution was bad and heavy. There was an air of strain and spasm throughout her performances, of that struggle for victory which never conquers."

Chorley was, of course, of the old school, and sympathetic to the Italian tradition which he saw violated and doubtless even threatened by Schröder-Devrient's flights into an unmusical declamation—and even into speech—just as later he would reject the violence of the early Verdi. But the course of European music was against him and his kind, and Schröder-Devrient was in the van. Some of us, even today, can side with Chorley, arguing that song is properly the lyrical extension of speech, declamation and poetry, and that recourse to declamation and speech in the lyric drama is, almost by definition, retrogressive, an admission of musical impotence. But others, notably Wagner, have seen it differently. In his *Über die Bestimmung der Oper*, Wagner discusses the moment when song surges toward the spoken word and says:

"It was to this solution that Schröder-Devrient was impelled at that moment of most frightful tension in *Fidelio*, where she points the pistol at the tyrant. In the phrase 'One more step and you are—dead!' with a ghastly accent of desperation she suddenly and literally spoke the last word. The indescribable effect struck everyone as a sudden plunge from one sphere into another, and its sublimity lay in the fact that—as during a flash of lightning—we had a fleeting glimpse of the nature of both spheres, of which the one was the ideal, the other the real." Heady stuff, and fateful for the vocal art!

In her personal life Schröder-Devrient was never able to keep the two spheres properly separate. With all the passion she expended on the stage, she still had more than enough left for less public indulgence. She had three marriages and many lovers. Her first marriage, to an actor named Karl Devrient, produced four children and a suit for divorce on grounds of adultery in which she was admittedly the guilty party. She resented the ensuing scandal, arguing that she could produce the extraordinary on the stage only because she experienced it in real life. It ill became the proper citizens of Dresden (her home), she said, to demand that she not transgress the narrow confines of their own dull lives, "for in that kind of life there is no grist for my art." She was pleading, in other words, for that privileged-artist status so persuasively advocated many years later by Wagner in his private life and in *Die Meistersinger* and by Strauss in *Feuersnot*.

Her attitude toward the ideal world of the theater, if not toward her more earthbound colleagues—with whom she tended to be impatient and caustic—was one of humility, devotion and dedication. "It's easy," she once said, "to discard the calling with the costume, and forget it all until the next performance. But I was never able to do it. How often has it happened, when the public applauded and showered me with flowers, that I would rush off to my room and ask myself: 'Wilhelmine, now what have you gone and done?' And the question would give me no rest. I would think about it day and night until I hit on something better."

And she was profoundly aware of her responsibilities as a German artist. Other Germans, notably Mingotti, Mara and Sontag, had made their names primarily in Italian opera. But when Schröder-Devrient first went to Paris in 1830, before her appearances in the Italian repertoire, it was with a German company offering German opera. "I had to represent German music," she recalled toward the end of her life, "and if the artist were to fail, it would be at the cost of Mozart, Beethoven and Weber. At the thought of such a thing I was so seized with anxiety that I was on the verge of cancelling my contract."

The German company was a success in both Paris and London, and she was in no doubt about her own decisive role. But what she contributed to the evolution of the vocal art could be grasped only when composers wrote to exploit the dramatic potentialities discovered by her kind of singing—what Rellstab called "the art of declamatory song"—or by her unique combination of singing and acting. She always felt that, as an example and as an influence, her accomplishments had been in vain.

"I have loved my art," she wrote to Clara Schumann in January, 1850, "and practiced it with a hallowed enthusiasm. Whether I accomplished anything, whether I have left anything for those who came after me, that is the question! My goal was ever the highest, and I have been happy to pass on the fruit of my experience where there was a desire for it and where I thought the soil fertile. Unfortunately, I can point to no results, and only throat-clearing and spitting succeed from time to time. The poverty of heart and spirit was too great, the soil too barren, to nourish the strong roots torn from my own heart."

Had Schröder-Devrient died at ninety-five instead of fifty-five, she could have discerned in the art of Luise Dustmann, Amalie Materna and Lilli Lehmann the luxuriant flower of those roots, and have been reassured about the fruitfulness of her turbulent existence. "Ich grolle nicht," she used to sing in the song dedicated to her by Schumann. She need not have complained. But she did. And it was in character for the great artist who was the first German dramatic soprano, and who had been celebrated in London as "the Queen of Tears."

· X ·

A New Kind of Tenor

DONZELLI · NOURRIT · DUPREZ

TAMBERLIK · TICHATSCHEK

A VARIETY OF circumstances combined to bring the tenor to the fore as the *primo uomo* of the vocal world in the early decades of the nineteenth century. The new status and the new responsibilities required a new kind of tenor. Conspicuous and decisive among these circumstances were the size of the opera house, the growing assertiveness and the rising decibel count of the opera orchestra, and the appetite of the new bourgeois public for gaudy and gory melodrama.

In order to be heard above the instrumental din of the new operas in the spacious auditoriums of Naples, Milan, Paris and London, and to bring conviction to the outsized personages of nineteenth-century romance, tenors—and not only they—had to sing louder and higher. Tenors had always sung high in falsetto, or in a kind of head voice, or *voix mixte*, but this was no longer enough. Rubini was the last of the tenor kings for whom a languishing cantilena and fanciful ornamentation would provide an adequately resplendent diadem; and even in Rubini's crown there was a full-voiced B-flat diamond among the other precious stones.

Opera, in the best works of Cherubini, Beethoven, Rossini, Donizetti, Bellini, Spontini, Auber, Halévy and Meyerbeer, represented a kind of theater closer to real life than the remote problems and crises of Metastasio's mythological and classical heroes and heroines. And even when treating the familiar mythological and classical subjects, these composers deserted the static forms of *opera seria* in favor of a more forceful exploitation of dramatic situations, following the example of Gluck and Mozart in drawing upon the resources of orchestra and chorus to complement the singers in building dramatic tension.

The castrato was inadmissible in such a theater, Velluti's participation in *Il Crociato in Egitto* constituting a freakish exception. And while it was still possible in the 1820s, and even in the early 1830s, for Pasta and Malibran to appear as Tancred and Othello, the acceptability of females as heroes hardly survived them. It is significant that the role of Tancred, written for a contralto in 1813, would be followed three years later by Othello, written for García and first sung by Nozzari, both tenors. The female soprano would still prevail—but as a heroine, not as a hero.

1. DOMENICO DONZELLI

Although some historians date modern opera from *Tancredi*, the anticipation of the dramatic tenor in *Otello* is possibly more significant than any of *Tancredi's* distinguishing features; nor should it be overlooked that *Otello* has not one but three principal tenors—Othello, Roderigo and Iago. The finest of the early Othellos was neither Nozzari nor García but Domenico Donzelli (1790–1873), who also created the role of Pollione in *Norma*.

Excelled purely as a singer by Nozzari, the younger David, García and Rubini, he was distinguished by vocal and histrionic characteristics and attainments that give him a greater historical importance as the forerunner of the grand-opera dramatic tenor, first fully revealed in the voice and action of Nourrit and in Duprez's high C from the chest.

He was not so appreciated in his own time. His contemporaries cannot be expected to have foreseen the royal line running from Nourrit through Duprez, Mario, Tamberlik, Tichatschek, Campanini, de Reszke and Tamagno to Caruso. But we, reading contemporary accounts of his Edgardo, Othello and Pollione, recognize the distinguishing characteristics of future dramatic tenors.

Some of the greatest dramatic tenors have begun life as baritones, notably de Reszke, Zenatello and Melchior, and most of them have had a baritone quality that gave tension and size as well as brilliance to their upper notes, providing their lower and middle registers with the weight and resonance requisite for forceful dramatic utterance and capable of dominating a clamorous orchestra and a vociferous chorus. Donzelli was such a tenor.

"He had," wrote Chorley, "one of the most mellifluous robust low tenor voices ever heard—a voice which had never by practice been made sufficiently flexible to execute Signor Rossini's operas as they were written, but who, even in this respect, was accomplished and finished if compared with the violent persons who have succeeded him. . . . The volume of Donzelli's rich and sonorous voice was real, not forced. When he gave out its high notes there was no misgiving as to the peril of his blood vessels; and hence his reign on the Italian stage was thrice as long as that of any of the worse-endowed, worse-trained folk who have since adopted the career of forcible tenor." (Chorley may be referring here to the fate of a tenor, Americo Sbigoli, who, while singing with Donzelli in a performance of Pacini's *Cesare in Egitto* in Rome in 1821, attempted to emulate Donzelli's full-voiced utterance of a certain passage and burst a blood vessel and died.)

This was in accord with the verdict of the *Allgemeine Musikalische Zeitung's* Vienna correspondent, covering Donzelli's Othello in 1823, when he was at the height of his powers: "He has a beautiful, mellifluous tenor with which he attacks the high A in full chest-voice, without once resorting to falsetto, while Signor David [who sang the Roderigo] rejoices in this higher voice and, on this occasion, once ascended to high F [above high C]. Donzelli's action is thoughtfully conceived, his interpretation well ordered, and full of vitality and expression, his declamation exemplary, particularly in recitatives."

These references to Donzelli's high A in full chest-voice *without once resorting to falsetto* are noteworthy as indicating that, even as late as the 1820s, a mere high A in full voice was unusual. The score takes Othello to many A's, and to B-flat in *fioritura*. The role of Roderigo, written for David, is conspicuously higher, with many high C's and, in *fioritura*, a dozen or so D's. David was renowned for his falsetto, and Rossini's writing for him undoubtedly reflects what was then the traditional concept of tenor virtuoso vocalism.

Rossini probably sensed that this kind of singing, a heritage of the castrati, would be unsuited to the character of Othello, and he may have pitched the role lower to obviate the necessity of falsetto. Even so, it may have been a bit high for García. This would explain why, at the première, he sang the role of Iago, which took him only to a G, with an optional B-flat in a duet with Roderigo. He sang the role of Othello subsequently, presumably resorting to falsetto.

About Donzelli critics of a more traditional disposition had reservations. Lord Mount-Edgcumbe's opinion was: "a tenor with a powerful voice which he did not modulate well." And Stendhal noted: "The tenor, Donzelli, is very fine. His voice, however, does not please me at all; it is veiled, and in the upper notes resembles a yell." They may have heard him on off nights; or it may have been a matter of point of view. To an early nineteenth-century traditionalist even Caruso's high C might have been heard as a yell.

The greatest tenors in their prime have produced high notes of irresistible splendor; but it has always been a hazardous undertaking, and even in Chorley's time the consequences, when attempted by the ill-prepared, the inadequately endowed, the indiscriminate, the foolhardy and the aging, had become evident. Chorley was correct enough in blaming the singers, specifically the tenors, the latter motivated "partly from a wish to split the ears of the groundlings, partly from that innate laziness which, together with the increased facilities in gathering gains during modern time, has corrupted the art."

But the fault is not wholly theirs. They have been encouraged, when successful, by the applause of the public and by critical praise. And even the composers have earned a full share of the blame by yielding to convention and requiring of their singers a kind of sustained singing above the normal vocal compass, which is always imprudent, even for the most abundantly gifted, and ruinous for all others.

2. ADOLPHE NOURRIT

When we use the term "dramatic tenor," it is usually to characterize a type of voice, heavier, more robust, more forceful and more resonant than a lyric tenor. But there is an implication that the dramatic tenor should also be an actor, indeed, a tragedian, since this type of voice lends itself to the big tragic or heroic roles; and the greatest dramatic tenors have all been great actors, or have become good ones—Nourrit, Duprez, Tamberlik, Tichatschek, de Reszke, Tamagno, Campanini, Slezak, Caruso and Martinelli. Most of them have been singers first, actors later—acting singers rather than singing actors. And since opera is primarily a singer's arena, a confrontation of the two types, assuming that the acting singer is a tolerably good actor, will usually be resolved in his favor. This was the personal tragedy of Adolphe Nourrit (1802–1839), who may well have been the greatest singing actor among all the dramatic tenors of opera history.

He was certainly the most creative. Among the roles written for him were Néoclès in *The Siege of Corinth*, Aménophis in *Moïse*, Arnold in *William Tell* and the Count in *Le Comte Ory*, all by Rossini; Masaniello in *La Muette de Portici* and Gustave in *Gustave III*, by Auber; Éléazar in *La Juive*, by Halévy; and Robert in *Robert le Diable*, and Raoul in *Les Huguenots*, by Meyerbeer. Other tenors may have created more roles, although it is doubtful. No other has created a comparable number of roles so substantial and so enduring. Indeed, until Verdi and Wagner came along, it could be said that Nourrit, virtually single-handed, had made a repertoire for the dramatic tenor. And singers of so recent memory as Caruso and Martinelli could thank Nourrit for Éléazar, in which each of them found one of his most congenial roles.

Certainly, and to his sorrow, Nourrit created a repertoire for Duprez. Nourrit's reign at the Opéra lasted from 1826 to 1837, when Duprez, who had hitherto made his career in Italy, was engaged for the Opéra and allowed to make his debut in Nourrit's role of Arnold in *William Tell*. This was too much for Nourrit. He withdrew from the Opéra and spent the remaining two years of his life touring the French provinces and Italy, while the public and the critics argued the merits of the situation and of the two tenors. Nourrit was disconsolate, feeling that the less sophisticated art of the acting singer had triumphed over his own more refined accomplishments as a singing actor. He never felt quite at home away from Paris, although he was successful enough, even in Italy. He developed symptoms of mental illness, and early in the morning of March 8, 1839, he jumped to his death from the window of his third-floor apartment in Naples.

In many respects his career had paralleled that of Schröder-Devrient, who was also his contemporary. Both were born into the theater. Schröder-Devrient's mother, it will be remembered, had been known as "the German Mrs. Siddons." Nourrit's father, Louis Nourrit (1780–1831), was the leading tenor at the Opéra until succeeded by Adolphe after the latter's triumph in *The Siege of Corinth* in 1826. While Schröder-Devrient's model had been her mother, Nourrit's was Talma, the great French tragedian. Although Nourrit studied singing with García, it used to be said of him that he "had been instructed by García, but inspired by Talma."

Talma's example led Nourrit far beyond the average actor's—or average singer's—range of intellectual curiosity and interest. He read widely, visited museums, studied the history of the theater and became an excellent musician. He also became a good poet. The words to "Rachel, quand du Seigneur" from *La Juive*—which Jan Peerce and Richard Tucker have sung so well in our own time—were written by Nourrit, as were translations of some Schubert songs which he was the first to intro-

The first of the full-voiced Italian tenors was Domenico Donzelli (above) as Pollione in *Norma*, a role which he created. His high A from the chest, which caused much astonishment at the time, would soon be overshadowed by Duprez's high C.

Adolphe Nourrit (below left), a pupil of the elder García, created almost single-handedly a repertoire for the dramatic tenor in the operas of Rossini, Auber, Halévy and Meyerbeer. He is shown (below right) as Robert in *Robert le Diable*, with the French bass Nicholas Prosper Levasseur and the soprano Marie Cornélie Falcon.

duce to the public in France. Here, too, were an enthusiasm and an accomplishment that he shared with Schröder-Devrient, who might have had some reservations about hearing *Die junge Nonne* as *La jeune religieuse*. He was an imaginative, all-around man of the theater, and his advice was sought and often accepted by both Halévy and Meyerbeer.

The elder Nourrit, in addition to being the leading tenor at the Opéra, was also a diamond merchant, and it was the latter trade that he proposed for Adolphe. The result, for his son, was a late start as a singer, a handicap he never entirely overcame. Thanks to his Italian schooling under García, he was able to cope with Rossini, but aside from *Otello*, he sang only in Rossini's later French operas, all written specifically for him. Rossini, with his extraordinary gift and predilection for tailoring his music to fit an extraordinary voice, never burdened him with the virtuoso requirements he had imposed upon David, Nozzari, Rubini and Donzelli.

Nourrit's was an agreeable, strong and expressive voice, capable of a brilliant, though not full-voiced, high C and resourcefully employed in diminuendo, *voix-mixte, voix de tête* and falsetto. Had he been an Italian, or had he been less concerned with the art of the actor, poet and pantomimist, he might have been a great singer in the older Italian style. But his preoccupation with every linguistic and dramatic nuance, his excellence in declamation and recitative, his determination that every syllable and every movement should contribute to his projection of the character he was portraying, were incompatible with the Italian concentration upon an uninterrupted melodic flow. He admired the great Italian singers, even the Italian-oriented Duprez, but he found their art one-sided and lacking in those refinements of vocal shading and poetic or dramatic utterance that so distinguished his own accomplishments as singer and actor.

When he went to Italy after withdrawing from the Opéra, he tried to adapt his singing to the Italian taste and to eliminate the nasality that marred certain of his tones. Donzelli's dark quality, or *voix sombrée*, which Duprez had adopted in Italy and which had contributed to his success in Paris, was Nourrit's goal. He even achieved it. But he was disturbed by his own success. "I hope," he wrote to a friend from Naples, "that with time I may be able to regain those fine nuances which are my true talent, and that variety of inflection which I had to renounce in order to conform to the exigencies of Italian singing." After his debut there he wrote again: "In truth, with the Italian inflection that I have cultivated, I have only one color at my disposal, and I find myself falling into precisely those errors for which we reproach the Italians."

Nourrit was a handsome man, with black curly hair, lively eyes and an intelligent and sympathetic countenance. He was burdened with obesity, but made up for it by the lightness and propriety of his movements and by great care in the choice and cut of his clothes and costumes. His circle of acquaintances, as might have been expected in a man of such diverse interests and accomplishments, extended well beyond the confines of the theater, and included both Chopin and Liszt, who introduced him to the music of Schubert.

Chopin was staying in Marseilles when Nourrit's body was brought through on the way to Paris. There was a funeral service at the church of Notre-Dame-du-Mont on April 24, 1839, and the organist was Chopin. During the Elevation he played Schubert's "Die Steine": "not," as George Sand wrote, "with the passionate and glowing tone that Nourrit used, but with a plaintive sound, as soft as an echo from another world."

3. GILBERT-LOUIS DUPREZ

One of the most engaging of Berlioz' *Evenings in the Orchestra* is a piece called "The Tenor's Revolution Around the Public, an Astronomical Study." Its hero, after initial good schooling, makes a premature Paris debut, then hies himself off to Italy. There his voice and his art develop; he does well, is exploited by all and sundry and returns to France, where he is re-engaged. On the night of his debut:

"A number comes during which the daring artist, *accenting each syllable*, gives out some high chest notes with a resonance, an expression of heart-rending grief, and a beauty of tone that so far no one had been led to expect. Silence reigns in the stupefied house, people hold their breath, amazement and admiration are blended in an almost similar sentiment, fear; in fact, there is some reason for fear until that extraordinary phrase comes to its end; but when it has done so, triumphantly, the wild enthusiasm may be guessed. . . . Then from two thousand panting chests break forth cheers such as an artist hears only twice or thrice in his lifetime, cheers that repay him sufficiently for his long and arduous labors."

All this is a reasonably accurate account of the early life and eventual Paris triumph of Gilbert-Louis Duprez (1806–1896). Berlioz goes on to give a far from flattering account of our tenor hero's ascendancy and decline. While riding high he is patronizing toward composers and jeopardizes the stability of the opera by exacting exorbitant fees. In decline he "has to decapitate every phrase and can sing only in his middle register. He plays fearful havoc with the old scores and imposes an insupportable monotony on the new ones as a condition of their existence." Finally comes a farewell appearance in *William Tell*, rather sympathetically told, and the crown passes to a new hero. . . .

Duprez had sung the title role in Berlioz' *Benvenuto Cellini* in 1838, and Berlioz, in his *Memoirs*, remembered: "Duprez was very good in any violent scene, but his voice had already ceased to lend itself to soft airs, long-drawn notes, a calm, dreamy music. For instance, in the air 'Sur les monts les plus sauvages,' he could not sustain the high G at the end of the phrase 'Je chanterais gaîment'; and instead of holding the note for three bars as he should have done, held it for only a moment, and thus destroyed the effect."

Berlioz also remembered Duprez's habit, in the air "Asile héréditaire" in *William Tell*, of always singing an F instead of a G-flat (enharmonic F-sharp). He once asked him why. "I don't know," said Duprez, "that note puts me out. It bothers me." Duprez promised to try singing it correctly once, just to please Berlioz, but he never did. "Neither for me, nor for himself, nor for Rossini, nor for common sense," wrote Berlioz, "did Duprez ever do the G-flat in any performance of *William Tell*. Neither saints nor devils could make him give up his abominable F. He will die impenitent."

It is unlikely that Berlioz had often heard Duprez at his best. The tenor was only thirty at the time of his sensational debut at the Opéra as Arnold in *William Tell* on April 17, 1837, but he had already been singing in Italy for nearly a decade. He had created the role of Edgardo in *Lucia* in Naples in 1835—the last scene of *Lucia* gives us some idea of what kind of singer he must have been at that time—and he had sung Arnold in the Italian première of *William Tell* at Lucca in 1831.

It was on this latter occasion that he discovered his potential as a dramatic tenor. Until then he had been just another lyric tenor, and small-voiced at that. When he first sang at the Odéon in Paris in 1825 it was said that one had to be seated in the prompter's box to hear him. He was selected for the role of Arnold only as an emergency replacement for Benedetta Pisaroni. He knew that the kind of voice he had employed heretofore would be inadequate for the big scenes of *William Tell*, and in his own words, as recorded in his *Souvenirs d'un Chanteur*, "It required the concentration of every resource of will power and physical strength. 'So be it,' I said to myself, 'it may be the end of me, but somehow I'll do it.' And so I found even the high C which was later to bring me so much success in Paris."

Duprez is referring here to the extraordinary passage in the stretta of the fourth act, following the "Asile héréditaire," in which the voice must twice ascend from G by way of A, B-flat and B-natural to a sustained high C. It was Duprez's stentorian and electrifying delivery of this passage that secured his success and supremacy in Paris and established his place in tenor history as the first to sing the high C from the chest.

Rossini did not like it. "That tone," he used to say, "rarely falls agreeably upon the ear. Nourrit sang it in head voice, and that's how it should be sung." Rossini had first heard Duprez's high C in his (Rossini's) own home, and had expressed his opinion by looking to see if any of his precious Venetian glass had been shattered. It struck his Italian ear, he observed, "like the squawk of a capon whose throat is being cut."

Duprez must have been, as compared with Nourrit, a conspicuously limited singer. His reliance upon the *voix sombrée* inhibited his mobility in rapid passages, and he was taken to task frequently for his habit of retardation. One caustic Paris critic observed of the passage "Suivez-moi!" in this same fourth-act stretta that Duprez would not have been difficult to follow at the pace he was taking. And the high C would appear to have been his absolute top. He simply omitted the C-sharp in the second-act duet, which Nourrit had taken easily in head voice.

Duprez assessed the comparison differently, of course. Nourrit, he conceded, "declaimed well; but his singing always impressed me as communicating less of compassion than of impetuosity and ardor. His voice had the quality of what used to be called a counter-tenor (*haute-contre*), and he could sing very high in a mixed register. When fate ruled that I should become his rival I knew perfectly well that the production of that voice, white and slightly gutteral, was totally incompatible with the method I had developed for my own. I also knew that my approach to recitative was entirely different from his and from other singers who had preceded me; for it had been their custom to *recite* rather than *sing*. They had looked upon recitative as a bridge from one vocal number to another. I, on the other hand, saw in recitative an essential element of composition, indispensable to the action and the expression, serving as a base for the ensuing aria, in which melody, harmony and rhythm inevitably take precedence over the words."

Duprez could thank the high C and the *voix sombrée* for the unique position he enjoyed as the interpreter of certain heavy roles; but the one probably shortened the life of his voice and the other deprived him of that variety of nuance and vocal color that had so distinguished Nourrit's singing of the same repertoire. Duprez may have been driven in this

Gilbert-Louis Duprez's high C from the chest drove Nourrit from the Opéra and set a precedent for stentorian high notes followed by dramatic tenors ever since. He is shown (left) as Othello and (above) as Arnold in *William Tell*, leading the Swiss against the Austrians, in a performance at Drury Lane in 1844. The two caricatures (below) give an idea of what the effort of his famous high C cost him.

Trom – pons l'es – pér – ance ho – mi – ci – de   ar – ra – chons___

It was this passage from the last act of *William Tell*, crowned by a sustained high C, that established Duprez's place in vocal history.

direction by an unconscious desire to compensate for his diminutive size. "What!" screamed a ballet girl when he appeared for the dress rehearsal of his first *William Tell* in Paris. "That toad? Impossible!"

But the intensity of his singing was compelling, and he learned, as so many singers have done, to make up for a voice no longer tractable by various devices of declamation, vocalization and action, some of them, doubtless, distasteful to a Berlioz. Even such resources are terminable. In 1849 Meyerbeer chose Gustave Roger (1815–1879) instead of Duprez for the role of John of Leyden in *Le Prophète*, and Duprez's reign was at an end. He was only forty-three, but he himself conceded that the freshness, brilliance and flexibility of his voice had diminished, and that, of the resources of his youth, only his strength remained.

Despite Berlioz' captious observations, Duprez seems to have had a compulsive integrity—although possibly not of a kind perceptible to a composer whose precious notation was being ignored. Chorley heard him do *Messiah* (in English) in 1845, and recalled how "this great French tenor, in the strength of his feeling for dramatic truth, propriety and (most of all) his determination never to present himself without doing the best of his best, could sing when his voice was half gone."

Roger heard an *Otello* in 1849 and noted in his diary: "Duprez, today, electrified us all. What daring! A terrifying old lion! How he hurled his guts in the audience's face! For those are no longer notes that one hears. They are the explosion of a breast crushed by an elephant's foot! That's his own blood, his own life, that he is squandering to entice from the public those cries of 'Bravo!' with which the Romans honored the dying gladiator. There is a certain nobility about it. For despite the inequalities of a voice more blemished by passion than time, his good schooling prevails, and he finds even in his deficiencies the means of sustaining style. When this man is gone the world will not hear his like again. I was amused by the critics and minor musicians talking about him in the foyer. Some find that he drags, that he opens his mouth too wide, and God knows what else. And what does it all mean? It's molten ore that he pours into those broadened rhythms, and when he opens his mouth so wide it is to show us his heart!"

Duprez lived to be eighty-nine, remaining active as a successful teacher and unsuccessful composer. One of his pupils was Marie Miolan-Carvalho (1827–1895), Gounod's first Marguerite and first Juliet. Among the diversions of his declining years was a little marionette theater set up in a corner of his living room where opera scenes were staged, the figures manipulated and their music sung by his son and daughter. Originally intended only for the amusement of family and friends, it achieved such celebrity that a special performance was commanded by Napoleon III. Shades of Guadagni, singing Orpheus behind the scenes of his puppet theater at Padua!

4. ENRICO TAMBERLIK

Although the line of the great Italian dramatic tenors is most conveniently dated from Donzelli, the first to display fully the vocal characteristics now commonly associated with Italian dramatic tenors was Enrico Tamberlik (1820–1889). Between Donzelli and Tamberlik had come the Frenchmen, Nourrit and Duprez, with a new repertoire provided for them by Rossini, Halévy, Auber, Berlioz and, of course, Meyerbeer. Tamberlik sang this French repertoire as well as Donzelli's great roles of Othello and Pollione, but he added to it a new kind of Italian role provided by Verdi. Among his Verdi roles were Manrico in *Il Trovatore*, the Duke in *Rigoletto*, the title role in *Ernani* and the role of Don Alvaro in *La Forza del Destino*, which he created in St. Petersburg in 1862. He also sang the title role in Gounod's *Faust* and the role of Ugo in the *Faust* of Louis Spohr.

This repertoire, which also included Don Ottavio in *Don Giovanni*, suggests both a considerable versatility and the kind of voice—midway between a lyric tenor and a heavy *tenore robusto*—that has been the glory of the greatest tenors, notably de Reszke, de Lucia, Caruso, Gigli, Lauri-Volpi, Fleta and Björling. These have all been singers who could bring virility as well as sweetness to lyric roles and leaven the vehemence of the most dramatic parts with lyrical singing. Tamberlik's repertoire makes it evident that he was such a singer. That he could also sing the baritone role of Alfonso in Donizetti's *La Favorita* indicates the baritone quality and the fullness in the middle and lower registers characteristic of the true dramatic tenor.

His high C and even a full-voiced C-sharp (interpolated in Rossini's *Otello*) were doubtless a decisive contribution to the high-note scourge. P. G. Hurst, in his *The Age of Jean de Reszke*, recalls the revival of *Otello* for Tamberlik in the London season of 1877, and how the evening's triumph was due to his famous C-sharp "ringing out with such extraordinary power and freshness that a repetition of the passage was demanded and granted." Tamberlik was then fifty-seven, suggesting that such ventures cost him less of his life's blood and vocal resources than they had cost Duprez. His voice showed signs of decay elsewhere, but at that age it could hardly be counted against the high notes alone. He belonged, apparently, to that lucky tribe among whom the high notes are the last to go.

Rossini, who had foreseen correctly that Duprez's high C from the chest would surely prompt someone to try the high C-sharp, was as little charmed by Tamberlik's accomplishment as by Duprez's, and he resented particularly its substitution for the A that he had written in the finale of *Otello*. The story was told that when Tamberlik wished to pay his respects to Rossini in Paris the composer sent word that he would be welcome but that he should leave his C-sharp in the vestibule and retrieve it when the visit was over.

It was Tamberlik, too, who added the high C's to "Di quella pira" in *Il Trovatore*. The public was delighted, but Tamberlik, possibly with Rossini's reproof in mind, sought Verdi's opinion before parading them at La Scala. Verdi was less stuffy than Rossini had been. It was not for the composer, he observed, to argue with the public. But he warned Tamberlik and all future tenors that the high C's had better be good.

As with most of the great dramatic tenors—excepting de Reszke, Caruso and Gigli—neither his voice nor its delivery was unblemished. "One may tell those of the future," wrote Chorley, "that the voice, howsoever effective, and in its upper notes capable of great power, can hardly be called a charming one—though warm with the south—nor regulated by an unimpeachable method. . . . Still, there was no hearing Signor Tamberlik during a single act of an opera without being aware that he was a man who could sway his public." Among his defects were a persistent vibrato and a tendency to sing out of time—but, then, a nice sense of rhythm has rarely been a tenor virtue. Assessing the available evidence, one imagines Tamberlik as having been closest to Bonci and Lauri-Volpi among the tenors audible on records.

If just too young to be called a product of Verdi, Tamberlik must have offered, nevertheless, at least a foretaste of what Carlo Gatti, in his biography of Verdi, calls "the new methods of singing developing out of his operas." These, according to Gatti, were "very different from those employed by his predecessors: sobs of grief, shouts of rage, transports of joy; methods that gave full rein to the Maestro's passionate feeling." Singers of the mid-century, brought up in the older tradition, or something close to it, must have found it difficult and even distasteful to imagine or fulfill Verdi's vocal requirements.

One suspects that the initial critical hostility to his early operas may have been attributable not only to the new violence of his style but also to the inadequacy of the available singers. One imagines that the older type of lyric singer may have prejudiced the listener against the obstreperous orchestra and the supercharged emotionalism of the dramatic situations by failure to surmount the one or fulfill the other; while singers sufficiently robust of voice and physique may have failed to perceive, or been unable to exploit, the lyricism inherent even in Verdi's most vehement utterances. Nor, initially, were the best singers available in Italy. They were off in Paris, London, Vienna and St. Petersburg, earning international fame and international currency in the older repertoire.

Tamberlik was among them. Although born in Rome, he seems to have sung little in Italy. He made his debut in Naples, but sang in Lisbon, Madrid and Barcelona before arriving in London in 1850, the only tenor of the time capable of survival against Mario. Thereafter he was regularly in London for the season. At other times he was in St. Petersburg or Madrid, or touring in North or South America. He had an affinity for Spain, and settled in Madrid at the close of his career, building a new life as singing teacher and—arms manufacturer!

5. JOSEPH TICHATSCHEK

If Verdi had his problems with singers ill-prepared by schooling, disposition or habit for the vocal requirements of a new kind of lyric theater, Wagner's problems were worse. He would stray farther from the old Italian vocal traditions than Verdi ever did. But of his earlier operas, *Rienzi* was related to Meyerbeer and *The Flying Dutchman* to Bellini; and he had two singers at his disposal, both well versed in the then modern Italian, French and German repertoire, who probably came closer to meeting his requirements than any singers the early Verdi had —although one might make an exception for Giuseppina Strepponi (1815–1897), his first Abigail, and Giorgio Ronconi (1810–1890), his

Enrico Tamberlik (above left) was famous for his high notes and his high stature. He is seen (above right) as Manrico with Francesco Graziani (as di Luna) and Jenny Ney (as Leonora) in the first performance of *Il Trovatore* at Covent Garden in 1855.

Joseph Alois Tichatschek, a protégé of Schröder-Devrient, was the first Rienzi and the first Tannhäuser. He is seen (right) as Tannhäuser.

first Nebuchadnezzar. Wagner's singers were Schröder-Devrient and the tenor, Joseph Alois Tichatschek (1807–1886). Indeed, their very existence encouraged Wagner in his decisions. "Dresden has now a large and worthy opera house," he wrote from Paris in September, 1840; "Tichatschek and Schröder-Devrient are the very people for my work; so I hope to succeed there." Tichatschek was to be his first Rienzi, his first Tannhäuser and his best, if not his first, Lohengrin.

Born in Bohemia, and well educated musically, Tichatschek came to Vienna to study medicine; but his enthusiasm for music and a striking high tenor voice led him to Giuseppe Ciccimarro (the name is variously spelled), who had been one of the tenors of Rossini's Neapolitan period. It may well be to Ciccimarro that Tichatschek owed an apparently effortless vocalism and an extraordinary vocal longevity. The young tenor served an apprenticeship in the chorus of the opera at the Kärntnertor Theater, then went to Graz to develop as a soloist. He returned to Vienna in due course as a leading tenor and was soon spotted by the directors of the court opera at Dresden. He made a sensational debut there in the title role of Auber's *Gustave III*, a forerunner of Verdi's *Un Ballo in Maschera*. A long-term contract was the result, and Tichatschek made Dresden his headquarters for the rest of his long life.

Chorley heard him there as Adolar in Weber's *Euryanthe* in 1839 and reported (in *Modern German Music*): "Few in any country have ever crossed the stage with an ampler proportion of natural advantages. He is of the right height—handsome—his voice was strong, sweet and extensive, taking the *altissimo* notes of its register in chest tones. Then, too, he possessed a youthful energy of manner calculated to gain the favor of all who hear and see him." Much later Chorley would say (in his *Thirty Years' Musical Recollections*): "I can recall no German tenor whom I have heard on a stage with much pleasure save Herr Tichatschek at Dresden."

This was also Wagner's view. Tichatschek was an ideal Rienzi. He lacked the intellectual sophistication to be an ideal Tannhäuser, as Schröder-Devrient had pointed out to Wagner even before casting had been completed. But there was no alternative. Tichatschek might deliver Tannhäuser's outrageous hymn to Venus into the ear of the presumably strait-laced Elisabeth—to whom else, Tichatschek may have inquired, should the leading man address himself if not to the leading lady?—but his voice and figure were magnificent. And what should a composer of such original and difficult music say of a tenor—of all people!—who could read his part at sight during rehearsals and memorize it as he went along? Not until Schnorr and Niemann appeared a generation later would Wagner have tenors capable of mastering his psychological subtleties and of moving securely in that no-man's-land between aria and recitative which was Wagner's invention, for better or worse, and which distinguished his vocal writing from all others'—unless one wanted to go back to Peri's *Eurydice* of 1600.

As late as 1867—with Schnorr, the first Tristan, dead, and Niemann refusing to sing without cuts—Wagner chose Tichatschek, then sixty, to be the Lohengrin in a special production for Ludwig of Bavaria in Munich. The result was a ghastly disaster. Tichatschek could still sing, but a fat old man was hardly the swan-born Knight of the Grail envisioned by Ludwig's youthful and fevered imagination. Ludwig observed the final rehearsal on June 11 through binoculars, and what he saw was not, in Ernest Newman's words, "the poetic Knight of the Grail of his boyhood dreams, but a sagging face painted and plastered into a simulacrum of youth, and an ancient body maintaining its uncertain equilibrium in the boat only by clinging to a pole let into the deck for that charitable purpose. He saw nothing he could call acting, only a succession of 'grimaces,' as he complained afterwards. Shattered was his dream of the spirituality of the Middle Ages; he had been fobbed off with the poorest theatrical make-believe."

It became a serious matter. Ludwig described Tichatschek as "the Knight of the Rueful Countenance." It had been unfair of Ludwig, Wagner countered, to use binoculars. Ludwig was adamant. He insisted that Tichatschek should not sing the performance; and he did not. Wagner withdrew to Triebschen, leaving Hans von Bülow to pick up the pieces and to coach a new—and younger—Lohengrin.

None of all this should cast any doubt upon the place in tenor history that Tichatschek had earned for himself in his youth and his prime. Both *Tannhäuser* and *Lohengrin* might have found heavier going with the German public had Wagner not had a tenor with the voice, appearance, musicianship and enthusiasm to make their heroes vocally thrilling and visually convincing.

Tichatschek was devoted to Wagner and even overlooked, or pardoned, his brochure "On the Performing of *Tannhäuser*," which exposed what Wagner regarded as certain inadequacies in the tenor's conception and exposition of the role. Theirs was not exactly the composer-singer relationship of the eighteenth century. The composers were gaining the upper hand. But singers and composers could still be colleagues in a common cause.

The Great Quartet

GRISI · MARIO

TAMBURINI · LABLACHE

As THE GREAT singers have never been disposed to sing only for their supper, it has been inevitable that they should tend to concentrate at the capitals of prestige and wealth and, once established, remain as long as their voices could reap a harvest of money and privilege.

They were to be found, throughout the eighteenth century, at the courts in London, Vienna, Berlin, St. Petersburg, Madrid and Lisbon. Following the French Revolution and the Napoleonic wars—and an awakening of a taste for Italian singing in France—the most lucrative centers were London, Paris and St. Petersburg.

Italian opera, sung by Italians in Italian, succumbed to a wave of nationalist opposition in the German-speaking capitals toward the middle of the century. With such composers as Weber, Spohr, Marschner, Lortzing, Flotow, Kreutzer and, finally, Wagner composing German opera for a new type of German singer, German became the language of the German lyric theater. Italian opera experienced a diminishing popularity, and Italian singers, rarely masters of any other language than their own, were welcomed only as guests. It would be some time before German singers, with the notable exception of the Italian-oriented Sontag, would become important on the international circuit.

Since the London season was in the spring and summer, it was possible for the true stars to shuttle between London and Paris, with an occasional season in St. Petersburg; and it was on this Paris-London axis that prospered the group of singers known to vocal history as "the great quartet." Its members were Giulia Grisi, the man known simply as

Mario, Antonio Tamburini and Luigi Lablache. Their reign endured for roughly twenty-five years, from 1835 to 1860, and the symbol of their identity and supremacy was *Don Pasquale*, written for them by Donizetti in 1843.

There were, to be sure, other excellent singers appearing with them— or against them: Fanny Persiani, Viardot, Jenny Lind, Henriette Sontag, Ilma di Murska, Marie Falcon, Alboni, Jeanne Castellan and Tamberlik. But the quartet comprised an elite of the elite. The three men were, in fact, unrivaled. Grisi was excelled by other ladies in certain roles, and toward the end of her reign she was probably excelled even in roles formerly reckoned her more or less private property; but she had political and diplomatic as well as vocal genius, and the security of her position was never in doubt so long as she chose to sing.

The quartet was also known as "the old guard," or—with their number augmented by certain of the other singers just named—"the commonwealth." A similar group, or clique, today would probably be known as an "establishment." As is common of "establishments" everywhere, this one had little taste for experiment or adventure. Their basic repertoire was Rossini-Donizetti-Bellini. The best work of all these composers was behind them. Rossini had written nothing for the theater since *Le Comte Ory* and *William Tell*. Bellini had died in 1835 and Donizetti would die, after a long illness, in 1848.

It was, therefore, a stagnant situation. Meyerbeer was represented by *Robert le Diable*, *Les Huguenots* and, after 1849, *Le Prophète*. But among the quartet only Mario distinguished himself in these operas. The general tendency among the quartet was to dismiss Meyerbeer's music as "Chinese."

The operas that would establish Verdi's reputation were to appear only toward the end of this period. Such of his earlier operas as made their way across the Alps—*I Due Foscari*, *I Masnadieri*, *I Lombardi*, *Attila*, *Nabucco and Ernani*—were not liked, and Verdi did not figure importantly among the achievements of "the old guard," granting an exception for Mario's success as the Duke in *Rigoletto*.

The term "quartet," as applied to this group, was, to be sure, largely symbolic. Its composition—a soprano, a tenor and two basses—was unorthodox, and its deployment limited. It had been derived from the casting of *I Puritani* in 1835, with Grisi, Rubini, Tamburini and Lablache, and until Mario replaced Rubini in 1839, it was usually referred to as "the *Puritani* Quartet." It was for the original quartet, i.e., with Rubini, that Donizetti had written his *Marino Faliero*, also in 1835, which included, as had *I Puritani*, a duet for two basses. Except in operas thus expressly written for them—notably *Don Pasquale*—they rarely appeared together as a quartet. But one or another of the basses was usually in the cast when Grisi and Mario sang.

1. GIULIA GRISI

Giulia Grisi's contributions to operatic history, i.e., in the form of enduring roles written for or created by her, were confined to the early years of her career, overlooking, of course, the hardly epochal role of Norina in *Don Pasquale*. She sang the first Adalgisa to Pasta's Norma in Milan in 1831, and she was in the première casts of *I Puritani* and *I Capuletti ed i Montecchi*. For the rest, her best parts were those forever identified with Pasta—Semiramis and Ann Boleyn—from whom she took them over, and upon whose interpretations she modeled her own. She was a memorable Lucrezia Borgia, and she excelled in lighter roles—Rosina, Norina, Susanna, Pamina and Elisetta (in *Il Matrimonio Segreto*)—but so also, surprisingly, had Pasta.

Her genius—if that is not too strong a word—was imitative rather than creative. When it was expended in areas compatible with her voice and dramatic temperament, she approached and may have matched the achievements of her models. Her endowment of voice and personal beauty was superior to that of either Pasta or Malibran, and her performances less likely to be blemished by effort or mishap. Simply because of the absence of any sense of hazard, they may also have been less exciting.

But she must have been a good actress. Jenny Lind, who rarely had a good word—or any word at all—to say about her contemporaries in the theater, heard her in Paris in 1841 and wrote: "There is an astonishing dearth of actresses here. Mlle. Rachel is the only one—after her, Grisi." A dubious compliment, perhaps, but, coming from Jenny Lind, high praise.

Grisi was certainly inferior neither to Pasta nor to Malibran in her ambitiousness, her taste for power, and her determination to have and to hold. Both her musical and vocal talents and her willfulness were apparent from the very beginning of her career. She was born—in Milan in 1811—into a musical environment. One of her aunts was Josephina Grassini (1773–1850), a leading contralto of the preceding generation. Her older sister, Giuditta, was an excellent singer, and a cousin, Carlotta, was a dancer in the category of Taglioni and Elssler: in other words, one of the great dancers of the century. Grisi seems never to have had any early vocal problems. Her debut in Bologna in Rossini's *Zelmira* at the age of seventeen was a great success. The younger David, with whom she sang in Florence in 1830, took an interest in her, as did Bellini and Pasta. And she was only twenty when her performance as Adalgisa established her as a singer of extraordinary promise.

It also confirmed her own estimate of her capacities. She promptly broke her contract at Milan and fled to Paris, where Rossini got her an engagement at the Théâtre-Italien. Such were her daring and her confidence that she chose Pasta's role of Semiramis for her debut there in 1832 (with Tamburini as her Assur). A year and a half later she conquered London in Pasta's role of Ann Boleyn (with Rubini and Lablache).

Her reign withstood and survived meteors and blunders. Among the meteors were Jenny Lind, who retired from the theater after a few seasons; Henriette Sontag, who returned from retirement as a replacement for Lind at the rival theater in London and then departed for America; Persiani, who sang Grisi's repertoire and was, in some respects, preferred by the connoisseurs, but was inferior in beauty of voice and person; and Pauline Viardot. It was the last who provoked Grisi's most damaging mistakes.

The roles in which Viardot triumphed were not Grisi's—Alice in *Robert le Diable*, Valentine in *Les Huguenots*, Fidès in *Le Prophète* and Rachel in *La Juive*. But Viardot's success was such—and to Grisi so disturbing—that she determined to make them her own, stopping only at Rachel. She survived the consequent disasters, but they left a blemish on the record of her achievements, establishing the limits of her realm more conspicuously than would have been the case had she been content to leave well enough alone.

Her fear of Viardot was demonstrated in less admirable ways. One could salute her daring, if not her judgment, in attempting Alice, Valentine and Fidès; but there was nothing to be admired in her attempts at sabotage. Grisi's will to have and to hold extended to the first tenor of the day, and in 1844 she had married Mario. When Viardot made her second London debut in 1848 as Amina in *La Sonnambula*, a role that had never been numbered among Grisi's best, Mario, who was to have sung with her, suffered a sudden diplomatic indisposition, and Viardot had to cope with a strange Elvino.

Again, in the same year, Mario's "indisposition" prevented his singing Raoul to Viardot's Valentine in the performance of *Les Huguenots* (more precisely, *Gli Ugonotti*, since the Italian "old guard" sang even Meyerbeer in Italian), scheduled for Viardot's benefit. Grisi suggested *Norma* as a substitute opera, "graciously volunteering" to sing the Norma to Viardot's Adalgisa. She had reckoned without the García will. Viardot proposed Roger as a substitute for Mario, adding: "If he cannot do it, then *Norma*, but I will sing the Norma." As it turned out, Roger could and did sing Raoul. Grisi saw to it that he never sang the part again in London, nor was Mario ever again indisposed when *Gli Ugonotti* was on.

Grisi tried once more. In 1850, when *La Juive* was revived for Viardot, with Mario as the Éléazar, the latter became indisposed a few hours before the première. This time Viardot was prepared. She had a substitute, a Belgian tenor named Enrico Maralti (Merelt) ready and waiting, and the performance went on. It was, of course, Maralti's last appearance in the part.

Grisi's reluctance to acknowledge any powers superior to her own was as pronounced toward time as toward man. The London season of 1849 was announced as her last. It was not. In 1854 a series of farewell performances proved a strong attraction at the box office. There was another series in 1855, and in 1860 there was a succession of twelve farewells, prompting J. W. Davison, critic of *The Times*, to inquire: "Does the word *last* bear an esoteric idiom in operatic parlance other than that ordinarily accepted?"

There were nine farewell appearances in 1861, and the London *Daily News* saw fit to observe: "We trust that she will not again be tempted by popular applause to swerve from what is now understood to be her settled purpose." She was supported in her resolve by a clause in her contract with Covent Garden binding her not to sing in public again for five years. This was also the year of Patti's London debut. But in 1866, when the five years had expired, she was still persuaded to try again, and she made a single appearance in *Lucrezia Borgia*. It was her last blunder. She died of pneumonia in 1869 in Berlin, where she had stopped on her way to St. Petersburg to join Mario.

When Pasta sang the first Norma in Milan in 1831, her Adalgisa was a young soprano named Giulia Grisi, soon to succeed her not only as Norma but also as the "Queen of Song" in London and Paris. She is shown (above left) as Norma early in her career. The Prince Consort of Grisi's reign was her leading tenor, a Piedmontese aristocrat known professionally simply as Mario (above right), whom she married in 1844. They were probably the handsomest couple in operatic history. Mario is seen here as Arturo in *I Puritani* (below left) and with Grisi in *Lucrezia Borgia* (below right).

2. MARIO

If Grisi added little to vocal history in terms of innovation, her husband added less, except for the simple fact of having been, for thirty years, the world's ranking tenor.

He created no roles of any historical account. In the Meyerbeer operas, which were among his best, he probably surpassed Nourrit, Duprez and Roger in beauty of voice and elegance of person, but he lacked their dramatic force and fervor. He sang Rubini's roles with less eccentricity than Rubini, but without his art and invention. As Chorley observed, Rubini, with whom the modern Italian tenor repertoire began, in roles written for him by Donizetti and Bellini, had been such an extraordinary virtuoso that composers were tempted to write for him what no one but Rubini could sing. And it was upon Mario that Rubini's mantle fell.

Like Grisi, he was endowed with a beautiful voice and a handsome person. Unlike her, he hardly had to make his own way. He entered music as an amateur; and he was simply so good that the profession embraced him. It was the opinion of some critics that he remained an amateur throughout his career, and that the characteristics of the amateur lent a unique charm to everything he did.

Alone among the great tenors, he was an aristocrat by birth as well as by instinct or cultivation. Son of a general in the Piedmontese army, he was born Giovanni Matteo Mario, Cavaliere di Candia, in Cagliari on October 17, 1810, and was trained for the career of an officer at the military academy in Turin. He came to Paris in 1836 and, when prevailed upon to sign a contract with the Opéra, had such misgivings about the propriety of his action that he wrote only his given name, Mario, as a signature. By that name he was known ever afterward. He made his debut at the Opéra in *Robert le Diable* in 1838. At twenty-eight he was a late beginner by the standards of the time—or any other time.

There was no apprenticeship. The Italian language and the Italian style were more congenial to him, and in 1840 he moved to the Théâtre-Italien. But having begun at the top, he stayed there. Obviously he gained professional polish, refinement and craftsmanship as he went along. He must have learned much from such true professionals as Grisi, Tamburini and Lablache. And Viardot, in particular, is said to have inspired him to unwonted heights as an actor, once Grisi had been defeated in her effort to deprive Viardot of his support.

But if he was not truly a creative singer, he established certain criteria

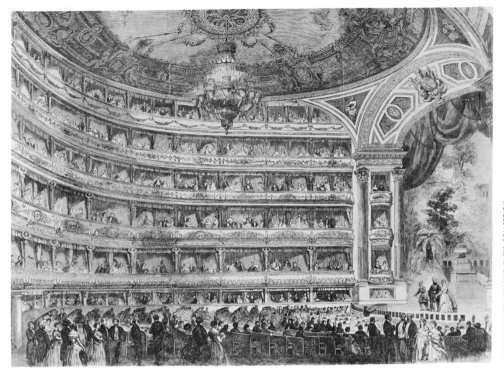

The capitals of Grisi and Mario's realm were Covent Garden in London (above) and the Théâtre-Italien in Paris (below). Note that at Covent Garden the conductor stands between the orchestra and the stage.

in matters of appearance, dress and deportment that were accepted as models by later tenors intelligent enough to acknowledge the validity of any criteria other than vocal. And he ranged more widely—or at least more successfully—than Grisi. Her ventures into the realm of Meyerbeer had been a catastrophe. Mario's were not. Nor was Verdi beyond him. His Duke in *Rigoletto* has been mentioned. He also sang Manrico in *Il Trovatore* and Riccardo in *Un Ballo in Maschera*, in addition to his participation in the abortive early productions of *I Due Foscari* and *I Lombardi*. He sang Éléazar to Viardot's Rachel and, late in his career, the Romeo to Patti's Juliet in Gounod's opera.

It is not by his accomplishments as an actor that he is remembered; but he may have been the prototype of the romantic tenor, more often imagined than seen. "The charm of personal appearance and graceful demeanor," said Chorley, "borne out by a voice the persuasive sweetness of which can never be exceeded, has fascinated everyone, the stern as well as the sentimental, into forgetting incompleteness and deficiency, which diligent and thoughtful study might have remedied ere Rubini's successor had been on the stage a couple of years. There has been no desire, no possibility of reckoning with one so genially endowed by nature, with so much of the poet and the painter in his composition, and of the nobleman in his bearing. Lines, rules, precedents, comparisons must sometimes be forgotten; and it is well."

Mario outlived Grisi by fourteen years, and with his voice in decline, he outlived his prosperity, too. A fortune had been dissipated, and his circumstances toward the end were so pitiable that in London a concert was given for his benefit. He died in Rome on December 11, 1883.

3. ANTONIO TAMBURINI AND LUIGI LABLACHE

It is convenient to discuss Tamburini and Lablache together, for it was the superlative quality of their accomplishments that brought respectability and something like equal status to the deeper male voice; and their close association contributed to the emergence of two separate and distinct categories: the baritone and the bass.

Antonio Tamburini (1800–1876) had the higher voice of the two. Its range was variously given as from C to G and from F to F. Both may be correct, the first applying to his youth, the latter to his maturity. As a young man his voice may, for a time, have had some of the characteristics of today's high baritones, although there were no parts for such a voice at the time. Later on, it must have been closer to what we now call a bass-baritone. An illustrative fact is his declining to sing the role of Don Carlo in *Ernani* on the grounds that it was too high for him. That was in 1847, when Tamburini was forty-seven, an age when most true baritones still have a G. It is also significant that the part was ultimately sung by Alboni, a mezzo-soprano. There simply were not, in those days, many true high baritones around.

Indeed, one is tempted to speculate that the high baritone, singing in the range required in Italian opera from Verdi onward, might be considered more accurately a mezzo-tenor than a high bass. Those of us who have heard any number of Italian baritones gasp out a feeble low A in the "Eri tu" from *Un Ballo in Maschera,* or opt for the A an octave higher, while ascending easily to the top G, would certainly hesitate to think of such voices as in any way related to the bass. This is not true, of course, of a bass-baritone with the F-to-F range common to German and Anglo-Saxon male voices; and attempts by bass-baritones to sing the Italian baritone repertoire have ruined some fine voices. With the German and American baritones who have prospered in the Italian baritone range—John Charles Thomas, Leonard Warren, Heinrich Schlusnus and Joseph Metternich—one has often suspected a tenor living safely.

What we know of the voices of Tamburini and Lablache prompts some speculation, too, on how they must have sung certain surviving pieces in their repertoire, especially the "Largo al factotum" from *The Barber of Seville.* Lablache, a true bass, whose range is given as E to E or E-flat to E-flat, could hardly have sung it with the full-voiced G's which are conventional today; and one wonders even about Tamburini. He was such a master of florid singing that he was known as "the Rubini of basses," and it seems likely that he used falsetto. As this famous aria was also a favorite salon item of Rossini's, the composer accompanying himself at the piano, it seems probable that it was conceived originally as a light patter song, with much comical falsetto and melodic alteration. It should be noted, moreover, that the original Figaro, Luigi Zamboni (1767–1837), was forty-eight or forty-nine in 1816. Even more curious is the "La Calunnia" aria, which today is always transposed a full tone down. What kind of voice can the original Basilio have had?

Tamburini and Lablache represented the maturity of a kind of singer

The "great quartet" included, curiously, two basses, Luigi Lablache and Antonio Tamburini. Lablache was noted for the prodigious dimensions of both his voice and his person, and he excelled equally in serious and *buffo* roles. He is shown (below right) as Duke Alfonso in *Lucrezia Borgia* in London in 1845 and as Figaro (below left) in *The Barber of Seville*, as caricatured by Dantan. Tamburini (above left) also excelled in both serious and *buffo* roles. He created the role of Riccardo in *I Puritani*, in which he is shown (above right), singing at the King's Theater in 1836.

spawned by *opera buffa* and formerly pretty much confined to it. Early in their careers they had traveled the *buffa* circuit from Palermo to Vienna, singing the same basic repertoire despite the difference in their voices. Both were famed for the lightness and agility of their movements, their accomplishments as comedians, their versatility, their musicianship —and their extraordinary popularity. In London, in 1840, when an impresario tried to save money by dropping Tamburini from the roster, there were riots in the theater.

Tamburini's father had been a bandmaster, and Antonio was a horn player before he was a singer. Even as a singer he was precocious. He was in an opera chorus when he was twelve, and was engaged as a soloist at the opera in Bologna when he was eighteen. His career was singularly devoid of significant incident. Much was written about him, but most of it in unmodified adjectives: "His execution was unsurpassed and unsurpassable," and so on. There is, however, the story of his assuming the costume and the role of a young soprano in Palermo who was too frightened to sing, a testament to his versatility and his falsetto. He retired in 1859.

Accounts of the career of Luigi Lablache (1794–1858) are similarly devoid of incident and even richer in superlatives. Everything about him seems simply to have been the greatest—his voice, his size, his strength, his intelligence, his art as singer and actor, and his personal decency and amiability. He was not, curiously, an Italian. His father was French and his mother Irish. But he was born in Naples, attended the Conservatorio della Pietà de' Turchini and began his career as a *buffo Napolitano*, acquiring a fluency in Neapolitan that subsequently colored his Italian and caused him some embarrassment.

He was in Vienna in 1827 when Beethoven died, and not only sang in the memorial performance of Mozart's *Requiem* but also paid the other singers. He was also one of the thirty-two torch-bearers who stood watch at the bier, which suggests that at thirty-two he had already achieved an eminence unprecedented for a bass, a possible exception being Fischer. He had sung the alto part of the *Requiem* in Naples in 1809 at a service commemorating the death of Haydn, and he sang the "Lachrymosa" at the funeral of Bellini in 1835.

Although formidable in tragic parts, he was most affectionately remembered as a comedian: Leporello (he used to carry away a sizable Masetto under his arm), Dr. Bartolo, Nemorino (in *Il Matrimonio Segreto*), Dulcamara (in *L'Elisir d'Amore*), Figaro (in *The Marriage of*

Figaro) and, above all, as Don Pasquale, thus described by Théophile Gautier in *Histoire de l'art dramatique en France*:

"The uncle, played by Lablache in the most fluttering manner, wearing a house coat of white dimity, nankeen trousers and a black silk bonnet, is like all uncles everywhere, very displeased with his rascal of a nephew. Following ancient and solemn precedent, he seeks to disinherit him. It is entirely just. Why should he be anybody's uncle? Don Pasquale, in spite of his sixty-nine years and his gout, finds himself still enough of a gay blade, still green enough to make heirs less collateral than M. Ernest. He consults Dr. Malatesta on this delicate point. . . . The doctor returns with a young woman wearing a dress of the most virginal *carmelite* and with a black lace veil that hardly lets one suspect her pretty face.

"To receive this angel of youth and beauty, Don Pasquale makes a most extravagant toilette: a superb peruke the color of mahogany dressed with ridiculous curls; a green frock with engraved gold buttons, which he could never fasten because of the enormous rotundity of his figure. All this gives him the look of a monstrous beetle that wants to open his wings to fly and cannot succeed. With the most gallant air, he advances with popping eyes, his mouth heart-shaped, to take the girl's hand. She emits a cry as though she had been bitten by a viper."

And so, more or less, the part has been played ever since. Lablache's accomplishment may have been approached by other basses, but not Donizetti's by other composers, unless just once, by Verdi in *Falstaff*. Puccini's *Gianni Schicchi* is a comedy, to be sure, but the fun is in the situations, rarely in the music. "For the present," wrote Chorley in 1862, "it may be feared that we have taken leave of mirth in Italian music. . . . We are becoming graver without becoming more learned; we are showing our ambition at the expense of our command over melody." Amen!

But to return to Lablache: It has been remarked that Jenny Lind's much publicized charity was rarely extended toward her colleagues in the form even of an acknowledgment of their existence. But she said of this singer: "Lablache is a genius. And what a voice! Oh, God in heaven! And the most perfect actor you could ever see."

Which is just about what everyone who ever wrote about him was trying to say.

· XII ·

The Nightingales

SONTAG · LIND · PATTI

THE TERMS "dramatic soprano," "lyric soprano" and "coloratura soprano" have long been used to designate certain types of voice. It is an inexact but unfortunately necessary categorization, symptomatic of a departure from the older criteria of *bel canto*, and attributable in large measure to Verdi and Wagner, who imposed requirements of volume, vehemence, endurance and range capable of fulfillment only at the price of one or another of the constituent elements of the singer's art.

Until the mid-nineteenth century every female singer was expected to be a mistress of coloratura, and it was also assumed that she could sing dramatically and lyrically. All sopranos sang the same repertoire. Certain singers were superior to others in coloratura, and more inventive in ornamentation. Others sang more dramatically or more lyrically. But a soprano was a soprano, as she—or he—had been since the seventeenth century. One notes the roles of Pasta, Malibran, Persiani, Grisi, Sontag and Lind—each an artist of distinctive vocal, dramatic and personal characteristics—and the repertoire is always basically the same, drawn from the popular operas of Rossini, Donizetti, Bellini and Meyerbeer.

From a singer's point of view it was the best repertoire ever, preserving some of the lyrical and ornamental virtues of the age of *bel canto*, while providing dramatic situations incompatible with the stereotype of *opera seria*. Fortunately, it has never been totally extinguished. *The Barber of Seville* and *Lucia* have survived; and *L'Elisir d'Amore, Don Pasquale, The Daughter of the Regiment, Norma* and even *La Sonnambula* have appeared and reappeared from time to time as mementos of an age of lovelier vocalism than our own. Nor has the art of singing it ever disappeared entirely, rare as the bird may be who can sing it properly.

We tend today to think of the coloratura soprano as a sweet-voiced girl with more or less secure high notes, and with agility and fluency enough to get through the arias of Zerbinetta and the Queen of the Night. But there have always been sopranos who could do more than that, women who had the passages and the coloratura, who could ascend to the high E or F without resorting to a detached, tricky head voice, and who, in lyrical and dramatic passages, could sing persuasively and beautifully. The line is easy to trace: Sontag, Lind, Patti, Sembrich, Melba, Tetrazzini, Galli-Curci and Lina Pagliughi. Sopranos of this admirable type have not been favored in the present century by the evolution of the repertoire. The Rossini-Donizetti-Bellini-Meyerbeer roles best suited to their capabilities have given way to meatier and supposedly more substantial fare.

It is important to distinguish between the numerous high-note singers who, today, are called coloratura sopranos and the very few who can sing true coloratura. The former, as students, have been the despair of landladies. As performing artists they have made the coloratura soprano a ridiculous figure. They have given florid song a bad name. The latter have sustained the glory of the singer's art, and the best of them have been the most admired of all singers.

Throughout the nineteenth century they inspired a delirium of enthusiasm never accorded any other type of singer, and paralleled in our own time only in the popular adoration of Frank Sinatra, Elvis Presley and the Beatles. Called nightingales by their worshipers, and warblers by more moderate admirers, they had beautiful voices that were lighter, more girlish, more virginal—even childlike—than the type of voice fashionable among sopranos today, and a special communicative quality suggesting a kind of sublimated and eternally youthful femininity.

The singular girlish sweetness and purity that characterized the voices of the great nineteenth-century coloratura sopranos may be attributable to the fact that so many of them started so young. It seems a reasonable speculation that they simply sustained into their maturity the sound which had never failed to delight their listeners at the outset of their careers. It has been a perverse habit of older singers of every generation to blame the low estate of contemporary vocalism on the impatience of the newcomers, on the unwillingness of the young to submit to years of disciplinary training, à la Caffarelli, before presenting themselves in public. This is nonsense—or was.

Throughout the centuries of vocal history the average debut age of the greatest sopranos—male and female—was sixteen or seventeen, and their prime was between twenty and thirty. Many of them began at even tenderer ages. The best of them never ceased to learn, but after whatever preliminary study they may have had, they learned in the toughest and most instructive of all schools—in the theater, before a paying audience and in the company of other professional singers.

And they had the advantage of singing for listeners with a taste for fresh young voices and usually in theaters small enough to allow a young lady's charms to make themselves felt across the footlights. Ears that had never heard the kind of dramatic soprano developed to meet the requirements of Wagner, Strauss and Verdi found nothing amiss in Agathes, Fidelios, Donna Annas, Lucias, Normas and Adalgisas not yet twenty.

Nor did the voices, as a rule, suffer any damage. Some singers, like Lind and Pasta, had their vocal crises, but these were exceptional cases. Others who began young, notably Grisi, Sontag and Lind, were singing well at fifty, or close to it, and Patti, who began at seven, sang in public at seventy-one. But Verdi, Wagner, Strauss and the Italian *verismo* composers conditioned our ears to more mature voices. That may be why youth in singers, and the youthful sound formerly sustained by older singers, is no longer treasured as it used to be, and why it is encountered so rarely, even in the best of today's coloraturas.

Three of the greatest coloratura sopranos of the nineteenth century—Sontag, Lind and Patti—were phenomenally early beginners. Their ages when they made their formal operatic debuts were not extraordinary—Sontag at fifteen, Lind at seventeen and Patti at sixteen, but Sontag and Lind were theater children, and they had a lot of singing in light opera behind them before they graduated to the big roles, while Patti had been concertizing for years when she made her opera debut in New York in 1859. And one is astonished at what they tackled.

Sontag was only seventeen when she created the title role in *Euryanthe* in 1823, and only eighteen when she sang in the première of the Ninth Symphony. Lind's debut role was Agathe in *Der Freischütz*, and Patti's was Lucia. That Sontag and Lind quite literally grew up in the theater probably contributed to an unstudied professionalism hardly to be acquired in any other way, and it doubtless accounted for a kind of instinctive showmanship that governed every word they said and every move they made even in their usually exemplary conduct in public off stage. At the same time it may help to explain their distaste for the theater. They both left it as soon as they could. It was the only world they had ever known. For them it could never have the glamour and the fascination it holds for those entering it from the outside.

Neither of them is remembered as a great actress, although there is nothing in the reams written about their performances in opera to suggest that they were not excellent. Theater craft was in their bones, and they never embarrassed themselves or their public with that awkwardness and indecision so often characteristic of the opera singer who has come to acting through the discovery of a voice. They were not possessed by the theater as were Pasta, Malibran and Grisi. But they were professionals through and through whether they liked the vocation or not.

1. HENRIETTE SONTAG

Sontag, daughter of a promiscuous actress and an alcoholic *buffo* bass, was born to the stage, and was very nearly born on it. Her mother played the part of Thekla in Schiller's *Wallenstein* in Koblenz on the night of January 2, 1806, and at six o'clock the next morning Gertrud Walburga Sonntag, the future Henriette Sontag, was born. The theater world in which she grew up was not edifying, beginning with her own family. When she was still an infant her father fell and broke his leg in a performance of Cherubini's *Lodoïska*. He spent the remainder of that evening deadening the pain with brandy instead of having the leg set. He became a cripple, and took leave of the stage, his family and, shortly afterward, his life. What Henriette's mother was may be gathered from the simple statistic that of her twelve offspring only three were assumed to be legitimate. But she was competent enough as an actress to be chosen as a replacement for Sophie Schröder in Prague in 1815, when the latter (and her daughter Wilhelmine) moved to Vienna.

Henriette made her operatic debut as the Princess of Navara in Boieldieu's *Jean de Paris* in Prague. She followed this with Rosina, Zerlina and Agathe, as well as many other roles from operas long forgotten. Word of this prodigy got to the impresario Domenico Barbaja, who brought her to Vienna for a trial. She made her debut at the Theater an der Wien, again as the Princess of Navara. Agathe and Rosina followed, and she was engaged for the next season. In 1823 she added Donna Anna, Pamina and Elena (in Rossini's *La Donna del Lago*) to her roles. Weber heard her in the last and offered her Euryanthe. Then came Beethoven.

Barbaja's company broke up in 1824, and Sontag accepted a contract

One of the best, and certainly the prettiest, of the early nightingales was the German Henriette Sontag. (Right) in *The Daughter of the Regiment* and (above) as she appeared in private life about the time of her early triumphs in Vienna, Berlin, Paris and London.

from the new Königstädter Theater in Berlin. Of her debut there in
L'Italiana in Algeri, on August 3, 1825, an account by the actress Karoline Bauer sets forth those particular vocal, physical and personal attributes that distinguished Henriette Sontag from every other singer of her
generation:

"Finally there appeared on the deck of the ship a slight, youthful,
graceful girl in a sky-blue skirt and a tiny white feathered hat framing a
charming, fresh, childlike forget-me-not face with blond curls, bright blue
eyes and an enchanting little-girl mouth, whose merry smile disclosed the
most beautiful pearly teeth. At rest or in movement, it was a delightful
picture of joyous youth and of harmonious charm and grace, but more
pretty than beautiful. . . . And then she opened that budding little
mouth, like a little woodland bird opening its bill, so naturally, so spon-
taneously, so gaily—and the sweetest, bright bird song echoed jubilantly
through the house.

"The voice was neither full nor strong, but pure as a bell, clear as a
pearl, silver-bright, mellifluous, particularly in the middle, flexible, distinctly articulated and of seductive sweetness. And how beautifully she
trilled—like the bright jubilation of a soaring lark. Then again there was
the brilliance of her singularly high head tones in the most difficult passages and roulades—as precise as a delicate musical clock. Incomparably
enchanting was her *sotto voce*. And it all came so easily, so effortlessly
from the charming little mouth that the listener had but to relax and
enjoy it, confident that nothing could go wrong.

"What took place in the months following this first, incredibly successful appearance, and in the ensuing years in Berlin—and not only in
Berlin—is absolutely unexampled in the history of the theater, a history
far from poor in extended ovations. It was generally expressed in the
term, 'Sontag-fever.' Berlin, normally so cold, so businesslike, so sober,
was a madhouse, full of insane rapture and enthusiastic, pure madness!"

One of the most profoundly smitten was the theater secretary and
house librettist, Karl von Holtei, who, forty years later, would write: "I
have seen more beautiful women, greater actresses, heard more powerful
voices, possibly even greater vocal virtuosity. But never have I experienced
so intimate a communion of charm, fascination, loveliness of sound, cultivation of all artistic capabilities, articulateness, sober exploitation of
given resources, and modest flirtatiousness. Yes, we were all a bit drunk.
. . . But the wine was good, pure and genuine."

Inevitably, this madness tried the patience of soberer heads, among them Ludwig Rellstab, then critic of the *Berliner Musikalische Zeitung,* whose merciless pen was later to drive Spontini from the Court Opera. Under the pseudonym of Freimund Zuschauer, he published in Leipzig a satirical pamphlet called *Henriette, oder die schöne Sängerin.* Sontag's fans were outraged. Some of them journeyed to Leipzig, confiscated all the copies in the publisher's stock and burned them. Rellstab was identified as the author, challenged to duels, tried for libel, sentenced to three months in the prison at Spandau—and served them. Curiously, he was himself a Sontag admirer, and once described her as "the most cultivated mistress of her art, a singer who, through the most industrious study, made the most of her gifts."

Although Sontag could hardly be numbered among those who have found celebrity distasteful, such adulation became too much even for her, and in 1826 she accepted a flattering contract for a two-months' trial engagement at the Théâtre-Italien in Paris. She made her debut in June of that year as Rosina. Tension was great, for not since Mara had a German singer survived comparison with the great Italians in their own roles. Rossini, Cherubini, Auber and Boieldieu were present. Her success was beyond question.

She returned to Paris in 1828, challenging comparison with Pasta as Desdemona in *Otello.* She triumphed again as Rosina and Cinderella, and measured her art with Pisaroni in *La Donna del Lago.* Of these encounters she wrote to Berlin: *La Donna del Lago* is my hobby, for in the first act Pisaroni sings me into the ground, and in the second act I do the same to her."

In April of that year she bowed in London at the King's Theater, again as Rosina, and was immediately the idol of society, into which she was accepted without the distinctions formerly drawn between artists and ladies. The example was set by the Duke of Devonshire, who invited her to a ball and subsequently proposed marriage. When she returned to Paris she was given a souvenir album of signatures collected by Sir Walter Scott. It contained the names of two dukes, twenty-three lords, eighty-seven earls, a hundred and sixty-eight knights, a hundred and thirteen gentlemen, fifty-nine authors, forty-three musicians, thirty-eight painters and twenty-six ladies, including four duchesses.

This was also the year of Malibran's return from America, and there began, in London and in Paris, one of those rivalries that have rejoiced the hearts and filled the pockets of impresarios, and inflamed the passions of opera lovers, since the dawn of vocal history. But in this rivalry there was no bad blood. "My God," Malibran is reported to have exclaimed when she first heard Sontag, "why does she sing so beautifully?" And on another occasion, defending Sontag against the charge of being without soul: "Say rather that she has had no sorrow. Her good fortune has been her misfortune. In unhappiness I am her superior."

Not as superior as she thought. Sontag had been publicly courted by Count Carlo Rossi, a secretary of the Sardinian legation, ever since her arrival in Paris. What the public did not and could not know was that the courtship had led, in 1827, to a secret marriage and a secret confinement. The Sardinian court at Turin refused to approve the marriage, and its becoming public knowledge would have ended the diplomatic career of Count Rossi. The court was finally persuaded to sanction the marriage, but only on condition that Sontag retire from the stage. King Friedrich Wilhelm III assisted by naming her a Freiin (Freifrau, or Baroness) von Lauenstein. She took leave of the theater in a performance of *Semiramide* in Berlin on May 22, 1830, and bade farewell to the concert stage with a tour to Warsaw and St. Petersburg, leaving the field to Malibran and Pasta.

The career of a diplomat's wife, upon which the Countess Rossi now embarked, belongs to political and social rather than to vocal history. Count Rossi was posted successively to The Hague, Frankfurt, St. Petersburg and Berlin. Suffice it to say that the new countess was not entirely silent. She sang a great deal privately, and sometimes, for charity, publicly. Only once did her singing get herself and her husband into trouble. Czar Nicholas I was much taken with her, and at his behest she sang *La Sonnambula* and *Lucia* at the Court Opera. There were immediate repercussions in Turin, and the czar's response came close to causing a break in diplomatic relations. "What the Countess Rossi does at my court, in accordance with my wishes," he wrote, "may never in any way be termed unfitting." The czar delighted in calling Sontag the "*Rossi-gnol*" (nightingale), but he was not the inventor of that pun, as inevitable, of course, as all the various combinations of Sontag and *Sonntag* (Sunday) that had delighted the Berliners and exasperated Rellstab.

The years in Berlin were difficult, however, especially at first. Berlin society, which had adored Henriette Sontag, was less eager to pay homage to the Countess Rossi, but her good nature and charm prevailed, and she even made news by being the first female to skate on the Spree. The example was followed with enthusiasm.

The political upheavals of 1848 and the attendant hostilities in Italy brought the abdication of Carlo Alberto as King of Sardinia in favor of his son, Victor Emmanuel II, and much belt-tightening at the Sardinian court. Eleven ambassadors were dismissed, and Count Rossi was given the choice of divorcing Sontag or retiring, probably on the reasonable assumption that he would choose retirement. He did.

The Rossis' circumstances were desperate. The expenses of a diplomatic establishment, much charity, a good deal of gambling and now inflation had wiped out Sontag's fortune. At this critical moment the London impresario Benjamin Lumley, proprietor of Her Majesty's Theater, came forward. Lind had, for religious reasons, deserted Her Majesty's for the concert hall; Mario and Grisi had left it for Covent Garden. Lumley, at his wits' end to replace Lind, offered an irresistible contract for a six-months' season.

Sontag reappeared at Her Majesty's on July 7, 1849, in *Linda di Chamounix*. "A more curious or noticeable event is not on opera record," wrote Chorley, referring to her reappearance after twenty years. "There was no need for misgiving," he added. "The first notes of Linda's *polacca* were sufficient to assure everyone who filled the theater that the artist was in her own place again. . . . All went wondrously well."

All continued to go well, in England, on the Continent and in America, where her tour and trials were a carbon copy of Lind's. It was money alone that drew her to America. It was money that sustained her through the not inconsiderable physical hardships of travel at that time. And it was money that persuaded her, on more than one occasion, to sing *The Daughter of the Regiment* in the afternoon and *Lucrezia Borgia* the same evening. Could she have sensed that time was running out?

Run out it did, in Mexico City, where she died of cholera on June 17, 1854.

2. JENNY LIND

Sontag is one of the most sympathetic figures among the great singers. Jenny Lind is not. Where Sontag seems always to have been friendly, outgoing, gracious and naturally amiable, Lind, behind a saintly exterior, was privately withdrawn, irritable, unpredictable, cold and calculating. Sontag's retirement from the public arena at the age of twenty-four represented a real sacrifice for the man she loved, requiring her to forgo not only the theater, which she may have disliked as much as she said she did, but all other public appearances, which no real singer dislikes, as well. Lind's retirement from the theater at twenty-nine was the arbitrary abandonment of something she felt to be unworthy of her.

There was always a smugness and primness about Jenny Lind, a readiness to judge and deplore and condemn, a constant dwelling upon her own virtue and high-mindedness. Her whole life was a series of pious, sanctimonious attitudes, relieved, when she chose to turn it on, by compelling charm. More astonishing than any of her vocal miracles is the plain fact that she could put these attitudes over. On the stage she may have been less than a great actress, although she was certainly a good one. Off the stage she was supreme.

The role of the simple little Swedish girl, a Hans Christian Andersen "Ugly Duckling," the insignificant, snub-nosed, plain, simply dressed, hesitant, unassuming poor-little-me, pining for the northern homeland, pure of heart and noble of thought, was the greatest of her roles. The legendary Jenny Lind was her own masterpiece. As a histrionic accomplishment it had only one flaw. It lacked the true artist's detachment. The public was taken in, and so were most of her friends and acquaintances; but so, also, was she.

The consequence was ambivalence, indecision and tortured rationalization. The woman behind the façade, strong-willed, ambitious, dauntlessly competitive, capable of ruthlessness and often inordinately pleased with herself, kept getting in the way. She was a conscientious, even a compulsive, letter writer. She may well have felt a requirement to explain or justify the inconsistencies of her performance as a woman, particularly the persistent ambivalence reflected in her behavior toward her suitors, her benefactors, her employers and the theater. Even her charity was piecemeal, unwisely diffused and tastelessly publicized; she may have been motivated by an unwitting desire to ennoble the pleasure she derived from her success as a singer.

Many of her letters have been preserved, and almost every one is a document of contradictions—ingenuous boasting flanked by disingenuous self-deprecation, gay pleasure in her triumphs modified by protestations of distaste for the theater and its people, longing for Sweden coupled with contempt for Swedish provincialism. Conspicuous between the lines —and sometimes in them—is a sense of her own unique vocation and goodness. She always seems to be thanking God that she is not as others are.

It should not be surprising, however, that a girl born (on October 6,

1820) into so inhospitable a world as hers, and conditioned as a child to life in the theater, with its emphasis on the exercise of fantasy, should have invented for herself a flattering role. She was the unwanted, illegitimate child of an ill-tempered, bigoted schoolteacher and a ne'er-do-well father. As an infant she was farmed out to foster homes until her voice, already striking at the age of nine, attracted attention and secured her admittance as an actress-pupil to the opera school of the Royal Theater in Stockholm. From that time on, although she lived intermittently with her parents, the theater was her only home and her only occupation. She appeared as actress or singer in twenty-two performances when she was thirteen, twenty-six when she was fourteen, and eighteen when she was fifteen, at which age she made her first appearance in grand opera. In 1837, aged sixteen, she was promoted to the status of a regular actress, and in that year she appeared ninety-two times.

By the time she was twenty-one she was a star of a magnitude that Stockholm had never known. She had added Euryanthe, Pamina, Julia (in Spontini's *La Vestale*), Alice (in *Robert le Diable*), Donna Anna, Lucia and Norma to her repertoire, and she was, not surprisingly, in need of vocal repair. She also sought refuge from an uncomfortable situation in the household of the Swedish composer Adolf Lindblad and his wife, who had taken her in. Lindblad had fallen in love with her. She went to Paris to study with Manuel García.

García—according to his own account to his pupil Mathilde Marchesi —told her: "Mademoiselle, you have an originality of style which requires training, but either your voice is worn or you never had one. You must take a few weeks of rest, after which I will hear you again." What followed is history. "I do not remember," García told Marchesi, "ever having had a more attentive, intelligent pupil. Never had I to explain anything to her twice." Jenny Lind's picture, according to Marchesi, was the only one he had on display in his studio.

She returned to Stockholm—and to the Lindblads, unwisely—with her natural endowment secured by technical mastery, and with a distaste for everything French that would endure throughout her life. She regarded the French, she told Ruskin in 1849, as a nation "shut out from the common portion of God's blessing upon men, and deservedly so." And she never sang in France—or, for that matter, Italy. She put it all on moral grounds; but she may have felt intuitively, and probably correctly, that the Jenny Lind show would have found a less credulous public in Paris than in London or Berlin.

Even more famous than Sontag was Jenny Lind, the "Swedish Nightingale":
(Above) as she appeared at the height of her operatic career; (below right)
as the more mature Jenny Lind-Goldschmidt; (below left) in the sleepwalking
scene from *La Sonnambula* at Her Majesty's Theatre in 1847.

From 1844 to 1849 she sang in Berlin, concertized widely in Germany, and made an opera debut in Vienna. She found the Germany of Mendelssohn and the Schumanns congenial and receptive to her own notions of the sanctity of art. And she was a sensation. But the centers of the operatic world were Paris and London. In Berlin, as Chorley put it, "her apparition was indeed a godsend among the clumsy and exaggerated women who strode the stage, screaming as they strode." And before Paris and London she faltered, as, indeed, she faltered at leaving Stockholm for Berlin and exposing herself in Vienna. Her provincial hesitancy to leap from a small pond to a larger one was probably genuine. And she paid for it.

Early in 1845, Alfred Bunn, then manager of the Drury Lane Theater in London, where opera was given in English, came to Berlin and offered her a contract to sing that summer in *La Sonnambula* and Meyerbeer's *Ein Feldlager in Schlesien*, in which the role of Vielka had been written for her. She accepted, and signed the contract. Subsequently she had doubts about learning the parts in English, and asked to be released. Bunn refused. She pleaded. "I possess neither the personal advantages, the assurance nor the charlatanism of other prima donnas," she wrote, a disingenuousness later held against her in court.

Her next offer from London came in 1846 from Lumley, whose Italian company at Her Majesty's Theater was competing with the company at Covent Garden, now managed by none other than Bunn. After much vacillation, and certainly with a bad conscience, she signed with Lumley and, in 1847, came to London, still under contract to Bunn. Her London successes produced a national delirium beyond anything in operatic history. They saved Lumley and hurt Bunn. He sued, and his suit was sustained. Lind was required to pay damages of £2,500. Lumley paid, but the stigma was hers.

She sang at Her Majesty's in the seasons of 1847–48–49, and the Jenny Lind legend dates from that engagement. It was not just her singing and acting, which were excellent enough. Far more compelling was her image, as we would say today. She was not what a singer, a woman of the theater, was expected to be. The fact that she was Swedish lent an exotic element to her identity. And then she was so good, so pure, so simple, so charitable, so spiritual! The image survived even the lawsuit, possibly because her defense had been that she was an innocent girl, unfamiliar with the English language, who had signed impulsively without knowing what she was signing.

She was also reluctant, or seemed to be. She talked incessantly of retiring from the theater, of singing only concerts and oratorios, and of devoting herself to charity. Before each season there was doubt about her appearance, and she was always a month or so late in appearing. She may have hated publicity, or been indifferent to it, as she said she was, but no other artist had her genius, probably intuitive, for making it.

Lumley, of course, knew how to make the most of the Lind legend, as did Phineas Barnum when she toured the United States and Cuba under his flamboyant but shrewd management in 1850–51. The instinct or intuition she had, but not the skill. Toward the end of her American tour she bought up the remainder of her contract with Barnum, thinking that she could do better for herself on her own. But without Barnum's management, without Barnum to interpose himself between Lind and the public, her irascibility and stubbornness emerged to soil the image.

As Joan Bulman, in her *Jenny Lind*, has put it, "she had owed more to Barnum's management than she realized. His showmanship had been exactly right for her. Someone congratulated him once on having 'always kept her angel face to the public'; he could afford to do that, and build her up as the angel in white, the incarnation of saintliness and charity, because his own reputation for wickedness countered hers for goodness, and added the necessary spice. They formed the perfect partnership. When she worked alone, she had to bear the limelight as the 'woman without a fault,' while at the same time those faults she had began to show—and they were not of a kind that Americans found endearing."

Having forsaken opera, she had only the concert as a setting, and the concert format of those days was far from today's recital: a few opera arias, some popular favorites such as "The Last Rose of Summer" and, in her case, some Swedish songs. Assisting artists were obligatory and not, as a rule, exciting. Such programs began to pall, and public apathy was turned to hostility by her stubborn championship of Otto Goldschmidt, her accompanist and, subsequently, her husband. Jenny's high opinion of his abilities as a soloist was not shared by critics and audiences. This displeased her, and she showed her displeasure, looking, on one occasion, "as stingey as a hive of wasps." She departed from New York on May 29, 1852, her halo awry.

The role that Jenny Lind played in real life, as effective and persuasive as it must certainly have been, was marred from time to time by sobering glimpses of an all too terrestrial femininity. This seems never to have been true of her singing or of her performances in the theater. Purely as a vocal virtuoso, she had her equals and probably her superiors, even among her contemporaries. But her voice had a quality which was hers alone, and which set her apart from every other singer. Critic after critic described it as possessing a certain woodland freshness, terrestrial, perhaps, but undefiled. Some thought it other-worldly.

Hans Christian Andersen, an unsuccessful suitor, said of her first performance as Alice in *Robert le Diable* in Copenhagen in 1843: "It showed me art in its sanctity—I had seen one of its vestal virgins." Mendelssohn and Clara Schumann reacted similarly. Many years later, in 1854, when her voice was showing some signs of deterioration, a far less impressionable commentator than Andersen, Mendelssohn or the Schumanns namely, the Viennese critic Eduard Hanslick—numbered her among "phenomena that approach the great manifestations of beauty in nature before which one can only stand still and gratefully proclaim their existence."

Of her performance of a song by Karl Taubert, "Ich muss nun einmal singen," Hanslick said: "An approximate imitation of the song of a bird, almost overstepping the boundaries of music, this warbling and piping becomes a thing of the most enchanting beauty in the mouth of Jenny Lind. All the fresh, natural woodland charm of the bird's joyous song reaches us here incredibly by way of the utmost technical bravura." And the tenor, Roger, who accompanied her on her tours of the British Isles, remembered "strains in her singing that threw off the scent of forest and moor."

So much for the quality and timbre of her voice, which were, of course, especially effective in Swedish songs and in certain passages of oratorio. Chorley, whose objectivity in his estimates of her art was interpreted as hostility by her admirers, offers the most reliable account of what her voice really was and what she did with it. Writing in 1862, long after the passions of 1847 and 1848 had subsided, he wrote:

"It can now, without treason, be recorded that Mdlle. Lind's voice was a soprano, two octaves in compass—from D to D—having a possible higher note or two available on rare occasions; and that the lower half and the upper one were of two distinct qualities. The former was not strong—veiled, if not husky, and apt to be out of tune. The latter was rich, brilliant and powerful—finest in its highest portions. It can be told that the power of respiration was possessed by Mdlle. Lind in the highest perfection; that she could turn her 'very long breath' to account in every gradation of tone; and thus, by subduing her upper notes, and giving out her lower ones with great care, could conceal the disproportions of her organ. . . .

"Her execution was great; and, as is always the case with voices originally reluctant, seemed greater than it really was. Her shake (a grace ridiculously despised of late) was true and brilliant; her taste in ornament was altogether original. In a song from [Bellini's] *Beatrice di Tenda*, which she adopted, there was a chromatic cadence, ascending to E in altissimo, and descending to the note whence it had risen, which could not be paragoned, of late days, as an evidence of mastery and accomplishment. She used her pianissimo tones so as to make them resemble an effect of ventriloquism. On every note that she sang, in every bar that she delivered, a skilled and careful musician was to be detected."

As an actress she could be charming, wistful, tender and pathetic, but not forceful, vengeful, grand or impassioned. Amina, Lucia, Adina (in *L'Elisir d'Amore*), Julia (in *La Vestale*) and Maria (in *The Daughter of the Regiment*) were among her best parts. Her Norma was much admired in Germany. But since she could not bear to associate herself with evil, even as an actress, she deprived the part of any suggestion of jealousy or hatred. Chorley was horrified. Her failure in this role, he said, was "something as entire, as aimless as it is possible for so remarkable an artist to make. The actress and the play had no agreement."

This could also have been said of her life. Jenny Lind and the woman she played off stage "had no agreement." The discrepancies became less apparent and less troublesome after her marriage, but this was rather thanks to Goldschmidt's combination of utter adoration and tact than to any fundamental change in her character.

She remained bigoted until the end of her days. Liza Lehmann, composer of "In a Persian Garden," remembered her reaction in Italy in 1871 to an Italian boy who served the muffins. "You see that boy?" Lind asked. "I am trying to conquer myself—to *bear* with him—but—he is a *Roman Catholic!*"

She was a remarkable artist and a remarkable woman—whoever she was. She died on November 2, 1887.

3. ADELINA PATTI

About Adelina Patti's identity there was never a moment's doubt—in her own mind or anybody else's. She was a *prima donna!* At the height of her fame her contracts excused her from attendance at rehearsals and required that her name appear on all posters in a separate line of large letters at least one-third larger than those used for the announcement of any other singer. She was at liberty to cancel in the event of an outbreak of contagious disease. Her farewells spanned decades and continents. And when she retired it was to a castle in Wales, complete with private theater.

She saw no evil in the theater. Neither religion nor politics nor the condition of the world at large was ever much on her mind. Nor does there seem to have been any evil in her. She could be petulant. There were flashes of anger. And she was as sticky about fees as about billing. But mostly she was amiable. "Graced by God with talent," Hanslick said of her, "she is, at the same time, one of the happiest of His creatures, simply by virtue of her inexhaustible joy in her vocation."

Nor were there ever any vocal complications. From her first appearance in 1850, at the age of seven, until her last in 1914, at the age of seventy-one, she never had a true vocal crisis. In the early years of her career the voice was comparatively weak at the bottom, and in later years it was weak at the top. But these were problems solved easily by discretion in the choice of repertoire and by transposition. "Time," said George Bernard Shaw in 1890, when she was approaching fifty, "has transposed Patti a minor third down." She was, moreover, a true singer, who could melt hearts with a simple ballad when she could no longer confound the imagination with the brilliance of her coloratura and her easy flights to the high F.

Her contentment with her calling and her vocal longevity were not unrelated. Fully aware that she was primarily a vocal phenomenon, and requiring no other distinction or distraction, she avoided anything that might impair her most precious endowment, including acting or even any very forceful singing. Clara Louise Kellogg (1842–1916), one of the early American sopranos, who sang with her through several London seasons in the 1860s and 1870s, tells, in her *Memoirs of an American Prima Donna*, just how careful Patti was:

"A great deal is heard about the wonderful preservation of Patti's voice. It *was* wonderfully preserved. How could it have been otherwise, considering the care she has always taken of herself? Such a life! Everything divided off carefully according to *régime*: so much to eat, so far to walk, so long to sleep, just such and such things to do and no others! And, above all, she has allowed herself few emotions. Every singer knows that emotions are what exhaust and injure the voice. She never acted; and she never, never felt!"

As one who had grown up on the stage and in the theater, she was used to routine, of course; and if she never acted much, she did not, at least, act badly. "While not being a great actress, she was always adequate in the histrionic side of her parts," said David Bispham (1857–1921), the American baritone, in his A *Quaker Singer's Recollections*, "though, after the fashion of her day, she invariably came to the footlights to sing her great arias regardless of the business of the stage: its occupants might do as they pleased as long as she had the undivided attention of the audience.

"She was, indeed, a songbird *par excellence*, and never allowed anything to upset either her equanimity or her comfort. I shall never forget her closing scene in *Aida*, where she and the tenor are supposed to be immured in a tomb of stone. At the close of the duet, Patti, who had instructed the stage manager to make her comfortable, would carefully adjust a sofa cushion which had been placed conveniently at hand, would kick with one high-heeled Parisian slipper a train around behind her, and, assisted by the tenor, would compose herself in a graceful position —and die."

And she dressed the part—of Adelina Patti. Bispham saw her at a gala performance during Queen Victoria's Diamond Jubilee. "Upon her corsage," he said, "there blazed a solid front of diamonds, and I was told that every gem in her possession had been carefully sewed upon the bodice of her dress. Ropes of pearls hung from her neck, her hands were covered with jewels, and a diamond tiara sat upon her graceful head. So valuable was the world-renowned prima donna that, besides her husband, she was guarded by several detectives, one of whom was with her in the carriage upon her way to the opera house, while another sat upon the box. One of these remained outside the door of her dressing room throughout the evening, while the other, with a companion, escorted her to the stage, remaining at her entrance and exit, guarding her as she returned to her dressing room and later to her hotel."

She was the successor of Grisi as "the Queen of Song," and the more splendid empress of the two. She reigned for forty-five years. Her dominion embraced not only Paris and London, but also Milan, St. Petersburg, Vienna and North and South America, and she had to sustain it against even more formidable challengers. Grisi's survival was assisted by the death of Malibran, by Jenny Lind's retirement from the theater

Adelina Patti (above left) became the most celebrated and durable nightingale of them all. Her reign covered 45 years. Among her most successful roles were Marguerite and Juliet. Her partner (above right) in *Faust* is none other than Mario, prince of tenors for a generation.

Among many other nightingales of Patti's long reign were the Croatian Ilma di Murska (below left) and the Canadian-American Emma Albani (below right).

and Sontag's death in Mexico City. Patti had to contend with Pauline Lucca, Ilma di Murska, Christine Nilsson, Emma Albani, Marie Cabel, Etelka Gerster, Marie Marimon and, toward the end, with Marcella Sembrich, Emma Calvé, Nellie Melba and Emma Nevada. All were long-voiced and normally long-lived, and untroubled by dreams of retirement.

Any one of these singers might have ruled in her own right in a less luxuriant age, and without a Patti secure upon her throne. They were like the many excellent tenors who had the misfortune to be contemporaries of Mario, de Reszke or Caruso. Each of them was probably Patti's equal or even her superior in one department or another, or in certain roles. But in none were combined all the constituent elements of the singer's art as they were in Patti. "I have heard greater artists as singers," said Hanslick, "and more brilliant voices. I recall more sophisticated actresses and more beautiful women. But Patti's charm consists in making one forget them. What she offers is so completely hers, so harmonious and lovable, that one allows oneself to be captivated and accepts capitulation with pleasure."

A singular aspect of this sudden flowering of virtuoso sopranos, all schooled in the tradition and objectives of *bel canto*, was its tardiness. A curious consequence was the artificial perpetuation of the Rossini-Donizetti-Bellini-Meyerbeer repertoire into the age of Wagner and the later Verdi. These singers were an anachronism, sustaining old-fashioned Italian opera into the twentieth century. Insofar as they ventured into the new repertoire, they did so hesitantly—and in Italian. Wagner, Meyerbeer and even Bizet and Ambroise Thomas were sung in Italian. To compound the foolishness, not one of these singers was Italian, except Patti, who was born in Madrid and brought up in the United States, and whose first language was American English.

Sontag had been German and Lind a Swede. Lucca was Viennese, di Murska Croatian, Nilsson Swedish, Albani Canadian-American (she took her name from the city of Albany), Cabel, Marimon and Calvé French, Gerster Hungarian, Sembrich Polish, Nevada American and Melba Australian. Di Murska, Gerster, Calvé, Nevada and Melba, moreover, were all pupils of Mathilde Marchesi, a German. Florid singing among Italian women seemed to have expired with Grisi, and the younger Italian singers had not yet fully mastered the new kind of dramatic singing required by Verdi. Even with Verdi, the first of the great dramatic sopranos was Teresa Stolz (1836–1902), a Bohemian.

Anachronistic it all may have been, but it was glorious for those who relished good singing, as it was also exasperating for the many who felt that the whole phenomenon was obstructing the acceptance of Wagner into public favor. Verdi suffered less. The basic repertoire was Rossini-Bellini-Donizetti-Meyerbeer, and the roles the same that had served prima donnas ever since the days of Pasta, Malibran, Persiani and Sontag. But while Patti's greatest roles were Linda, Rosina, Norina, Amina, Adina, Lucia, Zerlina, and so on, she also sang Violetta, Leonora and even Aida. Albani sang Elsa, Elisabeth and Eva, first in Italian, later in German. But she was an exception. The time for opera in the original language was yet to come, as were the singers who could move easily from one language and one repertoire to another.

Of those who deplored the display of vocal virtuosity, one of the most exasperated was the American, Henry T. Finck, then the young critic of the New York *Evening Post,* who had recently returned, after seven student years in Germany, an ardent Wagnerite. He was merciless in his denunciations of Patti, and lived both to regret them and to apologize.

"No doubt everything I said about Patti's shortcomings was true," he wrote in *My Adventures in the Golden Age of Music.* "She was infinitely more interested in showing off her lovely voice than in the music she sang. The composer was for her a mere peg to hang on her trills and frills. . . . But as a singer she was so glorious, so incomparable, that while under the spell of her vocal art the listeners forgot everything else and simply luxuriated in ecstatic bliss. I myself often wrote glowing paragraphs describing the charm of her voice and the ingratiating spontaneity of her singing. I consider myself fortunate in having been able to listen twice a week to the sweetest and most mellow voice the world has ever heard.

"It was like the singing of the nightingales I used to be enchanted with in the Tiergarten in Berlin. Patti was a nightingale; why ask more of her? In her way she was absolutely perfect, and perfection of any kind should be honored and extolled, without any of the buts and ifs on which I dwelt too much. In plain language, I made an ass of myself. . . . Oddly enough she also was longing to be different. She would have given one of her beautiful black eyes to sing and act Elsa, or Elisabeth or Eva. . . ."

Patti never sang a Wagnerian role, but she did sing "Träume" and the Prayer from *Tannhäuser* in concert—and in German. According to Shaw, who, as a militant Wagnerite, was particular about such matters, she sang them surpassingly well. "She attacks the Prayer," he wrote, "with the single aim of making it sound as beautiful as possible; and this being precisely what Wagner's own musical aim was, she goes straight to the right phrasing, the right vocal touch, and the right turn of every musical figure, thus making her German rivals not only appear in comparison clumsy as singers, but actually obtuse as to Wagner's meaning."

Shaw was always good on Patti. He despised her repertoire, but as one who had once studied singing he could not fail to acknowledge great singing when he heard it. As to her deportment, her prima-donna airs and habits, they were so much the expression of an essentially childlike nature that he could not suppress an affectionate and indulgent smile even while scolding.

"Madame Patti kissed hands last night, in her artless way, to a prodigious audience come to bid her farewell before her trip to South America," he wrote on January 23, 1889. "The unnecessary unpleasantness of the most useful of Mr. Louis Stevenson's novels makes it impossible to say that there is in Madame Patti an Adelina Jekyll and an Adelina Hyde; but there are certainly two very different sides to her public character. There is Patti the great singer: Patti of the beautiful, eloquent voice, so perfectly produced and controlled that its most delicate pianissimo reaches the remotest listener in Albert Hall: Patti of the unerring ear, with her magical roulade soaring to heavenly altitudes: Patti of the pure, strong tone that made 'God Save the Queen' sound fresh and noble at Covent Garden: Patti of the hushed, tender notes that reconcile rows of club-loving cynics to 'Home, Sweet Home.' This was the famous artist who last night sang 'Bel raggio' [from *Semiramide*] and 'Comin' thro' the Rye' incomparably.

"But there is another Patti: a Patti who cleverly sang and sang again some pretty nonsense from Delibes's *Lakmé*. Great was the applause, even after it had been repeated; and then the comedy began. Mr. [Wilhelm] Ganz, whilst the house was shouting and clapping uproariously, deliberately took up his baton and started Moszkowski's Serenata in D. The audience took its cue at once, and would not have Moszkowski. After a prolonged struggle, Mr. Ganz gave up in despair; and out tripped the diva, bowing her acknowledgments in the character of a petted and delighted child. When she vanished there was more cheering than ever. Mr. Ganz threatened the Serenata again; but in vain.

"He appealed to the sentinels of the greenroom; and these shook their heads, amidst roars of protest from the audience, and at last, with elaborate gesture, conveyed in dumb show that they dared not, could not, would not, must not venture to approach Patti again. Mr. Ganz, with well-acted desolation, went on with the Serenata, not one note of which was heard. Again he appealed to the sentinels; and this time they waved their hands expansively in the direction of South America, to indicate that the prima donna was already on her way thither. On this the audience showed such sudden and unexpected signs of giving in that the diva tripped out again, bowing, wafting kisses, and successfully courting fresh thunders of applause. Will not some sincere friend of Madame Patti's tell her frankly that she is growing too big a girl for this sort of thing? . . . No: the queens of song should leave the coquetry of the footlights to the soubrettes."

There is no way of knowing whether any of Patti's "sincere friends" acted on this suggestion. Probably not. She certainly never did. At the Metropolitan in New York, two years later, she had a piano pushed through the curtain after a performance of *The Barber of Seville*. She had sung Eckert's "Echo Song" and "Home, Sweet Home" during the lesson scene, and now she sang "Comin' thro' the Rye." All this showed "in a most forcible way," said Henry Krehbiel in the New York *Tribune*, "how genuine is the regard in which this great singer is held by her admirers, and Mme. Patti has every reason to feel glad and grateful at the admiring esteem which is awarded to her by the public of New York."

Nor was Shaw offering good advice. He, after all, was sitting in a press seat, and neither he nor his publication had contributed anything to the till. Patti, very sensibly, was guided by the audible and profitable approbation of the paying guests. She was not a sophisticated woman; and she might have found it difficult to agree that artists—or critics—should decide what the paying guest should receive for his money. And Patti was not cheap.

From Patti the patrons expected "Home, Sweet Home" and "Comin' thro' the Rye"; and they expected a proper prima donna, charmed to be coaxed, throwing kisses to her dear public and rewarding their devotion with the old favorites. In less austere times than our own the relationship between a prima donna—or a favorite tenor—and the public was a love affair. A thing of fantasy, of course, and in fantasy the partners never grow up.

Shaw should have understood that.

Patti did.

· XIII ·

The Mezzo Minority

PISARONI · VIARDOT · ALBONI

THE ORIGINS of the mezzo-soprano, as we understand the term and the species today, are difficult to trace in the confused transition of the lyric theater from *opera seria* to grand opera.

In the days of *opera seria* many of the castrati had been mezzo-sopranos, and were so designated, without prejudicing their standing or their celebrity. Most of the great female singers of the age of *bel canto* were sopranos, although many of them sang in a mezzo-soprano range when age had robbed them of their top notes. A lower female voice, designated alto or contralto, was condemned to secondary parts. And this habit of pejorative categorization persisted beyond the departure of the castrati, although male roles that would formerly have been sung by castrati were now frequently entrusted to lower-voiced females.

Rossini, to be sure, wrote some grateful *buffa* parts for singers designated as contraltos—Rosina in *The Barber of Seville*, the title role in *La Cenerentola*, Isabella in *L'Italiana in Algeri*, and Malcolm Graeme in *La Donna del Lago*. He wrote substantial parts for them in his serious operas, too, notably the title role in *Tancredi* and the role of Arsaces in *Semiramide*. But Tancred was appropriated by sopranos; and an Arsaces, however fine she might be, had a Semiramis above her, was overshadowed by the higher voice in duets, and condemned to fewer solo opportunities and to inferior billing. The singers of the early years of grand opera who are remembered specifically or categorically as contraltos, or as mezzo-sopranos, were those too limited in range, or too wanting in industry and determination, to tackle the great soprano parts.

Malibran is usually spoken of as a mezzo-soprano, but she sang the soprano repertoire. And the same was probably true of Pasta. It was certainly true of Caroline Unger (1803–1877), the Hungarian contralto who sang with Sontag at the première of Beethoven's Ninth Symphony. It was she who turned the oblivious Beethoven around to face the audience so that he might *see* the ovation. And it was she about whom Rossini said: "She has southern fire, northern earnestness, lungs of bronze, a voice of silver and a talent of gold." She sang for a long period as a soprano, mostly in Italy, and was considered by many to have been the supreme Lucrezia Borgia.

Mezzo-sopranos are better off today. They have Azucena, Amneris, Dalila, Carmen, Ulrica, Eboli, Orpheus, Laura, and Mignon, not to mention the Wagnerian parts—Fricka, Brangäne, Ortrud, Waltraute and Venus. And Richard Strauss has blessed them with Octavian and Clytemnestra. But with the exception of Carmen, Orpheus and Dalila, even these fat parts have sopranos above them; and big-ranged mezzos are tempted to try the upward leap, just as they were in the time of Malibran, Pasta and Unger—and for the same reason. The singer with the higher voice gets the top billing and the higher fee. Nor are the mezzo-sopranos secure even in their own inferior world. Many sopranos have found Carmen an irresistible temptation, among them Calvé, Patti, Lucca, Lilli Lehmann, Farrar, Ponselle and Jeritza. Sopranos have also found Octavian seductive. And Rossini's *buffa* parts, notably Rosina and Cinderella, are more often sung by sopranos than by mezzos or contraltos.

1. BENEDETTA PISARONI

The names of Malibran, Pasta and Grisi would be no more familiar than that of Benedetta Rosamunda Pisaroni (1793–1872) if they had confined themselves to Rossini's *buffa* parts and to Arsaces. And yet Pisaroni must have been quite a singer! An anonymous Milanese critic, writing in 1826, called her "that unique restorer of, and rightful heir to, the beautiful and enchanting song of Pacchierotti." And the far from anonymous Stendhal, three years earlier, had referred to her "superb contralto voice that executes the greatest difficulties with ease," and he regretted that several of Rossini's operas might be denied to Paris for want of "a contralto with sufficient technique to execute music written for Signorina Pisaroni." Among the roles written for Pisaroni was Malcolm Graeme in *La Donna del Lago*. She was not the first Arsaces, but she was considered to be the best as long as her voice prevailed, and she became uniquely identified with the role.

MUSEE DE L'OPERA

This portrait of Marietta Brambilla (left) makes it easy to agree with the unidentified cardinal who is said to have observed of her that "she has the finest eyes, the sweetest voice and the best disposition in the world."

Rosamunda Benedetta Pisaroni (below) was as famous for her homeliness as for the beauty of her voice and the compelling quality of her singing. This painting of Pisaroni, with her husband, does not show the pockmarks which disfigured her face.

MUSEO TEATRALE ALLA SCALA, MILAN

Pisaroni was another of those who triumphed over inferior vocal resources. At a time when females sang as sopranos if they possibly could, Pisaroni was a soprano who had to come down. This has been ascribed to a serious illness in 1813, presumably the attack of smallpox that left her so conspicuously disfigured that she used to send pictures of herself to managers interested in engaging her in order that they might be forewarned. The problem of introducing *Semiramide* to Paris was solved by introducing Pisaroni too, and Fétis has left a picturesque account of that debut in 1827:

"Never shall I forget the effect produced on the audience when, advancing up the stage with her back to the public, contemplating the interior of the temple, she enunciated in a formidable voice, admirably produced, the phrase, 'Eccomi, alfine, in Babilonia!' A transport of applause responded to these vigorous accents, this broad style, so rare in our days; but when the singer turned around, displaying features horribly disfigured by small-pox, a sort of shudder of horror succeeded to the first enthusiasm, many among the spectators shutting their eyes so as to hear without being condemned to see. But before the end of the opera her performance had gained a complete victory. After a few months the public thought no more about Madame Pisaroni's face, dominated as all were by her wonderful talent."

Among the several singers for whom Rossini wrote what we think of today as mezzo-soprano roles, only Pisaroni is remembered by any but purposeful researchers. But the music he wrote for them tells us how good they must have been; and the circumstances under which some of the roles came to be written suggest that they had more than merely vocal charms. For Marietta Marcolini, the first Isabella in *L'Italiana in Algeri*, according to Stendhal, Rossini turned his back on the great and influential ladies of Venice, while Marcolini, in turn, sacrificed Prince Lucien Bonaparte for Rossini. Maria Giorgi-Righetti, his first Rosina, and Adelaide Malanotte, his first Tancred, seem to have been similarly enchanting. And wondrous things were said at the time of Rosa Mariani, the first Arsaces.

A more familiar name is that of Marietta Brambilla (1807–1875), who created the roles of Maffio Orsini and of Pierotto in *Linda di Chamounix*, and was a famous Arsaces. It was she of whom some unidentified cardinal is said to have observed that "she has the finest eyes, the sweetest voice and the best disposition in the world." But the mezzo-soprano with whom began the dignity of that often ambiguous category was Malibran's younger sister, Pauline Viardot (1821–1910).

2. PAULINE VIARDOT

Pauline, at the outset of her career, sang the soprano repertoire, as Malibran had done, but she would never achieve a comparable stardom in the standard Rossini-Donizetti-Bellini roles. Halévy and Meyerbeer were her composers, and it would be through Meyerbeer that she would establish the prototype of the modern mezzo-soprano.

There were, to be sure, imposing triumphs. In 1839, when she was seventeen and eighteen, she presented herself in both Paris and London as Desdemona, Rosina and Cinderella. As the sister of Malibran and the daughter of García, she was assured of sympathetic attention. She was recognized immediately as a woman of extraordinary talent. But she was slower to mature than Malibran had been, and what she displayed in that first season, and in the seasons of 1840–41 and 1841–42, as impressive as it must have been, was not enough to safeguard a newcomer, even a García, against the tenacious and resourceful opposition of Grisi.

In 1840 Pauline married Louis Viardot, the director of the Théâtre-Italien, but Viardot, an impresario of uncommon probity, thought it improper to remain as director while he was married to an aspirant prima donna, and resigned. Thus early in her career, Pauline Viardot found herself without a stage in either of the world's two opera capitals. It turned out to be a blessing. During the 1840s she sang in Vienna, Dresden, Berlin and, principally, in St. Petersburg, expanding her repertoire, learning how to exploit the virtues and disguise the deficiencies of a singular voice, and developing her native endowment as an actress.

To these tasks she brought a combination of talent and intelligence possibly unexampled in the history of the lyric theater. Other great singers have been excellent musicians, but Pauline Viardot, who had studied composition with Anton Reicha (1770–1836) and piano with Liszt before she began to study voice seriously, still played so well in 1851, when she was thirty, that Ferdinand Hiller (1811–1885) was on the point of engaging her to head the piano department at the Cologne Conservatory, of which he was then the director. As a composer she arranged a number of Chopin's mazurkas as songs, and wrote presentable operettas for her pupils. She was also an excellent painter and a prodigious linguist.

But in Pauline Viardot the woman was as extraordinary as the artist. Her most congenial environment was the Parisian world of George Sand, Chopin, Alfred de Musset, Ary Scheffer, Berlioz, Rossini, Eugène Delacroix, Gustave Doré, Gounod and the political and philosophical thinkers of the time. In their society she moved not as a visitor from the alien world of opera but as a friend and confidante, a member in full standing of an intellectual elite.

Despite irregular features, she had that kind of beauty which is superior to prettiness, and more durable. She was loved by de Musset, Scheffer, Gounod and Berlioz. None of them found his love requited. But Ivan Turgenev did. He was a vital and often disturbing element in her life for forty years, the third party in one of the most enigmatic *ménages à trois* in literary or musical history. April Fitzlyon has called her study of this relationship *The Price of Genius*, implying that Pauline sacrificed the prospect of domestic bliss with Turgenev for her career as a singer. On the basis of what we know about Pauline, it is also possible to see in her refusal to leave her husband for Turgenev an accommodation rather than a sacrifice. She may well have preferred an equivocal situation that she could usually control to a domestic situation where control, by convention and law, would have passed to Turgenev. What the latter felt about it is reflected in his most famous play, *A Month in the Country*.

Pauline was also just a bit strait-laced. As a small girl she had witnessed her parents' wrath when her sister bore a child to de Bériot while still legally married to Malibran, and it had been a sobering experience. She never bore Turgenev an illegitimate child, nor is it even certain that their relationship was of such intimacy as to have produced one. But she made up for it curiously, and possibly symbolically, by accepting into her household Turgenev's own illegitimate daughter, born of a passing intimacy with the daughter of his mother's seamstress.

The most important figure in Pauline's musical, as distinguished from her private, life was Meyerbeer. He had been an admirer of her sister, and he admired Pauline even more. They met in Berlin in 1843, when he was director of the opera there, and he vowed that he would not allow any new work of his to be performed at the Opéra in Paris unless she appeared in it. In 1848, when negotiations were under way for the production of *Le Prophète*, he kept his word. The opera had originally been intended as a vehicle for Duprez in the role of John of Leyden, but by 1848 Duprez was no longer equal to such an enterprise. Meyerbeer, accordingly, reshaped the opera around Viardot in the role of Fidès, the mother forced to renounce her own son in order not to expose his mortality. Viardot, in 1849, was ready.

Indeed, even before the première of *Le Prophète* she had demonstrated her maturity by challenging Grisi once more, and in her own theater at Covent Garden. During her seasons in St. Petersburg and her visits to

Berlin, Dresden and Vienna, it must have become clear that the path to her goal would not be through the standard Rossini-Donizetti-Bellini soprano repertoire, but rather in roles, including soprano roles, requiring more than regular features, fluent acting and more or less perfect singing. In Berlin she had added Rachel and Fidelio to her repertoire, as well as Alice and Isabella in *Robert le Diable*. In Dresden she sang Valentine in *Les Huguenots* and in St. Petersburg Lucia and Amina.

In London and Paris in those earlier seasons she had sung Arsaces to Grisi's Semiramis and Romeo to Grisi's Juliet (in Bellini's *I Capuletti ed i Montecchi*). Now, in 1848, while still unable to down Grisi as Amina, she turned the tables with a stunning performance as Valentine in the first complete production of *Les Huguenots* in London. In the following season it was Fidès and in the year after that it was Rachel. This was terra incognita to Grisi, and when she ventured into it she came to grief.

Fidès was the accomplishment that established Pauline Viardot as one of the great singing actresses of operatic history. The role also disclosed a type of matronly heroine especially suited to the mezzo-soprano voice. There have been few singers since Viardot who combined the vocal and histrionic virtuosity to bring off this inordinately exacting role. Among them have been Marianne Brandt (a Viardot pupil), Sofia Scalchi, Ernestine Schumann-Heink and Margarete Matzenauer. The opera itself has been revived from time to time, only as a vehicle for such a singer, or for a tenor capable of making something of the essentially unpalatable John of Leyden.

Simply as a role, however, illuminated as it was by Viardot's voice and person, Fidès is assumed to have influenced Verdi in his design of the gypsy mother, Azucena, in *Il Trovatore*, while Viardot's accomplishment inspired Gounod to compose for her his *Sapho* and Saint-Saëns his *Samson et Dalila*. Thus, in a sense, Viardot, with an assist from Meyerbeer, established the mezzo-soprano as a first lady, capable of carrying a serious opera on her own shoulders. She rounded out her contribution to opera history with the title role of Gluck's *Orfeo*, restored to its original mezzo-soprano *tessitura* by Berlioz in 1859. And there was one more contribution, for some of us the most treasurable of all: Brahms's Alto Rhapsody, written for her, and first sung by her, in Jena on March 3, 1870.

A superior intellect was so important an element in Viardot's art, along with the force of a strong and original personality, that it is difficult to form an adequately precise image of how she sang and how she sounded. One can be certain that some inner radiance and intelligence informed

Pauline Viardot and Marietta Alboni, the two most celebrated mezzo-sopranos of the mid-19th century appeared together as Valentine and Urbain in *Les Huguenots* (below left) in London in 1848. This was before Alboni had assumed those proportions that prompted Rossini to call her "the elephant that swallowed a nightingale." Viardot (above) and Alboni (below right) as they appeared in private life in maturer years.

everything she did. Rellstab, in Berlin in 1843, when she was only twenty-two, conceding certain deficiencies in her voice, said: "But in it one senses a soul, a mind, or, if you like, what one might term the physiognomy of the voice, and it is this individual expression which moves the writer to such an extent." De Musset said: "She abandons herself to inspiration with that easy simplicity which gives everything an air of grandeur. . . . She possesses, in a word, the great secret of artists: before expressing something, she feels it. She does not listen to her voice but to her heart."

She was, in other words, as Malibran, Pasta and Nourrit had been before her, more than just a singer. But still, the voice was her instrument. How did she handle it? Chorley, habitually clinical in his evaluation of singers, is helpful. Speaking of her first appearance in London in 1839, he tells us: "Here and there were tones of an engaging tenderness, but here and there tones of a less winning quality. In spite of an art which has never (at so early an age) been exceeded in amount, it was to be felt that nature had given her a rebel to subdue, not a vassal to command, in her voice. From the first she chose to possess certain upper notes which must needs be fabricated, and which never could be produced without the appearance of effort. By this despotic exercise of will it is possible that her real voice—a limited mezzo-soprano—may have been weakened."

Viardot's natural range would appear to have been the two octaves from B-flat to B-flat, to which she added an upward extension to the high F and an extension downward to the G. In discussing this upward extension, and what it must have cost her, Chorley pauses for a few lines of digressive generalization; and since the problem is still with us—as he foresaw that it would be—it may be well to pause with him.

"Unless the frame be more than usually robust," he wrote, "the process is always more or less perilous. But in these days everyone will sing altissimo—basses where tenors used to disport themselves, tenors in regions as high as those devoted by Handel to his contraltos, while contraltos must now possess themselves of soprano notes, by hook or by crook, and sopranos are compelled to *speak* where formerly they were content to warble. There is no good in lamenting over this tendency; there is small possibility of controlling it; but its influence on the art of singing is hardly to be questioned."

When Viardot returned to London in 1848, even Chorley was so affected by the totality of her performance that he no longer spoke of her singing. He conceded that as Amina she could still not compete with Grisi and Persiani, but her Valentine, he said, "established a reputation different from, and superior to, that of any other prima donna within the compass of these recollections." Of her Fidès, introduced to London in 1849, shortly after the Paris première, he said that it "could set on the scene a homely burgher woman, with only maternal love and devotion to give her interest, and could so harmonize the improbabilities of a violent and gloomy story, and of music too much forced, as to make the world, for a while, accept it for its composer's masterpiece. . . . This originating faculty—in spite of many drawbacks, which are never to be lost sight of by those who admit while they admire—accompanied by great versatility, gives Madame Viardot a place of her own, not to be disputed."

In discussing Viardot's Orpheus, Chorley makes a curious reference to her bravura—curious, that is, to today's operagoer, who would certainly find any extraneous ornamentation in *Orfeo* impertinent and, in an artist of Viardot's vaunted integrity, unthinkable. But not Chorley, and he had his excellent reasons. The reference is to the air "Amour, viens rendre à mon âme," added to the close of the first act by Gluck himself for a production at Frankfurt am Main on April 3, 1764, as part of the festivities celebrating the coronation of Joseph II as Holy Roman Emperor. It was, for almost a century, generally attributed either to Ferdinando Bertoni (1725–1813), who had also composed an *Orfeo* to the same Calzabigi libretto, or to Guadagni, the original Orpheus.

"Her bravura at the end of the first act," Chorley writes, "showed the artist to be supreme in another light—in that grandeur of execution belonging to the old school, rapidly becoming a lost art. The torrents of roulades, the chains of notes, unmeaning in themselves, were flung out with such exactness, limitless volubility, and majesty as to convert what is essentially a commonplace piece of parade into one of those displays of passionate enthusiasm to which nothing less florid could give scope. As affording relief and contrast, they are not merely pardonable, they are defensible; and thus only to be despised by the indolence of the day, which, in obedience to false taste and narrow pedantry, has allowed one essential branch of art to fall into disuse."

Even in 1860, hardly more than a generation removed from the conventional decorative extravagance of Malibran, Pasta and Rubini, there were not many who felt as Chorley did. Viardot was frequently taken to task for the exuberance of her *fioritura*. In Berlin, in 1843, it had been too much even for Sontag, the then Countess Rossi, and in Moscow Viardot was scolded for her ornamentation of the music of Zerlina! But she was, after all, García's daughter, and had been brought up to regard

The British critic H. F. Chorley was ecstatic about Viardot's singing of this cadenza in the aria "Amour viens rendre à mon âme," from the first act of Gluck's *Orfeo*.

fioritura not as frippery but as an honorable and constituent element of expressive singing. Chorley, in assessing florid song, could distinguish between frippery and art. To his sympathetic and experienced ear, Viardot's *fioritura* was art, and his enthusiasm may well have been fired by a foreboding that she would be the last singer of whose virtuosity as much could be said.

The success of Viardot's Orpheus encouraged the directors of the Opéra to try a similar venture with *Alceste*. It was produced in 1861, with some success—and with much editing of the title role to accommodate her now severely limited range. She was only forty, but she was already paying the price for having exacted more from her voice than it could readily give. Her career as an opera singer was over, and her long career as a teacher—first in Baden-Baden, where she met Brahms, and subsequently in Paris—was about to begin.

"Don't do as I did," she used to tell her pupils. "I wanted to sing everything, and I spoilt my voice." She was not the last to hazard limited natural resources and pay the price. Nor was she the only one, either, who could have said, "Well, it was great while it lasted!" She had sung well for twenty-two years. Would another five or ten years have compensated for limited objectives and modest achievements? Probably not. Her career would have been more like that of Marietta Alboni (1826–1894), and less glorious; for Alboni had the finer voice.

3. MARIETTA ALBONI

If a beautiful voice, an immaculate technique and personal charm were all there is to singing, Alboni would be remembered more vividly than Viardot. But perfect singing alone does not guarantee a triumphant career. Those who wrote about Viardot rarely had much to say about her singing as such. The vocal accomplishment was incidental to the projection of a unique and exciting personality. Viardot offered a vocal portrait, or a series of portraits, in which certain flaws were an essential element of composition. Alboni had a flawless and sumptuous voice, managed with a classical virtuosity that she had acquired as Rossini's only pupil. She was an amiable woman, whose youthful beauty survived her subsequent obesity. As is so often true of such virtues, they tended, after the initial delight, to be a bit dull.

This, Chorley speculated, was why she traveled so much. As a singer she was the equal of Grisi, Rubini, Mario, Tamburini and Lablache, with whom she often sang, and probably their superior. The beauty of her voice and the perfection of her vocalism inevitably inspired rapture at a first encounter. But the very predictability of such perfection deprived her appearances of the suspense and tension that lend glamour and fascination to the accomplishments of the more creatively disposed, even those less generously endowed.

And so she wandered the length and breadth of Europe, wherever opera was sung and concerts were given. When Sontag arrived in New York in 1852, Alboni was already there. She returned to London and Paris from time to time, always welcome and always admired, but she never achieved, and probably never sought, the dominant position that made it possible for the "great quartet" to treat cities as citadels.

Like all the great low-voiced females of her generation, the scope of whose endeavors was circumscribed by the paucity of leading roles, she invaded the soprano repertoire. She even attempted Amina in *La Son-nambula.* But she lacked the tenacity and reckless energy required to bring it off. She may also have lacked the upper range. Chorley described her voice as a true contralto, extending two octaves from G to G, meaning, presumably, that this was its *natural* range. She certainly sang higher, and Clara Louise Kellogg, who heard her in London in 1871, when Alboni was in her mid-forties, assures us that she had an easy high C. But more than a high C was required of sopranos in those days, and besides, as every singer knows, it is one thing to be capable of producing the highest notes and quite another to use them habitually. Whether from indolence or good sense, Alboni did most of her singing in her own repertoire, and when, from time to time, she invaded soprano territory, she transposed.

Whether from indolence or good sense, Alboni, like Patti, took conspicuously good care of herself. She knew her assets and their value, and she safeguarded them jealously. She shared Patti's distaste for rehearsal. For singers of their disposition, rehearsal implied a raid on vocal capital. It was singing for nothing, which both Alboni and Patti found repugnant.

"My dear child," Alboni told Calvé, speaking of rehearsals, "they tire you too much nowadays with these ordeals. In my youth I very rarely attended rehearsals, and it saved me much wear and tear. Remember this," she added with a smile, touching her throat with the tips of her fingers, "what comes out here never goes in again. Don't let them work you to death!" She was then seventy, and Calvé had just heard her sing "with as noble and beautiful an organ as in her youth."

What a singer she must have been! When she first appeared in London as Arsaces in 1847, "our public was entranced," said Chorley, "to such spellbound delight as may be enjoyed in the island of lotus-eaters." And he remembered her in *La Gazza ladra,*" singing Pippo to Grisi's Ninetta, and in the duet, "Ebben per mie memorie," having to sing the entire first solo three times over—"not greatly to the satisfaction of the Ninetta." Rossini, who was capable of indelicacy even toward his favorites, called her "the elephant that swallowed a nightingale."

"If anyone were to ask me what piece of vocal music I had heard most perfectly executed in all the years I have been going to the theater," wrote A. de Rovray, the French critic, "I would answer without hesitation: the rondo from *La Cenerentola* as sung by Alboni. Art can go no farther. It is perfection carried to its outermost limits!"

· XIV ·

The New German Singer

LUDWIG SCHNORR · LILLI LEHMANN

OPERA IN Europe in the second half of the nineteenth century disclosed a curious dichotomy.

In Paris, London, Milan and St. Petersburg, well into the 1880s, the repertoire was essentially that of the 1840s plus Verdi, or even of the 1820s plus Meyerbeer. It was almost as if there had never been a composer named Richard Wagner.

It seems incredible today that *The Flying Dutchman*, first produced in 1843, should not have been heard in London until 1870 (in Italian), nor in Paris (in French) until 1897! *Tannhäuser*, produced in 1845, was first heard in London (in Italian) in 1876. After the Paris disaster of 1861 it was not heard there again until 1895 (in French). *Lohengrin*, produced in 1850, was first heard in London in 1875 (in Italian) and in Paris in 1887 (in French). *Tristan und Isolde*, produced in 1865, was first sung in London, by a German company, in 1882 and in Paris (in French) in 1897. The pattern in Italy was similar.

What kept the two worlds apart for so long was the fact that the vocal world outside Germany was dominated by Italian traditions and the Italian language, if no longer by Italian singers; and Wagnerian opera is fully effective only when sung in German. In those days, with such not able exceptions as Roger, Jenny Lind and Pauline Viardot, and the Americans, Minnie Hauk and Emma Albani, only German singers sang in German, and they were not held in high esteem outside Germany. Some were accepted; but in Paris and London, unless they were appearing with a visiting German company, they sang in Italian or French and were judged by Italian standards. What passed for good singing in Germany was thought uncouth elsewhere.

And it was probably pretty bad. When Italian opera had flourished in Germany and Austria during the eighteenth and early nineteenth centuries, it had been sung in Italian by Italians. Some of the early German singers, like Raaff and Ludwig Fischer, had been schooled by Italians or by Italian-trained Germans; but in Germany the *bel canto* traditions thus passed down were insufficiently durable to survive Rossini, Donizetti and Bellini sung in German, or the new vocal requirements levied, and the vocal license encouraged, by Verdi and Meyerbeer operas in translation. The combination of the German language, the German throat and the declamatory fustian of the German theater was too much for an alien tradition so tenuously rooted.

The repertoire of the German opera house, when Wagner had made himself known in the 1840s, was roughly the same as the repertoire of London, Paris, Milan or St. Petersburg, with greater emphasis, of course, on Weber, Spohr, Gluck, Beethoven and Spontini, the last of whom had composed German operas while director of the opera in Berlin. But the singing was not in the same class, and the occasional "guest" appearances of the great stars passing through on their way from Paris and London to St. Petersburg made it plain even to Germans just how bad it was.

The tendency, in Germany, was to blame the modern composers, specifically Meyerbeer, Verdi and Wagner, for an excessively declamatory style and for the employment of an orchestra so large and so loud that singers had to shout or scream in order to be heard. The directors of the German opera houses were also blamed for pandering to the popular taste for noisy operas and forceful singers, the latter thrilling enough so long as their voices had the incisive brilliance of youth, but insupportable once the youthful bloom was gone. An instructive insight into the mid-century state of vocal affairs in Germany is available from a surprising source.

Friedrich Wieck, Schumann's contentious but knowledgeable father-in-law, more usually associated with problems of the piano, denounced the state of vocalism in Germany in an open letter to the managers and directors of German opera houses in the *Fliegende Blätter für Musik* of Leipzig in 1853. He pleaded with the responsible authorities to cease accepting operas whose repeated performance would assure the ruin of voices, especially sopranos and tenors. He begged conductors to assume responsibility for the maintenance and supervision of young voices, suggesting that they begin by learning something about singing themselves. He called for a reduction in the size of the opera orchestra and a lowering of the orchestra pitch, already a full tone higher, he said, than it had been at the beginning of the century. And he proposed, finally, a school for the cultivation of "true tone and voice." To these admonitions he appended some fanciful projections of future opera notices as they might have to be written if the present state of singing in Germany should persist or deteriorate still further. Here is one of them:

"Miss L——'s Elisabeth in *Tannhäuser* was so beautiful and so deeply felt that one gladly forgave her consistent deviation from pitch, the mannered sliding and scooping (by which, to be sure, many songstresses give expression to their emotions under the guidance of emotional teachers), the breathy, throaty, greasy tone, etc. The Venus, too, seemed close to strangulation in her insuperable role; but, that aside, she was lovely to see. It was, nevertheless, a well-rounded, spirited performance. The chorus, to be sure, trying with might and main, but to no avail, to penetrate the orchestral masses, was frequently sharp, insofar as it could be heard at all; but this failing was gladly condoned in view of the surprising enthusiasm that animated all concerned. The Tannhäuser was in especially good voice, and in the first act seemed intent upon exhausting his resources, as if he wished to sacrifice himself to his noble mission as an artist. In the last act, however, there was visible and audible fatigue, with conspicuous departures from exact intonation, compensated by vigorous declamation."

Those who look upon Wagner's operas as anti-vocal might well observe that in just such circumstances he would not want for any number of singers suited perfectly to his requirements. But Wagner never looked upon his own music as anti-vocal. No more than Chorley or Lord Mount-Edgcumbe could he condone shouting, barking, shrieking, bawling, or strangled, out-of-tune singing. He treasured the rounded tone, the sustained vocal line, as much as anyone. But, alone among the German composers, he understood the musical physiognomy, so to speak, of the German language. He recognized the impropriety of German texts set to a pattern of recitative and aria based on Italian or French models. The result, he saw, was only slightly less abominable than French or Italian operas translated into German.

He sensed more acutely than other composers except Mozart the origin of music in the inflections and cadences of speech and poetry, and he knew that the German language required an indigenous declamatory and melodic idiom. The Italians and the French had evolved operatic idioms related to native linguistic idiosyncrasies. The Germans, except in the *Singspiel,* had not. Like English and American composers of serious opera today, they had tended to graft a text to the contours of foreign declamatory and melodic conventions, and what they wrote had the same hybrid characteristics that have always blemished native English and American opera.

One of Wagner's primary tasks, therefore, was to teach German singers to sing German in a new melodic-declamatory idiom derived from the multisyllabic and rarely lyrical German language. The best of the German singers of the mid-century, if only the best, had managed to grasp and master the vocal requirements of *Rienzi, The Flying Dutchman, Tannhäuser* and *Lohengrin.* They had all sung Meyerbeer, Spontini, Auber, Weber and the early Verdi in German, and these early Wagner operas were not so remote from what they had been singing right along.

Wagner's operas were longer and more strenuous, more original and more idiomatic; but they were not out of reach of singers adequately endowed and reasonably well schooled. But in the early 1860s, with *Tristan und Isolde, Die Meistersinger* and *Der Ring des Nibelungen* in preparation, even singers of the capacity of Tichatschek and Schröder-Devrient were no longer adequate.

In this predicament, and with the general state of singing in Germany as abysmal as it was, Wagner's salvation was the unique organization of the German lyric theater. Had he been dependent upon the resources of Covent Garden, the Théâtre-Italien or even the court operas of Vienna, Munich, Dresden and Berlin, he would have had more serious difficulties. But in Germany every sizable community had its own opera house, as is still the case today. Wagner could look beyond the great cities to Braunschweig, Magdeburg, Hannover, Bremen, Frankfurt am Main, Koblenz, Cologne, Darmstadt, Detmold, Mannheim, Essen, Nuremberg, Coburg, Stuttgart, Mainz, Wiesbaden, and others.

1. LUDWIG SCHNORR

The standard of performance in these theaters might be low, and it probably was. But some of the singers were young and promising, not set irrevocably in old habits of vocalism and stage deportment. Nor were the young singers entirely unfamiliar with Wagner. The early operas were all in repertoire. For the singers they represented the indispensable middle ground between *Les Huguenots, Il Trovatore* or *Faust* and the Wagner of *Tristan und Isolde* and *Der Ring des Nibelungen*. As early as 1856 Tichatschek had called Wagner's attention to a young tenor in Karlsruhe named Ludwig Schnorr von Carolsfeld, then only twenty years old. Wagner heard him as Lohengrin in 1862, and three years later Schnorr became the first Tristan.

That was in Munich on June 10, 1865. Schnorr was then engaged at the opera in Dresden, but the personal intervention of King Ludwig of Bavaria with the King of Saxony had procured his leave of absence for April, May and June. The tenor and his wife, Malvina Garrigues (a German soprano of French Huguenot descent), who was to be the first Isolde, had arrived in Munich on April 5, and rehearsals began immediately. From April 10 onward, Ernest Newman tells us in *The Life of Richard Wagner*, there were instrumental rehearsals of one kind or another in the Residenztheater under Hans von Bülow every morning and a piano rehearsal at Wagner's house every evening. The last scheduled rehearsal, a private performance before the king and some six hundred guests, took place on May 11. An extra and private rehearsal was held on May 13.

The first public performance was scheduled for May 15, but had to be postponed because of Malvina's hoarseness. She and Schnorr went to Bad Reichenhall on the Austrian border for her recuperation. Wagner urged Schnorr to return to Munich for performances of *The Flying Dutchman* and *Tannhäuser* on May 28 and June 1, but Schnorr refused to leave his wife. They returned to Munich on June 6. Rehearsals were held on the three following days. After the première on June 10, there were additional performances on June 13, 19 and 30.

Schnorr was given an extension of his leave from Dresden to sing Erik in *The Flying Dutchman* on July 9. At a concert under Wagner's direction on July 12 he sang the two big tenor scenes from the first act of *Siegfried*; then "Siegmund's Love Song" from the first act of *Die Walküre*, and he participated in the closing scene from *Das Rheingold* and the scene of Walther before the mastersingers from the first act of *Die Meistersinger*. On July 13 he and Malvina returned to Dresden. On July 15 he took part in a rehearsal of *Don Giovanni*. He should have sung the public performance the next day, but he was seized with a rheumatic fever, and on July 21 he suffered a stroke and died, aged twenty-nine.

Five hours before his death, Newman tells us, he had, in his delirium, burst into a paroxysm of song. His last words were: "Farewell, Siegfried! Console my Richard!" Wagner, after returning to Munich from the

A special niche in any vocal hall of fame should be reserved for Ludwig Schnorr (below right) and his wife, Malvina Garrigues (below left), the first Tristan and the first Isolde. They are shown (above) at a rehearsal for the first production in Munich in 1865. Schnorr was only 29, and he died six weeks later.

funeral, wrote to King Ludwig: "He was a fine, noble being, consecrated to me, faithful to me. The richly gifted *artist* became a theater singer to be of service to me, to be able to further my work. My King, in this singer I have lost much."

There were those who held that Wagner had killed him: an oversimplification, to be sure, even as a figure of speech. But any reader who has followed attentively Schnorr's schedule between April 5 and his death fifteen weeks later will agree that Wagner's requirements were, if not murderous, certainly monstrous. There may have been no way of easing the burden of rehearsals in the preparation of a work so difficult and so novel. But no one who has heard a performance of *Tristan und Isolde* can find Wagner's plea that Schnorr interrupt his short vacation at the end of May and return to Munich to sing Tannhäuser and Erik anything but outrageous, not to mention the gratuitous supplementary performance of *The Flying Dutchman* and the concert after the final *Tristan und Isolde* on June 30.

But Wagner's behavior toward others, including those closest to him, and to whom he owed the most, was almost habitually outrageous. On the very day when rehearsals for *Tristan und Isolde* began, under von Bülow's direction, as only one example, Cosima, then still married to von Bülow, presented her husband with Wagner's daughter. She was named, appropriately, Isolde. But it was proof of Wagner's unique importance that even those thus grievously injured never deserted him or lost heart in his cause. Certainly Schnorr never complained, nor suggested that he felt himself put upon.

There was simply something about Wagner that inspired selfless dedication and unmeasured self-sacrifice. Schnorr was not the only singer who gave of his time, his voice and his self to demonstrate, under the composer's guidance, that Wagner's music dramas could be sung, and sound beautifully when sung well. One thinks of Amalie Materna, the first Brünnhilde and the first Kundry; of Franz Betz, the first Hans Sachs and the first Wotan and Wanderer; of Georg Unger, the first Siegfried; of Albert Niemann, the first Siegmund; of Hermann Winckelmann, the first Parsifal; and of Emil Scaria, the first Gurnemanz. These roles are challenging enough even today for singers aided by example. What they entailed for those who created them, who had neither an established tradition nor aural memory to support their enterprise, is difficult to imagine.

But one feels that Schnorr's was the supreme achievement, that it was his example that made possible, or at least enhanced, the accomplishments of others. Clearly, he was more than just a singer. Voice he had, to be sure. It was described at the time as having the baritone quality ever characteristic of the great dramatic tenors. It was sonorous and brilliant. Robert Proelss, historian of the Dresden theater, remembered it as "curiously elegiac, somewhat veiled," but flashing out triumphantly when brightness was required, "like the sun breaking through passing clouds." Despite pathological corpulence, he was a good actor. But beyond all that he was also a cultivated musician, an excellent pianist, a poet and a man of uncommon artistic sensibility, inherited, no doubt, from his father, Julius Schnorr von Carolsfeld, a reputable painter.

It was this providential combination of vocal endowment, intelligence and fine personal attributes that made his accomplishment possible. His death, immediately following the fulfillment of his mission, and especially the Tristanesque circumstances—the delirious paroxysms of song upon his deathbed and the noble "Farewell, Siegfried! Console my Richard!"—suggest a kind of poetic or dramatic inevitability, as if the creation of Tristan, requiring more than could be expected of any man, had called down a fatal vengeance upon the youth who had defied and dared and prevailed. He who had given himself heart and soul to Wagner was vouchsafed a Wagnerian end.

For those who had been caught up for weeks and months in the exaltation of *Tristan und Isolde,* Schnorr's death may well have seemed the ultimate catastrophe in a drama more prodigious even than *Tristan und Isolde.* The music drama itself, once performed, could be performed again and again, as it has been for a century. But the drama of composition, rehearsal and production could never be repeated. And now the memory of the first radiant Tristan could not be blemished by subsequent performances less exalted and less exultant, nor the Tristan voice be soiled by wear and age.

Nor would the first Isolde ever sing the part again—or anything else. Malvina, too, was granted a real-life Wagnerian role, but it was closer to the sordid substance of *Der Ring des Nibelungen* than to the transfiguration of *Tristan und Isolde.* Through a series of misadventures arising from messages she believed herself to be receiving from her departed husband, she became entangled in the Wagner-Cosima-von Bülow triangle, and responded to Wagner's and Cosima's persecution by exposing to King Ludwig the intimacy of Wagner's relationship with von Bülow's wife, with consequences disastrous for all concerned.

Malvina was, in any case, nearing the end of her career. Indeed, she had thought it ended when her husband moved from Karlsruhe to Dresden in 1860. She was ten years older than he, and with his call to Dresden she relinquished her contract at Karlsruhe to devote herself to his career. Before her creation of the first Isolde she had been a German singer of no great celebrity. It is conceivable that a greater singer might have been unable to adapt herself so readily to the guidance and requirements of Wagner and von Bülow. Certainly the tension of that first production inspired performances beyond the normal capacity of the participants, and we have von Bülow's word for it that the accomplishment not only of Schnorr, but also of his wife, was "incredible!"

However tempting it may have been even for Wagner to see in Schnorr's death a poetic sublimation, the loss of this uniquely gifted tenor was serious, and it was, in Wagner's time, never made good. He had had Schnorr in mind as his Siegfried (hence, presumably, Schnorr's dying "Farewell, Siegfried," although it may have been addressed to King Ludwig), and Schnorr was, even in 1865, acquainted with much of Siegfried's music. Albert Niemann, five years older than Schnorr, and the first Siegmund, who had been the Tannhäuser of the Paris disaster in 1861 and would later be a memorable if somewhat senior Tristan, volunteered to sing the Siegfried of Götterdämmerung, but in 1876 he was forty-five, and Wagner decided upon Unger, a promising tenor from Mannheim, to sing both Siegfrieds. He later regretted not having accepted Niemann's offer.

From the point of view of the vocal historian, however, Wagner's problems in casting Der Ring des Nibelungen for Bayreuth in 1876 are incidental. The production of Tristan und Isolde in Munich, followed by Die Meistersinger in 1868, Das Rheingold in 1869 and Die Walküre in 1870, had established precedents and laid the foundations for a young tradition for singing Wagner. What remained to be proved was that anyone could sing Wagner consistently and still be able to sing Italian and French opera in a manner tolerable to non-German ears.

2. LILLI LEHMANN

It would be too much to say that any one singer alone had bridged this dichotomy. It required initiatives and breakthroughs from both sides. Decisive were the initiative and the accomplishments of Jean and

Édouard de Reszke in undertaking the great Wagnerian tenor and bass-baritone roles in German, if not in Germany, toward the close of illustrious careers in the French and Italian repertoire of Paris, London, Chicago and New York. Before them, and working from the other side of the divide, so to speak, was the German soprano Lilli Lehmann (1848–1929), whose accomplishments are documented indelibly in the records of the Metropolitan Opera Association for the season of 1891–92.

The Metropolitan had been since 1884—under the musical direction of Leopold Damrosch, and then of Anton Seidl and Walter Damrosch—a transplanted German opera house, the repertoire indistinguishable from that of any major German house, everything sung in German, and the roster reading like a German telephone book. As the soprano star of this company Lehmann had already made a great name for herself as all three Brünnhildes, Isolde, Venus, Marguerite, Fidelio, Rachel, Donna Anna, Aida, Norma and Carmen. Now, in the season of 1891–92, with a new international company drawn from the vocal elite of Paris and London singing the Paris-London repertoire of that time, Lilli Lehmann sang the Leonora of *Il Trovatore,* Norma, Aida, Bertha (in *Le Prophète*) and Donna Anna, all in Italian. She even sang the Leonore of *Fidelio* in Italian!

It was a tour de force, and characteristic of a woman for whom the tour de force was a way of life. She simply reveled in the accomplishment of the impossible; she accepted challenges with the self-destructive zest of a Malibran, with the advantage that hers was a more resilient constitution. Lehmann could be felled from time to time, as she was, not surprisingly, toward the end of that 1891–92 season, but her recuperative powers were as inexhaustible as her energy and ambition. She continued to sing in the United States, England, France and Germany for many more seasons, making her final operatic appearance as Isolde in Vienna in 1909 at the age of sixty. She went on to sing *Lieder* recitals past the age of seventy, and died in 1929, a few months before her eighty-first birthday.

Lilli Lehmann's repertoire included a hundred and seventy roles in a hundred and nineteen operas in German, Italian and French. They ranged from Suppé and Offenbach to Wagner and Meyerbeer, from Lucia, Lucrezia Borgia and Norma to Aida and Isolde. On tour in the United States with *Der Ring des Nibelungen* in 1889 she sang the three Brünnhildes every week for eight weeks, usually with a fourth major role added on Saturday evenings. At the Bayreuth Festival of 1896 she sang the Brünnhildes just a few days after having an egg-sized abscess removed from an ear. At the Metropolitan on January 27, 1899, she substituted for the indisposed Marie Brema as Fricka in a performance of *Das Rhein-gold*, taking over at four o'clock on the afternoon of the performance a part that she had never sung before. Bispham, who sang the Alberich in that performance, tells the story:

"On this occasion the great artist needed not only the prompter [she normally disdained any prompting] but all the prompting she could get, and every help was given her to get her through the evening as comfortably as possible. One or another of the assistant conductors stood ready to give the word at the least sign of trouble, to whichever side of the stage she moved. Her sister Marie [a singer of only slightly less brilliant accomplishments than Lilli] was rendering a similar service, and to her Madame Lehmann chiefly looked. The sister told me later that Lilli had sung in *Der Ring* so often and in so many parts that she was already somewhat familiar with the role; but let me say that there is not one artist in a thousand, perhaps not another in the world, physically, nervously, mentally and musically able to perform such a feat, or, if able to perform it, willing to do so to help another artist and assist the management in its duty to the public."

The circumstances of her very last appearance could not have been more appropriate. She had just concluded a guest engagement in Vienna, and was attending a performance of *Tristan und Isolde* in Gustav Mahler's box. A few minutes before the third act was to begin, the Isolde, Anna von Mildenburg (later Bahr-Mildenburg, the teacher of Lauritz Melchior), became hoarse and could not continue. Lehmann, who had not sung the part in four years, placed herself at Mahler's disposal, changed quickly into von Mildenburg's costume and finished the performance. Thus one came, she recalled in her memoirs, "to the 'Liebesklage' and 'Liebestod,' nor could one say that it had been unpleasant." For Lehmann, said Geraldine Farrar, for many years her pupil, "will was power."

Had her will been less powerful, she would hardly have become a singer and a personality of such eminence. The voice itself was not of the exceptional kind that can make unexceptional individuals sound like great singers. Her accomplishment was rather the product of an excellent instrument disciplined in the service of intelligence and industry and matured in a long apprenticeship. Had she not been blessed with an artistic sensibility extending far beyond the conventional attitudes of

OPERA NEWS

Among the most illustrious inhabitants of Valhalla were Amalie Materna (above left), the Brünnhilde of the first production of *Der Ring des Nibelungen* at Bayreuth and the first Kundry; and Franz Betz (above right), the first Bayreuth Wotan and Wanderer. He was also the first Hans Sachs and the first Kurvenal.

Lilli Lehmann's roles included Venus (below center), and Leonore (below left) in *Fidelio*. A Lehmannesque motto under the picture says: "Strive not for the noisy plaudits of the crowd but for the deepest insight and the utmost perfection." Albert Niemann was the first Bayreuth Siegmund, one of the greatest of all Tristans, and America's first (below right). (Opposite), he is shown with Lilli Lehmann when their singing days were behind them.

OPERA NEWS   AUTHOR'S COLLECTION

the German theater, and catholic enough to embrace Wagner without rejecting Donizetti and Bellini, or had she been a woman of less adventurous and determined disposition, she would have had a comfortable career as a dependable fixture of a leading German opera house—as, indeed, her sister did in Vienna.

Like so many earlier prima donnas, she was born and brought up in the theater. Both her parents were singers, and her mother, who seems to have been her principal teacher, later became a harpist in the orchestra of the German opera at Prague. Lilli made her debut there as the First Boy in *The Magic Flute* on October 20, 1865, a month before her seventeenth birthday. At a second performance two weeks later, the Pamina became hysterical following a row with the conductor, and Lilli, ready then as she would be later for any emergency, assumed the role.

She was engaged at Danzig, then Leipzig and finally Berlin, singing a wide variety of parts in the lyric and coloratura categories, and always with distinction and success. But like Kirsten Flagstad, half a century later, she was slow to arrive at absolute stardom. At Bayreuth, in 1876, when *Der Ring des Nibelungen* was first performed, Lehmann, then already just short of twenty-eight, sang only a Rhinemaiden and a Valkyrie. Her versatility may well have held her back. She was always ready for any contingency and any role; and, as so often happens with those who are ever ready and willing to serve, she came to be taken for granted.

Both her voice and her physical frame were light, and the management of the opera at Berlin was either unable or unwilling to discern the potentialities of which she herself was confident. It was probably all for the best. The voice was never damaged by premature exposure to roles of excessive weight, and when the time for weighty roles was at hand, she could manage them with such virtuosity and resourcefulness that there was never a suggestion of vocal inadequacy or vocal abuse. An example of the intelligent way she went about extending its capacity is provided in her own description of how she prepared for her first Isolde —in London in 1884, "singing every phrase hundreds of times, and then each act through from beginning to end three or four times running, gradually increasing my physical and vocal endurance." The suggestion of forging is encouraged by James Huneker's reference to her "steel-blue tones."

And she acknowledged a debt to Minnie Hauk, who was a member of the Berlin company from 1874 to 1877. Lehmann did not like Hauk, and had a generally low opinion of her work, but she never forgot her accomplishment in an unsuccessful production of Delibes's *Le Roi l'a dit*. As little as she had been impressed by Hauk in previous roles, the more she found to admire now. "What left the public cold," she remembered in *Mein Weg*, "was artistically much more resourcefully worked out than anything else she had done. The guttural quality of her lower voice was not disagreeable, as it otherwise was, and her singing and acting had more simplicity and dignity. It suddenly occurred to me that it is not necessary to roar; that one could sing well even with little voice if the sound were noble; that it was foolish, merely for the sake of competitive effort, to be led into exorbitant demands on one's strength by large auditoriums and the big voices of one's colleagues; that 'beauty' remains beautiful under all circumstances, even when recognized as such only by a few. I never forgot this intelligence."

Lilli Lehmann's career resembled Flagstad's in more ways than one. Not only did each begin as a light soprano, singing even in light opera and operetta, and moving only gradually into heavier and more demanding parts; they each first achieved full stature and recognition in America. But Flagstad was far from matching Lehmann's first New York season in 1885–86, when, in just over three months, Lehmann sang Carmen, Bertha (in *Le Prophète*), the Brünnhilde of *Die Walküre*, Sulamith (in Goldmark's *Queen of Sheba*), Venus, Irene (in *Rienzi*) and Marguerite (in *Faust*).

It is unlikely that Lehmann, even in her best years, ever commanded the glorious sound, the ability to open vocal floodgates, that so distinguished Flagstad from any other dramatic soprano of this century, or that she could call upon similar vocal resources. "Nature," said Hanslick, "denied her penetrating strength and sumptuousness of voice, and thus deprived her of the strongest, most immediate means of passionate communication, but it endowed her with a personality predestined not only for the stage, but particularly for tragic and noble roles."

As much could not be said so categorically of Flagstad, who could be phlegmatic on the stage as well as off. Flagstad could be inspired, to be sure, and then she was incomparable. But Lehmann was predictable. In her, said Hanslick, "refined artistic schooling outweighs strong immediacy of feeling. Her creations do not represent the improvisations of a great natural force; they are rather products of a superior mind which finds its way to the core of every interpretive problem and discloses the inner treasure in unblemished perfection."

This was an evaluation in which Lehmann herself would have been the first to concur. The cut of her features, as reflected in her photographs, does not suggest a personality ever troubled by ambivalence, indecision or doubt, least of all about her own worth. Prima donnas have rarely been noted for modesty, and in a woman of Lehmann's attainments and obvious awareness of them, modesty must have seemed an affectation. But she had a habit of insisting on her infallibility, of throwing it around, so to speak, in a way that was often exasperating to others and sometimes embarrassing to herself.

In her were concentrated all the familiar German virtues: industry, self-discipline, self-denial, conscientiousness, dependability, thoroughness, earnestness, responsibility, dedication and high idealism. Such an abundance of virtues can be tedious, and must have been so in her case; for she found it not only admirable but also exemplary, and she was impatient with the less gifted and less virtuous. She could be complacent, employing in her memoirs such terms as "musicians of our caliber" and "an elite circle," including herself, of course. And she lists illustrious casts of which she was a principal member, stooping to that most repugnant of cozy German euphemisms, *und meine Wenigkeit* (and my insignificant self). She could be rude, and she often was.

When Lillian Nordica sang Elsa at Bayreuth in 1894, for example, she approached Lehmann at a reception given by Cosima at the Villa Wahnfried and asked if she might call on her. Lehmann's response was hardly gracious. "I am not," she said, "taking any pupils this season." Nordica's biographer, Ira Glackens, paid her back, posthumously, by telling how Lehmann had been abandoned at a lonely railroad station in the wilds of America because she thought she knew more about connections than the train conductor. "*Esel!*" (ass!), she had said to the train conductor as she stepped down, timetable in hand, to await a connecting train that would never appear.

The story is given credibility by another, told by Lehmann herself in *Mein Weg*. In Toronto she was singing with an elderly conductor who, in her words, "knew so little about Mozart scores that after my *Entführung* aria, and in front of the committee, I called him, in English, to be sure, a veritable ass. He not only did not take it amiss; he begged my pardon. It was not very ladylike, I know, but I had the feeling that I should say it." She seems to have been fond of the term.

It should not be inferred that she was merely a bully. She challenged the biggest and most ferocious game. After her first successful season in New York she requested an extension of her leave from the opera in

Berlin. It might have been granted had she not accompanied the request with a threat to remain in America if it were refused. The leave was denied, and she made good the threat. As a consequence she was barred from German theaters for several years. And she lost her pension. In Bayreuth she crossed swords with the almighty Cosima, presuming to know more than Frau Wagner about certain details of *Der Ring des Nibelungen* as they had been executed in 1876, which she probably did.

Geraldine Farrar visited Lehmann in Salzburg shortly after the war, and Lehmann told her of a recent revival of *Tannhäuser* in Berlin. After the second act, a veteran critic had asked her opinion of the performance for publication. "With the air of an empress," as Farrar relays the story in *Such Sweet Compulsion*, "she rose, drew her cloak about shoulders, still statuesque, and announced, in no whispered undertones—as she made her way out—'Say that Lilli Lehmann leaves her loge in disgust at the travesty they call Art in this opera house!'"

Nor, for all her devotion and dedication to Wagner, was Lehmann a docile disciple. She could rationalize her singing of Bellini by citing Wagner's own early admiration for the composer of *Norma*, but Wagner's sanction was never extended to Donizetti, and not even his feelings about Bellini were shared by his militant following. It took courage and independence of mind and spirit for a great Isolde and Brünnhilde to sing not only Norma but also Lucia and Lucrezia Borgia.

To say that Lilli Lehmann bridged once and for all time—and for all singers—the disparity between the German and the non-German lyric theater would be to overstate the case. In both Italy and France the welcome extended to German opera in German has been hesitant, and to this day it is reserved for festival occasions and entrusted largely to the ensembles of German theaters or to German companies especially recruited for specific engagements. Italian singers have been reluctant or unable to sing in German, and French singers, with some exceptions, have been hardly more eager or flexible. Most adaptable of all have been the Americans, in a tradition established half a century ago in the careers of such splendid and versatile artists as Emma Albani, Minnie Hauk, Lillian Nordica, Olive Fremstad, Edyth Walker, Louise Homer, Emma Eames, Geraldine Farrar, Florence Easton, David Bispham and Clarence Whitehill. Two of these—appropriately, Farrar and Fremstad—were Lehmann pupils.

But many German singers, following the precedent set by Lehmann, have been less prone than their French and Italian colleagues to restrict their careers to the native repertoire or the native language. Even before Lehmann there had been Teresa Stolz and Maria Waldmann, the Aida and Amneris of the Milan, Naples and Paris premières of *Aida*, who sang the soprano and alto solos in Verdi's *Requiem* for the first time in Milan, Paris, London and Vienna. And there was Gabrielle Krauss, a Viennese pupil of Mathilde Marchesi, who was the Aida of the first Paris performance of *Aida* in French. But they were not Wagnerian sopranos.

Lehmann's distinction was in taking the big Wagnerian repertoire abroad and breaking out of it—and out of German. Among those who followed her example were Johanna Gadski, Milka Ternina, Ernestine Schumann-Heink, Emmy Destinn, Margarete Matzenauer, Frieda Hempel, Editha Fleischer, Maria Jeritza, Maria Müller and Elisabeth Rethberg among the ladies, and Leo Slezak, Karl Jörn and Hermann Jadlowker among the men, this list including some eastern Europeans brought up in the German theater.

The institution of so-called German, French and Italian wings in major English and American houses persisted until just before the last war, but this very coexistence in a single house was evidence that the earlier dichotomy was being bridged, if not ultimately healed. In the past twenty years modern air travel has given a new incentive to linguistic accomplishment and to the mastery of diverse idioms. The singer, today, who confines himself to one language and one repertoire is a provincial.

There are not many—probably not any—modern singers who can approach Lilli Lehmann's versatility and operatic universality. As an artist and as a personage she remains unexampled.

"There will be no replica of this daughter of Wotan in our time," said Farrar of her passing in 1929. "The gods received their own."

XV

Some Gentlemen of the Last "Golden Age"

MAUREL · TAMAGNO · DE RESZKE

THE LAST "golden age" may well have been the most golden of them all. It was certainly the most diversified.

The Rossini-Donizetti-Bellini repertoire was still sung, and it was sung well, although some of the old standbys stood no more. Meyerbeer's output had been augmented by *Le Prophète* and *L'Africaine*. The tradition of florid song had been nourished, not by Italian composers, curiously, but by the French, however anemically, in the operas of Gounod, Thomas, Delibes and Massenet. Bizet, with *Carmen*, had anticipated the *verismo* operas of the later Italians by a generation. Verdi's already substantial contribution had been crowned by *Aida*, *Otello* and *Falstaff*. Wagner's production was complete, and even his last works were making their way into the repertoire around the world. And Richard Strauss was in the offing.

Reviewing the names of the great singers of this period, one is struck immediately by a circumstance that distinguishes it from any other "golden age": the number and the celebrity of the males. The explanation is implicit in the repertoire. Opera composers of all pertinent nationalities had, throughout the century, sought increasingly to achieve a balanced casting. As they came to rely less on floridity, apparently acknowledging florid song to be unsuited to male voices, they developed a kind of vocal writing tailored to the masculine characteristics of wide-ranged tenors, baritones and basses. The new operas of Meyerbeer, Verdi and Wagner required a manly kind of singing appropriate to virile heroes and villains, and audible against big orchestras in big houses.

The male singer, not surprisingly in such circumstances, began to achieve parity of a kind with the female as a leading personality in the opera world and as an attraction at the box office. Beginning with Nourrit, Rubini and Duprez among the tenors, and with Tamburini and Lablache among the lower voices, and continuing through Mario, Tamberlik and Tichatschek, the male singer invaded, although he never occupied exclusively, what had, with the disappearance of the castrati, threatened to become a female realm, the one area in music where masculine strength and masculine dexterity, decisive in the playing of instruments, had not placed the female at a competitive disadvantage.

First Meyerbeer, and then Verdi, offered the male, including the lower-voiced male—opportunities unimagined by the composers of *opera seria*, and anticipated only haphazardly by Rossini, Donizetti and Bellini. The three tenors of Rossini's *Otello* constituted an isolated phenomenon, attributable, probably, to the providential availability of extraordinary virtuoso tenors. That the title role was subsequently also sung by female sopranos is proof that the inevitability of a male hero's being represented by a male singer with a masculine voice had not yet become obvious.

But the next two decades would see the tenor repertoire enriched by Arnold (in *William Tell*), Robert (in *Robert le Diable*), Éléazar (in *La Juive*), Masaniello (in *La Muette de Portici*), Edgardo (in *Lucia*), Pollione (in *Norma*) and Raoul (in *Les Huguenots*). Sopranos and mezzo-sopranos were unthinkable in such parts, and whoever conceived the idea of casting Pisaroni as Arnold for the Italian première of *William Tell* either could not have had his wits about him or knew nothing of the opera. The lower voices came into their own with William Tell and the Cardinal in *La Juive*, among others. And Meyerbeer, with the roles of St. Bris, Marcel and de Nevers in *Les Huguenots*, left an inheritance upon which basses and baritones would draw for nearly a century.

Verdi's contributions are more familiar to contemporary operagoers, and need not be noted beyond emphasizing his services to the lower voices in such fat roles as Nebuchadnezzar, Rigoletto, Macbeth, Simon Boccanegra, King Philip, Posa, the Grand Inquisitor, Iago and Falstaff. French composers followed suit with Mephistopheles, Hamlet, Escamillo, Herod, Athanaël, Don Quixote and Sancho Panza.

That French opera flourished then as never before or since explains the presence of so many Frenchmen, particularly basses and baritones, among the great singers of that last "golden age." French opera, at its best, calls for just those attributes that have commonly distinguished the finest French singers from all others—elegance of bearing and manner,

The last "golden age" was rich in French basses and baritones. Two of the finest were Pol Plançon (above), a vocal virtuoso of the kind one imagines Tamburini to have been, and Édouard de Reszke. Shaw said of de Reszke's Mephistopheles (left) that "the most timid child would climb straight up on his knee and demand to be shown how a watch opens when blown on."

sophisticated costuming, polished diction, declamatory finesse, subtlety of phrase, nuance and gesture.

These were requirements made to order for such actor-singers as Jean Lassalle, Victor Maurel, Pol Plançon, Maurice Renaud, Jean-François Delmas, Marcel Journet and Leon Rothier, all men of wide cultivation and profound students of singing and acting. They were continuing a tradition established by Nicolas Levasseur (1791–1871), Halévy's first Cardinal in *La Juive* and Meyerbeer's first Bertram in *Robert le Diable;* by Jean-Baptiste Faure (1830–1914), the most celebrated Mephistopheles of his time, and by Lucien Fugère (1848–1935), whose voice may be heard on records he made on his eightieth and eighty-second birthdays.

1. VICTOR MAUREL

Among these fine French basses and baritones of the last "golden age," the most illustrious was Victor Maurel (1848–1923), memorable forever as Verdi's first Iago and Falstaff, as the first Tonio and as the Simon Boccanegra of Verdi's revision of 1881. Others among them were better singers. Lassalle was often taken to task for overdependence upon a uniquely beautiful voice. Plançon, a better actor than Lassalle, rejoiced in a vocal virtuosity probably unmatched among the lower voices since Tamburini, and certainly unapproached by any subsequent basses or baritones.

It was not just that Maurel had created Iago, Falstaff and Tonio. Other baritones could have assumed these roles, just as scores of baritones have assumed them since Maurel's time, and just as there have been other Othellos than Tamagno. It was rather the concentration in Victor Maurel of certain rare attributes of intelligence, scholarship, insight and artistic integrity, combined with exceptional gifts and accomplishments as singer and actor, that predestined him for these historic assignments.

The indelible association of the names of Tamagno and Maurel with the roles of Othello and Iago is a curious phenomenon. No other roles in the opera repertoire are so identified with their creators. Thousands of opera enthusiasts know about Tamagno and Maurel who could not identify the first Manrico, the first Radames, the first Azucena, the first Tristan, the first Parsifal, or even the first Desdemona. It has more commonly been subsequent artists whose impersonations have earned them an exclusive or preeminent identification with certain roles.

We associate Feodor Chaliapin with Boris, for instance, although Chaliapin was not quite a year old when *Boris Godounov* was first performed on February 8, 1874. Leonore in *Fidelio* had to wait some fifteen years for Schröder-Devrient. We think of Maria Jeritza or Eva Turner as Turandot, although the role was created by Rosa Raisa, and of Giacomo Lauri-Volpi as Calaf, although the first Calaf was Miguel Fleta. Nor was Antonio Scotti the first Scarpia, nor Richard Mayr the first Baron Ochs, nor Lotte Lehmann the first Marschallin.

But those who come afterward have an example to depart from, to correct, or to improve upon. Those are the most admirable and the most memorable who, as originators of operatic roles, achieve characterizations so inevitable that they will live forever in the work of their successors, as with Mary Garden's Mélisande—and with the Othello of Tamagno and the Iago of Maurel. It speaks for what must have been the superb accomplishments of these two singing actors in roles difficult beyond all others in the sustained projection and articulation of subtle psychological insinuations and pressures.

No one was more aware of their excellence than Verdi. It was his own theater intelligence that had dictated their selection in the first place, but he did not much relish their subsequent harvest of celebrity. It injured his pride in his own achievement. When *Otello* was given successfully in Brescia six months after the Milan première with other singers, Verdi wrote to Franco Faccio, the conductor: "Well, well, so *Otello* is making out without the great singers who *created* the principal roles. I was so used to hearing of their glory that I thought *Otello* was ascribable to them alone. You are stripping me of an illusion when you say that the Moor can go over without benefit of stars."

This was but a reflection of a changing relationship between composers and singers. We have observed Handel and Hasse writing what they thought would be most congenial to their singers. We have seen Mozart catering to the capacities and tastes of Cavalieri, Raaff and Fischer. We have read of Rossini's horrified astonishment at Velluti's extravagance, but also of Bellini and Rubini working side by side to produce arias tailored to that extraordinary tenor's singular vocalism. We have learned what Berlioz thought of Duprez.

Now we find Wagner, in a letter cited by Newman, saying: "I do not know . . . an actor-singer of whom I could expect a proper realization of my dramatic figures unless I had taught him everything bar by bar and phrase by phrase." And we hear Verdi echoing the sentiment in a letter to Giulio Ricordi, his publisher: "I do not admit that either singers or conductors are capable of creating: this is a notion that leads to the abyss."

Victor Maurel was the first Tonio, Falstaff, and Iago (above right). The *Pagliacci* Prologue was added to the opera to accommodate him. Maurel's expression (above left) reflects what Shaw called his "restless cerebration."

Maurice Renaud (right) was a great French baritone singing actor in the Maurel tradition.

Let us grant that Wagner and Verdi had earned the right to insist upon a composer's prerogatives to the exclusion of all others'. But they set a hazardous example. We have looked into the abyss in our own century, and we were not led to it by singers—least of all by Maurel.

Maurel had, for a singer, curious notions about what opera should be, and about a singer's responsibilities; and they were not notions that any composer could fault who was serious about his calling. Maurel believed, for example, that there was more to opera than singing, and more to singing than a beautiful, big, exciting sound. He thought of the voice as a means of characterization, and he prided himself on his ability to color his own voice according to the requirements of the role and the situation. The voice was, in his view, just another element, along with makeup, costume, posture, bearing, movement, gesture and facial expression, in the projection of character and the illustration of that character's reactions to stress.

One speaks of "illustration" advisedly; for Maurel's artistic orientation was primarily pictorial. His father had been an architect, and Maurel himself, born in Marseille, had been schooled in architecture at the École des Arts et Métiers at Aix-en-Provence before the discovery of an extraordinary voice persuaded him to abandon architecture for music. At one brief period of his career, when he was at odds with the management of the Opéra in Paris, he abandoned singing to take up painting. And long after his singing days were over, he designed the sets for the Metropolitan's production of Gounod's *Mireille* in the season of 1918–19.

His sense of the pictorial is reflected in the story of his costuming of the role of Tonio, as related by Bispham. Maurel had complained about the lack of solo opportunities for Tonio, and suggested a prologue to be sung before the curtain. Leoncavallo complied with the now rather more than familiar war-horse. It had been Maurel's intention to sing it before the curtain in evening dress, but he found the conventional black and white insufficiently effective. He designed, instead, a clown's costume, which he then wore throughout the performance. Bispham disagreed with this conclusion, and did sing the Prologue in white tie and tails.

Among those who found Maurel's characterizations more pictorial than dramatic was Shaw, ever the first to detect a great artist's flaws while other critics were being distracted by his virtues. Of Maurel's Don Giovanni, for instance, Shaw observed: "Don Juan may be as handsome, as irresistible, as adroit, as unscrupulous, as brave as you please, but the one thing that is not to be tolerated is that he should consciously parade these qualities as if they were elaborate accomplishments instead of his natural parts. And this is exactly where Maurel failed. He gave us a description of Don Juan rather than an impersonation of him. The confident smile, the heroic gesture, the splendid dress, even the intentionally seductive vocal inflexion which made a success of 'Là, ci darem la mano,' were all more or less artificial. A Don Juan who is continually aiming at being Don Juan may excite our admiration by the skill with which he does it; but he cannot convince us that he is the real man."

Shaw had similar reservations even about Maurel's Iago, as to both his acting and his conception of the part. He noted "the excessive descriptiveness which is the fault of Maurel's method, resulting in a tendency to be illustrative rather than impersonative"; and about his conception of the role Shaw said:

"The chief objection to Maurel's Iago is that it is not Iago at all, but rather the Caesar Borgia of romance. As far as it is human, it is a portrait of a distinguished officer, one who would not be passed over for Cassio when he was expecting his step [promotion]. I am aware that this view of him falls in with the current impression in artistic circles that Iago was a very fine fellow. But in circles wherein men have to take one another seriously, there will not be much difference of opinion as to the fact that Iago must have been an ingrained blackguard and consequently an (if I may use a slightly Germanic adjective) obviously-to-everyone-but-himself-unpromotable person.

"A certain bluffness and frankness, with that habit of looking you straight in the face which is the surest sign of the born liar, male or female, appear to me to be indispensable to 'honest Iago'; and it is the absence of these, with the statuesque attitudes, the lofty carriage of the head, and the delicate play of the hands and wrists, that makes the figure created by Maurel irreconcilable with my notion of the essentially vulgar ancient who sang comic songs to Cassio and drank him, so to speak, under the table. There is too much of Lucifer, the fallen angel, about it—and this, be it remarked, by no means through the fault of Verdi, who has in several places given a quite Shakespearean tone to the part by nuances which Maurel refuses to execute."

Maurel may have been guided—or misguided, as Shaw would have it —by his taste not only for the pictorial but for the elegantly picturesque. The kind of Iago that Shaw wanted would probably have been too distasteful to Maurel, even as a task for the actor. Clara Louise Kellogg, whose *Memoirs* frequently give evidence of an acute critical intelligence, could say of him: "What an actor, and what an intelligence!" and go on to observe: "Curiously, he could never play parts of what I call elemental picturesqueness. His Amonasro was good, but it was a bit too clean and tidy. He looked as if he were just out of a Turkish bath, immaculate in spite of his uncivilized guise."

What we read about Maurel shows us a man of great ambition, high purpose and an admirable vision of the artist's calling. But he seems also to have been vain, self-centered and aggressive. "We are too great artists," he told Lilli Lehmann, "to waste time exchanging compliments; let's correct each other," an observation suggesting both vanity and integrity. Lehmann, who had a similar abundance of each, found him congenial company. "Maurel was the first singer and artist," she wrote in *Mein Weg*, "with whom one could talk about song and art; and in America, where we often had occasion to do so, we never lost a minute's opportunity to exchange views."

The glory of Maurel's Iago was blemished by his greedy eagerness to get the part. During rehearsals for *Simon Boccanegra* at Milan in 1881, Verdi had been so overcome by Maurel's artistry that he exclaimed: "If God grants me good health, I'll write Iago for you." Maurel interpreted this as a promise, and he promptly broadcast it, assuming, at the same time, that the opera would be called "Iago." And he kept pestering Verdi about it, to the latter's annoyance. But Verdi, guided rather by good theater sense than by affection, seems never to have considered any other baritone for the role.

Verdi was even more annoyed when Maurel demanded exclusive rights to the role of Falstaff for a certain period of time after the première. Verdi refused. And there is the story, possibly apocryphal, of Tamagno's reply when Verdi asked him whether he thought Maurel would make a good Iago. Maurel, Tamagno is supposed to have said, should be a good Iago on stage, too.

The attention given here to what may have been Maurel's shortcomings could seem an odd approach to an appreciation of a singer who was certainly a great artist. But one notes the respectful language in which the criticism is couched, and senses that Maurel was vivid and striking even in what may have been his mistakes. This is true only of the elect. Criticism tells us more than praise.

When W. J. Henderson tells us in the New York *Times* of Maurel's debut at the Metropolitan as Iago on December 3, 1894, that "he was a revelation to the public of the resources that go to make the art of a truly great singing actor," he tells us nothing about the substance of that art. Nor does Bispham, when he observes: "It is safe to say that for over a generation no baritone in Europe was his equal either as a singer or an actor."

But from Lilli Lehmann, at least, we get an idea of the effect that Maurel could achieve at his best. Speaking of a performance of *Faust* at the Metropolitan with Jean and Édouard de Reszke, Emma Eames and Maurel (the casting suggests that it must have taken place on either January 20 or February 13, 1899), she writes: "Maurel's death scene as Valentine moved us so deeply that we remained speechless for hours, savoring the overpowering inner impression that Maurel evoked with nothing that one could see or grasp, solely through spiritual expression."

From all that we read of Maurel, it must be plain that he employed more than that. But the function of art is to disguise art, or artifice, and if he could make so theater-wise and strong-minded a woman as Lilli Lehmann oblivious to his devices, the accomplishment speaks for itself. He may have been a bit too intellectual—Shaw refers to his "restless cerebration"—and too preoccupied with the pictorial effect; but the artist who could also render Lilli Lehmann speechless must certainly have been a master.

2. FRANCESCO TAMAGNO

Two more perfectly—and, for the purposes of *Otello*, more ideally— contrasted types than Maurel and Tamagno (1850–1905) can hardly be imagined. The one was French, the other Italian, the one all brains and art, the other all voice and elemental temperament. Maurel, had he not been a singer, would doubtless have achieved distinction as an architect, painter, writer or lecturer. Tamagno, son of a simple Piedmontese res- taurateur, would probably have ended his days as the proprietor of an inherited *trattoria* in Turin. Even as a singer, Tamagno, had it not been for *Otello*, would be remembered as no more than the possessor of the biggest—and, according to his detractors, the shrillest—high C in tenor history up to that time.

Bispham described his voice as seeming to be of "enduring brass." He recalled his singing the tenor part in Rossini's *Stabat Mater* at the Per- gola Theater in Florence. "The audience rose at him," Bispham remem- bered, "for no one was ever known to sing the 'Cujus Animam' with such a volume of tone as his." The "Cujus Animam," it should be added, rises to a high D-flat. Bispham was told subsequently that Tamagno had never sung the *Stabat Mater* before, and, until a fortnight before the performance, had not even heard of it. But high notes are a valuable asset, and Tamagno had them. Leopoldo Mugnone, who conducted for him often, remembered his adding five successive high C's to the stretta in the last act of *William Tell*.

Despite their association in one of the most momentous productions of operatic history, there seems to have been little love lost between Tamagno and Maurel. We have noted Tamagno's malicious observation about Maurel's qualifications for the role of Iago; Tamagno was doubtless aware of Maurel's aggressive tactics in attempting to secure the role. Tamagno, too, was an eager volunteer, but his letters to Verdi on the subject of his singing Othello have a persuasive humility. And in the performance he did not like Maurel's device of placing his foot on the chest of the prostrate Othello to punctuate the "Ecco il leone—here lies the lion," at the end of the third act. He seems to have felt it as a gratuitous bit of picturesque grandstanding. Maurel may well have had his own thoughts about Tamagno's singing the "Esultate" from the balcony of the Albergo Milano to the crowds paying homage to Verdi after the première.

But Tamagno had more than just a big voice, and both Verdi and he himself seem to have sensed it when *Otello* was being cast. At thirty-five (in 1886) he had already achieved celebrity in Italy and South America in such roles as Arnold, Ernani, Manrico, Radames, John of Leyden and even Éléazar (the French roles sung, of course, in Italian). But his dependence upon sheer voice, and particularly upon the unexampled ring of his top tones, had been noted by the critics. Verdi himself, who had become familiar with his work in the 1881 revision of *Simon Boccanegra*, had some misgivings, initially, about his ability to handle declamation and recitative.

Tamagno seems to have had none. He knew well enough that he was incapable of subtlety. He was stiff and ill at ease in the more or less stereotyped recitatives of most French and Italian operas, where subtlety, if any, must be supplied by the singer. But what Verdi wrote for his Othello has nothing in common with the recitative prototype of even his own earlier operas. Here the subtlety has been written into the music by the composer. It is characterization, pure and simple, requiring of the singer, assuming the requisite vocal and histrionic endowment and experience, only that he grasp the idiom and realize the composer's vision.

No one knew better than Tamagno himself that he was at his best in scenes of elemental intensity, in passionate situations where he could call upon his immense resources of voice and temperament for the expression of exultation, outrage, fury, resolve or despair. He had seen Othello played by the great Italian tragedian, Tommaso Salvini, and he was sufficiently familiar with the play to recognize that the part of a simple, proud, passionate man at the mercy of a brainy, cunning and conniving adversary was made to his order, that this role would discover more of the best that was in him than anything ever written for a tenor. He never had the slightest difficulty in fathoming what it was that Verdi was about.

There can hardly be any more illustrative phonograph records than those made by Tamagno of the scene of Othello's death and the "Ora, per sempre addio—Now, and forever, farewell!" in 1904. He was fifty-four in that year, the voice no longer fresh, nor always reliable. The production is primitive, and the piano accompaniment ludicrous. But the searing despair of his "E tu, come sei pallida, e stanca, e muta, e bella! —And you, how pale you are, and spent, and silent, and beautiful!", uttered after Othello has strangled Desdemona, is possibly unmatched by anything else on wax.

Tamagno was not a cultivated man, as Maurel was, but he must have been endowed with that intuitive intelligence and perception often encountered in fine artists who never did, nor could have done, well in school. Certainly no man could sing these lines as Tamagno sang them who did not both feel and understand feeling, or who lacked the inborn musicality to appreciate and exploit the expressive treasure of the Italian language.

One who has heard that hopeless farewell will find it less astonishing that the recreational passion of this big, simple man with the stentorian voice was butterflies. He simply found such delight in their delicate coloring that he gathered them wherever he went in Europe and in North and South America; and he left a collection of thousands of specimens to the community of Varese where, in 1905, he died.

3. JEAN DE RESZKE

Preeminent as he may have been in the single role of Othello, Tamagno was not the first tenor of his time. As a producer of high C's he was the successor of Tamberlik; but the king of tenors in Tamberlik's

The reigning tenor of the last "golden age" was Jean de Reszke, seen (above right) as Romeo and (above left) as the elegant Polish gentleman he was.

Francesco Tamagno, the first Othello in Verdi's opera, is obviously intent on murder (below left). In private life (below right) he wore a less sinister expression.

generation was Mario, and Mario's heir was Jean de Reszke, probably the greater artist of the two. De Reszke (1850–1925) was every bit as handsome as Mario had been, and more imposing of voice and presence. He sang a wider repertoire, and there was, of course, a wider repertoire available to sing: Radames, Don José, Vasco da Gama, Lohengrin, Walther, Tristan and the Siegfrieds, in addition to most of the roles that Mario had sung. He was, moreover, a Pole, a nationality that has always exercised an exotic fascination on western Europeans and Anglo-Saxons.

If any opera enthusiast or student of singing were asked to mention a single name symbolic of the last "golden age" the odds would favor his saying: Jean de Reszke. Or he might say: the de Reszke brothers. For Édouard, three years younger than Jean, was almost as preeminent among basses as Jean was among tenors. The de Reszkes have been, curiously, the only very famous brothers among male singers, excepting, possibly, Jan and Ladis Kiepura, although Ladis was not well known outside Poland. The baritone Carlo Morelli and the tenor Renato Zanelli were brothers, and there was Gustav Schützendorf, who was one of five brothers, all opera singers. Sisters have been numerous. Gabrielli, Sontag, Grisi, Patti, Tetrazzini, Giulia Ravogli, Lilli Lehmann and, in our own time, Rosa Ponselle, Anny Konetzni and Dusolina Giannini have all had singer sisters of the first class. This has probably been because so many of the female singers, unlike most of the males, have come of theater families.

Choose at random among the great casts of the last "golden age" and you will emerge with the names of Jean and Édouard de Reszke—certainly, at least, with the name of Jean—more predictably than with those of any of their celebrated female partners. Jean was, in addition to all else, so very much a creature of his time: elegant in manner and song, a romantic figure, the ideal Romeo and Faust; and he was the first tenor of the Italian and French repertoire to sing the mature Wagner in German. Ernest Van Dyck, a Belgian, was primarily a Wagnerian throughout his career. De Reszke had sung Lohengrin in Italian, as had many other tenors of the time, but for a man of his celebrity in the Italian and French repertoire to undertake Tristan and the Siegfrieds so late in his career was unprecedented. And it meant much at a time when the Wagner fever was at its height.

There were those among the nonbelievers who held that this venture cost him five or ten years of vocal life, and they blamed the Wagnerite critics, notably Shaw and Hermann Klein, critic of the London *Sunday*

Times, for having provoked him to it. There is some evidence to support the argument. Having once mastered Tristan and the Siegfrieds, he did not sing them often; and from about that time dated the indispositions that became frequent toward the end of his career. These were especially predictable when *Siegfried* was being performed, and critics unsympathetic to the Wagnerian cause spoke of "Siegfried-itis." Within six years of his first Tristan, Jean de Reszke was finished.

But it may be argued just as persuasively that in 1895, when he sang that first Tristan in New York, he was already forty-five, not young for a tenor. He had been, moreover, a late starter. He was twenty-four when he made his debut as a baritone in Venice in 1874. He withdrew after two years to make the change to tenor, and although he appeared as Robert in *Robert le Diable* in Madrid in 1879, he sang little until 1884, when Maurel prevailed upon him to take the role of John the Baptist in the Paris première of Massenet's *Hérodiade.* He was then thirty-four. The layoff may have contributed to the freshness of his voice, and it may have accounted for the durability that made possible the extraordinary achievements of his vocal maturity.

It may also have reflected a certain indolence. When he sang his first Othello (Verdi's) in London in 1891, the audience favored Maurel's Iago, and Shaw interpreted this as a manifestation of public displeasure with Jean's easygoing ways. "It is to his petulant laziness, and to nothing else," wrote Shaw, "that we owe the frightful waste of artistic resources at Covent Garden on stale repetitions of worn-out operas night after night when we might have been listening to *Siegfried* and *Otello!* . . . The height of his ambition would be attained, as far as we can judge, if he were permitted to maintain his status as leading tenor at the Royal Italian Opera by a single performance of Romeo every year."

These were harsh words to apply to a tenor who had already mastered Walther, although not yet in German, and who had just undertaken Othello. Laziness was doubtless too strong a word, although it is easy to understand how it might come to be applied to a tenor who found "Celeste Aida" inconveniently placed, and who sometimes omitted it. (Many years later he confessed to Martinelli that in his nineteen performances of Radames at the Metropolitan he had sung "Celeste Aida" only four times. "It was too difficult an aria to sing before I was properly warmed up," he said.) De Reszke seems, however, to have been of that type of man who is content to leave well enough alone unless spurred to extraordinary accomplishment by competition and provocation. Even

Shaw admitted that his third act in *Otello* showed, "like his Don José and other post-Van Dyck performances, that when the rivalry of younger men and the decay of his old superficial charm with advancing years force him to make the most of all his powers, he may yet gain more as an actor than he will lose as a singer."

The notion of singing Wagner in German may have been his own, however strongly encouraged he certainly was by Klein and provoked by Shaw. It was Klein who had visited the brothers and Jean Lassalle in Bad Ems following the Bayreuth festival of 1888, and given them such an enchanting account of *Die Meistersinger* that they proceeded at once to Bayreuth to see and hear for themselves. They were so delighted that Jean learned Walther in Italian and sang it at Covent Garden a year later with Lassalle as Sachs. Although Édouard did not sing in that production, he later became, in Bispham's opinion, the greatest Hans Sachs he had heard. Bispham had heard them all, and had sung—as Beckmesser —with most of them.

Klein was pardonably pleased with the results of his evangelism. "Looking back with calm reflection upon the Hans Sachs of Lassalle," he wrote in *Thirty Years of Musical Life in London*, "I must admit that his delineation of the poet-cobbler was too refined, too delicate, too 'gentlemanly,' to be altogether correct. Yet his noble voice and artistic phrasing imparted an added beauty to his music, and the benevolent, kindly spirit of the character has never been more delightfully portrayed.

"The very attributes of refinement and distinction that were out of place in Hans Sachs enabled Jean de Reszke to realize in ideal fashion the attractive personality of the Franconian knight, especially in the half-timid, half-angry moments when he rebels against the dull bigotry of the Nuremberg mastersingers. The entire embodiment presented features of originality that surprised by their freshness no less than by their truthful adherence to the Wagnerian conception; and as with his Lohengrin, so with his Walther, the vocal rendering of the part constituted a veritable revelation. The final rendering of the 'Preislied' on that hot July night was something that never before had been approached, and has not since been surpassed."

There are conflicting views as to what prompted Jean to take the next big step: to Tristan, Siegfried—and German. Klein, an intimate friend of the de Reszkes, was among those who thought it Jean's own idea. Even in the flush of his triumph as Walther, he was beginning, in Klein's words, "to rebel against the open vowels and soft consonants of the

Italian tongue as a medium for the utterance of the crisp, rugged verse, the expressive Teutonic sounds, the biting sibilants and gutturals of Wagner's original text. He felt that his declamation was losing force in the very act of giving it birth—that it had not yet acquired the intense dramatic quality that had so appealed to him in the enunciation of the Bayreuth singers." Klein, of course, was a Wagnerian. P. G. Hurst, author of *The Golden Age Recorded* and *The Age of Jean de Reszke*, was not. He thought that de Reszke had simply "bowed to the partisan clamor," the most insistent coming from G. B. Shaw. Taking the tenor's extraordinary artistic sensibility into account, one tends to believe Klein.

There can, in any case, be little doubt that de Reszke's first appearance as Tristan at the Metropolitan, with Nordica as Isolde, was the supreme achievement of his career. To the Wagner enthusiasts it was an inspiring and reassuring revelation. "Let one fact be pondered," said Henry E. Krehbiel, reviewing the production in the *Tribune: "Tristan und Isolde* was sung in tune throughout. Never before have we had a Tristan capable of singing the declamatory music of the first and last acts with correct intonation, to say nothing of the duet of the second act. . . . Mme. Nordica and M. de Reszke not only sang in tune, they gave the text with a distinctness of enunciation and a truthfulness of expression that enabled those familiar with the German tongue to follow the play and appreciate its dramatic value and even its philosophical purport. . . . As for M. Jean de Reszke, his voice was warm, and every note he sang a heart-throb."

He sang his first Siegfried in New York on December 30, 1896, and Krehbiel was even more ecstatic than he had been about his Tristan. His accomplishment, said Krehbiel, "was little short of a miracle. His every word, every tone, every pose, every action, was brimming over with youthful energy, vigor and enthusiasm. His Siegfried proved to be a worthy companion-piece to his Tristan, with which, last year, he enriched the experience of the friends as well as the foes of Wagnerian drama, but as an artistic creation it was even more amazing, more bewildering."

Krehbiel failed to note another accomplishment, recorded by Bispham, the Alberich of that performance. This had also been the occasion of Nellie Melba's one and only Brünnhilde, an undertaking described by W. J. Henderson in the *Times* as reflecting "ambition more potent than wise." Bispham has left us a piquant picture of de Reszke, "in the heavy fur coat of Siegfried, patrolling the forward part of the stage to keep the white-clad Melba from rushing to the footlights, over which she had so many times sung to delighted audiences." He does not mention Jean's supreme sacrifice: his mustache. De Reszke fans were outraged, and for his subsequent appearances as Siegfried in London he restored it.

One senses in the hyperbole expended on Jean de Reszke's triumph rather more than a hint of self-congratulation on the part of the critics. They were of the first Wagnerian generation. They had faced the fire of the conservatives and prevailed. But as long as the performance of the late Wagner remained more or less exclusively a German accomplishment, the new Wagnerian hegemony was geographically and aesthetically limited. Lilli Lehmann had shown that it was possible to sing both Isolde and Norma, but she was, after all, a German. De Reszke was not only a non-German, which could be said of Van Dyck, too; he was the leading tenor of the *other* repertoire, the successor of Mario.

There is no reason to doubt that he sang Tristan and Siegfried more beautifully than they had been sung before. In the Wagnerian view he had proved that Wagner's vocal writing did not preclude beautiful singing, that his most exacting roles could be sung without vocal damage. As Hurst put it, the entire operatic scene was changed in both England and America.

It is easy to see, in retrospect, that this was overstating the case. That Jean de Reszke's career as a singer was at an end just five years after his first Siegfried, and that it suffered a precipitous decline before it ended, cast some doubt on the effect of Wagner's heroic-tenor roles on their singers' vocal health. Even before de Reszke's vocal deterioration became conspicuous, it had been noted that his Romeo and Faust were not what they had been. Whether Wagner was responsible will remain forever a matter of opinion. But it is a fact that in the intervening half-century few non-German tenors of the Italian-French repertoire have chosen to follow de Reszke's example. Some of them have undertaken Lohengrin, Walther and even Tannhäuser. But Tristan and Siegfried have, as a rule, been left to the specialists, primarily Germans and Scandinavians. Notable exceptions have been Martinelli, who sang Tristan in German to Flagstad's Isolde in Chicago in 1948, and Ramon Vinay, who undertook Tristan at Bayreuth with splendid success.

One is reminded of Pauline Viardot. "I wanted to sing everything," she said, "and I spoilt my voice." But her career would not have been what it was had she been more thrifty. And this is true of de Reszke's. Even Hurst, who felt that he had committed vocal suicide, conceded that he may have genuinely wished to shine in the late Wagner roles, and an incident related by Klein would seem to dispel any suggestion of a reluctant hero.

Klein was in New York in 1896 when *Tristan und Isolde* was in repertoire, but he had to leave two days before a scheduled performance on April 27, and settled for a *Lohengrin*. There was supper afterward in Nordica's hotel apartment. The performance of *Lohengrin*, according to Klein, "touched at all points a very high level of excellence. I derived immense pleasure from the novel sensation of hearing Jean and Édouard de Reszke as exponents of Wagner's own text. Their conscientious enunciation of each syllable, their accurate diction and their admirable accent seemed to impart an added dignity alike to the music and to their impersonations."

After supper, Klein continues, "the distinguished tenor turned to Mme. Nordica and proposed that, as I was evidently not to be made to alter my determination [to leave the next day] the best thing they could do would be to 'bring the mountain to Mohammed' and sing some *Tristan* to me there and then. . . . They did not spare themselves, either, these generous friends. They sang with full voice; they went through not only the scene with which they had started, but the duet of the first act as well; and, from beginning to end, the exquisite beauty of their phrasing, the blending of their voices in perfect intonation and unity of color, the significance of their supreme dramatic interpretation constituted at once a marvel and a revelation."

The performance of *Lohengrin* to which Klein refers took place on April 15, and had a certain sentimental importance as the occasion when Nordica was presented with a tiara containing two hundred and thirty-three diamonds and valued at $5,000, which later became a sort of Nordica trademark. It might be noted, too, that during April, in addition to this *Lohengrin*, de Reszke sang Romeo on the 13th, Don José on the 20th, Faust on the 22nd, the third act of *Aida* and the fourth act of *Faust* at a gala on the 24th and Tristan on the 29th.

So it had been all season. Between November 18 and February 14 he sang twenty-five times, his roles including Romeo, Lohengrin (which he also sang in Italian), Tristan, Radames, Faust, Raoul, des Grieux, Don José and Walther. This averages a performance every three and a half days. In the following season he went beyond that, singing thirty-six times in ninety-seven days, or a fraction over a performance every two and a half days, and adding the young Siegfried, Roderigo (in *Le Cid*), Vasco da Gama (in *L'Africaine*) and Werther to his repertoire.

Lauritz Melchior, in his most strenuous seasons, 1938–39 and 1939–40, averaged a performance every four and a half days. He was singing only Wagner and only in German, and even his Wagner repertoire did not include Walther. As every singer knows, such contrasts as are represented by Werther and Siegfried, or Tristan and Faust, require a considerable vocal reorientation. The few singers nowadays who command anything like so wide a repertoire—Callas, for instance—demand, and get, ten days or two weeks between, say, a Tosca and a Lucia. But in that season of 1896–97, de Reszke sang Siegfried on January 2, Faust on January 4 and Werther on January 6. At the end of the season he sang Roderigo, Faust, Don José and Siegfried within a period of six days.

It is small wonder that his vocal decline dated from that time. He was, moreover, forty-six, and tenors who have approached the age of fifty without some evidence of vocal decay have been the exception rather than the rule. Certainly it would be unfair to blame it all on Wagner. The practice of singers, male and female, since then would indicate a consensus that, while the late Wagner can be sung without vocal damage by those attuned vocally to the idiom, it cannot be mixed with the Italian and French repertoire without some vocal dislocation. And few singers since de Reszke's time—probably none—have risked the juxtaposition of roles so disparate as Werther and Siegfried.

Bispham could well say of de Reszke: "Taking him for all in all, he was the finest artist of his generation, a tower of strength to our company, and a vocal and physical adornment to the stage he elevated by his presence."

XVI

Some Ladies of the Last "Golden Age"

NORDICA · MELBA · SEMBRICH

EAMES · SCHUMANN-HEINK

1. LILLIAN NORDICA

It was fitting that Jean de Reszke's partner when he sang his first Tristan should have been Lillian Nordica, singing her first Isolde.

For each of them this *Tristan und Isolde* was the pinnacle of a career, and doubly remarkable in that neither of them was a German, nor even primarily a Wagnerian. As splendid as de Reszke's achievement was, and conceding that he was probably the more finished artist of the two, Nordica's was, in certain respects, even greater. De Reszke was, at least, a European, and one of a family of opera singers. Nordica was an American, born Lillian Norton in Farmington, Maine, on December 12, 1857.

She was not, of course, the first American to make an international career in grand opera. Clara Louise Kellogg was a generation ahead of her, as was Annie Louise Cary, the first American Amneris. Emma Albani had long been a favorite in London when Nordica first appeared there in 1887, and Minnie Hauk was firmly established as one of the most celebrated of all Carmens.

Of her own generation were Ella Russell, Suzanne Adams, Emma Nevada, Marie van Zandt, Marie Engle, Frances Saville, Zélie de Lussan and Sybil Sanderson, for the last of whom Massenet wrote *Thaïs*. Among the great female singers of the golden age, Emma Eames, Edyth Walker, Marion Weed, Louise Homer and Geraldine Farrar were Americans, and Mary Garden, born in Scotland, and Olive Fremstad, born in Sweden, may be counted as Americans just as today we count Astrid Varnay, born in Sweden, and George London, born in Canada, as Americans.

Americans entering upon an operatic career in those days had essentially the same combination of advantages and disadvantages they have now. They were handicapped by the want of a native lyric theater. The American singer could not be born into the opera and grow up in an established opera house, as so many of the great European singers had done, nor was there a ladder of municipal, state and national theaters offering an aspirant the opportunity to begin at the bottom and work to the top. The American had, moreover, to assimilate an essentially alien idiom and master at least two, and preferably three, foreign languages.

But there were certain advantages in all these handicaps. Denied a native opera, and entering upon the operatic scene as strangers, the Americans could not be tempted, as so many Europeans were, to accept routine, to settle for local celebrity in a regional repertoire and the assurance of a pension. Tradition can as easily be a curse as a blessing, and the Americans, having none, could move more easily from one idiom, one language and one repertoire to another, from Italian to French to German. Because they had to crash the party, so to speak—not excluded, but uninvited—they had to beat the natives at their own game, and by a comfortable margin. None of all this could be accomplished without exceptional talent, compelling ambition, dauntless determination, assertive elbows and a capacity for hard work.

All these attributes were possessed by Lillian Nordica in an extraordinary degree. They carried her to triumphs more glamorous than those of any other American singer of her time, surpassed in their diversity only by those of Lilli Lehmann. Her repertoire extended from Gilda, Ophelia, Marguerite and Norina through Elvira, Valentine, Leonora (in *Il Trovatore*), Selika (in *L'Africaine*) and Aida to Elsa, Isolde, the three Brünnhildes and Kundry. At the peak of her career she could—and did—sing Violetta twenty-four hours after the Brünnhilde of *Die Walküre*. In 1903, when she was forty-six, she sang the Brünnhildes of *Die Walküre* and *Götterdämmerung* on February 12th and 14th and Marguerite on the 18th. In 1910, when she was fifty-three, she learned Isolde in French for a single production in Paris. These were Lehmann-esque accomplishments, and not even Lehmann could approach Nordica's itinerary as an operatic nomad.

Where Lehmann could learn her trade conventionally and consistently in the opera houses of Prague, Danzig, Leipzig and Berlin, Nordica was on the road most of her life, beginning with her first substantial professional engagement as soloist with Patrick S. Gilmore's band, a forerunner of the concert bands of John Philip Sousa and Arthur Pryor.

With Gilmore, as a girl of twenty-one, she toured throughout the United States and most of England, Ireland and western Europe. Later in her career, as an opera singer, she would appear at the principal houses of Paris, London, New York, Chicago, Boston and St. Petersburg, but she never really had a permanent theatrical home, and she spent a considerable part of her life with touring opera companies and with her own touring concert groups.

Leaving Gilmore in Paris in the summer of 1878, when she was twenty-one, she studied singing, acting, languages and repertoire, first in Paris and then in Milan, making her opera debut as Donna Elvira in a secondary theater in Milan in the spring of the following year. The shortness of the interval suggests cramming rather than study. She sang also in Brescia, Novara, Genoa, Monte Carlo, Nice and Aquila, her other roles being Gilda, Marguerite and Alice (in *Robert le Diable*). It was for these early engagements that she took the name of Giglio Nordica, *giglio* being the Italian word for lily. On the strength of provincial success in Italy she was engaged for St. Petersburg for the season of 1880–81.

Clara Louise Kellogg, who met her in Paris when she was still with Gilmore, and who was one of the company in St. Petersburg, pays a generous tribute to Nordica in her *Memoirs*, and in language that tells us more about Nordica's character and singing than can be found in pages of critical commentary. At the time of the Gilmore engagement, Kellogg recalled, "she was still a girl, but she dressed her hair in a fashion that made her look much older than she really was, and threw into prominence her admirably determined chin . . . A young person with a chin so expressive of determination and perseverence could not be downed.

"She told me at that early period that she always kept her eyes fixed on some goal so high and difficult that it seemed impossible, and worked toward it steadily, unceasingly, putting aside everything that stood in the path which led to it. In later years she spoke again of this, evidently having kept the idea throughout her career. 'When I sang Elsa,' she said, 'I thought of Brünnhilde—then Isolde.'

"My admiration for Mme. Nordica is deep and abounding. Her breathing and tone production are about as nearly perfect as anyone's can be, and if I wanted any young student to learn by imitation, I could say to her, 'Go and hear Nordica, and do as nearly like her as you can.' There are not many singers, nor have there ever been many, of whom one could say that. And one of the finest things about this splendid vocalism is that she has had nearly as much to do with it as had God Almighty in the first place.

"When I first knew her, she had no dramatic quality above G-sharp. She could reach the upper notes, but tentatively, and without power. She had, in fact, a beautiful mezzo voice; but she could not hope for leading roles in grand opera until she had perfect control of the upper notes needed to complete her vocal equipment. . . . It was not until after the Russian engagement that she went to [Jean-Baptiste] Sbriglia in Paris and worked with him until she could sing a high C that thrilled the soul. That C of hers in the 'Inflammatus' in Rossini's *Stabat Mater* was something superb. . . . She gained all and lost nothing. Her voice, while increasing in register, never suffered the least detriment in tone or timbre."

The high C was not the only essential of a soprano's equipment that was slow in coming. Nordica had had the advantage of sound vocal grounding under John O'Neill in Boston, with whom she commenced her studies when she was fourteen, and she learned the basic principles of showmanship as Gilmore's soprano soloist. But the interval between her leaving the band and her debut in Milan was too short. What could be done by the most intensive application she did, but opportunity ran ahead of her preparation, and she was not one to let opportunity pass. She sang her first Aida, for example, without stage rehearsal, and she prepared her first Valentine in a single week. There were inadequacies, and they were noted.

Shaw observed of her first Elsa (in Italian) in 1889: "Miss Nordica turned Elsa of Brabant into Elsa of Bond Street by appearing in a corset. She produces her voice so skillfully that its want of color, and her inability to fill up with expressive action the long periods left there by Wagner for that purpose, were the more to be regretted." And of a concert rendition of "Dich, teure Halle" two years later, he reported that Nordica had sung it in "a bright, bumptious, self-assertive and otherwise quite unmeaning way that was as exactly as possible the opposite of how it should be sung."

Philip Hale, the Boston critic, about the same time, was delighted with her vocalism in a performance of *Les Huguenots*, but went on to observe: "Valentine should arouse the sympathy of the spectator as well as the praise of the hearer, and Nordica did not touch the heart." In a moment of impatience, Hale once referred to her simply as "that woman from Maine."

Nordica was aware of her shortcomings, and she worked ceaselessly to overcome them. The most important influence in her artistic maturity seems to have been Cosima Wagner, with whom she studied Elsa, Isolde and the three Brünnhildes. Cosima probably had nothing to teach Lehmann—nothing, at least, that Lehmann needed to learn. Nordica, without Lehmann's previous firsthand experience of Wagner, needed all the good advice she could get, and she accepted Cosima's instruction as Gospel. Her appearance as Elsa in the first Bayreuth *Lohengrin* was a success. It was, in a sense, her debut as a complete artist.

Krehbiel, when she sang her first Isolde a year later, was probably writing from personal knowledge of the details of her career when he said that her performance "forced upon all a recognition of the lesson which Walther teaches Hans Sachs in the song-meeting in St. Catherine's Church—that ability comes with willingness and desire." And the formerly captious Philip Hale, toward the end of her career, found in her Marguerite "triumphs of dramatic instinct and dramatic intelligence, moments of vocally emotional beauty, phrases charged with longing, supreme happiness, terror, wild regret."

Lillian Nordica was an amiable woman, and that determined chin was a part of a memorably handsome countenance. She was not profound, certainly, and her intelligence was guided more by intuition and ambition than by intellect. She was proud, and, in her personal life, impulsive, which led her into three bad marriages, the women's suffrage movement, an ill-conceived notion of founding a Bayreuth-on-the-Hudson, a chauvinistic attack on the choice of Emmy Destinn to sing the première of *The Girl of the Golden West,* and an unprofitable row with Jean de Reszke, whom she accused, publicly and probably unjustly, of having conspired behind her back to secure Melba exclusive rights to the Brünnhilde of *Siegfried* at the Metropolitan.

But unhappy marriages, ill-conceived charities, and quixotic ideas of public service have not been uncommon among prima donnas. The singleness of purpose, the preoccupation with one's own ambitions, without which a woman is unlikely to become a prima donna, are difficult to reconcile with the woman's traditional role as wife, housekeeper and mother, nor are a prima donna's achievements in the theater any evidence of executive or administrative ability in the world of affairs. Not alone among female singers did Nordica find fulfillment in a congenial setting only on the stage.

Indeed, she couldn't live without it. Toward the end of her career she suffered from rheumatism, and David Bispham, who toured with her, recalled that she "was so ill during several concerts we gave jointly that she could scarcely struggle to her feet, but, once up, she went on unflinchingly behind the disguise of rouge, beautiful gowns and jewels to sing to audiences that adored her. Coming off, she sank into her easy chair, almost crying with pain, but when the audience thundered in delight she said to me: 'My favorite tree has always been tree-mendous applause. Listen to that! I must go and sing to them again. That is worth any suffering!' Once she added: 'Do you think, now I am getting old, I should be doing this if I didn't have to?' "

In 1913 she left for Australia with the company of assisting artists still considered essential for concertizing in those days. From Australia she planned to sing her way to Singapore, Manila, Hong Kong, Shanghai and, via the Trans-Siberian Railway, to St. Petersburg, and then go on to Paris and London. But following the Australian tour her ship struck a reef in the Torres Strait off Thursday Island. It did not founder, but the passengers had to remain on deck, and as a result of this exposure, Nordica, already ailing, caught pneumonia. In Batavia, Java, four months later, on May 10, 1914—a few hours after Franklin Holding, the violinist of her troupe, had played the Prize Song from *Die Meistersinger* and the Meditation from *Thais* for her—she died, aged fifty-six.

"At my funeral," she once said, "I want a baritone to sing 'Wotan's Farewell' and an orchestra to play the Funeral March from *Götterdämmerung*. For me that music has such dear memories. And then I want some great speaker to say . . . say . . . 'She did her damnedest!' "

None of this happened—probably because Lillian Nordica could no longer do her damnedest to see that it was done.

Nordica made forty-eight recordings for Columbia between 1906 and 1911, of which twenty-two were never released. Neither she nor Herman Klein, who supervised them, was satisfied that they gave a fair representation of her voice or her singing. Her own preference was for the "Tacea la notte" from *Il Trovatore*, made in 1906, a recording remarkable for, among other things, elaborate ornamentation devised by, or for, the German dramatic soprano, Therese Tietjens (1831–1877). Tietjens had been a special favorite of the London public between 1858 and her death, and rejoiced in a repertoire extending from Semiramis to Fidès.

This is not the only source of astonishment among Nordica's records. There is a "Miserere" from *Il Trovatore*, made on the same day as "Tacea la notte," which has an interpolated and long-sustained high C. It also

At the height of her career Lillian Nordica (above right) sang Isolde and the
three Brünnhildes, but her repertoire embraced such coloratura roles as Filine
in *Mignon* (above left). "A young person with a chin so expressive of determination and perseverance," said her older American colleague, Clara Louise
Kellogg, "could not be downed."

Nellie Melba is seen (below left) with her teacher, Mathilde Marchesi, whose
extraordinary understanding of the female voice also produced such great
singers as Ilma di Murska, Gabrielle Krauss, Etelka Gerster, Emma Nevada,
Sybil Sanderson, Emma Calvé, Emma Eames and Frances Alda. Melba must
have been a very solemn Marguerite (below right).

has an excellent tenor masquerading under the improbable name of Marcello Reseninil. The name suggests, but has not yielded, an anagram. Most striking of all the Nordica records, for some, is the aria from the second act of Ferenc Erkel's *Hunyadi László,* a marvelous display of vocal exuberance and extravagance in a woman of forty-nine.

2. NELLIE MELBA

Lillian Nordica, remarkable artist that she must have been, was not the greatest name among the ladies of the last "golden age." Nor was Sembrich, nor Tetrazzini, nor Ternina nor Lehmann. The greatest name was Melba. Victor Gollancz, in his reminiscent *Journey Towards Music,* remembers how Kirsten Flagstad sang her first Brünnhilde at Covent Garden and "at once leapt into the sort of fame reserved for a Melba, but never a Destinn, a Paderewski, but never a Schnabel, a Kreisler, but never an Ysaÿe. These popular acclaims, rarely based on comparative merit, and by no means on personality considerations, are wretchedly inexplicable."

They certainly are. But the very inexplicability of such phenomena is always a fascinating challenge to the observer. As those have passed in review whom we think of as the greatest singers, it has been recurrently noted that, purely as singers, they may have been surpassed by contemporaries less vividly remembered, and surpassed, possibly, as personalities, too. Certain artists, without ever intending it, or knowing how it happened, become institutions; and, once solidly institutionalized, they enjoy thereafter the indestructability of a legend.

They may be subjected to criticism. Their virtues may be re-examined and their failings exposed. It may be suggested that Paderewski had less technique than is required today to get into a first-class conservatory, and that Kreisler often played out of tune. It does not matter. Past a certain point of institutionalization, derogatory observations, even when their truth is acknowledged, become offensive, gratuitous, in bad taste. It is like suggesting that Billy the Kid was a cad and that the Indians did not, as a rule, attack wagon trains.

This legendary invulnerability has been enjoyed, among singers, by Catalani, Rubini, Lablache, Grisi, Jenny Lind, Patti, Mario, Jean de Reszke and Caruso—and primarily in Great Britain. No nation is immune to the requirement of institutions as a source of pride and reassurance. But the British, possibly because they have more institutions than anybody else, disclose the most profound understanding of what an institution is. They also know how to make one—or they instinctively know an institution when they see one—and they are unequaled by any other people in its care and maintenance, including living institutions.

Indeed, the British have a predilection for living institutions, treasuring them, presumably, as symbols of permanence. This may offer a key to the phenomenon which Victor Gollancz finds so wretchedly inexplicable. Great Britain's vocal institutions have all been vocally long-lived. Sims Reeves (1818–1900), for example, a British tenor admired primarily for his accomplishments in concert and oratorio, reigned supreme in that field for nearly fifty years. His singing in 1886 prompted Hanslick to observe that "to win the favor of the British public is not easy; to lose it impossible." The reign of the British baritone Sir Charles Santley (1834–1922), for whom Gounod added "Even bravest heart may swell" ("Avant de quitter ces lieux") to *Faust*, was even longer. Grisi ruled for nearly thirty years, and Patti for forty-five.

The whole purpose of an institution is that it be around for a while, preferably forever, and it may just be that the British public in the nineteenth century had a knack of sensing longevity in an attractive young voice. And one had to prepare for contingencies. Patti did not arrive in London until 1861, the year of Grisi's retirement, and London, at that time, came close to being without a vocal institution. There was no similar absence of a safeguarding overlap when Patti retired from public life in 1906. Nellie Melba was already in place. She had been singing at Covent Garden since 1888, and she would continue to do so until 1926.

Of all such institutions she would seem, at first glance, to have been the least explicable. She was, to begin with, an Australian (*née* Helen Porter Mitchell, 1859, near Melbourne), and Australia was an odd place for a singer to be from. Not surprisingly, considering her origin, she was also a late starter. She was well into her twenties, had married and borne a son, and had deserted her husband before she decided to be a singer. She was twenty-seven when she arrived in Paris to study with Mathilde Marchesi, and it was not until then that she saw and heard her first opera. But she made a debut at Brussels as Gilda after only nine months of study with Marchesi, and at the age of thirty she was a star in both London and Paris.

Her London debut was as Lucia, on May 24, 1888, and Klein, in the *Sunday Times*, noted "the extraordinary beauty of timbre and her exceeding brilliant vocalization." But he also found her deficient "in that indescribable something which we call charm. Her accents lacked the ring of true pathos," he continued, and, although she possessed admirable intelligence, "the gift of spontaneous feeling has been denied her." These deficiencies became less conspicuous as she gained experience. Shaw, two years later, noted that her heart, "which before had acted only on her circulation, was now acting on her singing."

But it never "acted on her singing" to any significant extent. Melba was not a great singing actress, and she probably never tried to be. Like Patti, she must have known, or sensed, that emotional involvement in singing shortens vocal life. She lacked Patti's theater background, and she had to acquire the basic routine that Patti had enjoyed by instinct or early experience. She learned to go through the motions with professional aplomb, although these motions were said by her detractors not to have gone beyond the raising of one arm in situations of some intensity and two arms for an outburst. She learned to color her voice, to produce a semblance of characterization. Her Mimi, especially, was thought to be moving.

Rossini is supposed to have said that the three things essential to a singer are voice, voice and voice. Melba had all three in generous endowment, plus the requisite competitive spirit—as well as the good luck to land in the hands of Mathilde Marchesi and the good sense to do as she was told. She was, said Marchesi, "one of my most industrious, pliant and talented pupils." This, from the woman who produced more prima donnas than any other teacher in vocal history, was high praise.

Marchesi's studios, first in Vienna and later in Paris, were the most efficient workshops ever designed for the developing of the female voice. Among her other pupils were Antonietta Fricci (Fritsche), Ilma di Murska, Gabrielle Krauss, Anna d'Angeri, Wilhelmine Tremelli (Tremel), Etelka Gerster, Emma Calvé, Sybil Sanderson, Emma Eames, Selma Kurz, Emma Nevada and Frances Alda. There was not an Italian in the lot, curiously, and Marchesi herself was a German, née Graumann in Frankfurt am Main. But if any teacher ever perpetuated the traditions of Italian eighteenth-century bel canto, it was she.

The voices of some of her pupils are preserved on phonograph records, notably those of Melba and Eames, and the hallmarks of the Marchesi schooling are readily identified. Common to all are an absolutely even scale, a lightness and precision of attack, an absence of any kind of forcing, an immaculate intonation, even in the most rapid passages, and a marvelous ease at the upper extreme of the vocal compass. The high notes are secure, but well within sensible dynamic limits. Voices so schooled were ideal for Rossini, Donizetti, Gounod, Thomas, Delibes, Massenet and some of Meyerbeer. On Verdi and Wagner they were expended at the owner's risk, as Melba discovered when she attempted the *Siegfried* Brünnhilde. Melba sang Aïda, but neither well nor for long. Elsa and Elisabeth were congenial, but it may be assumed that in *Tannhäuser* the "teure Halle" was greeted with restrained exuberance.

This kind of discipline was not for everyone. Its acceptance and practice qualified the pupil for a kind of singing probably closer to the art of Guadagni, Pacchierotti and Marchesi than anything we are likely ever to hear. It is a sexless kind of singing, girlish rather than boyish if you like, but rarely womanly in an earthy way—suited to Elisabeth and Elsa for obvious reasons, but not to Brünnhilde, Isolde or Kundry, or to Aïda or Leonora.

It was not, even in the 1880s and 1890s, truly contemporary, although the then fashionable French operas in which it was so effectively employed—*Roméo et Juliette, Hamlet, Lakmé, Mignon, Mireille* and *Faust* —gave it a deceptive sheen of contemporary validity. Even Pasta and Malibran, fifty years earlier, would probably have found it too disembodied. Farrar, who was urged by Melba to entrust herself to Marchesi, thought better of it, and wisely so. She would probably have been a superior singer, and have sung longer, but she wouldn't have been Geraldine Farrar—warm-voiced, impulsive, sometimes reckless.

"I have always regretted," wrote Farrar in *Such Sweet Compulsion*, "that I did not make use of a letter to that most noted vocal authority, Marchesi, but despite Melba's recommendation to her favorite teacher, there was little to be gained, we felt, in submitting to a dazzling treatment whereby all voices were taught to shame the flute in impossible sky-rocket cadenzas or fall by the wayside when unable to do so. I had no true coloratura register, and did not wish to change my own color in such mechanical attainment. I was even then aware of the monotony of beautiful, even tones, when all dramatic expression was sacrificed to sound only. This seemed to prevail in the French school of that period. Diction was excellent and clean-cut, but the voices were far from appealing in quality and expression. I may have been presumptuous in criticism, but I was firm in my decision as to my own procedure."

The first thing that Marchesi said to Melba, who had neither sung nor studied much at the time of her arrival in Paris in 1886, was: "Before you learn anything, you will have to unlearn everything you know. You take your chest voice too high." Although registers were indistinguishable in the singing of Marchesi's pupils, she believed in their existence (chest, mixed and head), as the old teachers of the Bolognese and Neapolitan schools of *bel canto* had, and she taught Melba to pass into the head register at about an F-sharp.

This precluded the big top notes demanded of Brünnhildes, Toscas, Butterflys, Turandots and Santuzzas, but it was a safeguard against wear and tear and the hardening of vital muscles and cartilages. One remembers that among the castrati there were those alleged to have lost their upper voices by singing divisions in full chest voice. And there can be no doubt that many voices are damaged today by being required to produce a bigger tone at the top than can be accommodated muscularly without destructive stress. On the other hand, as Farrar suggests, vocal chastity can be a bore. "God," said Gollancz when he first heard Joan Sutherland, "she's as dull as Melba!"

Melba could probably have produced as big a tone as anyone, but the unique characteristic of her voice was its beauty—Marchesi described it as "silvery"—and, aside from the one misstep with Brünnhilde, that beauty was never hazarded. She refused even to learn Madame Butterfly. Melba sang beautifully, and the beauty of her singing—the then young Victor Gollancz to the contrary notwithstanding—bred its own enchantment and excitement.

Mary Garden, in *Mary Garden's Story*, remembered hearing her at Covent Garden as Mimi: "You know, the last note of the first act of *La Bohème* is the last note that comes out of Mimi's throat. It is a high C, and Mimi sings it when she walks out the door with Rodolfo. She closes the door, and then she takes the note. The way Melba sang that high C was the strangest and weirdest thing I have ever experienced in my life. The note came floating over the auditorium of Covent Garden: it left Melba's throat, it left Melba's body, it left everything, and came like a star and passed us in our box and went out into the infinite. . . . That note of Melba's was like a ball of light. It wasn't attached to anything. It was out of everything. . . . My God, how beautiful it was!"

Krehbiel, describing Melba's Metropolitan debut as Lucia in 1893 for the readers of the New York *Tribune*, compared her favorably to Patti. Her voice, he said, "is charmingly fresh and exquisitely beautiful, and her tone production is more natural and more spontaneous than that of the marvelous woman who so long upheld the standard of *bel canto* throughout the world. . . . All that she wants lies in her voice, ready at hand. Its range is commensurate with all that can possibly be asked of it; and she moves with the greatest ease in the regions which are most carefully avoided by most of the singers of today. To throw out those scintillant bubbles of sound which used to be looked upon as the highest achievement in singing seems to be a perfectly natural mode of emotional expression for her. . . . Added to this, she has most admirable musical instincts."

One of her secrets was intonation, and Shaw may have been the only critic who sensed its importance. "You never realize," he wrote, "how wide a gap there is between the ordinary singer who simply avoids the fault of singing obviously out of tune and the singer who sings really and truly in tune, except when Melba is singing." Had Shaw continued as a music critic, he could have said the same of John McCormack and Richard Tauber. It was an acute observation.

This kind of appraisal from singers and critics who were no strangers to good singing explains how a woman from the Australian bush, already in her thirties, who had been on the stage for less than five years, could raise her voice in the company of Russell, Nordica, Lucca, Eames, de Lussan, Sembrich, Albani, Calvé and van Zandt and walk off with Patti's crown. As early as 1892, one spoke in London of "Melba nights," which brought high society to the opera, and usually members of the royal family. Paris, Milan, New York and Chicago followed suit. But the capital of Melba's realm was London, and this was gratefully acknowledged when she was made a Dame of the British Empire in 1918, the female equivalent of knighthood.

Under the stress of such homage, it is hardly astonishing that Melba's repertoire, never extensive, should have contracted as her renown increased. Nor was it entirely her fault. The kind of popularity and affection that Melba enjoyed breeds its own constraints. These can be more or less vexing according to the temperament of the idol. Melba was not indolent, but beyond her accomplishment in putting Australia on the opera map, she was no musical pioneer.

Her public wanted to hear her sing what she sang best, and they wanted to hear it again and again, with no experimental nonsense. And so she sang Lucia, Gilda, Marguerite, Juliet, Desdemona, Violetta and Mimi, draping the ample Melba frame in the costumes of these unfortunate ladies. When the show was over, a piano would be pushed through the curtain, and she would sing "Home, Sweet Home" and

"Comin' thro' the Rye" and Tosti's "Mattinata," just as Patti had done. Everything was splendidly permanent and imperishable. Queen Adelina, if not yet dead, was enjoying dowager status at her castle in Wales, so: Long live Queen Nellie!

She was a proper queen, too, handsome in a severe way, imperious, orderly, punctual, enjoying and providing good food and drink, wary of intimacy, as a queen must be, gracious when she chose to be, indignant when crossed, and prone to unceremonious candor and a kind of frontier humor that gave the total personal composition just the right leavening of eccentricity. She was, of course, inhospitable to rivals. The absence of Farrar, the early disappearance from the London scene of Eames, and the infrequent appearances of Selma Kurz, according to Desmond Shawe-Taylor, now music critic of the London *Sunday Times*, were attributed to the jealousies of Melba.

But she had an imperial taste for conquest. Following her initial triumphs in Brussels, Paris and London, she took on Milan in 1893, left the battlefield victorious, and never went back. That was that. Australia, to which she returned in 1902, was a walkover. The most glorious of her campaigns was fought at the Manhattan Opera House in New York at the side of Oscar Hammerstein in his wars with the Metropolitan between 1906 and 1910.

"At the Metropolitan," she said, "I should have had to sing when and where they wanted. My roles would have been dictated for me. No artist gives her best under those conditions. I said to myself, 'I am Melba. I shall sing when and where I like, and I shall sing in my own way.' It may sound arrogant, but arrogance of that sort is not a bad way to get things done."

The assurance of social stability and permanence that Melba, as an institution, had both served and symbolized was, of course, illusory, and Melba lived to experience the truth. When she returned to London to reopen Covent Garden in 1919, she was sixty and could still sing. But the social world and the social climate that had made a "Melba night" were gone, and she sensed it.

The best of all her roles was Nellie Melba, and she played it through to a memorable final curtain at Covent Garden on June 8, 1926, when she sang scenes from her favorite operas to a splendid audience headed by the royal family. Excerpts were recorded, including the "Salce, salce" and the "Ave Maria" from *Otello*, and there can be no doubt of an extraordinary accomplishment for a woman of sixty-seven. Also recorded was her farewell speech, in which she broke down and wept.

Emma Eames was one of the great Americans of the last "golden age." The Countess in *The Marriage of Figaro* (right) was one of her finest vocal accomplishments. She was married to the Spanish baritone Emilio de Gogorza (below right).

Marcella Sembrich (below), whose career overlapped those of Patti and Melba, was one of the few great coloratura sopranos of the time who was *not* a pupil of Marchesi, although she may have consulted her. She was one of the first singers to give entire programs devoted to *Lieder*.

That was not at all like Melba, but neither was abdication. She may have sensed that the occasion was more than an exchange of farewells between a prima donna and her devoted public. There was no heiress, present or apparent, no promise of continuity. Nineteenth-century opera would continue, but never again in a nineteenth-century setting, with a proper *prima donna assoluta* presiding as Grisi and Patti and Melba had presided. The new rulers would be conductors and stage directors and accountants, and even prima donnas would be expected to mind their p's and q's—and dotted notes. Melba would not have liked that.

She retired to Australia and died in Sydney in 1931.

3. MARCELLA SEMBRICH AND EMMA EAMES

As a singer Melba had outlasted the two ladies who were most conspicuously in her class in her repertoire. Sembrich retired from opera in 1909, concertized for a few years more, then settled in New York, continuing her career as a teacher at the Juilliard School of Music in New York and the Curtis Institute in Philadelphia. She died in 1935. Eames also left the Metropolitan in 1909, and made her last operatic appearances in Boston in 1912. She lived to be eighty-seven, dying in New York in 1952.

Sembrich, a Pole, born in 1858, and Eames, an American, born in China in 1865, were, in some respects, probably, Melba's superiors. An excellent pianist and violinist, Sembrich was one of the finest musicians among all the singers of history, and an artist of the most discriminating taste. But chronology was against her. Her vocal prime preceded the decline of Patti's, and it was past when Melba's ascendancy began. At a time when most singers, in their concerts, still held to the potpourri type of program, with assisting artists, Sembrich was one of the first to dare the solo recital in what has since become the conventional format, with the songs and arias sung in the order of their composition.

Eames, whose voice was thought by many to be more beautiful, even, than Melba's, and who sang a far wider repertoire, including Aida, Santuzza, and Tosca, was never able to approach Melba as a communicative artist. She was simply unable to shed a kind of prohibitive decorum. Shaw said of her: "I never saw such a well-conducted person as Miss Eames. She casts her propriety like a Sunday frock over the whole stage. . . . How I envy Miss Eames her self-possession, her quiet consciousness of being founded on a rock, her good looks (oh, those calmly regular eyebrows!)." And he was reminded of Thackeray's picture of a young lady, Charlotte, who, when she saw the remains of her lover,

> Borne before her on a shutter,
> Like a well-conducted person,
> Went on cutting bread and butter.

James T. Huneker once opened a review of Eames's Aida with the quip: "There was skating on the Nile last night."

4. ERNESTINE SCHUMANN-HEINK

Neither Eames nor Sembrich, as much as they may have been admired by the connoisseurs, was able to establish dominion and maintain it as Melba did, or to penetrate the consciousness and gain the affection of an enormous public extending far beyond the coterie of habitual opera and concertgoers. Ernestine Schumann-Heink did. As a contralto she was not a competitor of Melba's, and she never ruled as Melba had ruled. Nor, following her departure from the Metropolitan in 1903, did she have anything to rule over. She was never again associated permanently with any opera company. But as a concert singer and recording artist she came to be as legendary a figure in her motherly way as Melba was, particularly in the United States.

In the line of the great contraltos, or mezzo-sopranos, Schumann-Heink followed Marianne Brandt (1842–1921), one of Wagner's two original Kundrys (Materna was the other and the first), who introduced many of the great Wagner mezzo-soprano roles to England and America. Brandt sang the Azucena in a performance of Il Trovatore in Graz, Austria, which was the first opera performance that Schumann-Heink, née Roessler in 1861, ever heard. She remained Schumann-Heink's model and idol ever afterward.

Like Pisaroni and Viardot, whose pupil she was, Brandt was almost as celebrated for an ill-favored person as for the beauty of her voice and the compelling quality of her art. Wagner is supposed to have called her the ugliest woman he had ever seen walk across the stage, and she was discarded for the role of Sieglinde at Bayreuth in 1876 because it was feared that her homeliness would inhibit the ardor of Niemann's Siegmund. Wagner may not have put his opinion in just those words, but whatever he said, his comment got back to Brandt, and there was persistent bad feeling between them. She was not invited back for the performances of *Parsifal* planned for 1883.

Contraltos and mezzo-sopranos have not invariably been homely, although Schumann-Heink herself was of the opinion that they ought to be. Rossini's mezzos must have been very pretty. Alboni was a beauty until she grew fat, and Louise Homer, the splendid American mezzo-soprano (wife of the American composer Sidney Homer, and aunt of another composer, Samuel Barber) who succeeded to Schumann-Heink's roles at the Metropolitan, was a handsome woman. But there have been some ugly ducklings, and Schumann-Heink was one of them. Purposeful and intelligent as she was, she turned a liability into an asset, and compounded her plainness by a notorious indifference to what she wore. Actually, until she became fat, she may not have been so homely as she thought herself to be. If one may judge by her early pictures in costume, she was even pretty, if always rather solemn.

Her plainness, in any case, suited the role in which she cast herself: the plain Austrian *Hausfrau*—she had three husbands and seven children, not counting a stepson. The role served her well, especially during the First World War. A naturalized United States citizen since 1905, she sang generously for soldiers, at war rallies, and for liberty bond drives, and, subsequently, for disabled veterans. All this added immeasurably to her fame, and eased the embarrassment and grief she experienced in having sons serving on both sides. Her eldest son was lost on a German submarine.

As a singer, Schumann-Heink was distinguished from other lower-voiced females by being a true contralto. It will be remembered that in the time of Malibran, Pasta and Viardot, contraltos, or mezzo-sopranos, had to sing soprano roles in order to achieve stardom. And the roles subsequently written for them—Fidès, Azucena, Amneris, Dalila, Leonora (in *La Favorita*), Eboli (in *Don Carlos*), and so on—were high. Most of the women who sang them also sang soprano parts. Marianne Brandt, for instance, sang not only Kundry but also Fidelio, Donna Elvira, Rachel and Selika (in *L'Africaine*). Marie Brema (1856–1925), a contemporary of Schumann-Heink, born Minny Fehrman in Liverpool of a German father and an American mother, sang both the *Walküre* and *Götterdämmerung* Brünnhildes.

Schumann-Heink never ventured into the soprano realm, and this may have contributed to her vocal longevity. She sang most of the high

The role of Fidès in Meyerbeer's *Le Prophète* was one of Ernestine Schumann-Heink's best, but her favorite was that of the plain, motherly Austrian *Hausfrau*.

mezzo-soprano roles, including Fidès, and she had an astonishing virtuosity, which may be heard in her recording of the "Brindisi" from *Lucrezia Borgia*. But the glory of her sumptuous voice was at the bottom rather than the top, and her greatest roles were Erda and Waltraute. The extraordinary warmth and beauty of her middle register may be savored in her record of "Stille Nacht, heilige Nacht," the playing of which on Christmas Eve was, for a time, an American institution.

It is too bad that English-speaking audiences have so often been condemned to a limited experience of the best German singers. There have been exceptions, of course, notably Lilli Lehmann, Maria Jeritza, Elisabeth Rethberg and Maria Müller. But German artists good enough to be lured abroad have too often been confined to the German repertoire, primarily Wagner, and have had no opportunity to sing the roles for which some of them were most celebrated in Germany.

This constraint was pronounced with Schumann-Heink. As a young singer in Dresden, Hamburg and Berlin she had sung Azucena, Carmen, Amneris, Leonora, Orlovsky (in *Die Fledermaus*), for example. But at the Metropolitan, in the five seasons during which she was a member of the company, beginning with the season of 1898–99, the only major roles she sang were Ortrud, Erda, Fricka, Waltraute, Brangäne and Fidès. In her intermittent appearances thereafter she sang only Erda.

Within that limited repertoire, however, her art and voice cast a unique spell. Krehbiel observed of her debut as Ortrud on January 9, 1899: "If that feature [the character of a loveless woman] of Ortrud's nature has its strongest exemplification in its paganism, then Mme. Schumann-Heink realized it as it has seldom been realized in her invocation of the old Teutonic deities in the second act." Her low voice, he noted, was "exquisite in its union of volume and quality, and," he continued, "when she wins admiration for the passages in which Wagner thought neither of contralto nor soprano, but only of his Frisian creation, half woman, half witch and all wickedness personified, she compelled it by virtue of her thrilling use of tonal color, her giving out of Wagner's ideal which she had absorbed completely."

Almost precisely thirty years later, Olin Downes, in the New York *Times*, was saying of her Erda (in *Das Rheingold*): "Her brief address to Wotan projected itself over every other episode of the performance. . . . Nothing less than a great mistress of art suffices for this passage. The consciousness that was deep in the tone itself, in its every color and inflection, so impressed this listener yesterday [January 21, 1929] that it was some minutes after the disappearance of Erda that he was able to give his attention to the things transpiring before his eyes. This was the fault of Ernestine Schumann-Heink." She was then sixty-seven. There was more of the same three years later, on March 11, 1932, when she took her leave of the stage in the Erda of *Siegfried*. Few singers, male or female, have sung well into their seventies, and, of their small number, Schumann-Heink probably sang the best. She knew, for one thing, what to sing.

But she would not have been the Schumann-Heink of legend had she been content with the conventional operatic career of her time. She was a strong-willed, stubborn and impulsive woman, with a determination to go her own way in her own time that exasperated, in turn, her father, who was an Austrian cavalry officer, her husbands and her managers. It also prompted her to purchase her release from a contract with the opera house in Berlin that would have provided her, in due course, with that pension so treasured in those days by most German singers.

She had strong loyalties, too. One of them was to Maurice Grau, who had brought her to the Metropolitan. When he retired in 1903, she refused to sing under any other management. Another was the United States of America, and this was an enthusiasm that could not be satisfied in New York alone. Against the advice of everyone—including her second husband, Paul Schumann, an actor, whom she left behind in Hamburg, where he died—she toured for a year or two in an operetta *Love's Lottery*, by Julian Edwards. Thereafter, she roamed her new homeland in concert, maintaining residences in California and Chicago, and watering her operatic roots from time to time in Bayreuth, always addressed by Frau Cosima as "Erda." In Dresden, in 1909, she created the role of Clytemnestra in Richard Strauss's *Elektra*.

The great international singers had been touring the United States for years, but usually as members of touring opera companies, including the Metropolitan. Schumann-Heink preferred the more intimate contact of the concert, and the opportunities afforded for offstage acquaintance, uninhibited by membership in an operatic herd and subservience to an impresario. And thus she sang her way into the hearts of her new countrymen, singing the songs they liked to hear.

She was sometimes probably a bit corny, as one would say nowadays, but so were Kreisler and Paderewski—and Melba and Patti and McCormack and Richard Tauber and John Charles Thomas. Ernestine Schumann-Heink rejoiced, as the most universal artists have always rejoiced, in the consciousness of having made her lay listeners happy and their lives a bit richer. She died in Hollywood on November 17, 1936.

XVII

An Italianate Afterglow

RUFFO · TETRAZZINI · GALLI-CURCI

CARUSO · PONSELLE

GRAND OPERA, curiously, was never less Italian than during that last "golden age."

The repertoire was predominantly French and German. Wagner had arrived, and Meyerbeer had not yet left; he would endure as long as there were singers capable of sustaining the superficial glamour of *Les Huguenots*, *Le Prophète* and *L'Africaine*. At the same time, Gounod, Massenet, Thomas, Delibes and Bizet were represented by more than the lone masterpieces that keep their names more or less precariously alive today. Italian opera, even counting Mozart's Italian operas, comprised less than a third of the repertoire in New York, London and Paris, and those who sang the Italian operas outside Italy and South America were only exceptionally Italians.

The Verdi, Donizetti, Bellini and Rossini heroines were sung by Sembrich, a Pole; Melba, an Australian, Lehmann and Gadski, both Germans; and Albani, Eames, de Lussan, Van Zandt, Saville, Traubman and Nordica, all Americans. A Metropolitan *Aida* in 1895, for example, might include Jean and Édouard de Reszke, Nordica, Brema and Maurel. A Metropolitan *Don Giovanni* in 1899 would be cast with Lehmann, Sembrich, Nordica, Maurel, Salignac and Édouard de Reszke—not an Italian in the lot.

Melba was the Metropolitan's first Nedda and Mimi. Eames was the first Santuzza. The first Metropolitan Madame Butterfly would be Farrar, and the first Minnie in *The Girl of the Golden West* Destinn, a Czech. Lina Cavalieri, an Italian soprano more vividly remembered for her beauty and her amorous escapades than for her excellent voice, was the Metropolitan's first Manon Lescaut, Fedora and Adriana Lecouvreur.

For the rest, between Patti's last appearance in 1892 and the arrival of Claudia Muzio in 1916, and discounting the single seasons of Celestina Buoninsegna in 1906–07 and Luisa Tetrazzini in 1911–12, there was not a single proper Italian prima donna on the roster.

In the mezzo-soprano department the Italians were hardly better off. Giulia Ravogli appeared at the Metropolitan only in the season of 1891–92, and Sofia Scalchi made her last appearance in the season of 1895–96. There was, thereafter, only Eugenia Mantelli to hold up the Italian end against Rosa Olitzka, a German; Louise Kirkby-Lunn and Marie Brema, both English; and the Americans, Louise Homer and Edyth Walker. Mantelli's last season was 1902–03, and there would not be another Italian mezzo of the first class before the appearance of Bruna Castagna in 1935.

Italian tenors were almost as rare as Italian sopranos. Between the departure of Italo Campanini and Fernando de Lucia in 1893–94 and the arrival of Caruso in 1903, the great "Italian" tenors at the Metropolitan were de Reszke; Andreas Dippel, a German; Francesco Viñas, a Spaniard; and Albert Alvarez, Thomas Salignac and Albert Saléza, all French. Only among the baritones, in Mario Ancona, Giuseppe Campanari and, after 1899, Antonio Scotti, did the Italians have singers capable of holding their own with non-Italians in the Italian repertoire.

But just before and just after the turn of the century, a variety of circumstances conspired to correct the inferior status of the Italian repertoire and the Italian singer. Wagner and Meyerbeer were, to begin with, uncongenial bedfellows. With the Wagnerians in the ascendancy, Meyerbeer could not long survive; and his oblivion was hastened by the departure—through retirement or death—of the great Meyerbeer singers. When it was no longer possible to produce *Les Huguenots* with Nordica, Scalchi, Melba, Plançon, Maurel and Jean and Édouard de Reszke, Meyerbeer's day was done. Other operas of the French repertoire proved similarly incapable of survival without the support of glamorous and uniquely qualified singers.

It was just at this time that there emerged a new generation of Italian composers—Leoncavallo, Mascagni, Puccini, Giordano, Catalani and Cilèa—and a new idiom of Italian opera, which reflected the influence of both Wagner and Verdi but was closer to the soil, closer to the often cruel and violent realities of everyday life among more or less ordinary people: the idiom known as *verismo*. Here were roles, too, that were closer to the Italian nature than Raoul, de Nevers, St. Bris, Marcel, or Faust and Romeo—or any of Wagner's medieval and prehistoric creatures with their obscure and complex psychological motivation. One need mention only Turiddu, Canio, Tonio, Rodolfo, Andrea Chénier, Gerard (in *Andrea Chénier*) and Scarpia among the men, and Santuzza, Nedda, Mimi, Tosca and Madame Butterfly among the women.

These were simple people, animated by an immediacy of situation and reaction congenial to Italian audiences—and not only to Italians—and comprehensible to Italian singers. And suddenly the Italian singers were there, particularly the males: Antonio Scotti, Enrico Caruso, Riccardo Stracciari, Giuseppe de Luca, Pasquale Amato, Titta Ruffo, Giovanni Zenatello, Alessandro Bonci, Giovanni Martinelli, Bernardo de Muro and Aureliano Pertile among the men; Rosina Storchio (the first Madame Butterfly), Gemma Bellincioni (the first Santuzza and the first Fedora), Cesira Ferrani (the first Mimi and the first Manon Lescaut) and Claudia Muzio among the ladies. It should be added that among these ladies only Muzio sang at the Metropolitan.

It was not that these singers were restricted to the new operas. Most of them sang the Italian repertoire from Mozart and Rossini to Puccini, Giordano and Cilèa. Such versatile artists as Scotti and de Luca were at home in the French repertoire, too. Caruso, particularly, ranged far and wide. Among his greatest parts were des Grieux in Massenet's *Manon*, Samson, Raoul, John of Leyden and Éléazar. But it was the popularity of the new operas, redressing the imbalance of Italian representation in the repertoire, and the exciting manner in which Italian singers sang them, that gave Italians a new status in international opera companies.

One is tempted to assume also that these singers—particularly the men—brought into fashion a new kind of singing, or, at least, a new kind of vocal sound—fat, round, opulent, warm, and well-focused right up to a full-voiced and resonant top. We cannot know how Mario and Tamberlik sounded, or how large and how beautiful were the voices of such early baritones as Giorgio Ronconi and Francesco Graziani. But neither anything written about these older singers, nor the records of the earlier male singers of the last "golden age," taking into account the quality of recording and the ages of the singers when the records were made, suggests voices of the size and richness of Caruso's tenor or Ruffo's baritone.

Certainly the new operas, with their immediacy and unremitting high tension, encouraged a forceful and emphatic kind of singing as violent in contrast to Verdi as Verdi had been to Rossini, Donizetti and Bellini half a century earlier. Floridity had as little place in this kind of opera as in Wagner. Verdi, in his early operas, had not immediately forsaken florid song, least of all for his heroines, but there is little call for it in the

The declining years of the last "golden age" were rich in Italian baritones. The finest vocalists were Giuseppe de Luca (left) as Rigoletto, and Mattia Battistini (above), whose fear of the ocean prevented his coming to the United States.

Riccardo Stracciari (below) was thought by many to have the most beautiful voice.

De Luca described the voice of Titta Ruffo as "a miracle." Others called him "the Caruso of baritones." Hamlet, in Ambroise Thomas's now forgotten opera, was one of his greatest roles (right).

operas of his middle period, and in *Aida, Otello* and *Falstaff* virtually none. The new composers took the hint. They wrote for voices ample, sumptuous and free, with compelling high notes. And it was among the baritones, curiously, that a revival of Italian vocal preeminence first became conspicuously manifest.

The names alone, with the years of birth, will give some idea of the dimensions of this baritone prosperity: del Puente, 1841; Campanari and Antonio Magini-Coletti, 1855; Battistini, 1856; Ancona, 1860; Scotti, 1866; Sammarco, 1873; Stracciari, 1875; de Luca and Ruffo, 1876; Eugenio Giraldoni (the first Scarpia) and Domenico Viglione Borghese, 1877; Amato, 1878; Danise, 1883; Mario Stabile and Luigi Montesanto, 1888.

1. TITTA RUFFO

Of the older singers Scotti is the best-known, if only because he survived at the Metropolitan until 1933. As a singing actor he was the most remarkable of them all, succeeding—and, in the opinion of some, surpassing—Maurel as Don Giovanni, Iago and Falstaff, and unrivaled as Scarpia. But it is among the group born in the 1870s that one senses, on their records, the new kind of singer. And towering above them all—or bellowing, as his detractors insisted—was Titta Ruffo.

He was not the finest singer of the lot. That was de Luca, who sang at the Metropolitan from 1915 to 1935 and then returned in 1939–40, still an exemplary vocalist at sixty-four. He appeared again in the season of 1945–46, demonstrating a vocal longevity equaled in baritone history, probably, only by Battistini, Antonio Cotogni, Lucien Fugère and Sir Charles Santley. The most beautiful voice of all may well have been Stracciari's, although some who heard them both in their prime preferred Amato's. But Ruffo's was simply the grandest voice in baritone history. The only male voice of comparable grandeur was Caruso's, and the one record the two men made together, the "Si, pel ciel" from *Otello*—recorded in 1914, when both were in their prime—stands alone as an example of sheer vocal wealth, unmatched and unapproached among the great documents of vocal recording.

They never appeared together as Othello and Iago, nor, for that matter, did Caruso ever sing Othello, which remains inexplicable in view of the promise of that one record. Neither did they appear together often anywhere else, and certainly not at the Metropolitan. Ruffo's first appearance there was in the season of 1921–22; in other words, not until after Caruso's death. It is assumed, but not documented, that the management did not wish to embarrass Caruso by engaging another male singer so nearly unique and in so nearly the same way, granting Caruso a superior musicality.

Ruffo was never a house baritone. He was a star, a box-office attraction in his own right, entitled to equal billing with the prima donna and the *primo tenore*, and he commanded commensurate fees. Among his great roles were Don Carlos (in *Ernani*), Hamlet, Rigoletto, Figaro, Tonio, Gerard, Barnaba (in *La Gioconda*), Neri Chiaramantesi (in Giordano's *La Cena delle Beffe*) and Cascart (in Leoncavallo's *Zaza*). He was not a great actor, but the enormous voice proceeded from a big, robust body and a massive head, and his movements on the stage had something of the assertive, compelling, overpowering force of his singing.

Critics and fellow baritones alike were at a loss to describe the sound he made—but they tried. De Luca called it "a miracle," and let it go at that. Emilio de Gogorza spoke of "a black voice." The critic Henry T. Finck thought of a "baritonal Tamagno." Lauri-Volpi called it "a leonine voice," and Maurel used to say that Ruffo's D-flat, D, E-flat and the following notes to the top A-flat were the most glorious baritone sounds he had ever heard. Anyone who has listened to his cadence on C-sharp, A, D at the end of his recording of the "Nemico della patria" from *Andrea Chénier* will know what Maurel was talking about, and anyone who has heard his "Brindisi" from *Hamlet* will know what they all were talking about.

Ruffo's first appearances in the United States were with the Philadelphia-Chicago Company in Philadelphia on November 4 and New York on November 19, 1912. By the time he arrived at the Metropolitan he was forty-five, and the voice, while retaining its size, was beginning to lose some of its concentrated resonance. By the mid-twenties it had a hollow sound, as if the center had been blown out. It was still big, but the metal —variously described as bronze or brass—was gone. He retired in 1929 and died in Florence in 1953.

2. LUISA TETRAZZINI and AMELITA GALLI-CURCI

Great Italian singers of this period were less numerous among the females than the males. There were fine singers, to be sure—Storchio, Bellincioni and Buoninsegna—but non-Italians surpassed them in the heavier dramatic and even in the dramatic-lyric roles—or were preferred to them in Paris, London and New York. Italian dramatic sopranos, at that time, rejoiced in the display rather than the disguise of separate

Luisa Tetrazzini was a true coloratura and a notably buxom one, possibly thanks to the chicken recipe (with spaghetti) which still bears her name. She is seen here as Rosina in *The Barber of Seville* (above left).

"Like a pansy in the velvet of its medium scale" was the way Geraldine Farrar described the voice of Amelita Galli-Curci. She is shown (above right) as she appeared at the height of her career.

Among the great early-20th-century tenors were Beniamino Gigli (below left) as Vasco da Gama in *L'Africaine*, and Giacomo Lauri-Volpi (below right) as Radames.

registers, and their booming, sometimes almost baritone chest tones, particularly, were felt as vulgar and grotesque by non-Latin audiences. And so most of them sang in Italy, Spain and South America.

But in two spectacular instances Italian women enjoyed reputations hardly less lustrous than those of the men. The ladies were Luisa Tetrazzini, born in 1871, and Amelita Galli-Curci, born in 1882. Neither of them, significantly, was a dramatic soprano. Nor were they in any way a reflection or a product of the new developments in contemporary Italian opera. They represented, rather, the continuation of the older Italian tradition of florid song, a responsibility that had not been fulfilled by Italian female throats since the prime of Giulia Grisi, discounting Patti, of course, who was born in Madrid and reared in America, and who neither studied nor served an apprenticeship in Italy.

Although it is impossible to fix a date when the coloratura soprano came to be regarded as a creature distinct and apart from her lyric and dramatic sisters, one is tempted to speak of Tetrazzini and Galli-Curci as the first true coloratura sopranos in the sense that the term is used today. Patti, Albani, Melba and Eames, to be sure, all sang the roles of Gilda, Lucia, Rosina, Violetta, Juliet, Amina, Valentine, and others that Tetrazzini and Galli-Curci sang. But they also sang much else—Elisabeth, Elsa, Eva, Aida and Desdemona; Albani even sang an Isolde. And these same roles were sung by other women hardly thought of as coloraturas, notably Lehmann and Nordica.

Tetrazzini and Galli-Curci sang nothing but coloratura parts, and it was the breathtaking ease and brilliance with which, in their prime, they mastered the virtuoso demands of such roles, rather than any compelling dramatic expression or histrionic excellence, that distinguished their performance and sustained their celebrity. *Fioritura*, with the earlier sopranos, had been accepted as one of many constituent elements of the singer's art, with the extreme high notes, say D and above, an attractive option for those who could produce them. With Tetrazzini and Galli-Curci *fioritura*, crowned by E-flats, E's and F's at the end of a cadenza, was a vocal way of life. It was a kind of singing symbolized more recently by Lily Pons.

It should come as no surprise, therefore, that each had her limitations. Both had lovely, clear, limpid voices—Farrar described Galli-Curci's as "a voice of rare timbre, like a pansy in the velvet of its medium scale"— and they prospered in the rarefied atmosphere above high C; but Tetrazzini's glorious top was not matched by any comparable glory below, and Galli-Curci had difficulties with pitch that became conspicuous well before the end of her career. Tetrazzini rarely deviated from pitch, but her deviations from taste in what she chose to add to the written score were frequent and sometimes startling, as may be confirmed in her recordings.

The kind of singing in which they specialized and excelled is the province of youth, and it may be assumed that they both sang better, or at least with less waywardness and eccentricity, in the earlier years of their careers than they did at the height of their fame. This would be particularly true of Galli-Curci, who reached her peak in Meyerbeer's rarely heard *Dinorah* in her mid-twenties. Her famous recording of the "Shadow Song" from that opera is an astonishing tour de force.

Tetrazzini was thirty-seven and had fifteen years of operatic campaigning behind her when she arrived at Oscar Hammerstein's Manhattan Opera House in 1908, hailed as a new Melba; she was forty, and had passed from plump to fat, when she reached the Metropolitan for a single season in 1911–12. There was no sign of vocal decay in those areas of the compass where she had always been most comfortable. Indeed, she continued to sing well for another twenty years. But her already great celebrity probably encouraged her to regard certain musical excesses as a prima donna's inalienable prerogative.

Galli-Curci was forty when she reached the Metropolitan in the season of 1921–22, and she was already suffering from a goiter which inhibited muscular freedom in her throat. The critics, who had applauded her earlier appearances in New York with the Chicago Company in 1918, noted a tendency to sag from pitch, as well as evidence of labor in the taxing passages. The exceptional beauty of her voice was unimpaired, but it was no longer fully responsive. The goiter was removed some years later, but she never regained her former facility. She died in 1963.

In the short span of her prime she became a legend, and her name a household word. When "Red" Grange was making nonmusical history at the University of Illinois as one of the greatest running backs of American football, someone once suggested to Bob Zuppke, the Illinois coach, that Grange was deficient, or negligent, in other departments of the game, that all he could do was run. Zuppke is supposed to have replied: "All Galli-Curci can do is sing." Of such fame are legends made.

The season of 1929–30 was her last at the Metropolitan, and the following season was Lily Pons's first.

3. ENRICO CARUSO

For all the fine achievements of the baritones and coloratura sopranos, the most enduring and the most glorious symbol of Italy's survival as a

Caruso's favorite debut role in his early career was the Duke in *Rigoletto* (right).

He appears more at ease (below left), possibly listening to one of his own more than 200 records. Although more familiarly associated with heavier dramatic parts, Caruso was a natural comedian, and he particularly enjoyed the role of Nemorino in *L'Elisir d'amore* (below right).

source of great singers was Caruso, born in 1873, who reigned supreme among singers of all categories from the beginning of the century until his death in Naples in 1921, the rightful, undisputed heir to the throne of Jean de Reszke. It is generally conceded that there never was a tenor voice comparable to his in its harmony of size, brilliance and warmth. Possibly because of its combination of resonance and a velvety smoothness, it lent itself to phonograph recording more satisfactorily than most other voices of that pioneering epoch in the recording industry, and the result is a legacy of some two hundred and fifty records, providing a complete account of his career and covering every aspect of his vocal art from the simplest Italian and Neapolitan songs to the most demanding arias of the opera repertoire.

Many singers have achieved immortality of a kind by their excellence in a restricted area, or by their association with particular roles—Tamagno as Othello, Maurel as Iago and Falstaff, Scotti as Scarpia, Jeritza as Turandot and Tosca, Mary Garden as Mélisande, Lotte Lehmann as the Marschallin, Chaliapin as Boris, for example. Others, like Melba and Tetrazzini, having achieved fame, were content to go on for year after year repeating the roles in which their fame was won. Caruso, although he never attempted de Reszke's feat of singing Wagner in German, sang an extraordinarily wide and varied French and Italian repertoire, ranging from lyric to dramatic, from Nemorino to Éléazar. He sang the new Italian operas of Puccini, Mascagni, Leoncavallo, Giordano and Cilèa, but he also sang the older repertoire—*Le Prophète, L'Africaine, Les Huguenots, William Tell, Faust,* and so on—and, of course, the Verdi operas.

In the line of Italian tenors Caruso followed Tamagno and de Lucia, but he was unlike either of them—more lyric than Tamagno, more straightforward than de Lucia, although sharing with both the intensity and immediacy of vocal utterance that have always distinguished the great Italian singers at their best. What we read of de Lucia, and what can be heard of him on records, are evidence of a more old-fashioned kind of vocalism than Caruso's, with a marked vibrato and much use of mixed voice, head voice and falsetto contrasted with full, ringing high notes. These devices of contrast Caruso rarely employed. Some other tenors have employed them until comparatively recently, notably Lauri-Volpi, Richard Tauber, and Fleta. There was none of this in Tamagno's singing, of course, which, in comparison with Caruso's, was primitive.

Among Caruso's Italian contemporaries, only Alessandro Bonci (1870–1940) and Giovanni Zenatello (1876–1949) approached him in a limited repertoire, Bonci in lighter, lyric roles, some of which Caruso did not sing, and Zenatello in certain dramatic parts, especially Othello, in which he shared preeminence with Leo Slezak between the decline of Tamagno and the assumption of the role by Martinelli in 1937. Neither Bonci nor Zenatello left anything like Caruso's imprint on vocal history, but they were certainly fine singers.

Bonci, a distinctive stylist, has been described by Hurst as seeming to have solved "the entire problem of voice production, leaving the uninitiated listener with the impression that there was no problem to solve, and he took the high D with the utmost ease." In Zenatello's case it is worth noting that his renown was inhibited by the fact of his never having sung at the Metropolitan, undoubtedly because of Caruso's presence there. Of his Othello, Victor Gollancz goes so far as to say that "opera-goers too young to have heard Zenatello's piercingly clean but ample and rounded 'Esultate,' with its grace-note glory, sung to thrilling perfection, can have little idea of what that music can mean."

But whatever the virtues of other tenors, they paled beside Caruso's. He had everything as a singer and learned much as an actor. For all the size of his voice, he even had an astonishing agility, as documented in his cadenza in "La donna è mobile." If hardly a profound musician, he was nevertheless profoundly musical, with a Neapolitan's inborn compulsion to musical communication. Thus, his singing was never just vocally exciting. It was always ennobled by sympathy and compassion.

He had the big high notes, but he was never a mere high-note singer, as many of his imitators have been. He had exceptional vocal amplitude, but he was not a bellower. His pathos was sometimes blemished—for Northern ears—by an all too explicit Neapolitan exuberance; but he was, after all, a Neapolitan, and one may argue that vocal communication is not necessarily enriched by making a dogma of transalpine and Anglo-Saxon restraint. And Caruso could sing lyrically without a trace of that preciousness that often passes for artistry in the singing of the more sophisticated.

Indeed, the stunning glory of Caruso's voice probably overshadowed the sheer beauty of his singing, which was a pity; for the secret of its beauty lay not in the voice alone, nor even in this singer's extraordinary, probably intuitive, sense of form in the shaping of every phrase and of every song and aria, but rather in the fact that there were most marvelously united in Enrico Caruso a beautiful voice and a beautiful nature. The radiance that illumined his singing did not originate in the throat or the head. It originated in the man. No one understood this, or could have understood it, better than his American wife, Dorothy; and in her tribute to him, *Enrico Caruso, His Life and Death,* she has explained it in prose of a simple eloquence worthy of her husband:

"Enrico's nature was not only uncomplicated; it was actually elemental. He was made in large blocks of essentials. His humanity was deep, his humor was broad, his faith was high. . . . His complete absorption in his own work left him neither the time nor the desire to indulge in the usual and useless commentaries on events and people. . . . His manner was perfect . . . at the same time affable and impenetrable. . . . Nor did he depend on others to advise, amuse, comfort or inspire him, since he knew that his source was uniquely within him. . . . His consciousness of being his own source was the force which spurred him toward perfection. . . . He didn't preach tolerance, kindness, generosity, justice, resourcefulness—these requisites of wisdom were the elements of which he was made."

When asked what were the requisites of a great singer, Caruso once said: "A big chest, a big mouth, ninety percent memory, ten percent intelligence, lots of hard work and something in the heart."

Something in the heart! How had Tosi put it two centuries before?

"Oh, how great a master is the heart! Confess it, my beloved singers, and gratefully own that you would not have arrived at the highest rank of the profession if you had not been its scholars; own that in a few lessons from it you learned the most beautiful expressions, the most refined taste, the most noble action and the most exquisite graces; own (though it be hardly credible) that heart corrects the defects of nature, since it softens a voice that is harsh, betters an indifferent one, and perfects a good one. Own, when the heart sings you cannot dissemble, nor has truth a greater power of persuading. And lastly, do you convince the world that from the heart alone you have learned that pleasing charm that so subtly passes from vein to vein and makes its way to the very soul."

Caruso's voice being what it was, his heart was little burdened with correcting the defects of nature, softening harshness or bettering indifference. It could concentrate on the perfection of the good. Since the heart was big, and the voice nearly perfect to begin with, the lyrical communication was an unexampled combination of excitement and warmth.

One of the attractions of singing, for the vocally gifted, is a kind of sensuous pleasure experienced by the singer in the production of sound, an autointoxication, if you will, induced not only by the sound alone but by the physical vibrations which produce it. One senses this pleasure in

Caruso's singing; but being the simple, warmhearted, generous man he was, he could never be content with selfish enjoyment. He acknowledged in his extraordinary vocal and musical endowment an obligation to share his gifts, his accomplishments and his pleasures with others.

The public was his partner in the fulfillment of a mission, and his role in the partnership was to give the best, and all of the best, that was in him, even if this meant singing through a hemorrhage, as he did in a performance of *L'Elisir d'Amore* at the Brooklyn Academy of Music the year before he died, a manifestation of the abscesses of the lung that killed him. To decline to sing if he could sing, or to give less than his best, was not just failure but betrayal. And one senses in his finest accomplishments, of which there are many on records, not just a singer rejoicing in the glory of the sound he makes but rather his profounder satisfaction in sharing a providential bounty.

Caruso was not without Italian heirs. Martinelli had joined the Metropolitan in the season of 1913–14. Beniamino Gigli arrived in 1920–21 and Giacomo Lauri-Volpi in 1922–23. Each of them, had there never been a Caruso, would have been a candidate for recognition as the greatest tenor of the century thus far. They had strikingly distinctive voices: Martinelli's intensely concentrated and brilliantly penetrant; Gigli's all silver and produced, in its prime, with such marvelous ease that he used to sing Rodolfo's "Narrative" seated, not rising from his chair even for the high C; Lauri-Volpi's less beautiful than Gigli's, but with a persuasive sensual quality and an exultant top that made the *Turandot* arias and the last act of *Andrea Chénier* unforgettable.

These tenors provided the Metropolitan with a supplementary "golden age" decade as far as Rodolfo, Cavaradossi, Pinkerton, Andrea Chénier, Vasco di Gama, Arnold, the Duke, Manrico and Radames were concerned. Martinelli not only took over Éléazar from Caruso, giving it a special distinction all his own, but, in 1937, earned his place in history as one of the great Othellos. Among the lower voices there were still Ruffo, de Luca, Danise and Mario Basiola, and, after his debut in 1926, Ezio Pinza to match the luster of their tenor counterparts. In 1940 the arrival of Salvatore Baccaloni brought the welcome assurance that the genre of the Italian *basso buffo* was not extinct.

4. ROSA PONSELLE

But for many the most striking personality of this decade—and, in certain respects, the most strikingly Italian—was an American, Rosa Pon-

Although she was American-born, there was Italian blood in the veins and an Italian spirit in the art of Rosa Ponselle. As Norma (left), one of her greatest roles.

Among the Italian ornaments of the post-"golden age" were Giovanni Martinelli (below right), who succeeded to Caruso's role of Éleazar in *La Juive*, and Ezio Pinza (below left) as Don Giovanni, now most vividly and affectionately remembered for *South Pacific* and "One Enchanted Evening."

selle, born Rosa Ponzillo in Meriden, Connecticut, on January 22, 1897. Hers was an Italian dramatic soprano of a kind—excepting Muzio's, perhaps—that had not been heard since the time of Buoninsegna: dark, brilliant, ample, with those lower tones which, when exploited with discretion, have ever been the glory of the great Italian sopranos, and with a flexibility that made available to her some of the roles associated with the great Italians of a century earlier: Pasta, Persiani and Grisi.

All this seems to have come to her naturally. From the obscurity of vaudeville and moving-picture houses, where she and her sister Carmela had been singing as "the Ponzillo Sisters," she emerged suddenly on the stage of the Metropolitan on November 15, 1918, at the age of twenty-one, singing Leonora to Caruso's Don Alvaro in *La Forza del Destino*. "*Place aux dames*," wrote Huneker in the *Times*. "She is comely and she is tall and solidly built. A fine figure of a woman . . . added to her personal attractiveness, she possesses a voice of natural beauty that may prove a gold mine; it is vocal gold, anyway, with its luscious lower and middle tones, dark, rich and ductile."

She was not quite ready for such celebrity or for such expectations, least of all in a company that still included Muzio, Destinn, Farrar, Alda, Easton and Bori, all singing roles that would subsequently be hers. When she sang the Rachel to Caruso's Eléazar in her second season, Richard Aldrich, in the *Times*, could say only that "Ponselle is also given some opportunity to sing well, some of which she accepts." But in the ensuing seasons she added Elizabeth (in *Don Carlos*), Santuzza, Leonora (in *Il Trovatore*), Elvira (in *Ernani*), Selika (in *L'Africaine*) and Maddalena (in *Andrea Chénier*). When *La Vestale* was revived for her in 1925 she was approaching her vocal maturity, and Lawrence Gilman told the readers of the *Herald Tribune*:

"Here was a singer who could sing Spontini's long, gravely sculptured melodies with the required sense of line and dignity of style, and with the formal and somewhat stilted pathos that is their quaint and special mark—as in her second-act aria 'Tu che invoco con orrore'; for Miss Ponselle sang these passages of cantilena with admirable phrasing, with loveliness of tone, and severity of style, and she was no less admirable in those moments of true dramatic expression with which the score abounds."

The peak of her career was reached two years later with Norma, a role that has been revived at intervals for almost a century and a half as the ultimate test by which the truly great sopranos could distinguish themselves from the merely very good. Ponselle was one of them. Her voice, wrote Olin Downes in the *Times*, "is probably the most beautiful of any soprano of her generation." And it was a generation that included Jeritza, Muzio and Rethberg!

Ponselle's last new role was Carmen. She had been coached in it by the Spanish mezzo-soprano, Maria Gay, and she incorporated in her characterization some of the vulgarity for which Gay had been taken to task when she sang the role at the Metropolitan in the season of 1908–09. The New York critics found this attempt at realism no less offensive in 1935. But she moderated it after the unsatisfactory première, and it came to be regarded as one of the finest achievements of a career to which she put a timely and dignified end by retiring after the season of 1936–37.

By that time the Italianate afterglow had already begun to fade. The Great Depression was on. At the Metropolitan the Italians were reluctant to accept lower fees as dictated by the failing economy, and in the early thirties they drifted off, one by one: Danise, Gigli, Lauri-Volpi, de Luca. The aging Scotti retired in 1933. Only Martinelli and Pinza held on among the great Italian names, to be joined by Bruna Castagna. The future of Italian opera, in America, at least, rested largely with non-Italians, many of them Americans—Lawrence Tibbett, John Charles Thomas, Mario Chamlee, Sydney Rayner, Richard Bonelli, Charles Kullmann, Richard Crooks, Leonard Warren, Robert Weede, Jan Peerce and Richard Tucker; and, of course, with the Pole, Jan Kiepura, and the splendid Swedish tenor, Jussi Björling.

Among the ladies, neither Gina Cigna nor Maria Caniglia was able to erase the memory of Muzio and Ponselle, or hold her own against the Croatian Zinka Milanov; nor could the American Dusolina Giannini, whose voice and features were as Italianate as Ponselle's. Giannini's greatest successes were achieved in Europe. At the Metropolitan, Castagna was alone among the Italian mezzo-sopranos, but elsewhere Ebe Stignani disclosed a voice of comparable magnificence and a similarly eloquent dramatic utterance. An Italian consolation in New York was the arrival of Licia Albanese for the 1939–40 season to take over the lyric roles long and affectionately associated with the Spanish Lucrezia Bori and the Brazilian Bidú Sayão.

The great Italian singers of the first three decades of the century, particularly the tenors and baritones, have not, for those who heard them in their prime, been rivaled by their more recent Italian successors.

· XVIII ·

The Singing Actresses

CALVÉ · GARDEN · FARRAR

"IT IS SAFE to say," wrote Krehbiel in the *Tribune* of a performance of Ambroise Thomas's *Hamlet* at the Metropolitan Opera House on December 4, 1895, "that no Ophelia who has been seen here in years, on either the lyric or the dramatic stage, has expressed what Mme. Calvé expressed in this scene [the Mad Scene].

"Her face was full of simplicity, childish sweetness and wistful wonder, but its simplicity was not that of a happy and intelligent child; it was that of vacancy. Her eyes and her lips had no mind behind them. Her motions seemed to have no guidance. They were sudden, capricious and constantly changing, yet always full of grace and prettiness.

"At the end of her aria she sank in a shapeless heap, and the ushers thought it a fitting time to throw bouquets at her. The members of the chorus brought them to where she lay, but she would have none of them. Then she started up, caught at the bouquets, tore them to pieces and almost buried herself in them. Such an incident with a singer who was less an artist would have destroyed the effect, if she had succeeded in making any. Mme. Calvé made it all a part of her scene, treated it consistently in her own mood and made it contribute to the purpose of all that she had done hitherto and to the result that followed. A wonderful artist, indeed, is this woman, and a wondrous pity it is that the operatic list which she has made her own is so circumscribed."

This extraordinary scene would seem to be as appropriate an introduction as any to a kind of prima donna that emerged at the turn of the century and came to be called the "singing actress." Calvé was not, of course, the first great singer to be so designated, or to qualify for the designation. Pasta and Malibran probably sang too well to be thought of as actresses first and singers afterward. The term would more likely have been applied to Pauline Viardot, and certainly to Schröder-Devrient. What conspired to bring Emma Calvé, Mary Garden and Geraldine Farrar to the fore, and to set them apart from other singers of their time, was a new repertoire in which vocal virtuosity of the traditional sort was deprecated in favor of a more emotionally immediate kind of singing.

The Rossini-Bellini-Donizetti-Meyerbeer-Verdi repertoire had begun with vocal virtuosity. More than virtuosity might be added; but without it the singer simply could not perform. He had no business being on the stage. And even Wagner, for all his eschewal of ornamentation and *fioritura*, required a lot of sheer voice. The operas of the new repertoire, concentrating more upon the projection of a personality than upon the exploitation of vocal virtuosity, enabled certain singers to achieve greatness without being great singers by standards previously prevailing.

The *verismo* operas of the young Italian composers were of this sort, and made to order for such a singer as Calvé, whose Santuzza quickly eclipsed Bellincioni's original; and for Farrar, whose Madame Butterfly was unrivaled as long as she was present and in form to sing it. But there was also a parallel French idiom, centered, usually, on the projection of exotic and otherwise fascinating females, that provided an even more congenial setting for the art of Calvé, Garden and Farrar.

It is difficult for us to comprehend this idiom today, for it was short-lived. Most of the operas and, in some cases, even the composers are virtually forgotten. The name of Jules Massenet, of course, is remembered. *Manon* is still in the repertoire. But what of *Sapho, Hérodiade, Esclarmonde, Grisélidis, Thaïs, La Navarraise* and *Cléopâtre*? We still hear *Samson et Dalila*, but what of Saint-Saëns' *Hélène*, and *Phryné*? *Mignon* is still heard from time to time, but who knows a note of Thomas's *Hamlet, Psyché* or *Le Songe d'une Nuit d'Été*?

Gustave Charpentier lives intermittently as the composer of *Louise*. *Carmen* seems to be imperishable, but Bizet also wrote *La Jolie Fille de Perth, Djamileh* and *Les Pêcheurs de Perles*. Totally forgotten are Camille Erlanger's *Aphrodite*, Henri Février's *Monna Vanna*, Xavier Leroux's *La Reine Fiammette*, Félicien David's *Lalla-Roukh*, Victor Massé's *Une Nuit de Cléopâtre* and Gabriel Pierné's *La Fille de Tabarin*. With them in limbo languish such non-Gallic items as Leoncavallo's *Zaza*, Giordano's *Madame Sans-Gêne* and *Fedora*, Mascagni's *Lodoletta* and *Iris*, and Humperdinck's *Die Königskinder*.

But still remembered are the three extraordinary ladies whose art en-

dowed them with a fleeting but glamorous vitality. The sturdier operas—
Carmen, Manon, Cavalleria Rusticana, Pagliacci, Tosca, La Bohème
and *Madame Butterfly*—are still effective as sung by a more traditional
kind of opera singer. The others required more than that, and if the
likes of Calvé, Garden and Farrar are about today, they are not in the
opera house.

1. EMMA CALVÉ

Calvé, the first on the scene—she was born in 1858—was also the slow-
est starter, possibly because she had no operatic model, as Garden and
Farrar subsequently had in Calvé. She sang for a good many years in
Belgium, France and Italy without fully satisfying either her listeners or
herself, and in Milan she was even hissed. But Maurel, apparently sensing her potential, chose her to appear with him in Théodore Dubois's
Aben-Hamet at the Théâtre-Italien in 1884, and from him she received
invaluable advice and assistance. "I have always been deeply grateful to
Maurel," she wrote in *My Life*, "for the lessons in lyric declamation
which I received from him and which have greatly influenced my career."

A subsequent influence was Eleanora Duse, the Italian actress. "Her
art," Calvé remembered, "simple, human, passionately sincere, was a
revelation to me." Calvé followed her from town to town in Italy, ob-
serving, studying, but never presuming to meet her. That a young singer
should have chosen an actress rather than another singer as a model
shows where her instinctive predilections lay. One is reminded of Nourrit
and Talma. And it can have been no accident that her first great success
was as Santuzza, which had been one of Duse's most celebrated accomplishments on the stage.

But Calvé's was not a merely imitative success. In realizing Santuzza
as an operatic heroine she was, of course, guided by Mascagni's music as
well as by the character of Giovanni Verga's play. Bispham, who saw
both Duse and Calvé in the part in London in 1895, found Duse "all
intelligence" and Calvé "all fire," which would suggest the influence of
Bellincioni as well as of Duse. Shaw, when Calvé sang the first Santuzza
in London in 1892, found her "irresistibly moving and beautiful, and
fully capable of sustaining the inevitable comparison with Duse's impersonation of the same part."

Calvé learned much from Marie Miolan-Carvalho, a pupil of Duprez
and Gounod's first Marguerite, and much, too, from her ultimate voice

teacher, Rosina Laborde, a singer whose memory went back to Malibran, Pasta, Sontag, Tamburini and Lablache. She probably owed more to Marchesi, with whom she had studied in 1882 and 1883, than she chose to acknowledge. From Marchesi, to be sure, she would never have learned the kind of dramatic vocal coloration that made her Santuzza and, subsequently, her Carmen so memorable. But unlike Garden and Farrar, she was a superb vocalist, with a voice ranging from A below middle C to the E above high C, and it seems likely that she retained throughout her career certain fundamentals of virtuoso vocalism that she had learned from Marchesi.

A vocal phenomenon in any case, she was equally comfortable in the soprano and mezzo-soprano ranges, which would explain her vocal affinity for Carmen; but she never achieved the kind of even scale from top to bottom that Marchesi doubtlessly toiled to impose upon her, although she might well have achieved it had she remained with Marchesi longer. Indeed, Calvé used to say that because of her "two voices," she never had to strain the one in order to reach the other. She could sing just about anything. In *The Marriage of Figaro*, for instance, she sang, at one time or another, Cherubino, Susanna and the Countess; and in Massenet's *Hérodiade* she sang both the contralto Hérodias and the soprano Salomé.

She spoke, sometimes, of four voices, referring to a third, or head voice, and to the unearthly, disembodied "fourth voice" that she had learned from Mustafà, the next to last castrato at the Sistine Chapel. "You have only to practice with your mouth tight shut for two hours a day for ten years," Mustafà had told her, "then you may possibly be able to do something with it."

Calvé mastered the trick in three years, and Massenet provided for it in *Sapho*, which she created in 1897. It may be heard on two of her records: the aria "Charmant oiseau," from David's *La Perle du Brésil*, and a folk song, "Ma Lisette." Calvé said that she had never been able to pass it on to any of her pupils; but those who observed the way Lily Pons used to close her mouth to produce her highest notes have speculated that Pons, by accident or instruction, may have approximated the technique.

Calvé sang a wide repertoire, including such traditional roles as Lucia, Amina, Pamina, Marguerite, and Juliet, but her success as Carmen, Santuzza and Ophelia at the height of her career was such that she was given little opportunity to sing anything else, hence Krehbiel's reference to a circumscribed repertoire; and these were the roles by which she is

Emma Calvé is shown (above) as Ophelia in *Hamlet*: "Its simplicity . . . was that of vacancy. Her eyes and lips had no mind behind them," wrote H. E. Krehbiel. Carmen has attracted hundreds of sopranos and mezzo-sopranos and has eluded most of them. Calvé caught her (left)—and didn't like what she caught.

remembered. The names of the famous singers who have tried Carmen would fill a column or two of a telephone book. That the name of Calvé remains indelibly associated with the part to this day testifies to a unique accomplishment.

But it was Santuzza which first made her an international celebrity. Following her success in the première of *L'Amico Fritz* in Rome in 1891, she was engaged to be the first Santuzza at the Opéra-Comique. By now her singular combination of intelligence, originality and determination was beginning to mature.

"My interpretation of the role of Santuzza," she recalled, "astonished my comrades. My spontaneous and apparently unstudied gestures shocked them. Even the costume, which I had brought with me from Italy, the clothes of a real peasant woman, coarse shirt, worn sandals and all, was considered eccentric and ugly. I was unmercifully criticized and ridiculed. . . . 'Come what will,' I thought, 'I shall act the part as I feel it.' I went on the stage, and I was . . . the naïve and tragic Santuzza, the passionate, impulsive peasant girl of Italy. It was a triumph!"

Carmen followed. If, as Santuzza, she had defied certain general traditions of dress and decorum, as Carmen she defied specific traditions of costume and performance in a role that had already had many distinguished interpreters, including Marie Galli-Marié, who had created it in 1875 and was still living in Paris. An inveterate traveler and always a curious observer, Calvé had visited Granada and seen the gypsies and their dances. She had studied their dress, gestures and movements; and she now strove for authenticity in her own impersonation.

"I insisted," she wrote in *My Life*, "on wearing the fringed shawl which is called in Spain the *mantón de Manila* instead of the bolero and short skirt in which the part had always been costumed. In the matter of the dance, also, my ideas and those of the directors did not agree! They wanted me to learn the steps which had been danced with such grace and charm by Galli-Marié. 'How do you expect me to imitate Galli?' I protested. 'She was small, dainty and an entirely different build. I am big. I have long arms. It is absurd for me to imitate anyone but the gypsies themselves.' Whereupon, I showed them the true dance of the *gitanas*, with its special use of the arms and hands—a manner of dancing for which the Spaniards have invented the expression *el bracear*."

Her success was enormous, and, by her own admission, it went to her head. "If I was criticized out of all measure before these two successes," she remembered, "after them I was praised with equal lack of restraint. Everything I now did was right. Unfortunately for me, no one dared utter a word of criticism: and in consequence, I was carried away by my passion for realism. It became an obsession, and occasionally I overstepped the mark. Later, however, I learned wisdom and moderation."

She could not yet have experienced this enlightenment when Shaw witnessed her Carmen in London in 1894. His comments may have assisted her to it. Shaw was, by his own admission, immoderately pro-Calvé. She was a woman, he wrote, "whose strange personal appearance recalls Titian's wonderful *Virgin of the Assumption* at Venice, and who has, in addition to the beauty of aspect, a beauty of action—especially of that sort of action which is the thought or conception of the artist made visible—such as one might expect from Titian's Virgin if the picture were made alive."

But he found her Carmen shocking, and in no flattering sense of the word. This Carmen, he reported, "is a superstitious, pleasure-loving good-for-nothing, caught by the outside of anything glittering, with no power but the power of seduction, which she exercises without sense or decency. There is no suggestion of any fine quality about her, not a spark of honesty, courage, or even of that sort of honor supposed to prevail among thieves. All this is conveyed by Calvé with a positively frightful artistic power of divesting her beauty and grace of the nobility—I had almost written the sanctity—which seems inseparable from them in other parts. . . .

"Her death-scene, too, is horribly real. The young lady Carmen is never so effectively alive as when she falls, stage dead, beneath José's cruel knife. But to see Calvé's Carmen changing from a live creature, with properly coordinated movements, into a reeling, staggering, flopping, disorganized thing, and finally tumble down a mere heap of carrion, is to get much the same sensation as might be given by the reality of a brutal murder. . . . Nothing would induce me to go again. To me it was a desecration of a great talent. I felt furious with Calvé, as if I had been shown some terrible caricature by Hogarth of the Titian."

Calvé may have been encouraged to mend her ways by Shaw, but she had obviously not been sobered by the wry comments of the New York critics, who had written similarly, if less vividly, six months earlier. Subsequent Carmens have made Calvé's seem tame, notably those of Gay, Jeritza and Ponselle, all of whom indulged in a purposefully rude and vulgar kind of exhibitionism that would probably have shocked Calvé.

It has not been, with *Carmen*, a question of who was closer to Meilhac and Halévy, Bizet's librettists, or to the Merimée original; it has been rather that the vogue of the *verismo* operas of the end of the century made possible an impersonation closer to an unromanticized gypsy than was previously thinkable either in literature or on the stage. And to ambitious prima donnas the notoriety of a shocking success was irresistible.

Calvé herself seems to have shared Shaw's aversion to the character she offered as Carmen, and it was not her favorite part. She found it antipathetic, redeemed only by truthfulness and bravery, qualities she seems not to have communicated to Shaw. It must have been her own concern for truthfulness that persuaded her to treat it that way. Once fashioned and perfected, it was so popular that she became her own creature's slave and would continue to be so throughout a long career.

The Calvé of real life is elusive. She may have belonged, like Garden, to those who live in the parts they play. Memoirs often tell much, sometimes unwittingly, but Calvé's betray little except her eager curiosity about all that she saw and experienced in her extensive travels. In her relations with other people she was considered capricious and difficult, although capable of much charm. And she had a southern temper. Bispham tells of a quarrel she had with the tenor Alvarez during a performance of *Carmen* when Bispham was relieved, as the final curtain fell, to find that Don José's knife had not been planted firmly between her shoulder blades. She died in Millau, in southern France, in 1942.

2. MARY GARDEN

Mary Garden, born in Aberdeen, Scotland, in 1874, but raised in America, and Geraldine Farrar, born in Melrose, Massachusetts, in 1882, resembled Calvé in their concept of the voice and singing as constituent elements of an actress's equipment and art, and in their taste for original and realistic theater, emancipated from tradition. For the rest, they were as different from Calvé as Scotland and New England are different from the south of France. They differed conspicuously from one another, too, but they had much in common besides an American upbringing.

They were both exceptionally well-favored. They were both strongwilled, stagestruck and ambitious, which has been true of most prima donnas. What they shared in an extraordinary degree was the indefinable quality which today we call glamour. And it was this quality, probably, that enabled them both to begin at the top and stay at the top. Stardom was not something they worked up to through a proper schooling and apprenticeship. It was immediate. They were born for it, and when opportunity offered it, they seized it. Garden made her first appearance on any stage at the Opéra-Comique as Louise on April 13, 1900, when, at the second act, she replaced the indisposed Marthe Rioton, who

Thaïs, conceived by a Frenchman for the Opéra-Comique, has been singularly associated with Americans. Sybil Sanderson was the first, and Geraldine Farrar the prettiest; Mary Garden (above) was probably the greatest. Among Garden's favorite roles was the title role of *Le Jongleur de Notre-Dame* (below left), originally written for a tenor. She was not quite the first Louise. That was Marthe Rioton (below right), whose indisposition gave Garden the opportunity for her first and greatest role.

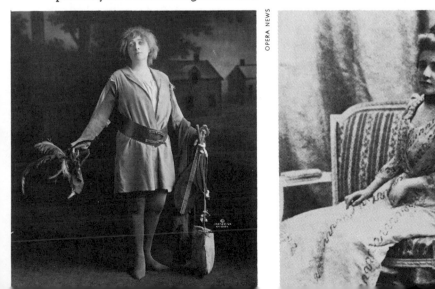

had created the role two months earlier. Farrar began her operatic life as Marguerite in *Faust* at the Royal Opera in Berlin on October 15, 1901, aged nineteen.

Both were fascinating women as well as fascinating actresses, and it was not their celebrity alone that proved so attractive to celebrated men. Garden was loved by André Messager, the conductor of her debut as Louise, by Albert Carré, director of the Opéra-Comique, and by Debussy. Farrar, in Berlin, was distinguished by the attentions of none other than the German crown prince. Among her subsequent admirers were Scotti and, it is said, Toscanini. Garden, who never married, insists that men fell in love not with her but with the women she created on the stage With Farrar, who had an unsuccessful marriage to the Dutch movie actor, Lou Tellegen, the physical beauty of the real-life woman cast its own spell.

Each, by her own admission, was too preoccupied with self and career for consistent and wholehearted reciprocation. Both seem to have belonged to that type of female, not uncommon in the theater, who finds fulfillment vicariously on the stage, preferring the kind of emotional involvement from which the fall of the curtain brings release. This might help to explain their success as unschooled actresses. Their feminine instincts were theater-oriented. "Others acted a role," Garden recalled. "I was the role. She who was Mary Garden died that it might live. That was my genius . . . and my sacrifice. It drained off so much of me that by comparison my private life was empty. I could not give myself completely twice."

They had their own ideas of how certain characters should be played, and their ideas were sound. They defied conventions—and stage managers—as Calvé had done. Their notions of costuming were original, and arrived at through intimate knowledge of their own physical assets. They knew that physical beauty, to be appreciated, must be seen, and they went beyond the customs of the time in making it visible. And they understood better than any singers since Jenny Lind's time the uses of publicity. Farrar, in her memoirs, is explicit about this:

"It has been the accepted fact in opera circles that rival sopranos and tenors must necessarily be at each other's throats and reputations. The wild conjectures and spicy gossip would seem to be part of the glamour surrounding the public favorites. I believe Mary Garden shared with me (since neither of us has ever been accused of vacuum above the eyebrows!) the sporting instinct to profit from whatever value the credulous public drew from the headlines."

Mary Garden sang little in the standard repertoire—Violetta, Manon,

Marguerite and Tosca—and that little without making indelible history. But she earned immortality not only with Louise, which she did not create—to use one of her favorite words—but also with Mélisande, which she did. The memory of her Mélisande has been obliterated neither by Maggie Teyte nor by Lucrezia Bori, both vividly identified with that elusive heroine for operagoers of later generations.

"Her Mélisande," wrote Frances Alda many years later, in *Men, Women and Tenors*, "remains immortal. She was so still. Just that one little phrase: *Il fait froid ici*, as it came from her lips, and you shivered under the chill winds that blow between the worlds of the real and the unreal. Contrasted with it, Bori's rendering of the line sounded like a schoolgirl who steps out of bed without her slippers."

Beyond that, while still in Paris, she took over Thaïs from Sybil Sanderson, the American soprano for whom Massenet had written the part, and created a kind of fringe repertoire of her own with such odd items as *La Reine Fiammette*, *La Fille de Tambarin*, *Aphrodite* and Lucien Lambert's *La Marseillaise*, arousing considerable innocent merriment in the latter with her conspicuously accented cry of *"Je suis française!"*

Singing for Oscar Hammerstein at the Manhattan Opera House in New York between 1907 and 1910, she added Salome (in French, of course, and dancing it herself) and the juggler in *Le Jongleur de Notre-Dame*, an audacious choice, since the part was written for, and had always been sung by, a tenor. This, oddly enough, was not her idea but Maurice Renaud's. And she set tongues wagging and heads shaking with her costuming, if not her singing, of Thaïs. Like almost everybody else in those days, she also sang Carmen.

She never sang with the Metropolitan. According to her own account, she was never asked to. She sang only once in London, a disastrous Juliet, and, like Farrar, she never sang in Italy. After Hammerstein's withdrawal from New York, she followed her colleagues to Chicago, and made her headquarters there, keeping her own kind of French opera alive long after it had begun to fade elsewhere. She was, for a time, director of the Chicago Opera Company, or directa, as she called it. She retired in 1930.

The secret of Mary Garden's accomplishments as a singing actress would seem to have been a unique capacity for total identification with the character she was projecting. Indeed, "projecting" is hardly the word for her kind of acting; it implies an artistic procedure, and, if we may take Garden at her word, there was none.

When asked how she interpreted Louise, for instance, she replied: "I didn't. I just walked on the stage as Louise." And elsewhere she says: "Salome, Thaïs, I knew them all. That sort of thing was always happening to me—the feeling of being someone else, of having been somewhere else. I never 'studied' any of these roles. I never had to rehearse, really." With such a penchant, or requirement, for working from a state of trance, it should not be surprising that she never suffered from nerves.

Her statement about never having "studied" her roles requires some qualification. Mary Garden's impersonations were obviously the realizations of an extraordinarily rich and active fantasy, and we can believe easily enough that she had no requirement for study in the sense of plotting out her roles step by step, gesture by gesture, attitude by attitude. Her approach to the theater was too inspirational for that. But there was plenty of intelligent thought behind everything she did. It is reflected in her own description of how she prepared *Le Jongleur de Notre-Dame*:

"Mr. Hammerstein assigned me that part during my first season at the Manhattan, and I studied it the following summer in Paris, together with Salome. I was the first woman ever to sing the role of the boy juggler who did homage to the Madonna in a humble way of his own. Now this was one of my strangest and most problematic creations. Here was a little boy of fifteen, a sexless child, with a voice that wasn't yet broken, and there was Salome, with a voice of passion and color, and I had to take my voice and make it that other thing. I couldn't put into that boy passion of any kind. The voice had to be pure and high, like a choir boy's before it changes, and how it tired me! It wasn't easy, but it was a part, the *Jongleur!* The critics and the public all loved it. They never even thought about the fact that it was a woman doing it."

In this constant preoccupation with vocal color as a means of characterization she would seem to have been the child of Maurel and the great-granddaughter of Nourrit. "Every one of these women I sang had a special quality of her own," she remembered, "and in every one of them I had a different singing voice. In Fiora [in *L'Amore dei Tre Re*] the quality was passion and terror, and I put these things in my voice. I should like to say again and again that I used my voice the same way a painter uses his brush. He throws the colors he wants onto his canvas. I threw color into my roles in the different tones that I sang. Fiora was full of the red passion of Italy. Salome was vice personified; the *Jongleur* was sexless; Louise was *l'amour libre*; Mélisande was mystery, secrecy; Sapho was the cocotte of Paris, common, and I made my voice that. Aphrodite was a cold, brilliant diamond, her quality being that she wanted what she couldn't get."

But all this thinking was mere preparation for the casting of a spell, with herself the first to be spellbound. It is a dangerous kind of acting, doomed to be ridiculous unless the spell is extended to the audience, and Mary Garden seems never to have appeared ridiculous. She was always able to convince the audience of the reality of her vision, and to make the audience a participant in her experience. She believed, and she made converts of those exposed to her belief.

She belonged to that curious group of singers who—in the theater, at least—sound better than they sing. They prosper only in the theater, where the ear may be numbed, or beguiled, by a compelling impersonation. One hears such a singer in concert or on records and wonders if *that* can be the same voice. Mary Garden's records surprised even Mary Garden. "I just loathe them," she wrote. "I can't bear it when someone plays a trick on me and turns them on."

They are not, in fact, that bad. Some early recordings, notably those made with Debussy at the piano in 1902, are tolerable only as curiosities; but later examples show her to have been wonderfully resourceful in the manipulation of an essentially indifferent instrument. The "Depuis le jour" from *Louise*, for instance, recorded in 1910, is magical. The voice is touched so lightly with the breath that the fast vibrato, a blemish in an instrument employed less skillfully, becomes a lovely shimmer. The thinness of the high notes is disguised by a probably contrived thinness elsewhere, so that color and quality are uniform throughout the range, and all is appropriate to the reflective rapture of a frail, unsophisticated girl. A slow tempo is sustained from beginning to end with that total repose which is the hallmark of a great artist.

3. GERALDINE FARRAR

Geraldine Farrar was more the opera singer than Mary Garden. Her repertoire included Madame Butterfly, Violetta, Marguerite, Nedda, Leonora, Juliet, Mimi, Zerlina, Carmen, Tosca and Elisabeth. And in roles especially identified with Garden—notably Manon, Louise and Thaïs—she could draw upon a superior vocal endowment and make her effects by more conventional vocal means, although she, too, was a vocal colorist. But she shared Garden's aptitude for projecting an exotic and glamorous heroine, for bringing life to inferior musical and dramatic material unresponsive to routine and workaday stagecraft. And she had a compelling asset in her own physical beauty. Small and slender, with delicate, finely cut and finely proportioned features, she was simply an overwhelmingly pretty girl.

She knew this—and she loved it. The strain of narcissism detectable in most singers was, in Geraldine Farrar, pronounced. One senses it in the title of her book, *Such Sweet Compulsion*—so different from, say, Alda's boisterous *Men, Women and Tenors*, or Lilli Lehmann's abrupt *Mein Weg*. And it is conspicuous in her disingenuous device of having part of the story told by the spirit of her mother, who died in 1923, thus admitting many flattering and intimate observations unthinkable in first-person discourse.

"On that breath-taking night of October 15, 1901," the mother's spirit tells us of Geraldine's debut in Berlin, "the curtain revealed this angelic form as Marguerite . . . lovely in her medieval costume, natural in bearing and gesture." And of her Violetta: "Her Parisian dresses were exquisite and original. She was slender as a birch, and a mania for freedom of the throat and shoulders kept me constantly alert for misplacement of tulle and ribbon which she would toss carelessly aside as if no flesh were thus exposed."

References of this sort to beauty of person and attire are a sort of refrain throughout the book, and colleagues are exposed to unflattering comparison, not all of it in the third person. Recalling her own performances as Elisabeth in Berlin, with Emmy Destinn as Venus, Farrar shows us Destinn "swathed in voluminous folds of a particularly horrendous shade of pink satin; a red wig rose from her forehead . . . further burdened by a wreath of violent red roses. We managed, even so, to present ourselves with dignity and effect." Elsewhere she describes Destinn's Salome as looking like a misplaced Valkyrie. And of Jeritza's "Vissi d'arte," sung prone on the stage, she writes: "I obtained no view of any expressive pantomime on her pretty face, while I was surprised by the questionable flaunting of a well-cushioned and obvious posterior."

More pertinent to Farrar's attributes as an artist, however, are the mother's accounts of the rehearsals for that first Marguerite, particularly when she tells how Geraldine "obtained many concessions on the stage in her very personal conception of Marguerite, which was her own, born of a lively fancy and youthful impulse." She was, it should be remembered, all of nineteen, and without any previous stage experience. A debutante's "very personal conceptions" can hardly have been welcome in the German theater of those days, any more than they would be welcome today. That Farrar was not criticized for such impudence was attributable to precocious imagination, daring and determination—and

Unlike most American singers of the last "golden age," Geraldine Farrar began her operatic career in Berlin, where Manon (above right) was, understandably, one of her most successful roles. And she was as beautiful offstage (above left) as on. Farrar was the first American Madame Butterfly (below left), and at the Metropolitan the role was for fifteen years virtually her private property. The very first Butterfly was Rosina Storchio (below right).

also, quite probably, to the approval of the crown prince, whose affectionate attention—and, presumably, protection—she was understood to be enjoying (which may also have had something to do with the fact that she was permitted to sing in Italian).

But Farrar was speaking the truth when she said that she and Mary Garden had never been accused of vacuum above the eyebrows. They had faults and limitations, but neither stupidity nor obtuseness was among them. If there was tough resolution beneath the surface of Farrar's lovely features, there was also an acute intelligence behind her brashness. It counseled her wisely against accepting the Marchesi mold. It guided her to Lilli Lehmann, it protected her against her own ambition in the choice of roles, and it counseled the abandonment of roles that proved beyond her powers, such as Leonora in *Il Trovatore*.

That she could profit from Lehmann's guidance without accepting Lehmann's dictation, and eventually win Lehmann's admiration and affection, must be counted an accomplishment of both diplomacy and will. Had she been a less contentious pupil she might have sung better and longer, but she would not have been Geraldine Farrar. She seems, from the very first, to have sensed that she was destined to be a singing actress rather than a virtuoso vocalist.

Lehmann, she remembered, "was a hard taskmaster, and demanded the ultimate; but found in me an energy equal to her own, if not quite to her physical resistance. I earned her respect much later. We argued frequently, for she often urged upon my vocal apparatus measures illsuited to its particular reaction; where she would force obedience, I would obtain results by less strenuous efforts. Technical control to her meant everything, while emotional color was my natural asset and delight. We had to effect compromises, which in the course of time became my necessary response to her lofty ambitions for the art of song.

"Having evolved from her own light vocal endowment a repertoire that ran the gamut from dizzy coloratura to the noble sweep of Donna Anna, Norma and Isolde, she could not understand the more limited and very sensitive instrument that lay in my own throat. With her, Will was Power; in me, she was obliged to acknowledge the particular asset of adaptability, to careful choice of roles and *Lieder*. Thus, though no true dramatic soprano, I could so manipulate as to convey the accent of drama in my phrases. I early realized that for my own best result, the power of suggestion rather than actual tone volume could operate to the advantage of vocal resources never to become over-strong."

What she sang, and where and when, reflect the same sober, dispassionate and shrewd estimate of assets and liabilities. In the course of a twenty-year operatic career, she sang about two dozen roles in the standard operas. Some she discarded immediately, among them Leonora, Gilda, Maddalena (in *Andrea Chénier*) and Queen Elizabeth (in *Don Carlos*). At the Metropolitan, which she joined in the season of 1906–07, she sang, but soon discarded, Violetta, Nedda, Micaëla, Juliet, Zerlina and Cherubino. She added Tosca in 1909, and thereafter, with the exception of Carmen in 1914, she took on nothing new from the standard repertoire. She seems simply to have settled on Tosca, Madame Butterfly, Mimi, Marguerite, Manon and Carmen. She would have liked to retain Elisabeth in *Tannhäuser*, which she regarded as one of her best parts, but Elisabeth was considered, at the Metropolitan, to be German property.

But she was insatiable in her search for new material tailored to her specifications, and her eye for roles was matched only by her eye for clothes. One has only to see the pictures of Farrar as the Goose Girl (with live geese) in Humperdinck's *Die Königskinder*, as Anita in Massenet's *La Navarraise*, as Suor Angelica, as Caterina in Giordano's *Madame Sans-Gêne*, as Thaïs, Louise and Zaza, to appreciate her taste, her judgment and her discretion. The phonograph records tell the rest, insofar as it can be grasped without one's having experienced her in the theater.

When she made her debut at the Metropolitan, as Juliet, Krehbiel wrote in the *Tribune* that "she appeared as a beautiful vision, youthful, charming in face, figure, movement and attitude. She sang with a voice of exquisite quality in the middle register, and one that was vibrant with feeling almost always. She acted like one whose instincts for the stage were full and eager. . . ." Aldrich, in the *Times*, came closer to what the phonograph records reveal when he said: "Her voice is a full and rich soprano, lyric in its nature and flexibility, yet rather darkly colored, and with not a little of the dramatic quality and with a power of dramatic nuance that she uses, in the main, skillfully."

Nuance, or coloring, as she calls it, was her secret, applied with the most admirable and decisive musicianship. Her records leave no doubt about who was directing pace and phrase when she was singing, nor about her qualifications for the exercise of such authority. One understands, and even applauds, her defiance of Toscanini when the latter came to the Metropolitan in the season of 1908–09. "Italia vs. New England," she called it. Their confrontations prompted Toscanini to observe, for Farrar's benefit, that the stars are in heaven. She was unrepentant. "There was also," she says, "a human constellation that trod the Metropolitan boards to the renown of that institution and the gratification of the public; not to mention the box office."

But what is most surprising about Farrar's records—and the evidence is confirmed by those who heard her in the flesh—is the sheer intensity of her singing. Her pictures suggest a creature almost too lovely to be real, and too conscious of her beauty ever to expose it to the wear and tear of emotional involvement. But the singing, particularly in the *Madame Butterfly* and *Carmen* records, for all the vocal fragility of which she was ever aware, is warmly communicative, profoundly feminine and sometimes reckless in its expense of every resource and its disregard of physical limitations.

She paid the price. Toward the end of her first decade at the Metropolitan her voice began to fail, and she had to undergo an operation for the removal of a node from a vocal cord. She made a good recovery, and resumed her career, but it can hardly have been the same again. She retired from the Metropolitan at the close of the season of 1921–22, at the age of forty, but concertized for some seasons thereafter.

It would appear, in retrospect, that in Farrar the will triumphed over the intelligence. She was always aware of her physical and vocal frailty; but careful and shrewd as she was in her selection of roles, she simply could not sing cautiously certain of the parts best suited to her—notably Madame Butterfly and Tosca—and produce the characterization that she felt and wanted. Nor could she spare herself in the frequency with which she sang them. Next to Caruso she was the most popular singer at the Metropolitan, and a wise diva does not leave her celestial throne unoccupied.

The new roles that she created, and those revived for her, were, of course, hers exclusively as long as she wanted them, and Madame Butterfly and Carmen were virtually her private property. She sang Madame Butterfly ninety-five times during her sixteen seasons at the Metropolitan, not counting out-of-town performances, and Carmen fifty-eight. Throughout her career at the Metropolitan she averaged between twenty-five and thirty-five performances a season in New York alone.

She was more circumspect than Viardot and Jean de Reszke had been in their selection of roles, but in whatever she sang she gave all that was in her. Had she given less she would not have been the exciting artist she was, nor could she have sustained the supremacy that her competitive spirit required. As with Viardot and de Reszke, it was worth it.

XIX

Some Gentlemen Who Stand Apart

CHALIAPIN · McCORMACK
TAUBER · TIBBETT

THERE HAVE BEEN among the great singers, particularly in more recent times, certain individuals who defy categorization. They have been without precedent, and have had no successors of comparable distinction.

Feodor Chaliapin was one. His Boris Godunov and Don Quixote have remained unexampled as vivid vocal and histrionic portraits. There were John McCormack and Richard Tauber, whose celebrity as singers of popular music, Irish and German, has obscured their attainments as two of the finest vocalists among tenors of any time or category. And there is Lawrence Tibbett, who was catapulted from minor roles to stardom by a Metropolitan audience's response to his performance as Ford in *Falstaff* on the evening of January 2, 1925, and whose subsequent success in early sound pictures made him an American institution.

1. FEODOR CHALIAPIN

Born in Kazan in 1873, Chaliapin was a primitive—and a Russian, the first singer of that nationality to establish a great international reputation. He was big—his voice, his movements, his nature, his art as singer and actor, and his escapades. He was what the Germans call an *Original*, that is, a character; everything about him was original. His Boris has been imitated, if hardly duplicated. But in roles from the standard repertoire—Mephistopheles, Don Quixote, Leporello, Don Basilio—his characterizations have been acknowledged as not only original but

319

unique, unbecoming to any other singer or actor. They were outsized and often enough outlandish, projected in broad, bold and daring strokes, in comic parts often bordering on caricature and slapstick—or crossing the border.

When he first appeared outside Russia—in Milan in 1901, in Monte Carlo in 1904 and in New York in 1907—*Boris Godunov* was not in the repertoire of any of these companies, nor, of course, was any other Russian opera, and Chaliapin had to make do with Mephistopheles, Leporello and Don Basilio. In these parts he was a sensation. But it was not until Diaghilev brought *Boris Godunov*—with Chaliapin—to Paris in 1908 and to London in 1913 that he could, in this portrait of a Russian tyrant in a Russian opera by the most Russian of all Russian composers, establish himself fully as the great artist he was.

Such was his reputation thereafter that excesses in other parts were granted him as a prerogative, although there were always some operagoers who found them deplorable. In non-Russian roles his elemental Russianness and his irrepressible pictorial exuberance were sometimes felt to be incompatible with French and Italian style and tradition. His characterizations were always outstanding, but even persons who relished them per se conceded that they often stood out too much.

It is instructive to look back, from time to time, to the reaction excited by an extraordinary artist before critical asperity—and critical acuity, too —have been moderated by awe and deference. The New York critics, when Chaliapin made his debut in Boito's *Mefistofele* on November 20, 1907, were more surprised than pleased by this sudden confrontation with a Slavic devil.

"The newcomer's impersonation of Mephistopheles is startling in its picturesqueness, and would make a gaudy picture book for children," said Krehbiel in the *Tribune*; "but with Goethe's conception of this particular devil, or even Boito's, it has as little to do as it has with the Pater Seraphicus of Goethe's final scene. Mr. Chaliapin's notion of the devil is merely carnal. When he throws off his cowl he is the fantastic devil of the picture books, a figure that could fright the soul of any human creature. When he appears among his kindred on the Brocken he is bestiality incarnate. In the presence of his *Maestro divino* he bares his breast and arms with decorum; but in the company of his fellows he casts off a cloak resembling Papageno's parrotlike habiliments and bares himself to the rump. It is stupendously picturesque, of course, for the man is of marvelous stature and amazing plasticity of pose and gesture; but calls

Chaliapin

Chaliapin's Boris Godounov (above) was unprecedented and has never been surpassed. He had graphic gifts as well. The portrait (right) is not by his famous artist son, Boris Chaliapin, but by himself. His family was always puzzled as to how he could have seen himself so accurately from that angle.

to mind, more than anything else, the vulgarity of conduct which his countryman Gorki presents with such disgusting frankness in his pictures of Russian low life."

One wonders what Krehbiel and other critics might have thought of his performances as Gounod's Mephistopheles at the Marinsky Theater in St. Petersburg ten years earlier, in which, according to Chaliapin himself, he had "made the mistake of gross exaggeration in an ineffectual attempt to escape the commonplace. In trying to avoid the conventional gesture," he admitted, "I was no doubt bizarre and uncouth." He did not, however, agree with the New York critics of 1907, and he left at the end of the season, not to return until the season of 1921–22, and then as Boris, and to hymns of praise. "All that we have heard of the greatness of his impersonation . . . was made plain," said the same Krehbiel. "It was heartbreaking in its pathos, terrible in its vehemence and agony."

Krehbiel had, in 1907, caught some of the essential elements of Chaliapin's art, particularly his predilection for the pictorial. In this Chaliapin probably resembled Maurel; and he was, like Maurel, a talented graphic artist. His sketches and caricatures are probably as good as Caruso's, and there is a famous self-portrait, accomplished in no more than two dozen thin lines, that is a little masterpiece by any standards. This, rather than his voice or a profound musical instinct, was his gift to his son Boris, subsequently to achieve fame for his *Time* magazine covers.

What Krehbiel had failed to note was the original thinking that lay behind everything that Chaliapin did, making it appear so native to him that it conveyed a sense of inevitability, however much at odds it may have been with tradition. Nor did Chaliapin's private deportment suggest a profoundly thoughtful person. He was a *bon vivant* and raconteur, unruly, fond of vodka and congenial company—and enormously attractive.

"A great blond cherub of a man" is the way Farrar describes him, recalling their meeting in Monte Carlo in 1904. "Of superb physique, he had an uncanny gift for cosmetic metamorphosis, and adding to dramatic gifts a magnificent voice that rolled out like melodious thunder, it was easy for him to equal the triumphs of even Caruso those days! And what a fellow with the ladies! In this motley crowd of surfeited grand dukes, wearied kings incognito, phlegmatic John Bulls, American millionaires new to this international playground, and sophisticated Parisian elegants, it was not easy to overlook this fascinating barbarian whose sentimental attacks were along lines quite unusual to the traditions of overpolite society, and so, eminently successful."

Chaliapin's approach to the lyric theater was that of Calvé, Garden and Farrar. He was of their generation and disposition, and in his passion for dramatic and pictorial truth he defied theater conventions and traditional characterization. This was, to the critics of those days, gamy fare, and Chaliapin was at a disadvantage. Aside from the Russian opera, for which there was only a limited acceptance outside Russia, he had no new repertoire congenial to his view of the theater. And his approach to the theater was not always congenial to tradition-laden roles.

Like Calvé, Garden, Farrar, Maurel and Renaud, he was never primarily a singer. He had a voice—more bass-baritone than bass—of great size and splendor, but until he learned to adapt its employment to the actor's rather than the singer's art it brought him neither satisfaction nor satisfactory success. This was true even of his singing of Moussorgsky's songs. "I sang his romances according to all the canons of singing," he remembered in his thoughtful book *Man and Mask*, "but in spite of this my renderings were lifeless. I was particularly dismayed by the realization of my inadequacy in his 'Song of the Flea'; my version of it was so mediocre that for a long time I refrained from singing it in public."

Even as the Miller in Dargomyzhsky's *Rusalka*, in which he achieved his first real triumph, he felt his performance to be inadequate, and he confided his doubts to Mamont-Dalski, a celebrated Russian actor. Dalski diagnosed his trouble as failure to find the suitable inflections [Chaliapin's translator uses "intonation," but "inflection" seems to be meant]. "The inflections by which you interpret your character are false," Dalski told him. "That explains the whole thing. You utter the Miller's reproaches and complaints to his daughter in the accents of a petty tradesman, although the Miller is a steady-going peasant, the owner of a windmill and other property." Chaliapin took the hint:

"I was cut to the quick by Dalski's criticism. I grasped the truth of what he said immediately, and while I was ashamed of my unsuitable renderings, I was nevertheless glad that Dalski had given form to my confused ideas. Inflection—that was the essential. I was justified in my dissatisfaction with the 'Song of the Flea'; the entire value of a song lay in the correctness of the inflection. Now I understood why *bel canto* nearly always gives rise to boredom.

"I thought of singers I knew, with magnificent voices, so perfectly trained that at any moment they could sing *piano* or *forte*, but who nearly all sang notes to which the words were merely of secondary importance. In fact, so little stress was laid on the words that more often than not the audience could not make out a syllable of what they were supposed to be saying. Singers in this category sing in an agreeable manner, their voices never sound strained, and are produced effortlessly; but should they have to sing several times in an evening, no one song would sound very different from the other. Love or hate—there is really nothing to distinguish them! I don't know what impression this makes on the average listener, but I do know that I am bored after the second song on the program."

From that time on, Chaliapin, then in his early twenties, spent his free evenings in the theater rather than in the opera house. Actors rather than singers were his models, and he even thought for a time of becoming an actor. But not for long. "I was bound to opera by my very heart-strings," he recalled; "for my heart bore forever the 'divine stigmata' of music, as Pushkin expresses it."

He also spent much time in art museums and with painters. An older friend had discouraged his early enthusiasms for pictures that gave merely an admirable *reproduction* of an object. The camera, the friend had said, was a wearisome invention; it cannot make the forest path or the garden alley eloquent. It can only accurately represent them. And so Chaliapin studied the Russian moderns—Vroubel, Sierov, Vasnetsov and Riepin. And "now I understood that care must be taken not simply to copy . . . in order to make the maximum effect. The Logos, or Word, might be found in color, line, gesture, speech; and from this new-found knowledge I drew conclusions relevant to my own art as an opera singer."

With this feeling for line and color, for artful distortion, it was inevitable that Chaliapin would be a master of makeup. But he was also aware that makeup is only an auxiliary. Its chief value, he used to say, is that it hides the actor's own features; and he gave more importance to what he called "psychological make-up." There was no achievement of which he was more proud than a performance he gave at a dress rehearsal of *Boris Godunov* in Paris in 1908. The costumes had not arrived, and he played the part without makeup and in street clothes.

"Perhaps I should never have realized how natural my words and monologue sounded," he tells us, "had I not heard, at the moment when I rose up, glancing fearfully toward a corner of the stage, to declaim:

'What's that? There's something in the ingle-nook,
Something that stirs . . .'

had I not heard, I say, a strange sound in the auditorium that disturbed
me. I looked askance to see what was happening, and this is what I saw:
the spectators had risen to their feet, some of them were even standing
on their seats, and all were gazing toward that corner of the stage toward
which I myself was peering. . . . I was singing in Russian; my words
were incomprehensible to them, but from the expression in my eyes,
they were aware that I was afraid of something."

This independence of makeup had much to do, of course, with the
success as a recitalist of a man so essentially of the theater. Chaliapin's
programs, like his performances in opera, were strikingly unconventional.
He never followed a printed program. The audience was required, instead, to buy a booklet, available at the entrance to the hall, containing
translations of a repertoire from which he would select at his discretion,
and according to his mood and vocal condition, announcing each song
by number as he went along. Whoever had not bought the book was out
of luck. Chaliapin favored songs of character, and such was his art of
inflection at the height of his career that it survived the glory of his
voice by many years.

He was at his best, of course, in Russian music, where his purposeful
distortions proceeded from an inborn affinity with style, text and language. In other music, particularly German, his conceptions of a song
could be wildly at odds with notation, tradition and even the sense of
the words. Gerald Moore, as a young man, was his accompanist for a
time, and learned to be ever on the alert for the unexpected, the improbable and even the improper. But Moore, now long established as a dean
of accompanists, concedes that the most fastidious admirer of Schubert
and Schumann could be swept away by Chaliapin's dramatic art and
persuasive power of suggestion.

He remained to the end of his days a kind of overgrown, precocious
boy—capricious, spoiled, moody, impulsive and unpredictable. He was
more than a great showman. He was more even than a great show. He
was the whole show, and his deportment was governed accordingly. He
would walk away from the piano, for instance, while the accompanist
was still playing an important postlude, and it could be much the same
in the theater.

"Alas," noted Richard Aldrich in the *Times*, when Chaliapin sang his first King Philip in *Don Carlos* at the Metropolitan in 1922, "the great dramatic master is subject to the operatic temptations of the weaker brethren and sisters. At the end of the monologue there was great applause; and though nobody else in the company, in obedience, apparently, to a newly promulgated principle, acknowledged applause on the scene, Mr. Chaliapin not only acknowledged his warmly, but also finally came forward to the footlights, told the conductor where to begin again, and straightway repeated the last stanza of his monologue—with what effect upon the dramatic illusion need not be described. He did it differently, as if to show that his resources were not used up. No doubt he could have done it a third time still differently; and the picture having once been shattered, he might as well have."

It is easy to imagine that a man so accustomed by disposition and privilege to being a law unto himself must have been an uncomfortable revolutionary, assuming that he was not leading the revolution. Chaliapin's relationship with the Russian Revolution was equivocal, as became an apolitical idealist. Accustomed to thinking of himself as a man of the people, he was basically sympathetic to socialist aspirations. He remained, initially, in St. Petersburg, a member of the Marinsky Theater company, and he was, at one time, even named president of the theater's Committee of Arts. But his first administrative act was to decree that rehearsal hours would no longer be fixed, that rehearsals would last until the work was done. This ended not only his presidency but also, for a time, his membership in the company.

He was subsequently invited back and given the title of Premier Singer to the Soviet People. But he was always an irrepressible individualist, and he found Communist regimentation as distasteful as Romanov regimentation had been. He went into exile in 1922 and was subsequently denounced as an "anti-revolutionary" and deprived of all his Russian property and titles. He died in Paris in 1938.

2. JOHN McCORMACK

There were, between Chaliapin and John McCormack, born in 1884, certain significant similarities. Both were primitives—boisterous extroverts, willful, self-indulgent, contentious, impatient of direction and resentful of correction and criticism. They were essentially conscientious, and they set themselves high standards, but these standards were their own. And, as is often true of gifted primitives, prompted by instinct

Lawrence Tibbett's Iago (above left) suggested to one critic a kind of Venetian Robin Hood. He looks even less sinister (above right) with his prize hens, Tabitha and Mehitabel.

Richard Tauber didn't look like Richard Tauber without the monocle (below left).

John McCormack (below right) at the height of his career as recitalist and recording artist.

BETTMANN ARCHIVE   RCA VICTOR RECORDS

rather than by the consciousness of insight, they could address themselves to ordinary people with an immediacy of communication rarely
achieved by artists of more intellectual background and disposition.

What distinguished McCormack, in his time, from other singers with
a similarly enormous popular following—Harry Lauder, for example—
was his ability to excite a parallel admiration among the most exacting
connoisseurs of opera and *Lied*. He is remembered today primarily as a
singer of Irish ballads and folk songs. Many who treasure his recordings
of "Kathleen Mavourneen," "Macushla," "The Rose of Tralee," and
so on, would be surprised to learn that during the first decade of his
career he was primarily an opera singer—in London, New York, Chicago,
Boston, Philadelphia and the major cities of Australia. They would also
be surprised to learn that his records of such hallowed items as "Il mio
tesoro intanto," "O Sleep, Why Dost Thou Leave Me," "Where'er You
Walk," some of them made as many as fifty years ago, are held by some
collectors to have remained unsurpassed in the perfection of their style
and vocalism.

This span of repertoire confounded even McCormack's contemporaries. Throughout his long career, he was plagued by critics who,
while acknowledging the beauty of his voice and the elegance of his
singing, deplored his taste and judgment in the selection of what he
sang. His response was always that to sing nothing but the best music
was a form of snobbery. "It isn't everyone," he used to say, "who appre-
ciates the more artistic music. The world is full of men and women with
humble thoughts and simple sentiments, and who shall despise them—
for are they not men and women?" His reward for this democracy was
an earned income of about a million dollars a year.

There were those who felt that McCormack lowered himself to make
money; and he played into their hands by a notoriously extravagant way
of life. He presided over luxurious establishments in Ireland, California,
Connecticut, New York City and London. He owned, at one time or
another, twelve Rolls-Royces, and in a life as full of wine as of song, he
drank nothing but champagne. A Stradivarius and a Guarnerius were
among his possessions, although the only thing he could play on a violin
was "Killarney." One of his most persistent ambitions was to own a
Derby winner. It remained expensively unfulfilled.

The critics were encouraged in their view of his self-debasement, para-
doxically, not only by the inclusion in his programs of what they felt to
be bad, but also of what they knew to be good. Two groups were always

devoted to such composers as Bach, Handel, Haydn, Mozart, Schubert, Schumann and Hugo Wolf. The critics were thus reminded continually of how well—and how tastefully—he could sing the best music. It only aggravated their scorn for the sentimental Irish ballads and songs that came at the end—and drew the throngs; and the scorn was not moderated by the fact that he sang this music beautifully, too. Such singing of such stuff, they insisted, was prostitution.

One might argue—and some did—that McCormack, like Fritz Kreisler, possessed the art of turning lesser metals into gold. There was, certainly, never a trace of condescension toward anything he sang. The same attention to line, tone, phrase, diction and intonation was expended upon the plainest Irish or other popular ditty as upon "Oh, Sleep Why Dost Thou Leave Me." McCormack's art as musician and vocalist was always admirable, whatever he sang, and, as such, a source of aesthetic pleasure. But he was hurt by the criticism, and was always touchy on the subject of repertoire. "I suppose you think," he said in 1923 to Sir Compton MacKenzie, then editor of the magazine *Gramophone*, "that I sing nothing but muck!"

He might have sung more of it than he did, and not as well, had it not been for Caruso. What distinguished John McCormack from other singers of Irish ballads was an Italian schooling from which he derived not only a disciplined vocalism but also taste and experience in a wide repertoire. And to this schooling he was prompted by hearing Caruso at Covent Garden in 1904. McCormack was twenty then, and just beginning a career as a professional singer. "I will never rest," he said to a friend after that performance. "I will work and train and pray, and someday there will be two men singing like that . . . Caruso and me." Money was raised through concerts and donations, and off he went to Milan. Three years later, on October 15, 1907, he made his London operatic debut as Turiddu at Covent Garden.

He sang the lyric roles—Edgardo, Don Ottavio, Alfredo, Rodolfo, Pinkerton, and others—and was sought as a partner by Melba, who took him to Australia, and by Tetrazzini, who took him to Hammerstein's Manhattan Opera House in New York. He was soon spoken of as the "Irish Caruso." But he was no Caruso, and nobody knew it better than he. His veneration of Caruso survived many years of friendship. When, after Caruso's death, a friend suggested to him that he was now the world's greatest tenor, he said: "I object to that title. The greatest tenor is dead, and the next one has not arrived."

As a result of his intensive Italian schooling, coupled with a fine imitative ear, McCormack remained, in terms of vocal style, an essentially Italian tenor. All those who heard him sing, or who have listened to his records, have been more or less amused by what appeared to be, when he sang in English, an ineradicable Irish brogue. Some of the British critics, however, thought these linguistic idiosyncracies more Italian than Irish, and they deplored his habit of making *give* rhyme with *leave*. The critic of the London *Times*, in an appreciation of his career, following his death in 1945, went so far as to say:

"Unfortunately, his Italian training had not equipped him thoroughly for the difficult art of singing the English language, and the pleasure to be got from the purely vocal side of his art was modified by his failure to produce with any appearance of naturalness the vowel sounds contained in such a phrase as 'If with all your hearts.' Fortunately, Italianate vowels did not contaminate the Irish intonation of his native folk songs."

Whether right or wrong, McCormack's vowel sounds were always pure, and his consonants distinct. Hardly another singer has combined so successfully an immaculate enunciation with an immaculate melodic line. This was one of the secrets of his art, particularly in music of an inferior order, where the melody, however compellingly voiced, was not sufficiently communicative to stand alone. Where Chaliapin had "acted" a ballad, McCormack "told" it. Chaliapin's art was the lyrical extension of the actor's sustained speech and declamation, assisted by facial expression and gesture. McCormack's was rather an Italianate extension and refinement of the Irish minstrel's storytelling.

"Next to his pleasant and well-produced voice," wrote Edwin Evans, critic of the London *Daily Mail*, in 1934, "he owes his popularity to the fact that of all singers now before the public, he is probably the most intelligible. He is, perhaps, the only singer whose patrons might economize on the 'book of words' without losing the thread of any song."

It was this knack, possibly stemming from a predilection to talk, to be listened to, and to convince, that predestined him for the recital hall. He was, in private life, gregarious, garrulous and disputatious, with a penchant for holding forth on any and all subjects. In the recital hall he had, of course, a captive audience, and he relished it. This was his natural habitat.

That he would have made a great career as an opera singer is unlikely. The top notes, above a B-flat, were not his by divine right, and he did not have them for long. He never was, and never would have been, a good actor. In the recital hall he could sing what he sang best, in congenial surroundings and in congenial keys. In the opera house, whatever the role, he had never been anyone but John McCormack. In the recital hall, to be just John McCormack was enough.

That there was always something boyish about this John McCormack may have accounted for the preponderance of females among his fans. Originally tall and lanky, and darkly handsome, he put on weight at an early age, and made a portly figure on the stage, or assisting in Roman Catholic ceremonies, resplendent in his uniform of a Papal Chamberlain. He might properly be addressed as Count McCormack, but he never entirely shed the manners of a provincial Irish mill-town boy. He may have sensed this and resented it, for his relationship with Athlone, his birthplace, was neither close nor cordial.

An awareness of provincialism may also have contributed to his ostentatious social habits and to his prodigality with money. He was an indefatigable celebrity hunter, and his own legitimate celebrity made it an easy chase. He was drawn particularly to the world of sports. Bill Tilden was among his friends, and McCormack and his wife were among the guests at the wedding of Gene Tunney. His compulsion to excel was pronounced, and he was, in game or argument, a bad loser.

There was also, probably, an element of incredulity in the whole performance, as if the phenomenon of John McCormack might not be true, or could not last—and must be relished while it did. He suffered more than most singers from pre-recital nerves. He visited the nearest Catholic church before every appearance—he called it "saying grace for music." Before leaving his dressing room he would stand for a few minutes in silence, gripping a rosary.

And he was an eager admirer of his own records. Even at the height of his career he was continually astonished at how good they were, and he enjoyed his astonishment. Toward the end of his life, when nothing but the records was left, he would play them again and again, exclaiming happily, and a bit wistfully—possibly even a bit incredulously: "I was a damned good singer, wasn't I?"

He was.

3. RICHARD TAUBER

So was Richard Tauber (1892–1948), who, like McCormack, achieved such legendary fame as a singer of popular music that his accomplishments in opera and *Lied* are often overlooked. He is identified forever with the exuberant "Dein ist mein ganzes Herz" from Lehar's *Das Land des Lächelns,* which he sang as no other tenor ever did, or will. But those who have also heard his recording of the quiet "Aus Apfelblüten einen Kranz," from the same operetta, are in a better position to know how great an artist he was.

Irresistible and inimitable though he was in operetta, and in his singing of popular German and Austrian songs, Tauber's profoundest affinity was with Mozart. Like McCormack, he made an exemplary record of "Il mio tesoro intanto." If the two tenors were to be judged solely on their singing of this single aria, McCormack would have the edge, thanks, probably, to his Italian schooling. But in Mozart's German operas Tauber was —and, on records, is still—in a class by himself. There can hardly be another recording so sheerly *bezaubernd* (enchanting) as Tauber's of "Dies' Bildnis ist bezaubernd schön" from *The Magic Flute.*

The voice was less beautiful than McCormack's, and hardly as large. One cannot imagine Jan Kubelik, the violinist, saying of Tauber, as he once said of McCormack: "The man must have a Stradivarius in his throat." It was not, with Tauber, the beauty of the instrument. It was rather his way with it. And his way was that of the supreme musician, more widely versed in music and musical literature than McCormack, and more sophisticated. He was the greater virtuoso in the mastery of his voice as the instrument of an extraordinarily imaginative musicality. McCormack's voice may have had more of the sound of a violin, but Tauber was closer to the violinist in his use of the voice he had.

In English-speaking lands he is remembered primarily as a recitalist, although he sang in opera in London, and was much admired as Florestan, Tamino, Belmonte and Don Ottavio. It was in London, indeed, that he made his last public appearance, on September 27, 1947, rejoining his Viennese colleagues—he had spent the war years in London—in a single performance of *Don Giovanni.* He was operated on for cancer shortly afterward, and died three months later.

He was an exuberant recitalist, standing very erect, as small, stocky men tend to do, the German military effect heightened by a monocle, his entrances and exits cocky and ebullient. His audiences' delight in certain vocal tricks, especially his contrasting of *piano* and *forte,* led him into irresistible temptation, and he sometimes overdid them. But few have excelled him in his ability to establish rapport with an audience. He always seemed to be having fun; and his audiences always did. His distinctly individual vocal production and his idiosyncrasies in attacking a note and turning a phrase have been imitated by scores of later German tenors. Some of them have approximated his mannerisms, none of them his art.

4. LAWRENCE TIBBETT

If Richard Tauber was imitable, up to a point, Lawrence Tibbett was not. It is difficult to think of another singer in whom the voice, the singing and the man were so much of a piece. Other German tenors, for instance, although they cannot sing like Tauber, can sometimes sound like him. No other baritone has ever sounded like Tibbett. And, short of an improbable duplication, none ever will.

This distinctive individuality of voice and personality may have accounted, in part, for a largely individual repertoire. But there were other reasons. When Tibbett achieved stardom so suddenly in 1925, the Metropolitan's baritones included Ruffo, de Luca, Scotti and Danise, shortly to be joined by Mario Basiola. In the German wing were Friedrich Schorr, Michael Bohnen, Gustav Schützendorf and Tibbett's own countryman, Clarence Whitehill. There were few plums, in such company, with which to reward a twenty-nine-year-old American baritone who had suddenly made Ford seem more important than Falstaff.

Nor would he have been prepared for the plums had they been his to choose from. Unlike earlier American baritones, notably David Bispham and Whitehill, and unlike even his own contemporaries, John Charles Thomas and Richard Bonelli, Tibbett, born in 1896, had come to the Metropolitan in the season of 1923–24 with no previous operatic experience anywhere. That was one of his most important distinctions. But it was also a handicap. Thomas and Bonelli, when they reached the Metropolitan, were seasoned performers, having sung leading roles in Belgium, France, Germany and Italy. Tibbett, when he brought down the house with Ford in *Falstaff*, had appeared previously only at the Metropolitan, and only as Valentine, Silvio and the Herald in *Lohengrin*, not counting such distinctly minor roles as Morales in *Carmen*, the Marquis d'Orbigny in *La Traviata* and Fleville in *Andrea Chénier*. For all the sensation excited by his triumph as Ford, he was hardly qualified to take over Rigoletto from de Luca, Scarpia from Scotti, Gerard from Danise, Barnaba from Ruffo or Tonio from Basiola.

He would, in due course, sing most of these roles. Rigoletto and Scarpia became pretty much his private property after the departure of the Italians in the early thirties. But few would contend that he ever effaced the memory of the great Italian baritones in their best parts, not even as Iago, Falstaff and Gianni Schicchi. Only as Simon Boccanegra did his accomplishment stand alone in the Italian repertoire. His memory is indelible in roles tailored to his measure: Brutus Jones in Louis Gruenberg's *The Emperor Jones*, Eadgar in Deems Taylor's *The King's Henchman* and Colonel Ibbetson in the same composer's *Peter Ibbetson*, Wrestling Bradford in Howard Hanson's *Merry Mount*, and Guido in Richard Hageman's *Caponsacchi*.

And he is remembered for many accomplishments outside the opera house. It used to be said of McCormack that he arrived when everybody had a gramophone and nobody a radio. A similar accident of chronology brought Tibbett to the fore just as the moving pictures were discovering sound. His startling seizure of the show as Ford, and his subsequent success in native opera—*The King's Henchman, Peter Ibbetson* and *The Emperor Jones*—made him a national figure. Hollywood was looking for things to do musically with its newly found voice, and there was Tibbett —still young enough, hardly handsome, but good-looking in a manly, round-faced, country-boy (Bakersfield, California) way, and not only a much publicized opera star but home-grown, too.

The result was a series of pictures: *The Rogue Song, New Moon, The Southerner, Cuban Love Song* and *Metropolitan*. They were hardly cinematic masterpieces, and Tibbett was subsequently eclipsed as a singing moving-picture idol by Nelson Eddy; but they contributed immeasurably to Tibbett's fame, and they did a lot, also, to bring an awareness of opera and an operatic way of singing to the remotest corners of North America. The effect was undoubtedly heightened by the fact that this opera singer was so unmistakably and indubitably American.

It was not just that Lawrence Tibbett *was* home-grown; it was rather that there was always something so engagingly home-grown in his appearance, and this had a lot to do with the appeal he had for American audiences. John Charles Thomas and Bonelli were just as much native-born Americans as he; but, possibly because of their European training, their Americanism was not so pronounced. They arrived at American opera houses in New York, Chicago, Philadelphia and Boston, moreover, as stars, and their fully legitimate success was wanting in the essential element of surprise.

Despite this effective Americanism, however, and despite the familiarity proceeding from his moving pictures and radio appearances, Tibbett was never a popular singer in the way that John McCormack was popular, or Nelson Eddy, or even John Charles Thomas. A majority of Nelson Eddy's fans, probably, would have been surprised to learn that he sang Wolfram, Silvio, Amonasro, Gianni Schicchi, Gunther and many other roles during six seasons with the Philadelphia Civic Opera Company. Neither McCormack nor Thomas is remembered primarily as an opera singer. Tibbett is. A later generation must be reminded, or told, that he once appeared in a moving picture called *The Rogue Song*, and that he used to sing something called "The Glory Road."

There was something about the commanding resonance of Tibbett's voice, its manly sonority and mellow warmth, and there was something about his professional way with a song, something about his imposing physique, his dress, his posture and his movements, that spoke of dignity and high aspiration. He was not purposefully forbidding as a recitalist, or in concert. He could be friendly with an audience, and he usually was. But neither his manner nor his singing was intimate. McCormack could sing to an audience heart to heart, seeming to take his listeners into his confidence. And so could Thomas. McCormack's innate artistry usually saved him from banality. Thomas could be banal, which was the more exasperating because he was also capable of exemplary refinement. Tibbett was always the celebrated visitor from the Metropolitan, giving the best that was in him. The performance was a bit stiff; not standoffish, or condescending, but self-conscious, and the audience remained self-conscious, too.

There was something of this self-consciousness in his acting. He had begun his professional life as an actor, gaining experience in summer stock, and he was always essentially a man of the theater, a singing actor rather than a vocal virtuoso. But it was never easy for him to escape the distinctive features and bearing of Lawrence Tibbett. "A person whose features are too marked," said Chaliapin, in *Man and Mask*, "is at a disadvantage as an actor." And this was true of Tibbett. A conspicuously round face and open countenance, set in a head rather too small for the body, were hard to mask, and he was readily identifiable whatever the costume and the makeup.

He was at his best, accordingly, in roles to which his native dignity and upright aspect were most becoming, or where his physique was an asset, as in *The Emperor Jones*. His Iago, for example, vivid and picturesque, was too hale and hearty. Lawrence Gilman, in the *Herald Trib-une*, possibly influenced, too, by a green costume and a cap with a feather, was reminded of Robin Hood. Nor were the brutality and ruthlessness of his Scarpia leavened by the requisite subtlety. Neither costume nor makeup nor gesture could make Lawrence Tibbett credible as a devious, scheming, cunning or conniving character. But he was always an excellent and sympathetic king, capable of conveying authority, or anguish and remorse, with a patrician sense of propriety.

It is difficult to place him in historical perspective without distorting history. Any appraisal of his influence is likely to make him appear to have been more of a pioneer than he was. Because of the publicity attending his explosion into stardom from the ranks at the Metropolitan, and the fame proceeding from his moving pictures, there was a popular tendency, at the time, to regard him as America's first great opera singer.

He was, of course, nothing of the sort, although he was the first American baritone to sustain leading roles at the Metropolitan in the Italian repertoire. A score or so of American singers had preceded him to operatic fame. But of these only Nordica and Farrar had previously approached Tibbett's preeminence as a national figure, and that was thirty years before moving pictures began to talk. Tibbett, in his pictures, was exposed to a public of millions, most of whom, if they had ever heard of Nordica, had probably thought that she was Italian.

It has been assumed by some that Tibbett's unique distinction was his having been entirely home-grown and home-trained. But Ponselle, who preceded him to leading roles at the Metropolitan by six years, was just as exclusively home-grown and home-trained as he. The impact of her achievements was modified, however, by her Italian parentage and by the fact that she began at the top. It was the circumstance of Tibbett's sudden emergence from the ranks that was unique. It made him a legendary figure, and legends can be more telling and more enduring than mere facts.

Tibbett's example, and the publicity surrounding it, magnified immeasurably by his moving pictures, encouraged hundreds, even thousands, of young Americans to aspire to a career in opera. And in this respect it is probably no exaggeration to say that he inaugurated a new era in American singing.

XX

And Two Ladies

ANDERSON · FLAGSTAD

1. MARIAN ANDERSON

As with Tibbett, so also with Marian Anderson is the historical perspective somewhat distorted by legend. But if she is thought of popularly as the first Negro to achieve international prominence in an international repertoire, which she was not, it has been through no fault of her own. She has always been the first to point out that the Negro tenor Roland Hayes, almost a generation ahead of her, had done just about everything that she ever did except sing at the Metropolitan, be excluded from Constitution Hall and become a national institution.

Many who heard Hayes in his prime would rate him Marian Anderson's peer in musical art if not in vocal endowment. But his was a different case. Educated at Fisk University and Harvard, he was, almost from the first, a sophisticated singer. There was nothing about his performance of the classics that inspired in his white listeners any astonishment that a Negro could sing them so well. His appearance, bearing and manner suggested as much before he opened his mouth. And so, when he sang with most of the important orchestras of Europe and the United States, his truly extraordinary achievements were taken for granted. For all the impact he made upon the public consciousness as a Negro, Roland Hayes might as well have been white.

Marian Anderson's journey to the top was long, and her arrival dramatic. Her humble origin in a Negro quarter of Philadelphia, where she was born in 1902, and her lack of formal education, provided the proper setting for an American success story, and the fact that recognition and acceptance were slow in coming gave the story the essential ingredients of determination and perseverance in the face of disappointment and frustration. And she had a truly great voice.

337

She was also, and still is, more universal in her appeal than Hayes ever was. He was an artist's artist, a musician's musician, ever the idol of the connoisseurs. There was finish in his vocalism, art in his phrasing and elegance in his diction. But he lacked Anderson's compelling, elemental simplicity and strong dramatic instinct that informed everything she sang.

It was not merely that Marian Anderson's voice was more ample and more beautiful. It was, indeed, neither exceptionally large, nor, in every part of an extensive range, exceptionally beautiful. The upper notes tended toward stridency, and the Stygian darkness of the lowest notes was not to everyone's taste. But it was always distinctive; and its distinctiveness was exciting. It was also distinctively Negroid. The result, when it was applied to German, French and Italian music and text, was rather more than slightly incongruous, an exotic juxtaposition of black Africa and Europe, the violence of the contrast rendered tolerable by an American filter. This incongruity was more apparent, of course, to European audiences; and, since it was further moderated by her very considerable musical intelligence, the Europeans, particularly the Germans and Scandinavians, found it both charming and moving.

It has often seemed, and it has often been said, that American critics and American audiences were inexcusably tardy in their recognition of Anderson's greatness; and there has been a tendency to assume that this tardiness had something to do with her being a Negro. This assumption would seem to be negated by the earlier example of Roland Hayes. It wasn't all that simple. Anderson's voice was recognized as early as 1925, when she was selected from a field of three hundred contestants in a competition for an appearance with the New York Philharmonic Orchestra at the Lewisohn Stadium. She was then twenty-three. But she was far from the artist she would be when she returned from Europe ten years later.

It was not so much that Marian Anderson was slow in achieving recognition; she was also slow in achieving artistic maturity. She had enjoyed excellent vocal schooling in her native country, but with a girl of so limited an educational background, it is doubtful if she could ever have attained the requisite grounding in languages and style without residence and experience as a public performer in Europe. This was the advice of her own intelligence, and she followed it resolutely, returning to Europe again and again between 1925 and 1935. When she came back to America to make that memorable debut at Town Hall on December 30, 1935, she was ready. She had not been ready before.

Accounts of her successes in Scandinavia and central Europe, and particularly in Vienna and Salzburg, had been circulated at home. Much publicity had been given to the comment of Toscanini, when he had heard her in Salzburg: "Yours is a voice such as one hears once in a hundred years." And now the American public was ready, too.

An accident became a blessing on that occasion. During the crossing from Europe she had fallen down a flight of steps on shipboard and broken an ankle. The injury, she felt, should not have any effect on her singing, but the ankle was in a cast, and she did not wish to hobble from the wings to the piano on crutches. Accordingly, she took her place at the piano behind drawn curtains. No announcement was made, and a long dress hid the cast. The story became known, of course, and added to the drama—and the publicity—of what had been, in any case, a dramatic debut.

Although she was not the first Negro singer to achieve an international reputation, nor even the first to sing in opera, she was certainly the first to appear at the Metropolitan. When she sang that precedent-setting Ulrica in *Un Ballo in Maschera* on January 7, 1955, she was fifty-two and past her prime. Her career as an opera singer did not go beyond two seasons and the one role; but the consequences are felt to this day in the careers of many Negro singers who have since sung and are now singing at the Metropolitan and other opera houses around the world.

2. KIRSTEN FLAGSTAD

"The voice itself is both lovely and puissant. In its deeper register it is movingly warm and rich and expressive, and yesterday it recalled to wistful Wagnerites the irrevocable magic of Olive [Fremstad] the immortal. The upper voice is powerful and true, and does not harden under stress.

"Her acting is noteworthy for its restraint and poise," continued Lawrence Gilman in his review, in the *Herald Tribune*, of Kirsten Flagstad's debut at the Metropolitan as Sieglinde on February 2, 1935. "She does not indulge in those imbecile operatic gestures which Wagner detested —he called them 'swimming exercises.' Mme. Flagstad expresses volumes with a turn of her head or a lifting of a hand. She was, at times, a bit inflexible yesterday; but that may possibly have been due to nervousness."

It may also have been due to the fact—of which Gilman was possibly unaware—that she had sung the part for the first time only eight months before. Long experience of Metropolitan Isoldes had not prepared him for a European without years of Berlin, Vienna, Munich and Bayreuth behind her. "She is not," he noted incredulously, "another of those autumnal sopranos who passed their prime when the Kaiser was a boy, and whose waistlines have gone to that bourne from which no slenderness returneth."

Olin Downes, in the *Times*, was similarly impressed: "To the Metropolitan Association came yesterday a new singer who made an immediate and irresistible appeal to the audience. No Sieglinde of the past ten years [and they had included Maria Müller, Elisabeth Rethberg, Maria Jeritza, Florence Easton, Grete Stückgold, Gertrude Kappel, Elisabeth Ohms, Dorothee Manski and Göta Ljungberg] has made such an impression here by her voice, stage business, her intelligence and dramatic sincerity, and by her evident knowledge of Wagner. . . . The net results of this performance arouse keen anticipation of the enactment of the part of Isolde which Mme. Flagstad will take on Wednesday evening." And Downes, too, noted a break with Metropolitan tradition. "It appears," he observed, "that for once the Metropolitan has engaged a singer who is in her prime and not in the declining years that follow success."

With the ensuing Isolde, a role which Flagstad had sung previously only a few times in Oslo, and in German, all critical restraint was swept aside. "A transcendentally beautiful and moving impersonation," said Gilman, "an embodiment so sensitively musical, so fine-grained in its imaginative and intellectual texture, so lofty in its pathos and simplicity, of so memorable a loveliness, that experienced operagoers sought among their memories of legendary days to find its like. They did not find it."

Lawrence Gilman was then fifty-seven and had been a newspaper critic in New York since 1896, the year before Flagstad was born. His Isoldes would have included Nordica, Ternina, Marion Weed, Gadski, Fremstad, Melanie Kurt, Margaret Matzenauer, Easton, Nanny Larsen-Todsen, Kappel, Ohms, Ljungberg, Anny Konetzni and, most recently, Frida Leider. He may even have heard Rosa Sucher, the first Bayreuth Isolde (1886), who sang the role in a special Damrosch season at the Metropolitan Opera House in 1895. One wonders which of these ladies he had in mind when, in commenting favorably on Flagstad's appearance and deportment, he observed that "there is no reason implicit in Wagner's

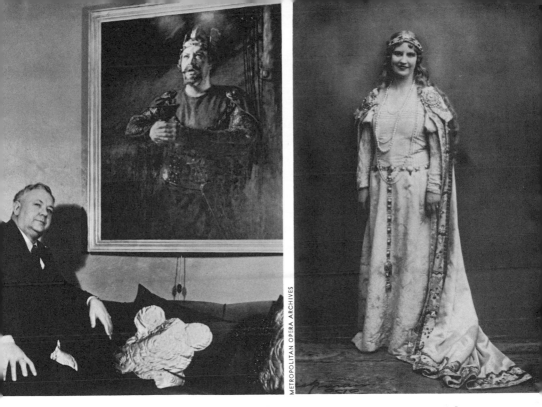

The greatest Wagnerian soprano of the century was fortunate in having the greatest *Heldentenor* as her contemporary. Lauritz Melchior's Tristan may well have been the finest of them all (above left). Kirsten Flagstad, like Lilli Lehmann and Lillian Nordica before her, found the entrance to Valhalla in New York. But she also sang the more lyric roles, such as Elsa (above right). Flagstad drinks coffee during an intermission in Los Angeles (below left). After the performance the libation would be champagne.

Marian Anderson's natural habitat was the recital hall, but her engagement at the Metropolitan established a historic precedent. She is shown (below right) being welcomed to the opera house by Rudolph Bing.

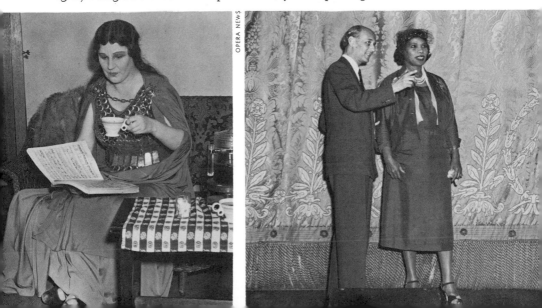

text why Isolde should be represented as an elderly and semaphoric *Hausfrau* in a red wig."

Downes was similarly ecstatic: "Then came the sweeping climax of the first act, when, Heaven be praised, the soprano had the voice to achieve the musical apotheosis of the situation. That voice soared; the sustained A carried the thrill that only the human voice, of all instruments, communicates. . . . Mme. Flagstad, whatever vicissitudes the Metropolitan may be facing, should be retained here for seasons to come. She is an artist young enough to develop in the grandest roles, and give them what they imperatively require."

This artist "young enough . . . to develop in the grandest roles" was just five months short of her fortieth birthday. She had previously sung Isolde and Sieglinde in German and Eva, Elsa and Elisabeth in Norwegian and Swedish. In what remained of that first season at the Metropolitan she sang for the first time anywhere Kundry and the Brünnhildes of *Die Walküre* and *Götterdämmerung*. Only illness prevented her from doing the *Siegfried* Brünnhilde, too, which she sang for the first time the following autumn in San Francisco.

Obviously, she was a quick study, and blessed with a secure memory. She had learned Isolde in Norwegian in six weeks. But she did not undertake such an appalling enlargement of her repertoire as a tour de force. It was required of her because the Metropolitan wished to exploit her newly discovered potentiality as an attracter of audiences, and she did what had to be done. Edward Johnson, who had just come in as general manager of the Metropolitan, remembered Lilli Lehmann and wanted Flagstad to do Norma, but she was not at ease in Italian, and the project was dropped. During the war years, in Europe, she added Alceste and Rezia (in *Oberon*). Her last new role was Dido in Purcell's *Dido and Aeneas*, in London, toward the end of her career.

Although new to most of the Wagner repertoire, she was no beginner. Just a little more than a year before her arrival at the Metropolitan she had celebrated her twentieth anniversary in the theater. But there had been nothing in her career to predict the eminence to which she was elevated so suddenly and so dramatically in America. She had sung almost exclusively in the Scandinavian theaters and in the Scandinavian languages. And she had sung the conventional repertoire of a provincial theater, including operetta.

In Oslo her roles had included Nuri (in d'Albert's *Tiefland*), Nedda, Amelia (in *Un Ballo in Maschera*), Minnie (in *The Girl of the Golden West*), Micaëla and Marguerite, and she had sung Desdemona to Slezak's Othello. In Göteborg, Sweden, she had added Agathe, Mimi, Eva, Aida, Elsa and Tosca. None of this seemed to point the way to her destiny as the greatest Wagnerian soprano of the century, nor had she shown any special affinity for Wagner. In Vienna, just five years before her New York debut, she had heard *Tristan und Isolde* for the first time and had, by her own admission, been so bored that she could hardly stay awake.

Hers had been, in other words, the typical career of a provincial Continental opera singer. Such a career, for the majority of those who led it in pre-jet days, differed strikingly from the opera career of popular British and American imagination. Its glamour was confined to the performance in the theater. An artist was an employee of the crown, state or municipality. He resided in the city where the opera house was situated, and spent most of his time there, enjoying—or not enjoying, as the case might be—a life in no way different from that of any other employed citizen. A prima donna was a *Hausfrau* like any other woman, and was normally indistinguishable from any other in her offstage dress and deportment. Such a woman was the Flagstad encountered by Edwin McArthur, her future accompanist and conductor, when he met her for the first time at a cocktail party given in her honor by NBC Artists' Service shortly after her Metropolitan debut.

"Flagstad herself gave me something of a shock," he has written in his *Flagstad, a Personal Memoir*. "Naturally, I was excited to meet her. But after having heard her at the Metropolitan in striking costumes and in opulent operatic settings, I was not prepared to meet such a strangely unglamorous woman. She was nothing like most other divas I had known. There is no denying, however, that she attracted attention despite her almost excessive simplicity. Like her husband [Henry Johansen], she was tall, but she was not beautiful. And at this party of distinguished people gathered to swoon, she gave little if any impression of the glamorous celebrity who had been expected.

"*Plain* is the only word I can use to describe her. Her dress was unattractive—she wore a hat fit only for a woman to wear to market—and, not having learned how to play the role of a famous woman, and obviously feeling self-conscious at meeting so many strangers, she didn't smile at all. I remember standing aside for a few minutes just looking at her, naturally with admiration for what she was, and praying that my ambition to become her accompanist would be realized, but at the same time trying to persuade myself that such a woman could really be *Flagstad*."

And so she would remain for some time. Toward the close of her first American concert tour, and just before her first Carnegie Hall recital, she sang a special matinee at the Junior League in New York. Frances Alda was in the audience, and went backstage to congratulate her, but was barred from the dressing room on Flagstad's orders, along with everybody else. Alda was not pleased, and she telephoned McArthur the next day to complain about everything, including Flagstad's lack of nail polish. "Tell that Norwegian peasant," she said, "that her singing is great, but she had better learn how to dress her hair and put some polish on those rough nails."

She learned it all, eventually. McArthur says the dawning awareness of herself as a prima donna, and an awareness, too, of a prima donna's prerogatives, began in 1938, about three years after her Metropolitan debut. She never became genuinely sophisticated, he says, but "in being exposed more and more to the upper levels of society, she developed more accurate taste in her clothes and in her mode of living. Up to this time, it had been possible to walk down a street with her without any-one's taking notice. As she came to be recognized, she feigned irritation, and complained that the public 'will not let me live a private life.' The truth of the matter is that she enjoyed every shred of attention that came her way. And as a prima donna, she was acute enough to know that she had to dress and play the part."

Alda's reference to Flagstad as a peasant was an oversimplification. Flagstad was no phenomenon fresh from the farm. Her parents were, in fact, professional musicians, and her father had been conductor at the Central Theater in Oslo. But the family was of peasant stock, and Flag-stad's personality and behavior reflected many peasant traits, among them a stubbornness described by McArthur as "granitic," and a persist-ent reluctance to admit error. There was something almost childlike, also, about her delight in the exercise of power, once she discovered how much power she had, and in her abuse of it, too. An example of such abuse, as McArthur acknowledges, was her determination to promote his career as a conductor. She repeatedly made his engagement a condition of her own.

Her approach to the theater was curiously detached. Had she come to it straight from the farm, or from a prosaic middle-class life, it might have held an irresistible fascination for her. But having grown up in it, she could, like Jenny Lind or Henriette Sontag, take it or leave it. She was strongly bound to family and home. After each of her two marriages, she left the theater for a time. In 1941, with her husband in occupied

Norway already suspected of Quisling associations, she turned her back on American success, prosperity and fame, and returned to him, against the advice of her American friends, with ghastly consequences.

Only the sturdiest peasant resiliency, stubbornness and faith could, after the war, have carried her through her husband's death in prison and enabled her, subsequently, to persevere against the hostility that awaited her upon her return to the United States. She had to face a virulent campaign against herself in the press. There were picket lines and, in Philadelphia, stink bombs and a near riot in the Academy of Music. That she was able to maintain her poise and sustain her art under such circumstances was evidence of an elemental feminine courage more often encountered in the defiant heroines of opera than in the women who merely sing their roles. And she fought it through. In the end she was welcomed back to the Metropolitan and to the New York Philharmonic Orchestra and was made Directress of the Royal Opera in Oslo.

Against the fortitude—one is tempted to say nobility—that emerged when Flagstad's mettle was tested, her occasional rudeness, tactlessness, ungraciousness and capriciousness were trivial blemishes, though not always accepted as such by the victims. She could be small in small matters, not so much childlike as childish. But in big matters she was big.

One sensed something of all this in her operatic impersonations. Her accomplishments as an actress had little to do with traditional histrionic artifice, nor were they the product of a superior intellect. Flagstad was, indeed, anything but an intellectual. Her favorite reading when she first came to America, according to McArthur, was movie magazines—he thought that her pose of resenting any invasion of privacy was modeled on Greta Garbo—and her favorite game was solitaire, which she played constantly and with passionate concentration.

Her communication as an actress was rather the expression of a self-contained personality reacting to dramatic and musical stimulation with an intuition both acute and sure. It is doubtful that she ever investigated with any thoroughness the psychological labyrinth of Wagner's texts. But, as she was both profoundly musical and profoundly feminine, she was responsive to a composer's guidance. With composers as articulate and compelling as Wagner and Beethoven, this was enough.

There was a certain element of dormancy about Flagstad. The fact that she sang for twenty years in Europe without exciting much attention is evidence of it. The artistic greatness that lay concealed within her was awakened only by exposure to the most demanding roles— Isolde, Sieglinde, the Brünnhildes, Kundry, Senta and Leonore—which, for more than half her professional life, she had deemed not for her, if, indeed, she had thought of them at all. Her greatness as a person was disclosed only by exposure to emotional fires fed by war and persecution.

There was a dormant element in her voice, too, a kind of extra dimension, rarely tapped in recital, which only the surging Wagnerian orchestra and the insistent challenge of Melchior's plangent tenor would move her to reveal. Then, and not until then, would one realize that here was the grandest soprano within memory—one suspects that only Materna, among the great Wagnerian sopranos of history, may have had a voice of comparable amplitude. And then one would speak of the opening of floodgates without cringing at the cliché. There seemed no other way to describe that transcendent sound.

The most accurate measure of the degree and the qualitative implications of Flagstad's preeminence was the company in which she achieved and sustained it. The German wing at the Metropolitan when she arrived in 1935 was one of the strongest in the annals of that institution. Melchior, of course, was among the great Tristans, Siegfrieds, Tannhäusers, Lohengrins and Parsifals of Wagnerian history, not a great actor, perhaps, but not a bad one either, his voice unexampled in its size, richness and brilliance by any other Wagnerian tenor of the century. The baritones and basses—Friedrich Schorr, Michael Bohnen, Gustav Schützendorf, Ludwig Hofmann and Alexander Kipnis—were also supreme, each in his way. (It had been Kipnis, incidentally, who called Flagstad to the attention of the Metropolitan's directors.) The mezzo-sopranos were formidable, notably Karin Branzell, Maria Olszewska, Kerstin Thorborg and the American, Kathryn Meisle. And the sopranos—!

During her prewar years at the Metropolitan, Flagstad shared Sieglinde with Lotte Lehmann, Kappel, Maria Müller, Rethberg and Helen Traubel; the Brünnhildes with Kappel, Easton, Konetzni, Marjorie Lawrence and Ljungberg; Isolde with Kappel, Konetzni and Easton; Elisabeth with Lehmann, Ljungberg, Irene Jessner and Traubel; Kundry with Kappel; and Elsa with Lehmann, Rethberg and Dorothee Manski. That she could reign supreme among nearly a dozen of the finest dramatic sopranos of the century speaks for itself.

Destinn and Ponselle enjoyed a similar supremacy, but against inferior and less numerous competitors. Only Patti, Melba and Caruso achieved a comparable immunity from comparably formidable competition.

Rudolph Bing was not overstating the case when he referred to Flagstad as "the Caruso of our time."

· XXI ·

Cadenza

CONTEMPORARY PROBLEMS

AND PROSPECTS

FASHIONS IN singing, and the accomplishments of the great singers, have been governed for the past century by trends in musical philosophy and musical taste and by the requirements levied by composers in their efforts to influence taste—or cater to it.

Throughout the seventeenth and eighteenth centuries, as we have seen, the singers were generally masters of their own destinies in terms of what was expected and required of them. Operatic composition was tailored to vocal fashion and to the predilections and capacities of individual singers. This was true of a good deal of vocal composition well into the nineteenth century.

Beginning with Verdi and Wagner, however, and continuing through Strauss and the *verismo* Italians, fashion in the lyric theater was determined by the interaction of composer and public, with the singer only one of several executive agents. Such exceptional artists as Grisi, Patti and Melba could perpetuate the older relationship of singer and public, in which the composer served the singer's courtship of the listener; but the repertoire that favored this relationship could not withstand the popularity of the new operas. With the public's acceptance of the composer rather than the singer as the dominant figure in the lyric theater, and of the conductor as the composer's plenipotentiary, the singer's formerly more or less exclusive intimacy with the public came to be regarded as improper and even indecent.

The singer's margin of creative and imaginative freedom was inevitably inhibited. If the eighteenth century had been the century of the singer in the opera house, the nineteenth was the century of the orchestra; and as composers, particularly Wagner, began to impose upon the orchestra an interpretive as well as an accompanying and supporting function, the singer became a single element in a vast ensemble subject to the conductor's direction, guidance and control.

Great singing was still possible within this complex organization, and individual singers were spurred to extraordinary achievements by the challenge of new horizons disclosed by composers of extraordinary genius. But just as fashions and accomplishments in singing reflected the influence of great composers upon the repertoire in the latter half of the nineteenth century, so does singing today reflect the stagnation into which the repertoire has fallen since the death of Puccini.

There seems to be something about stagnation of repertoire that breeds stagnation of performance. With constant repetition of the same works, certain approaches to their interpretation are found preferable to others and become more or less standard. Performers, thereafter, defy convention at their own risk. Most observers would agree, probably, that there has been the same inhibition of striking individuality among today's singers as has been noted in the work of orchestras, solo instrumentalists and conductors. The level of competence is high—possibly higher than ever—but its effectiveness is compromised by uniformity.

Today's singer is appallingly restricted whether he knows it or not. From his earliest student days he is subjected to a kind of musical guidance grounded in a Germanic philosophy of the sanctity of composition and the immutability of the written note. Singing teachers rarely attend to much beyond vocal technique. Interpretation—and, too often, even vocal technique—is in the hands of pianist-coaches. From the beginning to the end of his career the singer's every utterance is supervised by that "police escort" which the virtuosos of the end of the eighteenth century discerned in Mozart's orchestral accompaniments.

Nor does today's singer have a viable contemporary music—as the popular singer does—in which he could feel sufficiently at home stylistically to do as he pleases. The contemporary serious composer offers challenges enough in a kind of music excruciatingly difficult to sing; but his music has not found its way to the hearts of the general public, and it is excluded therefore from the standard repertoire. The singer who masters the difficulties is rewarded by the applause of only a small coterie of devotees. Not surprisingly, the most successful singers have not appraised this kind of challenge as an attractive investment of time and vocal resources.

And there are other restrictive factors. Not only is the repertoire of the opera house stagnant; the popularity of the song and *Lieder* recital is declining. It was never a particularly satisfactory institution except in the hands of the greatest artists. It was slow to emerge as something suitable for a large public, and it was quickly stereotyped. The older format for a singer's appearance outside the opera house had called for an orchestra and assisting artists. This offered greater variety and an effective sequence. The appearance of the star performer at the close of each half of the program was an event, appropriately prepared. The recital, with the singer alone at the bend of the piano, solemnly progressing from the seventeenth century to the twentieth through four or five groups, with only the piano as an accompanying instrument, is a trial both for the singer and for the public.

Today's singer is further handicapped by being virtually cut off from the main stream of popular music. In the eighteenth century, and well into the nineteenth, the arias from the operas of Rossini, Donizetti, Bellini and Meyerbeer were the popular music of the time. Singers offered them without shame as the principal items of their concert programs, and instrumentalists capitalized on their popularity by paraphrasing them in elaborate virtuoso potpourris.

The conventions of our own time require that a recitalist be serious with a capital S. The singer may not lower himself to please a paying public with what a paying public might like to hear. This is pandering, a compromise of artistic integrity, and the critics will go after the sinners just as they went after John McCormack and Richard Tauber. But there is more to the problem than artistic snobbery. The singer of today could not be truly popular even if he had a choice; for popular music is now idiomatically different from the music he has been taught to sing.

The opera, oratorio, concert or recital singer who wishes to sing popular music is confined pretty much to the semiclassical literature and to songs from the "musicals." The popular music of our time is sung—and often sung very well—by a different kind of singer influenced by the jazz musician's way of shaping a phrase around the buoyant and explicit beat of jazz. Very few "serious" singers can do this—Eileen Farrell has come closest—nor would their audiences like it if they did. The idioms are incompatible.

There are other problems—many of them. The jet age has condemned the best singers to be forever airborne. The old leisurely pace of their nomadic existence—long seasons in residence in one place linked to other seasons in other places by pleasant ocean voyages—has become frantic. The summer vacation has been sacrificed to the lucrative festival phenomenon. The singer is in New York today and in London, Milan or Vienna tomorrow, with appearances scheduled the following week in Buenos Aires or Rio de Janeiro and the following month in Tokyo, Melbourne and Sydney.

The case of the baritone—Hans Hotter—who worked in performances in Colorado between two appearances at Bayreuth in a space of ten days may have been exceptional, but it was not unique. The international circuit imposes severe strains on the singer in the form of sudden changes of climate and time and the sheer fatigue of constant travel. And once he has achieved that level of prominence where his services are in demand around the world, he can no longer afford to settle back and enjoy life. If he won't fly, his competitor will.

Recording has created problems, too. With records being made from a selection of the best of several "takes," and with more or less splicing, the singer may find himself hard put to live up to his records in his public appearances. He is at a disadvantage as his own competitor. And the strain and nervous tension of recording sessions is an additional tax on vocal and other physical resources, not to overlook the frustrations of having a conductor and a good many other functionaries passing judgment on his performance and telling him what to do and what not to do, and of having to do certain passages over and over again because of his own or somebody else's mistakes.

But the basic problem is repertoire. And with the contemporary composer failing to provide a contemporary style congenial to the general operagoing public, the singer seeking an escape from the endless repetition of favorite operas of Mozart, Verdi, Wagner, Strauss and Puccini has followed the example of many instrumentalists in retreating into the past.

The leading and most influential figures in this retreat—or revival—have been Maria Callas and Joan Sutherland. Thanks to their example, the public has been awakened suddenly to the nearly lost art and the all but forgotten delights of florid song. The old war-horses of Pasta, Malibran, Persiani and Grisi are being trotted out: *Norma, Il Pirata, I Puritani, Lucrezia Borgia, Maria di Rohan, Anna Bolena, Roberto Devereux, Semiramide, La Sonnambula,* for example. And everyone is agreeably surprised at what these old operas can still yield to the singer who has revealed their secrets and mastered the idiom and its technical requirements.

Maria Callas rediscovered the dramatic elements of *bel canto* and the art of Pasta, Malibran, Grisi and Viardot. She is seen (above left) as Lucia, in Naples.

Joan Sutherland explored more deeply the nearly forgotten art of improvisatory embellishment. As Norma (above right).

What Callas and Sutherland started is carried on by Teresa Berganza (below left), a mezzo-soprano of the type for which Rossini wrote *The Barber of Seville* and *La Cenerentola*; by her compatriot Montserrat Caballé (below center), a soprano of more dramatic disposition; and by the American Marilyn Horne (below right), whose success in music by Lampugnani and Simone Mayr may forecast further Baroque excavations.

What Callas and Sutherland have accomplished may be a mere beginning if younger singers take the hint and do their homework. The eighteenth century, excepting Mozart and the Handel and Gluck revivals, remains virtually untouched. There are hundreds of operas by scores of composers awaiting excavation and investigation. This is a singer's realm, and its successful recovery is primarily the singer's responsibility. Others may help. But the essential substance of this music is a melodic line. It is not enough that this line be sung merely correctly, in time and in tune. It must be shaped, varied and embellished, and it must be sung persuasively, movingly, excitingly and convincingly. This will require more creative initiative and invention, more imagination and individuality, and a greater self-respect and self-reliance than has been required—or permitted—of singers for a century or more.

Singers for whom this archaeology is attractive will have to become, to some extent at least, musicologists. They will have to use libraries, consult old scores and pictures, learn to read in more than two clefs, study embellishment and the art of constructing effective and tasteful cadenzas, just as the instrumentalists do who are exploring the treasures of baroque. And the singers have one important advantage. Old vocal recordings made by older artists around the turn of the century offer clues denied to the instrumentalist.

Baroque instrumental music suffered virtual extinction during the nineteenth and early twentieth centuries, and such music as survived—that of Mozart, Haydn, Bach and Handel—was disfigured by subjection to nineteenth-century fashions in performance and arrangement. Baroque vocal styles were more persistent, thanks to the perpetuation of the basic traditions of florid song in the operas of Rossini, Donizetti and Bellini, and thanks, also, to the magic worked by such singers as Sontag, Lind, Grisi, Patti, Sembrich and Melba in an old-fashioned repertoire kept alive by the singers' popularity and excellence. One senses—but cannot prove, of course—that the records of Patti and de Lucia, for example, provide a more vivid and more reliable signpost to the eighteenth century than anything available on records to the instrumentalist who would like to know how Bach or Rameau or even Mozart really played.

There have already been some astonishing accomplishments. Not only Callas and Sutherland but also such younger singers as Berganza, Horne and Caballé have shown what can be done by those willing and able to project themselves back a century and a half or more in time and master the severe technical and stylistic requirements. They have shown, too, how much pleasure and excitement this older vocal music can still yield when sung with the essential combination of virtuosity, affection and conviction. Horne has even gone back beyond Rossini to such forgotten masters as Giovanni Battista Lampugnani (1706–1781) and Simone Mayr. Others will surely follow her example.

It should be a rewarding enterprise. Quite aside from the pleasures of scholarship and research, and the public's delight in the rediscovery of true virtuosity, it offers the singer his only chance of emancipation from the dictatorship of composers, conductors and coaches, his only hope of regaining that freedom to pace and phrase according to his own impulse and insight now enjoyed, among vocalists, only by the popular singer. That it also imposes severe responsibilities would seem to go without saying.

Throughout the nineteenth century the harmonic fertility of the great German composers encouraged a philosophical view of music as organized sound, and of instrumental music as somehow more respectable than vocal music, as something superior to mere song. This view overlooks the fact that the human voice is the most beautiful and expressive of all musical instruments, and that all other instruments are essentially vocal substitutes. But under the impact of such overwhelming composer personalities as Wagner and Verdi the creative prerogatives and responsibilities of the singer passed to the composer and conductor by unwitting default.

The orchestra, in Wagner's and Verdi's operas, provided much of the dramatic impulse and color formerly left to the singers, and the extent, complexity and success of the orchestra's participation left the singer no choice but to accept subservience and dependence. It has occurred to few of them, probably, that they were, at the same time, letting the composer, the conductor, and the orchestra do much of their own work, and that their own creative imagination was condemned to extinction.

The public and the critics have applauded the abdication. For the singers to have done otherwise than submit would have been to oppose prevailing taste and opinion. There would have been little applause at any time in the past half-century for any singer whose insistence on a prima donna's prerogatives had prompted a reputable conductor to remind her—as Toscanini reminded Farrar—that the stars are in heaven. But something has been lost!

A lovely example of the Germanic attitude toward the kind of music in which the singer rules is offered by Robert Schumann in his postscript to a review in his *Neue Zeitschrift für Musik* of a concert appearance by the soprano Francilla Pixis, the adopted daughter of the pianist Johann Peter Pixis (1788–1874), in Leipzig in 1835:

"A word more before Florestan comes in. After Francilla's concert I heard Jonathan say to Florestan: 'If I am not mistaken, Florestan, I saw something moist on your cheek after the Donizetti aria.'

" 'Possibly,' Florestan replied, 'but it was only perspiration.'

"Back home I heard Florestan pacing furiously up and down in his room, exclaiming in disjointed phrases:

" 'O, eternal shame! O, Florestan, have you lost your senses? Have you studied Marpurg, dissected the 'Well-tempered Clavier' and learned Bach and Beethoven from memory only to weep at a miserable aria by Donizetti, heard for the first time after many years? And this Jonathan has to see it! If those tears were still there I would crush them with my fist.' "

"At this he rushed to the piano and proceeded to play the aria as though it were a beer cellar ditty, ludicrously and grotesquely, so that he was finally able to calm himself and say:

" 'Truly, it was only the tone of her voice that so went to my heart. . . .' "

As if to be moved to tears by a mere melody well sung were somehow sinful!

It is still customary, even among lovers of fine vocalism, to take a patronizing view of the Rossini-Donizetti-Bellini repertoire—not to mention older *opera seria*—as dramatically preposterous and vocally merely pretty when sung well.

This is to ignore Maria Callas' most important contribution. Whatever her vocal shortcomings, she has reminded us that a long vocal line with a simple, unobtrusive accompaniment, or a brisk cabaletta delivered with conviction and scintillant virtuosity, are empty only if left empty by singers. To the singer of truly creative disposition they offer a scaffolding within which may be fashioned a musical edifice of the loveliest proportions, of compelling beauty and overpowering drama.

The key to the secrets of baroque and early nineteenth-century opera is not merely the mastery of the technical requirements. That is essential. But beyond technical mastery lies imagination. The singer must translate into musical phrase and cadence the emotions of character under stress, as Pasta and Malibran did—and as Callas has done. And conductors must learn to encourage and support the singer's imaginative flight, which will not be easy for this increasingly literal-minded breed, nor congenial to their autocratic disposition.

The most tasteful embellishment will hardly kindle enthusiasm in the kind of conductor who forbids the insertion of appoggiaturas in Mozart's operas (arguing that if Mozart had wanted them he would have written them) or who refuses to hasten the tempo at that point in "Là ci darem la mano," for instance, where the time changes from two-four to six-eight as Don Giovanni, sensing that Zerlina's resistance is weakening, cries: "Andiam, andiam mio bene"—in other words, "Come, come, my little one, let's be off!" Time was when composers felt it superfluous to spell out the obvious.

We are speaking, of course, of a singers' world. If this will strike many as monstrous, it is only because our musical orientation is still basically Teutonic. We tend to react as Florestan reacted to tears provoked by Francilla Pixis' singing of an aria by Donizetti. If it may strike others as pessimistic, due to the implied retreat into the past—well, that is up to the contemporary composer. The charm and the success of good singing may remind him of his artistic base in communicative vocal melody.

Handel, Haydn and Mozart, as well as Rossini, Donizetti and Bellini, all worked with and for good singers. Liszt, Chopin and Anton Rubinstein all acknowledged their debt to great singers as influences in their interpretive art as instrumentalists. And Wagner said that he owed everything to the revelation of Schröder-Devrient's Fidelio. Is it pessimistic, then, to hope that great singers of our own time may lead us back to musical health and sanity?

That they will have to go back first to the eighteenth century to do it is only because what we call serious music has lost contact with its melodic roots. Only through industrious and intelligent archaeology can we rediscover our elemental musicality. The instrumentalists have provided an example in their investigation of baroque music. But the great instrument of baroque was the human voice, and the lessons of baroque can best be communicated vocally.

A singer's world is monstrous only under the government of sterile singers. May it be the calling of the great singers of the last third of our century to remind us that music is song, and that it is the privilege—and the responsibility—of the singer to be the supreme musician!

Coda (1981)

READING THIS "Cadenza" after an interval of sixteen years, and the chapters immediately preceding it, I find little that I would wish to change. Indeed, little in the singer's world of opera, concert, oratorio and recital has undergone any substantial change, and there are few among the singers who have entered that world during the interval, or grown to maturity, whom I would wish to add to my gallery of the great, covering a span of nearly four centuries, which is not to say that among the others there have not been, and indeed still are, many excellent and admirable singers.

I should preface whatever may follow by stressing that my listening experience during these sixteen years has been confined almost wholly to what has come my way in London. But given the Royal Opera, the English National Opera and Glyndebourne, and the fact that today's outstanding singers constitute a kind of international touring company, with London an almost obligatory stop, I have probably heard most of those now enjoying international reputations.

An exception is Beverly Sills, who made her career almost exclusively in America, and whom I heard live only once, under trying circumstances, as Lucia in her only visit to the Royal Opera. She dominated the American scene as did no other singer of her generation, and on reputation and undoubted accomplishment deserves an honorable place in these pages.

Among those who have emerged or achieved their highest standards during these years, pride of place goes unquestionably, in my view, to

Beverly Sills, seen here as Violetta in *La Traviata*, "dominated the American scene as did no other singer of her generation," while Leontyne Price, seen here as Tosca, has enjoyed an international career of similar distinction.

the tenors, although not, certainly, to Wagnerian tenors. A generation that has produced or witnessed the prime of Franco Corelli, Carlo Bergonzi, Nicolai Gedda, Alfredo Kraus, Jon Vickers, Placido Domingo, José Carreras, Luciano Pavarotti and James McCracken need offer no apologies to the vocal past. I have heard them all, most of them in a variety of roles. I have admired them all, and have enjoyed them all.

If I were to single out one as standing somewhat above a distinguished company, it would be Domingo, whom I have heard often at the Royal Opera and on television, if in a relatively small sampling of his extraordinary repertoire. Listening to him, I almost invariably find myself asking: "Did Gigli, Martinelli, Pertile, Lauri-Volpi and Bjoerling sing any better?"

I think not. In some matters of style, taste, musicianship and immaculate vocalism they did not—as I remember them—sing as well. But the voices were more individual, more distinctive and, in Gigli's case, more beautiful. Domingo's voice, goodness knows, falls mellifluously and persuasively upon the ear, but it hasn't quite the burnished silver quality of Gigli's, the incisive metal of Martinelli's, the ardor and fervor of Pertile's, the sensual insinuation of Lauri-Volpi's in his younger years, nor the sheer brilliance of Bjoerling's.

But I have treasured memories of all these more recent tenors: of Pavarotti's evident and contagious pleasure in the sound of his own effulgent voice and in the pleasure he knows it gives to others; of Bergonzi's innate and intuitive, if unabashedly Italianate, sense of style; of Kraus's elegance in movement, posture, attitude and enunciation; of Gedda's harmonization of warmth and refinement; of Carreras' irrepressible and richly voiced lyricism; of McCracken's deeply felt and vividly projected Othello (I wish that I might have heard his Tannhäuser at the Met, of which I have heard only superlative accounts); of Vickers' Aeneas, Othello and Peter Grimes (I missed his Tristan, of which, too, I have heard only superlative accounts), and so on.

If something is missing from this catalogue of tenor prosperity, it is the truly dramatic, heroic tenor. The last dominant figure in that category would be, I suppose, Del Monaco. All those named above, with the possible exception of Vickers, fall rather into the category of *spinto*, lyric tenors capable of undertaking successfully the dramatic roles as Gigli, Pertile and Lauri-Volpi did. Of the true *Heldentenor* for the Wagnerian repertoire there has been none to efface or even challenge the memory of Melchior, or even of Max Lorenz in his prime. That same

"Among those who have emerged or achieved their highest standards during these years, pride of place goes, unquestionably . . . to the tenors. . . ." Here Placido Domingo as Othello, Jon Vickers as Samson, Nicolai Gedda as Lenski in *Eugene Onegin* and Luciano Pavarotti in recital, exhibiting "the evident and contagious pleasure in the sound of his own effulgent voice and in the pleasure he knows it gives to others."

is true of Wagnerian sopranos. There has been only Nilsson to compete with one's memories of Flagstad and Leider.

Among baritones, with Tito Gobbi now retired, there has been only Sherrill Milnes to stand out among many excellent, if hardly legendary, singers. The standard among baritones is high (as is their vocal range), but they have not been of the kind, either as singers or actors, whose names become household words.

The same would seem to be true of sopranos of all categories, many of them excellent—Kiri Te Kanawa the most vocally distinctive, Edita Gruberova the most vocally accomplished—in an opera world that remembers Callas and can still hear Sutherland, Leontyne Price, Victoria de los Angeles, if no longer in their vocal prime. Some of us, of course, remember Jeritza, Milanov, Ponselle, Raisa, Rethberg, Sayão, Albanese, Easton and Turner (the list could easily be extended), while in Italy and South America, as well as in North America, older opera-goers have similarly vivid and as yet uneclipsed memories of Caniglia, Cigna, Giuseppina Cobelli (the latter little known in the English-speaking world, if only because she never sang there, and recorded only two sides) and Magda Olivero. This view might be disputed in America on behalf of Renata Scotto, whose successes there I have not experienced.

Of true contraltos one can hardly speak, now that Kathleen Ferrier is no longer with us. They seem to be an extinct species, although, curiously, almost all the finest female popular singers—Ella Fitzgerald, Sarah Vaughan, Peggy Lee and Cleo Laine, for example—are or have been contraltos, right down to the low D. In their place we have mezzo-sopranos, themselves forever tempted, as Pasta, Malibran, Viardot —and, in my opinion, Callas!—were, to shed the *mezzo* from their designation, and move up the scale vocally and financially. Such has been the case with Grace Bumbry, Shirley Verrett and, from time to time, Janet Baker, the latter rejoicing in a command of coloratura—and the art of making it make musical and dramatic sense—shared most conspicuously with Horne and Berganza. Frederica von Stade has so far resisted, or possibly not yet experienced, the upward urge, but she, too, is no more a true contralto than her sisters. In the Italian repertoire my memories of Castagna, Stignani and Simionato remain unchallenged, as do my memories of Branzell and Thorborg in the German.

True basses, too, would seem to be a threatened species. There are fine bass voices aplenty, but they tend to be bass-baritones rather than

"Among baritones . . . there has been only Sherrill Milnes, [seen here as Rodrigo in *Don Carlo*] to stand out among many excellent . . . singers," while among basses Nicolai Ghiaurov, seen here as King Philip in the same opera.

basso-profundos. They all have a high G, but sound as though nearing bottom at the low G. Among them, with George London no longer singing, and Jerome Hines nearing the end of a splendid career, Nicolai Ghiaurov and Martti Talvela stand—and sing—pretty much alone.

A number of factors have contributed to the disappearance or relative weakness of the low notes among contraltos, mezzos, baritones and basses, most obviously a rising pitch, the growth in the size and importance of the orchestra, requiring singers to raise their voices both in pitch and intensity in order to make themselves heard, and the competitive urge of singers, especially the men, to sing higher and louder than others, an urge conducive to sounds often having more to do with athleticism than musicality. Taste and fashion have also been contributing factors, especially with respect to female voices. The booming, baritonal bottom notes, the glory of contraltos of yesteryear, and of some sopranos, too, are no longer felt to be seemly. The few singers who still have them exhibit them at the risk of critical censure.

Prevailing pitch, now internationally standardized at A-440 (oscillations per second), has risen, with many local variations and fluctuations, by about a semitone since the turn of the last century, and by a whole tone from that prevailing until then in southern Italy. For a Konstanze tackling "Martern aller Arten" in *Die Entführung aus dem Serail,* for example, or a Fiordiligi faced with "Come scoglio" in *Così fan Tutte,* or a Florestan in his taxing dungeon aria in *Fidelio,* a semitone can make an enormous difference.

Singers, too, have contributed to the vocal mischief, interpolating high notes that quickly become traditional and, in effect, obligatory, however dubious their propriety. Composers noted the singers' predilection—and the public's favorable reaction—and obliged by writing accordingly, *vide* Zerbinetta's aria in *Ariadne auf Naxos* and what Puccini asked of his Turandot and Calaf. Both factors, a rising pitch and the singers' own high note interpolations, comprise a sorry phenomenon of higher vocal altitude, excluding many excellent singers from roles they could sing easily at the pitch prevailing at the time and place of composition, without the now expected high note interpolations, and rendering more taxing and exacting the requirements for those who do sing them, damaging many voices and shortening the life of others. To make matters worse, the pitch in many orchestras and opera houses is edging upward from A-440. Instrumentalists like it that way. It makes for greater tonal brilliance. But voices cannot be adjusted

by valves, by the lengthening of the necks of fiddles, and by the substitution of steel strings for gut.

Paradoxical as it may seem, while voices have been working higher,
if not necessarily rising higher, they have also been getting heavier, the
singers putting more weight of breath upon the vocal cords in order to
produce a bigger sound. Within the past decade, the release on LP of a
thousand or so 78s, many of them dating from the first decade of the
century, and made by singers born as far back as the 1830s, 1840s and
1850s, has made it possible for the student of vocal history, as well as
the collector of rare discs, to hear for himself how voice production has
been affected and influenced by larger orchestras, larger expectations
and increasingly restrictive vocal categorization. The developments
have meant, in turn, that most singers today begin, or at least emerge,
later than they used to do. Certainly they come to the heavier roles later.

Not only the old records of older singers speak for themselves. So do
facts. It may be well to recall here some of those set forth in earlier
chapters. Milder-Hauptmann, when she sang the premiere of *Fidelio*
in 1805, was twenty. Schröder-Devrient, when she put *Fidelio* on the
map, so to speak, in the Vienna revival of 1822, was a month short of
eighteen. Henriette Sontag was eighteen when she sang the premiere
of Beethoven's Ninth Symphony, and she had already, a year earlier,
created the title role in *Euryanthe*. Lind made her debut as Agathe in
Der Freischütz at seventeen, Patti hers as Lucia at sixteen, and Lilli
Lehmann hers as Pamina at seventeen. Grisi sang the first Adalgisa to
the Norma of Pasta when she was twenty. Pasta herself was a veteran
at thirty-one. Most astonishing of all, perhaps, is the fact that Schnorr
von Carolsfeld, when he created the role of Tristan in Munich in 1865,
was twenty-nine, and that he died in Dresden just over five weeks later
after singing a rehearsal of—Don Ottavio!

These great singers at those ages could not have produced the vocal
sounds we associate with those roles today, and the records of those
who lived to make them, most notably Patti, Calvé, Albani and Lehmann,
suggest that they preserved a youthful vocal quality throughout long
careers. Yet Albani sang Isolde; Patti sang Aida; Eames sang not only
Aida, but also Santuzza, as did Calvé, who was also the most famous
Ophelia (in Ambroise Thomas' *Hamlet*) of her time, as well as the
most famous Carmen. Lehmann sang just about everything.

Irene Abendroth's fine 1902 recording of "Bel raggio lusinghier" from
Semiramide hardly suggests the first German Tosca and a great

Sieglinde. Margarethe Siems's sensational recording of "Beau pays" from *Les Huguenots* does suggest the singer for whom Strauss composed Zerbinetta's *tour de force*, but hardly the first Chrysothemis and the first Marschallin, any more than Schumann-Heink's bravura "Brindisi" from *Lucrezia Borgia* suggests the first Clytemnestra and Cosima Wagner's favorite Erda.

The same is generally true of the men, although inevitably they started later, if still considerably earlier than is the rule today. Until the baritones born in the 1870s came along, most notably Ruffo, the vocal sound of baritones was lighter and brighter, more suited to elegance than to power. Compare the recordings of Battistini and Scotti, for instance, with those of Ruffo and his contemporaries and successors! With pre-Caruso tenors, excepting, possibly, Tamagno, the recorded evidence is much the same. It is on the records of De Lucia, Bonci, Tito Schipa and even early Lauri-Volpi that we gain an echo of a lighter and more virtuosic past. And on McCormack's early operatic records, too. His teacher in Milan was reminded, he told McCormack, of Mario.

All this suggests that the traditions and criteria of bel canto and florid song, established and passed on by the castrati, long survived the new requirements and exactions of Meyerbeer, Wagner, Verdi, Strauss and the Italian verismists. Singers were still schooled according to the older disciplines. They sang the then new music, and the best of them must have sung it well, greatly assisted, obviously, by thorough and arduous technical grounding. But they can hardly have produced the sounds we have learned to expect from the examples of Caruso, Ruffo, De Muro, Flagstad and Melchior.

The older tradition would seem to have survived, at least among the women, longest and most vividly in Germany and Austria, as reflected in the records of Abendroth, Schumann-Heink, Siems and—as we hear on records she made in the early 1920s—Maria Ivogün. It has not entirely vanished, but specialization and categorization, now most conspicuously and disastrously in Germany and Austria, rule out the widely ranging repertoire open to, and welcomed by, the older singers. It probably means that the heavier roles, while they may now be sung more effectively, are sung less beautifully, with less sovereign command of vocal resources, and with a narrower margin of vocal security.

In earlier chapters I have discussed the inhibition of the singer's former creative prerogatives, first by composers, from Rossini (rather ineffectively) through Verdi and Wagner, and then by conductors, led by Mahler and Toscanini. This imposition of executive authority and supervision has done much to obliterate the individuality that once made singers instantly recognizable not only by the sound of their voices, but also by their way with a phrase, often a singularly wayward way.

Today's idolatry of composers—it would have struck composers prior to Verdi's time as idolatrous—will not countenance such liberties and idiosyncrasies, and neither will conductors. This has had much to do, I suspect, with what seems to me a distressing homogeneity in modern vocalism, along with the jet-propelled internationalism of today's opera world that has largely erased what once were fascinating, sometimes exasperating, national, cultural and regional approaches to song and singing. I once played De Lucia's famous recording of "Ecco ridente" from *The Barber of Seville* for a conductor friend of mine. He said: "Well, it's marvelous, but of course I wouldn't stand for it." In De Lucia's time, with an artist of his stature, it was the singer, not the conductor, who decided what would be stood for. The singer's world—and the public's, too—assuming the singer to be also an artist, was the better, the more exciting and the more rewarding for it.

Now, in the interval since this book was written and published, another and more sinister villain has appeared on the scene, or rather advanced to a position where he is permitted, even encouraged, to run roughshod over singer, conductor, composer and librettist. I refer, of course, to the new generation of producers, fathered by Wieland Wagner in Bayreuth and Walter Felsenstein in East Berlin, who seem to feel that in order to keep an aging repertoire alive, operas should be restaged in accordance with contemporary theater and cinematic fashion, and in the light of a contemporary political and social climate.

The resultant stylistic abominations are not here my subject, but again the singer is denied yet another prerogative, not this time as musician, but as singer-actor, becoming, as one of them has put it, a mere puppet on a string manipulated by the all-powerful producer. And so we get not the composer's opera, nor even the conductor's—let alone the singer's!—but the producer's.

As for televised opera—what with producers trying to present opera in terms of modern cinematic fashion and conventions, and scared witless at the prospect of letting composition and singers get on with their job in an appropriate amphitheatrical environment. God help us! Zoom in on tonsils, lips, tongue, molàrs, inlays and moles! Change camera angles in mid-aria, put the viewer down in the midst of the chorus, and heaven knows what other cinematic mischief, not to mention the egregious and inept lip-synching of prerecorded European studio productions. Opera belongs in the opera house, and the most acceptable telecasts are those that put the viewer there—and keep him at his distance.

This Coda, and the earlier chapters, too, have been concerned almost exclusively with opera singers. If I have neglected those thought of primarily as recitalists—most of them splendid opera singers as well—it has been partly a matter of personal predilection in favor of opera and partly a matter of vocal history. The solo song or Lieder recital as we know it today is of comparatively recent origin, dating roughly from the last two decades of the nineteenth century, as is true, too, of the solo instrumental recital. The format is severe, and has become more severe since the earlier years of this century with the banishment of the assisting artists, opera arias and popular songs that contributed variety and even a bit of fun to the programs of such popular favorites as McCormack, Tibbett, Crooks, Tauber and John Charles Thomas.

But it would be an injustice to fine artists and fine vocalists, and to their admirers, of whom I have been one, to close these pages without— speaking only of those of recent or present memory—paying tribute to the noble artistry of such superlative recitalists as Karl Erb, Kathleen Ferrier, Dietrich Fischer-Dieskau, Elena Gerhardt, Hans Hotter, Gerhard Hüsch, Lotte Lehmann, Julius Patzak, Peter Pears, Hermann Prey, Heinrich Schlusnus, Peter Schreier, Elisabeth Schwarzkopf, Maggie Teyte and, most recently, Elly Ameling.

These past years have brought about a welcome widening of the operatic—if hardly of the recital—repertoire by revivals of operas long lost to sight and hearing in the mists of nineteenth-century operatic history. This was predictable, and widely predicted. As far as enrichment from contemporary sources is concerned there has been, also predictably, nothing worth discussion, and that goes for the recitalist's repertoire, too. There won't be until composers stop putting clusters of notes in singers' mouths that emerge less musically than the nuances and cadences of speech, and see their way clear, at long last, to give opera and song back to singers, providing them with something to sing to their own and their listeners' hearts' content.

H.P., London, June 1981

Glossary

Accademia. An early term for concert, corresponding to the German *Akademie* and the French *concert spirirtuel.* A contemporary approximation would be the symphony concert with soloists. Where prominent singers (or instrumentalists) were concerned, however, the orchestra, rather than the soloist, was the "assisting" element, and there were customarily other "assisting" artists.

Akademie. See *Accademia.*

Appoggiatura. A term derived from the Italian *appoggiare,* meaning to lean or support. It is a note inserted between two other notes to assist, support, or give emphasis and/or elegance to a melodic or harmonic progression.

Aria d'agilità. An air of lively and brilliant character, giving the singer an opportunity to display his agility in execution.

Aria di bravura. Essentially similar to the *aria d'agilità.*

Aria cantabile. A slow air, usually of pathetic character, offering the singer an opportunity for the display of a long, flowing line, expressive phrasing and vocal coloration, with or without appropriate embellishments.

Aria da capo. Da capo means "from the beginning," and an *aria da capo* is an air in three parts, the second being in contrast to the first, and the third being a repetition of the first. In the age of *bel canto* this repetition would be embellished, and it would end with a more or less extensive *ad libitum* cadenza. The standard thirty-two-measure popular song is a derivative of the *aria da capo,* the eight-measure "bridge" corresponding to the second part, but without embellishments or cadenza.

Aria di mezzo carattere. An air midway in character between the *aria cantabile* and the *aria d'agilità.*

Aria parlante. An air of recitative or declamatory character.

Arpeggio. Literally, "harplike," designating a passage in which the voice (or instrument) sounds the successive notes of a chord.

Bel canto. Literally, "beautiful song." See Chapter I for a discussion of its origin and application.

Benefit. An opera performance or a concert in which all receipts accrued to an individual singer or composer and all expenses were borne by the management. In the eighteenth century, and well into the nineteenth, most prominent singers' contracts guaranteed a benefit.

Buffo(a). The term was applied both to the genre of Italian comic opera and to the singers who specialized in it, e.g., *opera buffa* and *basso buffo.*

Cabaletta. A short air with a pronounced rhythm, suited to repetition with variations. In the nineteenth century the term came to be applied generally to the closing brilliant section of an elaborate aria or duet.

Cadence. From *cadere*, meaning "to fall," applied in music to the close, not necessarily falling.

Cadenza. The Italian word for cadence, but designating in general musical terminology a brilliant virtuoso episode written or *ad libitum*, preceding the cadence proper, when applied to vocal music. A cadenza in an instrumental concerto is, of course, a much more elaborate affair.

Cantata. A term applied originally to vocal compositions, other than opera, of the monodic type that came into fashion in Italy about the turn of the seventeenth century. While opera was sung in costume in a theater, cantatas were sung in the salon, or chamber, or in church, hence *cantata da camera* or *cantata da chiesa*. The term came to be applied to more extended works involving chorus and concerted numbers, of which the cantatas of Bach are an example.

Cavatina. A short air. The use of this term, rather than "aria," varied greatly from time to time and from composer to composer.

Chest voice. See Registers.

Coloratura. Literally, colored. The term was originally used as a synonym for florid song, or *canto figurato*, referring to the employment of divisions, embellishments, elaborate cadenzas, and so on. In modern terminology it refers to a kind of light soprano, presumably able to sing a coloratura kind of music. It was not so used in the age of *bel canto*, when every singer was expected to be an expert in coloratura.

Concert spirituel. See *Accademia*.

Continuo. The term refers to an accompaniment from a "figured bass"; i.e., the harmonic bass is enunciated by the bass notes with figures (numerals) added by the composer to indicate how the chords should be completed. It was left to other instruments, essentially the harpsichord, to fill in the unwritten notes *ad libitum*. The accompanying role of the piano and double bass in a jazz combo is identical with the *continuo* of the seventeenth and eighteenth centuries.

Countertenor. A male alto, or falsettist, as opposed to the female contralto. The term was sometimes, but not generally, applied to castrato contraltos and mezzo-sopranos.

Division. An older term for a roulade or passage, derived from the fact that such lengthy, brilliant excursions consisted of the division of the essential notes of a tune by adding a number of incidental, or passing, notes, usually in a sequential order, thus achieving a rudimentary kind of variation. Handel's operas and oratorios, particularly, contain many familiar examples, notably the bass "divisions" in "Why do the nations rage?"

Embellishment. Synonymous with "ornaments" or "graces," the term refers to notes added to decorate or "embellish" the given melody. In the seventeenth and eighteenth centuries embellishment was left largely to the invention and discretion of individual singers and instrumentalists. The conventions of embellishment, and what was expected of the singers, at the turn of the nineteenth century may be studied in the operas of Rossini and Donizetti, who wrote out much that had previously been regarded as the inventive prerogative of the singers.

Evirato. Literally, emasculated, a synonym for castrato.

Falsetto. A kind of vocal production, now normally applied only to males, by which the upper range is extended and takes on the character of the female (or boy) alto or soprano. Not everyone agrees about how it is accomplished, beyond the fact that it shuts off chest resonance and requires a high larynx position. Nor does everyone agree on just where a "legitimate" head voice ends and falsetto begins. A rule of the thumb is that while progression from head voice to falsetto is possible, the reverse progression is not. The rule's validity is dubious. In the age of *bel canto* the term was also applied to certain registers of the females and castrati; and to make the picture hopelessly confusing, some of the old masters placed the falsetto register *between* the chest voice and the head voice.

Fioritura. Literally a flowering; in other words, a flowery kind of embellishment.

Grace. See Embellishment. As applied to the singers of the seventeenth and eighteenth centuries, the term does not refer to grace notes as the latter are now understood. The grace note was simply one of many graces.

Haute-contre. See Countertenor.

Intonation. Derived from *intonare*, to intone, it is now understood as referring to the singer's adherence to the proper pitch, in other words, to singing in tune. *Intonare*, as it appears in older documents, has sometimes been translated as "to intone," "to tune," and "to attack." But that the early Italian masters also had pitch in mind is indicated by their use of *stonare*, the reverse of *intonare*, in reference to singing out of tune.

Kammersänger(in). The German equivalent of *virtuoso(a) di camera.* It is still employed in Germany and Austria as an honorary title.

Kapellmeister. The German equivalent of *maestro di capella.* It is still used in Germany and Austria to designate the head of a musical establishment. But the *Kapellmeister* title is now inferior to *Generalmusikdirektor* (general musical director) and *Dirigent* (conductor), and may even have a pejorative connotation.

Legato. From *legare*, meaning to bind or tie, and referring to a smooth (bound) passage from one note to another in contrast to a detached or non-legato movement.

Lirico spinto. From *spingere*, meaning to push, drive or propel, and applied to a lyrical voice pushed toward the robust (*robusto*) or dramatic.

Maestro di capella. *Capella* means chapel, and the term *maestro di capella* originally referred to the director of music in a dignitary's chapel. Over the years, however, the term *capella* (Ger. *Kapelle*) came to refer to any band of musicians, and *maestro di capella* (Ger. *Kapellmeister*) to its conductor.

Martello. The Italian word for hammer, referring, in seventeenth- and eighteenth-century vocal music, to notes repeated rapidly. The word "trill" (*trillo*) was originally applied to this device, but as trills came to mean the alternation of two notes, the term *martello*, or *martellato*, was substituted.

Messa di voce. From *mettere*, meaning "to put in place," and referring to a soft attack and an extended crescendo (swelling out of a tone) and decrescendo. It was a basic device of the castrati, whose extraordinary lung capacity enabled them to sustain the exercise over an astonishing period of time. See Chapter I for a more detailed discussion. It should not be confused with *mezza voce*, or half voice.

Musico. A common euphemism for castrato, later applied to female contraltos and mezzo-sopranos specializing in male roles.

Opera seria. Literally, serious opera. The term was applied in the baroque era to operas treating serious subjects as distinct from *opere buffe*.

Ornaments. See Embellishments.

Pasticcio. Literally, a pudding. The term was applied in the age of *bel canto* to operatic performances composed of scenes or arias from a variety of operas by several composers.

Portamento. From *portare*, to carry, a device by which the voice is carried from one note to another, especially a distant note, without break, and gliding over the intervening notes.

Recitative. A term applied to a kind of singing or a kind of melodic writing more declamatory than songful. As a noun it refers either to the more or less extended episodes in baroque opera where the plot was advanced between arias, or to the declamatory exposition preceding and setting the stage, so to speak, for a set aria or concerted number.

Register. A term used to designate a certain area of the vocal range, or compass, and the type of vocal production and vocal color congenial to that area. Vocal registers are customarily (but not invariably) termed "chest," "middle" (or "mixed"), and "head." Throughout the history of singing there has been considerable disagreement about the physiological phenomena involved, and even the existence of separate registers has been questioned.

Ritornello. The term, as employed in baroque opera or other vocal music, refers to the return to the instrumental portion of a composition, commonly the instrumental introduction.

Roulade. See Division.

Scala trillata. A scale passage in which each note of the scale is trilled.

Slur. A kind of exaggerated legato as opposed to the tidy passage from one note to the next.

Sotto voce. Literally, "under the voice," cutting off both chest and head resonance.

Stretta. Literally, "tightening." It is applied in vocal music to an accelerated passage or episode at the close of a scene or aria.

Tessitura. Literally, "texture," but used in vocal music to designate the prevailing, or average, pitch of a song or a role. A song or a role may, despite the absence of extraordinarily high or low notes, be taxing because of the prevailing range, or *tessitura.*

Trill. From *trillo,* and referring to the rapid alternation of two adjacent notes.

Turn. A four-note embellishment of a given note, employing the note above, the note itself, the note below, and ending on the note itself. The Italian term is *gruppetto.* It may also begin on the lower note.

Virtuoso(a) di camera. See *Maestro di camera.* The German equivalent (for singers) is *Kammersänger(in).*

Vocalise. As a verb the term refers to the exercising of the voice; as a noun it refers to a composition designed to give the voice an appropriate exercise.

Voix mixte. A kind of vocal production involving the mixture of registers. It is employed most commonly to relieve the weight and tension of the "chest voice" by an admixture of "head voice" or vice versa. The French term *voix mixte* is more usual than the Italian *voce mista,* possibly because the French were expert in its employment, and partial to it.

Voix sombrée. A kind of vocal production in which the vocal color is darkened. It is encountered notably in references to such tenors as Donzelli and Duprez, who carried a "chest" production higher than had been the practice of earlier tenors.

Bibliography

Alda, Frances, *Men, Women and Tenors*. Boston, Houghton Mifflin, 1937.

Aldrich, Richard, *Concert Life in New York, 1902–1923*. New York, G. P. Putnam's Sons, 1941.

Allgemeine Musikalische Zeitung. Leipzig, Breitkopf und Härtel, 1798–1848, 50 vols.

Ancillon, Charles d', *Traité des eunuques*, 1707; translated anonymously as *Eunuchism Displayed*. London, 1718.

Anderson, Emily, *The Letters of Mozart and His Family*. London, Macmillan & Co., Ltd., 1938, 3 vols.

Anderson, Marian, *My Lord, What a Morning*. New York, The Viking Press, Inc., 1956.

Arteaga, Stefano, *Le rivoluzioni del teatro musicale italiano dalla sua origine fino al presente*, 2nd edition. Venice, 1785, 3 vols.

Arundell, Dennis, *The Critic at the Opera*. London, Ernest Benn, Ltd., 1957.

Ashbrook, William, *Donizetti*. London, Cassell, 1965.

Bauer, Karoline, *Nachgelassene Memoiren*. Berlin, 1880, 3 vols.

Berlioz, Hector, *Evenings in the Orchestra*, translated from the French by Charles E. Roche. New York and London, Alfred A. Knopf, 1929.

Berlioz, Hector, *Memoirs of Hector Berlioz 1830–65*, translated by Rachel (Scott Russell) Holmes and Eleanor Holmes, annotated and the translation revised by Ernest Newman. New York, Tudor Publishing Co., 1935.

Bie, Oscar, *Die Oper*. Berlin, S. Fischer Verlag, 1919.

Bispham, *A Quaker Singer's Recollections*. New York, Macmillan, 1920.

Bulman, Joan, *Jenny Lind*. London, James Barrie, Publishers, Ltd., 1956.

Bülow, Hans von, *Briefe und Schriften*. Leipzig, Breitkopf und Haertel, 1899, 8 vols.

Burk, John, *Clara Schumann, a Romantic Biography*. London, James Barrie, 1956.

Burney, Charles, *A General History of Music 1776–89*, edited by Frank Mercer. New York, Harcourt, Brace and Company, 1935 (first published 1776–1789), 2 vols.

Burney, Charles, *The Present State of Music in France and Italy*. London, T. Becket and Co., 1771.

Burney, Charles, *The Present State of Music in Germany, the Netherlands and United Provinces*, 2nd edition. London, T. Becket, J. Robson and G. Robinson, 1775, 2 vols.

Calvé, Emma, *My Life*. New York and London, D. Appleton and Company, 1922.

Caruso, Dorothy, *Enrico Caruso, His Life and Death*. New York, Simon and Schuster, Inc., 1945.

Chaliapin, Feodor, *Man and Mask*. London, Victor Gollancz Ltd., 1932.

Chorley, Henry F., *Modern German Music*. London, Smith Elder & Co., 1854.

Chorley, Henry F., *Thirty Years' Musical Recollections*, edited with an introduction by Ernest Newman. New York and London, Alfred A. Knopf, 1926.

Corsi, Mario, *Tamagno, il piu grande fenomeno canoro dell' ottocento*. Milan, Casa Editrice Ceschina, 1937.

da Ponte, Lorenzo, *Memoirs of Lorenzo da Ponte*, translated by Elisabeth Abbott, edited and annotated by Arthur Livingston. Philadelphia and London, J. B. Lippincott Company, 1929.

Dent, Edward J., *Opera*. London, Penguin Books, Ltd., Revised Edition, 1949.

Deutsch, Otto Erich, *Handel, a Documentary Biography*. New York, W. W. Norton & Company, Inc., 1955.

Deutsch, Otto Erich, *Mozart, a Documentary Biography*, translated by Eric Blom, Peter Branscombe and Jeremy Noble. California, Stanford University Press, 1965.

Duprez, Gilbert-Louis, *Souvenirs d'un Chanteur*. Paris, 1888.

Einstein, Alfred, *Gluck*, translated from the German by Eric Blom. London, J. M. Dent & Sons, 1936.

Einstein, Alfred, *Mozart: His Character, His Work*, translated by Arthur Mendel and Nathan Broder. London, Cassell, 1946.

Farrar, Geraldine, *Such Sweet Compulsion*. New York, Greystone Press, Inc., 1938.

Fétis, François Joseph, *Curiosités historiques de la musique*. Paris, 1830.

Finck, Henry T., *My Adventures in the Golden Age of Music*. New York and London, Funk and Wagnalls, 1926.

Fitzlyon, April, *The Price of Genius, a Life of Pauline Viardot*. London, John Calder, Ltd., 1964.

Foxall, Raymond, *John McCormack*. London, Robert Hale, Ltd., 1963.

García, Manuel, *Traité complet de l'art du chant*. Paris, 1847.

Garden, Mary and Biancolli, Louis, *Mary Garden's Story*. New York, Simon and Schuster, Inc., 1951.

Gatti, Carlo, *Verdi, the Man and his Music*, translated from the Italian by Elisabeth Abbott. New York, G. B. Putnam's Sons, 1955.

Giustiniani, Vicenzo, *Discorso sopra la musica*, translated by Carol MacClintock. American Institute of Musicology, 1962.

Glackens, Ira, *Yankee Diva: Lillian Nordica and the Golden Days of*

Opera. New York, Coleridge Press, 1963.

Gollancz, Victor, *Journey Towards Music, a Memoir.* New York, E. P. Dutton & Company, Inc., 1965.

Griesinger, G. A., *Biographical Notes Concerning Joseph Haydn,* translated and with introduction and notes by Vernon Gotwals. Madison, Wisconsin, University of Wisconsin Press, 1963.

Grout, Donald Jay, *A Short History of Opera.* New York, Columbia University Press, 1947.

Grove's Dictionary of Music and Musicians, editions of 1880 and 1949. London, Macmillan & Co., Ltd.

Haböck, Franz, *Carlo Broschi Farinelli, die Gesangskunst der Kastrat. n.* Vienna, Universal Edition, 1923.

Haböck, Franz, *Die Kastraten und ihre Gesangskunst. Eine gesangsphysiologische Kultur- und musikhistorische Studie.* Stuttgart, Berlin and Leipzig, Deutsche Verlags-Anstalt, 1927.

Hanslick, Eduard, *Vienna's Golden Years of Music 1850–1900,* selected, translated and edited by Henry Pleasants. New York, Simon and Schuster, Inc., 1950.

Hedley, Arthur, *Selected Correspondence of Fryderyk Chopin,* abridged from *Fryderyk Chopin's Correspondence,* collected and annotated by Bronislaw Edward Sydow, translated and edited with additional material and a commentary by Arthur Hedley, London, Melbourne and Toronto, Heinemann, 1962.

Helm, Ernest Eugene, *Music at the Court of Frederick the Great.* Norman, Oklahoma, University of Oklahoma Press, 1960.

Heriot, Angus, *The Castrati in Opera.* London, Martin Secker and Warburg, Ltd., 1956.

Hogarth, George, *Memoirs of the Opera in Italy, France, Germany and England.* London, Richard Bentley, 1851, 2 vols.

Hurst, P. G., *The Operatic Age of Jean de Reszke; 40 Years of Opera 1874–1914.* London, Christopher Johnson, 1958.

International Cyclopedia of Music and Musicians, edited by Oscar Thompson, 4th edition, edited by Nicolas Slonimsky. New York, Dodd, Mead & Company, 1946.

Jellinek, George, *Callas, Portrait of a Prima Donna.* New York, Ziff-Davis Publishing Company, 1960.

Kellogg, Clara Louise, *Memoirs of an American Prima Donna.* New York and London, G. P. Putnam's Sons, 1913.

Kelly, Michael, *Reminiscences of Michael Kelly.* 2nd edition, London, Henry Colburg, 1826.

Kirkpatrick, Ralph, *Domenico Scarlatti.* Princeton, N. J., Princeton University Press, 1953.

Klein, Hermann, *Thirty Years of Musical Life in London 1870–1900.*

New York, The Century Co., 1903.

Kühner, Hans, *Genien des Gesanges aus dem Zeitalter der Klassik und Romantik*. Basel, Trias-Verlag, 1951.

Landon, H. C. R. (Ed.), *Collected Correspondence and London Notebooks of Joseph Haydn*. London, Barrie and Rockliff, 1959.

Lawton, Mary, *Schumann-Heink, the Last of the Titans*. New York, The Macmillan Company, 1928.

Lee, Vernon (Violet Paget), *Studies of the Eighteenth Century in Italy*. London, 1880.

Lehmann, Lilli, *Mein Weg*. Leipzig, S. Hirzel, 1913.

Lobe, C. G., *Fliegende Blätter für Musik, Wahrheit über Tonkunst und Tonkünstler*. Leipzig, Baumgaertner's Buchhandlung, 1855, 2 vols.

Loewenberg, Alfred, *Annals of Opera 1597–1940*, 2nd edition. Geneva, Societas Bibliographica, 1955.

Marchesi, Mathilde, *Marchesi and Music, Passages from the Life of a Famous Singing Teacher*. New York and London, Harper & Brothers, 1898.

Marx, Adolf Bernhard, *Gluck und die Oper*. Berlin, Verlag von Otto Jancke, 1863.

McArthur, Edwin, *Flagstad, a Personal Memoir*. New York, Alfred A. Knopf, 1965.

Moore, Gerald, *Am I Too Loud?*. London, Hamish Hamilton, Ltd., 1962.

Moscheles, Ignaz, *Aus Moscheles' Leben*. Leipzig, von Duncker & Humblot, 1872, 2 vols.

Mount-Edgcumbe, Richard, *Musical Reminiscences of an Old Amateur*, London, W. Clarke, 1823.

Musikalisches Conversations-Lexikon, bearbeitet und herausgegeben von Hermann Mendel. Berlin, Verlag von L. Heimann, 1870, 11 vols.

Newman, Ernest, *The Life of Richard Wagner*. New York, Alfred A. Knopf, 1933–1946, 4 vols.

Pirchan, Emil, *Henriette Sontag, die Sängerin des Biedermeier*. Vienna, Wilhelm Frick Verlag, 1946.

Quicherat, L., *Adolphe Nourrit, sa vie, son talent, son caractère*. Paris, Librarie de L. Hachette et Cie., 1867, 3 vols.

Radiciotti, Giuseppe, *Aneddoti rossiniani autentici*. Rome, 1929.

Riemann, Hugo, *Musik-Lexikon*, Berlin. Max Hesses Verlag, 1919.

Rosenthal, Harold D., *Two Centuries of Opera at Covent Garden*. London, Putnam, 1958.

Schauensee, Max de, *The Collectors' Verdi and Puccini*. Philadelphia and New York, J. B. Lippincott Company, 1962.

Schenk, Erich, *Wolfgang Amadeus Mozart, eine Biographie*. Zürich,

Leipzig and Vienna, Amalthea-Verlag, 1955.

Scholes, Percy A., *The Oxford Companion to Music*, 9th edition. London, New York, Toronto, Oxford University Press, 1955.

Seltsam, William H., *Metropolitan Opera Annals, a Chronicle of Artists and Performances*. New York, The H. W. Wilson Company in association with the Metropolitan Guild Inc., 1949.

Shaw, George Bernard, *Music in London 1890–94*. London, Constable and Company Limited, 1949.

Smart, Sir George, *Leaves from the Journal of Sir George Smart*, edited by H. Bertram Cox and C. L. E. Cox, London, Longmans, Green and Co., 1907.

Spohr, Louis, *The Musical Journeys of Louis Spohr*, selected, translated and annotated from Spohr's *Selbstbiographie* by Henry Pleasants. Norman, Oklahoma, University of Oklahoma Press, 1961.

Stendhal (Henri Beyle), *Life of Rossini*, translated by Richard N. Coe. London, John Calder, 1956.

Strunk, Oliver, *Source Readings in Music History*. New York, W. W. Norton & Company, Inc., 1950.

Tosi, Pier Francesco, *Opinioni de' cantori antichi e moderni, o sieno osservazioni sopra il canto figurato*, Bologna, 1723, translated as *Observations on the Florid Song, or Sentiments of the Ancient and Modern Singers* by John Ernest Galliard. London, J. Wilcox, 1743, reprinted by William Reeves Bookseller Limited, 1926.

Toye, Francis, *Giuseppe Verdi: His Life and Works*. New York, Alfred A. Knopf, 1931.

Wechsberg, Joseph, *Red Plush and Black Velvet: the Story of Melba and her Times*. Boston and Toronto, Little, Brown & Company, 1961.

Weinstock, Herbert, *Donizetti and the World of Opera in Italy, Paris and Vienna in the First Half of the Nineteenth Century*. New York, Pantheon Books, 1963.

Worsthorne, Simon T., *Venetian Opera in the Seventeenth Century*. London, Oxford University Press, 1954.

Yorke-Long, Alan, *Music at Court: Four Eighteenth Century Studies*. London, George Weidenfeld and Nicolson, 1954.

Index

Page numbers in italic type refer to illustrations.

ABOUT THE AUTHOR

HENRY PLEASANTS has made his mark in the field of books about music not only with the highly controversial *The Agony of Modern Music* and *Serious Music—and All That Jazz!* but also with his distinguished translation and editing of the musical criticisms of Eduard Hanslick, Robert Schumann and Hugo Wolf and of the autobiography of Louis Spohr.

But his first and most enduring enthusiasm has always been singing. As a boy soprano he sang in various churches of Philadelphia's Main Line suburbs, and at seventeen he won a scholarship as a baritone at the Curtis Institute of Music, the audition jury including Marcella Sembrich and Emilio de Gogorza. His own teacher was Horatio Connell, a pupil of Julius Stockhausen, who had been a pupil of Manuel García. But it was the classes in English composition conducted by Professor William Harbeson of the University of Pennsylvania that inspired him to become a writer.

At nineteen he was already a music critic on the Philadelphia *Evening Bulletin*; four years later he was elevated to musical editor; and in 1942 he entered the army. But all the time he continued his musical studies —singing with Giuseppe Boghetti (the teacher of Marian Anderson), piano with Isadore Freed in Philadelphia and Ivan Engel in Budapest, and composition with Tibor Serly. During the 1944–45 Italian campaign he took advantage of leaves to study with one of the great baritones mentioned in this book—Giuseppe de Luca.

After the war he entered the foreign service, and from 1945 to 1955 also served as European music correspondent for *The New York Times*. In a professional capacity, then, it is no exaggeration to say that Mr. Pleasants has heard nearly all the great (and most of the not-so-great) singers who were still singing in the 1920's as well as those who have made their mark since.

Mr. Pleasants retired from the Foreign Service in 1964. He and his wife, the American harpsichordist and fortepianist Virginia Pleasants, now make their home in London, where he remains active as London music critic for the *International Herald Tribune* and as London editor of *Stereo Review*.